Uncle Sam and You Curriculum Package

How do elections work? What does the President do all day? Who decides where stop signs go? What is Labor Day? *Uncle Sam and You* is a one-year civics course that answers these questions and many more. Designed for students in grades 5-8, this curriculum guides you on an engaging tour of American government. Learn about elected leaders and everyday citizens who have important roles to fill in making our country work.

All of the instructions for how to use the course are included in Part 1 and Part 2, so you do not need a separate teacher's manual. At the beginning of each weekly unit, an introductory page gives an overview of the unit, a list of the lessons, and a list of what additional books the student will be using while studying that particular unit. Each unit has four daily lessons, followed by a holiday lesson you choose. While this course is designed for children in grades 5-8, younger children can listen to the lessons and participate in the family activities.

The lessons are richly illustrated with full-color photographs and historic illustrations. At the end of each regular (non-holiday) lesson is a list of several supplemental activities. You may choose which activities to assign. Depending on how many activities you assign, most students will need 45-90 minutes to complete one lesson. One special family activity is assigned each week that corresponds with the holiday lesson you choose for that unit. These activities include craft and art projects, themed meals, and other multi-age activities.

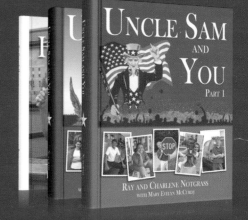

The full curriculum package includes:

- *Uncle Sam and You Part 1*
- *Uncle Sam and You Part 2*
- *The Citizen's Handbook*
- *Uncle Sam and You Answer Key*

Eight works of literature are assigned in the *Uncle Sam and You* curriculum to give your child a richer perspective on the various topics studied. Two optional additional resources are the *Student Workbook* and *Lesson Review,* each of which provides a way to review material in each lesson. The *Answer Key* that comes with the curriculum package has all of the answers needed for grading.

For more information, visit notgrass.com or call 1-800-211-8793.

UNCLE SAM AND YOU

PART 2

Previous Page: City Hall in Savannah, Georgia

Uncle Sam and You Part 2
by Ray and Charlene Notgrass
with Mary Evelyn McCurdy and Bethany Poore

ISBN 978-1-60999-047-3

All product names, brands, and other trademarks mentioned or pictured
in this book are used for educational purposes only.
No association with or endorsement by the owners of the trademarks is intended.
Each trademark remains the property of its respective owner.

Unless otherwise noted, scripture quotations taken from the
New American Standard Bible, Copyright 1960, 1962, 1963, 1971, 1972, 1973,1975, 1977, 1995
by the Lockman Foundation. Used by permission.

Cover design by Mary Evelyn McCurdy
Interior design by Charlene Notgrass
with Mary Evelyn McCurdy

Printed in the United States of America

Notgrass Company
975 Roaring River Road
Gainesboro, TN 38562

1-800-211-8793
www.notgrass.com
books@notgrass.com

Table of Contents
PART 2

St. Joseph, Missouri

Williamson County, Texas

UNIT 16 – THE UNITED STATES MILITARY

BOOKS USED IN UNIT 16

- The Citizen's Handbook
- Basher Five-Two
- Student Workbook (optional)
- Lesson Review (optional)

2011 graduates of the United States Military Academy at West Point celebrate their graduation.

The United States MILITARY I

Nuristan Province, Afghanistan
Afghan boy holds the hand of an Arizona National Guardsman during a medical and humanitarian assistance mission, 2007.

Aboard the USS *Peleliu*
Marine Corporal moves a pallet of disaster relief supplies being sent to flooded regions of Pakistan, 2010.

The military forces of the United States exist to defend our country. They defend American civilians and embassies in other parts of the world. They also defend other countries who are allies of the United States. The U.S. military performs many acts of compassion and service to people around the world who are in need, in times of peace and in times of war. See examples at left and on page 515.

The military is a clear example of civic involvement because it is made up of citizens who serve all other citizens by defending the very existence of our nation. Members of the military sometimes serve to the point that they lay down their lives for our country.

All members of the military receive training on a continuing basis so that they are prepared for the work they do each day and the work they may be called upon to do in case of war. Some citizens use training they have already received and continue those careers in the military. Examples are military doctors and ministers serving as military chaplains. Chaplains are pictured in the center photo on page 515. Other citizens receive training for new careers after they join the military and later use the skills they learn in their lives as civilians.

The four branches of the United States military are the Army, Air Force, Navy, and Marines. The President is Commander in Chief of the military. The Secretary of Defense is responsible for daily operations. Working under the Secretary of Defense are the Secretaries of the Army, Navy, and Air Force. The Secretary of Defense and the Secretaries of the Army, Navy, and Air Force are civilians. The fact that civilians oversee the military is an important part of how our democratic government operates. Even our military forces are subject to the American people and their elected officials.

Most U.S. Presidents have served in some branch of the military. See chart below.

Presidents in the Military

U.S. Army

General of the Armies of the U.S. George Washington (American Revolution)
Major James Monroe (American Revolution)
Major General Andrew Jackson (War of 1812)
Major General William Henry Harrison (War of 1812)
Major General Zachary Taylor (Mexican War)
Brigadier General Franklin Pierce (Mexican War)
Private James Buchanan (War of 1812)
Brigadier General Andrew Johnson (Civil War)
General of the Army Ulysses S. Grant (Civil War)
Brevet Major General Rutherford B. Hayes (Civil War)
Major General James A. Garfield (Civil War)
Brevet Brigadier General Benjamin Harrison (Civil War)
Brevet Major William McKinley (Civil War)
Colonel Theodore Roosevelt (Spanish-American War)
Colonel Harry S. Truman (World War I)
General of the Army Dwight D. Eisenhower (World War II)
Captain Ronald Reagan (World War II)

U.S. Navy

Lieutenant John F. Kennedy (World War II)
Commander Lyndon B. Johnson (World War II)
Commander Richard M. Nixon (World War II)
Lieutenant Commander Gerald R. Ford Jr. (World War II)
Lieutenant Jimmy Carter (Korean War, Cold War)
Lieutenant, Junior Grade George H. W. Bush (World War II)

State Militias

Colonel Thomas Jefferson (Virginia)
Colonel James Madison (Virginia)
Captain John Tyler (Virginia)
Colonel James K. Polk (Tennessee)
Major Millard Fillmore (New York)
Captain Abraham Lincoln (Illinois)
Brigadier General Chester A. Arthur (New York)

Air National Guard

First Lieutenant George W. Bush (Texas)

Dillingham Airfield, Hawaii
Soldiers look over a map during training.

Windhoek, Namibia
Two U.S. Army chaplains (left and right) spent a week in Namibia leading a conference related to health in 2010. Attending the conference were four Namibia Defence Force chaplains, one prison chaplain, and fourteen chaplain assistants. One is pictured in the center. One of the purposes of the conference was to encourage members of the Namibian military to be faithful to their spouses.

Khwazahkela, Pakistan
A U.S. soldier works alongside members of the Pakistan military as they help Pakistani flood victims off a U.S. Army Chinook helicopter.

The United States Army

The Army is responsible for military actions on land. Its mission is "to serve the American people, to defend the Nation, to protect vital national interests, and to fulfill national military responsibilities." The Army began on June 14, 1775, when the Continental Congress created a national army and named George Washington as its commanding officer. Prior to this, American fighting forces were the members of various state militias. The Continental Army was disbanded after the American Revolution, but was reformed in the 1790s to defend the western territories of the United States.

Washington, D.C.
*Congressman Alexander Pirnie reaches
into a container of draft numbers
at Selective Service Headquarters, 1969.*

The All-Volunteer Army

Members of the U.S. Army have taken part in every war in our nation's history. Most soldiers have been volunteers; but sometimes men have been drafted to serve. Some states used a draft during the Revolutionary War. Both the Union and the Confederacy used drafts during the Civil War, but they were unpopular in both places. In 1917-1918, men were drafted to serve in World War I.

The first peacetime draft began in 1940. The Federal government wanted America to be ready in case it became involved in World War II, which was already being fought in Europe and Asia. The draft was discontinued two years after World War II but begun again in 1948. The draft continued throughout most of the Vietnam War.

Young men register for Selective Service when they turn eighteen. During the Vietnam War, days of the year were randomly assigned draft order numbers. This was used to determine who would be drafted into the military. Young men whose birthdays had lower draft order numbers were more likely to be drafted into the Army. Notice the photograph above. The last Americans were drafted in 1972; they reported for duty in 1973. Afterwards, the American military became an all-volunteer force. In the photo at left a soldier voluntarily re-enlists.

Central Iraq
*A soldier re-enlists while standing
in the Euphrates River, 2008.*

The National Guard and the Army Reserve

In addition to soldiers on active duty, the United States Army also includes the National Guard and the Army Reserve. The National Guard is the modern version of state militias. Personnel in the National Guard serve under each state's Governor, but they can be called into active duty with the Army when a need arises. The Army Reserve is made up of two groups: men and women who have served for a period of time on active duty and agree to continue to be available as needed on a part-time basis, and also men and women who volunteer specifically for the Reserve. Guard and Reserve members train one weekend per month and for two weeks during the summer. The President can call up Guard and Reserve members for active duty when he sees a need. See guardsmen and reservists below.

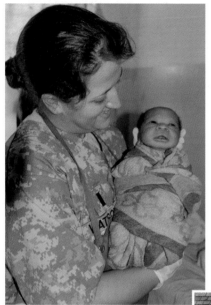

Bagram Airfield, Afghanistan
Army Reserve soldiers arrive in Afghanistan for a one-year tour of duty, 2011.

Rural Uganda
A U.S. Army Reserve nurse holds a 5.5-pound baby boy just minutes after he was born, 2009.

San Vicente, El Salvador
An Army Reservist gives a woman medical care, 2010.

Sandy, Utah
Utah National Guardsmen wait to be hoisted into an Air Force Pave Hawk helicopter during training, 2007.

Kosovo
Army Major General Kenny Montoya (left), adjunct general of the New Mexico National Guard and Air Force General Craig McKinley view Kosovo from a Black Hawk helicopter, 2011.

Army Equipment

The Army uses a wide range of weapons, including rifles, machine guns, artillery, and rockets. The basic Army vehicle is the High Mobility Multipurpose Wheeled Vehicle, usually called the Humvee (see photo below); but the Army also uses tanks, rocket-launching vehicles, armored personnel carriers, and other vehicles. It also has some aircraft and sea vessels.

Women in the Army

Women have served alongside the Army since the Revolutionary War, for many years mostly as nurses, cooks, and seamstresses. About 35,000 women served during World War I in office jobs as well as in the traditional roles

Kandahar Province, Afghanistan
A Chinook helicopter sling-loads a Humvee on Christmas Day, 2009.

just mentioned. During World War II, the Army formed the Women's Army Auxiliary Corps, which became the Women's Army Corps, often called WACs. These women continued to serve in support roles, although the Corps became a part of the regular Army after the war.

Also during World War II, about 1,000 female pilots flew Army aircraft within the U.S. They transported cargo and also flew planes from manufacturing facilities to military bases. These female pilots came to be called Women's Airforce Service Pilots or WASPs. This service freed male pilots to fly in combat. In the 2010 photo below, a former WASP is about to receive the Congressional Gold Medal, the highest award a civilian can receive.

When the Army became all-volunteer in the 1970s, women in the Army began to be treated equally with men. They now receive the same basic training and receive combat training. The Women's Army Corps was disestablished in 1978.

An Army Hero

Alfred Rascon was born in Chihuahua, Mexico, in 1945. He and his parents immigrated to California when Alfred was a child. When Rascon graduated from high school in 1963, he joined the Army and was trained as a medic.

Fairbanks, Alaska
General Norton A. Schwartz, Chief of Staff of the Air Force, visits with Nancy Lee Baker. Ms. Baker flew military aircraft during World War II.

Rascon was sent to Vietnam. On March 16, 1966, his battalion came under heavy enemy attack. Several soldiers were wounded. Three times during the battle, Rascon went to help wounded soldiers while the enemy continued to fire. He received many injuries. When the fighting stopped, Rascon ignored his own injuries and helped treat other soldiers until he was on a helicopter to be evacuated. Rascon spent six months recovering from his injuries.

Captain Rascon receives the Medal of Honor from President Bill Clinton.

Rascon was discharged from the Army in 1966 and joined the Army Reserves. In 1967 he became a U.S. citizen. Three years later, Rascon graduated from Officers Candidate School as a Second Lieutenant and returned to Vietnam as an advisor. He was discharged again in 1976 as a captain and served in the Reserves until 1984. Rascon later served in various government positions. Concerning America, Rascon has said, "I'm Mexican by birth, American by choice."

As seen in the photo above, Rascon received the Medal of Honor in recognition of his bravery in Vietnam. In 2002 he became director of the Selective Service. Later that year Rascon returned to the Reserves as a Major. He served in the Army Medical Service Corps in Iraq and Afghanistan. By the time Rascon retired, he had achieved the rank of Lieutenant Colonel.

Greater love has no one than this, that one lay down his life for his friends.

John 15:13

Lesson Activities

Thinking Biblically — Read Numbers 1:1-4 and 1:44-46 to learn about the army of the nation of Israel.

Literature — Read "A Better Day for Humankind—Here and Everywhere" in *The Citizen's Handbook,* page 82, and "U.S. Military Code of Conduct," "High Flight," and chapter 1 in *Basher Five-Two.*

Creative Writing — In your notebook, write a paragraph answering the question: What do you think is the motivation of people who serve in the United States military?

Find Out! — How many members of your extended family have served in the U.S. military?

Student Workbook or Lesson Review — If you are using one of these optional books, complete the assignment for Lesson 76.

The United States MILITARY II

While the U.S. Army is responsible for military activities on the ground, the Air Force is responsible for those in the air, the Navy for those on the seas, and the Marines for those between the sea and the land.

The United States Air Force

The Aeronautical Division of the U.S. Army Signal Corps was founded on August 1, 1907, less than four years after the Wright Brothers flew their first successful flight at Kitty Hawk, North Carolina. After a series of name changes, the flight section of the Army became the U.S. Army Air Forces in 1941. In 1947, two years after World War II, the United States Air Force was separated from the Army and became a separate branch.

Alzey, Germany
Air Force Colonel jumps from C-17 Globemaster III, 2010.

The mission of the Air Force is "to fly, fight, and win in air, space, and cyberspace." All branches of the military use advanced technology, but the high-tech equipment used by the Air Force has been especially important during the wars in Iraq and Afghanistan. By using this equipment, the U.S. military can depend less on soldiers fighting on land. This saves many American lives.

See Air Force personnel at work on this page and on page 521. The Air Force Reserve and the Air National Guard help the active duty Air Force. Each of the fifty states has an Air National Guard.

Bagram Air Field, Afghanistan
Hospital chaplain hugs an injured Afghan child treated at an American military hospital, 2012.

An Air Force Hero

You may have seen *Mr. Smith Goes to Washington*, a movie about the U.S. Senate. Pennsylvanian Jimmy Stewart was the male lead in the movie. The popular movie star was drafted into the Army in 1940. Though he did not weigh enough to be accepted at first, Stewart worked successfully to gain weight and was assigned to the Army Air Corps.

Turku, Finland
The Thunderbirds, the U.S. Air Force Air Demonstration Squadron, perform in Finland for the first time, 2011.

Stewart had already earned a pilot's license in 1935 and a commercial license in 1938. At first the Army protected him from dangerous situations; but Stewart asked to be sent overseas and into combat. He was stationed in England. Stewart flew twenty dangerous missions in various roles: as command pilot, wing commander, and squadron commander. He received the Distinguished Flying Cross and other medals. By the end of the war he was a colonel.

After the war, Stewart returned to acting. In 1946 he starred in the popular Christmas movie, *It's a Wonderful Life*. As he continued his acting career, Stewart remained in the U.S. Air Force Reserves. In 1959 he became a brigadier general. He retired from the Reserves in 1968 when he reached the mandatory retirement age and was awarded the Distinguished Service Medal.

Civil Air Patrol

In the late 1930s, civilians interested in aviation banded together to form an organization of volunteers who wanted to help defend their country. They formed the Civil Air Patrol (CAP) just one week before the Japanese attacked Pearl Harbor in December of 1941. During the war, they flew more than 500,000 hours while helping protect Americans. They worked tirelessly and successfully to help protect Americans from attacks by German submarines along U.S. coasts. In 1948 the Civil Air Patrol became an official auxiliary of the Air Force.

Today the headquarters of the Civil Air Patrol is at Maxwell Air Force Base in Alabama. The organization has three main functions:

Emergency Services — CAP helps save the lives of almost one hundred people each year through its search and rescue efforts. The organization helps with transportation and communication during disasters, such as hurricanes and tornados. It also helps the U.S. Air Force with transportation and communication.

Cadet Program — Young Americans aged twelve through twenty-one participate in the CAP Cadet Program. They have the opportunity to advance through a sixteen-step program

Texas
Homeschooling Cadet receives a Civil Air Patrol promotion.

which includes aerospace education, training in leadership, physical fitness, and morality. Cadets who become cadet officers can enter the Air Force as an airman first class. The CAP Cadet Program has become a popular homeschool activity. See photo at left.

Aerospace Education — In addition to the aerospace education provided for cadets, CAP provides aerospace education for the general public and also aerospace educational materials for public schools.

CAP has many opportunities for adult volunteers, for pilots who want to use their skills to serve, and for members of the clergy who serve as CAP chaplains. Chaplains help with the moral training of cadets and help disaster victims who are served by CAP members.

The United States Navy

On October 13, 1775, General George Washington informed the Continental Congress that he had obtained three armed ships to stop British ships that were headed to Boston. Congress approved what Washington had done and commissioned two more ships. With these actions, the United States Navy was born. The British Navy was the strongest in the world, but individual U. S. ships won several victories in one-on-one battles against British ships in the Revolutionary War and the War of 1812. One of the first American ships was the USS *Constitution*.

Charlestown, Massachusetts
Sailors assigned to the USS Constitution march in the annual parade at the Bunker Hill Monument which honors Americans who fought in one of the first battles of the American Revolution, June 2012.

The size of the U.S. Navy rose and fell at various times depending on the military needs of the country. An important event in the history of the U.S. Navy occurred in 1854, when Commodore Matthew Perry sailed to Japan and opened that country to American trade. Many ships were built and added to the Navy in the late 1800s. In 1907 President Theodore Roosevelt sent most of the Navy's battleships around the world on a fourteen-month tour to show other countries the strength of the United States.

Today the Navy has giant aircraft carriers with runways where planes can take off and land. It has amphibious assault ships (which can travel on water and land), battleships, cruisers, destroyers, frigates, and submarines. The purpose of these ships is "to maintain, train

Washington, D.C.
Sailors march in the inaugural parade
for President George H. W. Bush, 1989.

Camp Shaheen, Afghanistan
A U.S. Navy Hospital Corpsman practices English
with children of Afghan National Army soldiers, 2010.

and equip combat-ready Naval forces capable of winning wars, deterring aggression, and maintaining freedom of the seas." The Navy has always been an all-volunteer force. Part of the Navy's forces are the U.S. Navy Reserves. See sailors at work on this page.

Women's service in the Navy is similar to that of the Army. Women filled support roles for many years. During World War II, they were officially the U.S. Naval Reserve (Women's Reserve), but they were often called Women Accepted for Volunteer Emergency Service, or WAVES. Women became part of the regular Navy after the war, and the WAVES designation was discontinued in 1978.

Presidents Theodore Roosevelt and Franklin Roosevelt both served in the civilian role of Assistant Secretary of the Navy. The only other President who has served as a civilian leader of military forces was William Howard Taft, who was Secretary of War from 1904 to 1908, during the presidency of Theodore Roosevelt (after World War II, the title of Secretary of War was changed to Secretary of Defense).

A Navy Hero

Michael Thornton, a native of South Carolina, enlisted in the Navy in 1967. He was accepted into the Navy's special operations force called SEALs (for SEa, Air, and Land operations). Between 1968 and 1973 he served several tours of duty in Vietnam and Thailand. On October 31, 1972, Petty Officer Thornton was on an intelligence gathering operation

Arabian Sea
A Naval plane captain carries out a pre-flight inspection
of an F/A-18C Hornet aboard the USS Carl Vinson
aircraft carrier, 2011.

against an enemy river naval base. He and the men with him came under enemy fire. His superior officer, a lieutenant, was hit and feared dead. Thornton returned to the lieutenant's location, fought off two enemy combatants, and carried the lieutenant (who was injured but alive) to safety. Thornton got into the water, inflated a life jacket, and kept his superior officer above water for two hours until they were rescued. All of the patrol members survived the incident. Thornton was awarded the Medal of Honor. He continued to serve, through the Desert Storm operation in Kuwait and Iraq, and retired as a lieutenant in 1992. Thornton received the Purple Heart and many other combat medals.

The United States Marines

The first units of Continental Marines were authorized by Congress on November 10, 1775. They protected the Navy's ships and crew and served as sharpshooters in battle. They also went ashore from ships to seize British supplies in what are called amphibious (between sea and land) landings. The Marines were made a separate unit of the military in 1798. They have served throughout American military history, but they were an especially key force in the islands of the Pacific during World War II. The Marines helped keep the Japanese from gaining victories and helped push them back toward Japan.

Lakehurst, New Jersey
Marines and Airmen practice a sling load operation, 2012.

Today's Marines work with the Navy to accomplish landings in dangerous territories. These amphibious landings are often the first invasions by American forces. The Marines are able to perform rapid air and ground assaults on short notice during times of crisis. See Marines at work at right and on page 525.

The Marines serve under the Secretary of the Navy, but they train and do their work as a separate branch of the U.S. military. The Marine Corps also has a reserve. The Marines have always been an all-volunteer branch of the military.

A Marine Hero

At age 11, Joe Foss saw Charles Lindbergh at an airshow near his home in South Dakota in 1926. Joe had to drop out of school to help run the family farm at age 17 when his father died. However, he later went to college, working to support himself and getting help from his family. Foss graduated from the University of South Dakota in 1940 with a business degree and a civilian pilot's license. Foss enlisted in the Marine Corps Reserve and requested to be sent into combat. He was assigned to the Pacific, and during World War II he flew more than sixty missions. His leadership in air combat was crucial in the fighting at Guadalcanal, which was a turning point in the war in the Pacific. Foss received the Medal of Honor in 1943.

Following the war, Foss helped to organize the South Dakota Air National Guard. He was elected to the state House of Representatives, but he was recalled to duty during the Korean War. He attained the rank of colonel. Foss later became commander of the South Dakota Air National Guard and retired as a brigadier general. In 1954 he was elected Governor of South Dakota and was re-elected two years later. In 1959 Foss was named commissioner of the new American Football League (AFL). He remained in this position until just before the AFL merged with the National Football League in 1966. Foss later hosted two different outdoor programs for television. He served as a director of the U.S. Air Force Academy and was president of the National Rifle Association for two years. Foss died in 2003.

Alexandria, Egypt
U.S. Marines demonstrate an amphibious beach assault during Bright Star, a multinational exercise involving military forces from Egypt, Germany, Jordan, Kuwait, Pakistan, and the United States, 2009.

Dhaka, Bangladesh
A Marine Sergeant shows schoolchildren a video of his daughter on his iPad. His Marine unit was in Bangladesh as part of an Engineering Civil Action Program to improve the relationship between the U.S. and Bangladesh by building a second story to a high school, 2012.

Organization of the Military

The Joint Chiefs of Staff are the senior military officers who are responsible for making sure that the U.S. military is ready for any situation. The Joint Chiefs plan what the military does, and they also advise the President, the Secretary of Defense, the Homeland Security Council, and the National Security Council on military matters. The Joint Chiefs of Staff is composed of a chairman, a vice-chairman, the Army chief of staff, the Air Force chief of staff, the chief of Naval operations, the commandant of the Marine Corps, and the chief of the National Guard Bureau.

The Army, Navy, Marines, and Air Force are four of the seven uniformed services of the United States that commission officers. The United States Coast Guard is part of the Department of Homeland Security, but it can be transferred to the Department of the Navy by the President at any time or by Congress during time of war. We will study the Coast Guard when we discuss homeland security. The other two uniformed services are the United States Public Health Service Commissioned Corps, which is within the Department of Health and

Human Services, and the National Oceanic and Atmospheric Administration Commissioned Corps, which is part of the Department of Commerce.

The members of the United States military have served proudly and well for over two centuries. Most members of the military serve for a few years, while others make a career of military service. For many years the great majority of those who served in the military were single adults. However, many men and women who serve today have families. Their families make significant sacrifices.

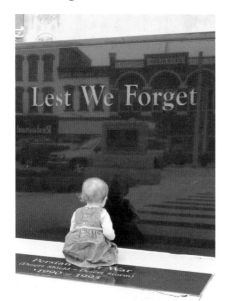

Greensburg, Indiana
War Memorial

We must never forget that the heart of the United States military, the reason for its effectiveness, is the sons and daughters, the brothers and sisters, the dads and moms of our fellow Americans. May we never forget their service and always be thankful for it. What our military does both within our borders and around the world helps us to do what we do in our country. However, we must not place our trust in soldiers, but in God who created all things and who is King of all the nations.

The king is not saved by a mighty army;
A warrior is not delivered by great strength. . . .
Our soul waits for the Lord; He is our help and our shield.
Psalm 33:16, 20

Lesson Activities

Thinking Biblically — Copy Psalm 33:16-20 into your notebook.

Vocabulary — In your notebook, make a drawing for each of these words that illustrates what it means: technology, combat, mandatory, auxiliary, chaplain. Write the word under the drawing. Check in a dictionary if you need help with their definitions.

Literature — Read "1918 Resolution" in *The Citizen's Handbook,* pages 83-85, and chapter 2 in *Basher Five-Two.*

Find Out! — Where is the military base nearest to your home?

Picture This! — Draw a picture of a person in the U.S. military in training, in combat, giving aid, or being honored for his or her service.

Student Workbook or Lesson Review — If you are using one of these optional books, complete the assignment for Lesson 77.

Four Years at
WEST POINT

American military bases are spread across the United States from Maine to Hawaii, but the oldest continuously-occupied military post in America is in West Point, New York. Since 1802 it has been the home of the United States Military Academy, commonly referred to as West Point.

History of the U. S. Military Academy

General George Washington believed West Point, New York, about fifty miles north of New York City, to be the most important military site in the country. In 1778 he gave Colonel Thaddeus Kosciuszko the responsibility of designing a fortress at that location. Kosciuszko had come to America from Poland to volunteer his services to the Continental Army. The following year Washington moved his headquarters there. In 1780 he gave Major General Benedict Arnold the command of West Point. In an act of treason, Arnold offered to sell West Point to the British. He also scattered the Continental troops under him to make the fort weak. On September 23, 1780, Americans captured the messenger Arnold was using to communicate secretly with the British. Thus the traitor was found out, and West Point was saved.

President George Washington, Secretary of the Treasury Alexander Hamilton, Secretary of War Henry Knox, and President John Adams all believed that the United States should establish an institution that would teach the art and science of warfare. The U.S. Military Academy at West Point was finally established in 1802 when President Thomas Jefferson signed legislation creating it.

In its early years, the teaching at West Point emphasized civil engineering. For many years, graduates of West Point oversaw the building of most of America's bridges, harbors, railroads, and roads. In the second half of the nineteenth century, the school began teaching more subjects.

A naval school was founded in 1845 in Anapolis, Maryland. It became the U.S. Naval Academy in 1850. The U.S. Air Force Academy was founded in 1954 in Denver, Colorado.

527

Many of America's most famous generals have been West Point graduates, including Robert E. Lee, Ulysses S. Grant, Dwight D. Eisenhower, Douglas MacArthur, and George Patton. After World War I, MacArthur served as the Superintendent of West Point. He emphasized physical fitness and athletics for West Point students. Science and technology training became a more important part of the curriculum after World War II. The number of students enrolled at West Point increased in the 1960s. Today the number is 4,600. The first female students enrolled in 1976; sixty-two women graduated in 1980.

A West Point Education

If a student decides he wants to go to West Point, he must prepare long before finishing high school. West Point trains an elite group of men and women for service to the United States. It wants only those who are ready for the challenge. Over 10,000 young people apply each year, but only about 1,300 of them are chosen.

What must a student do in high school to have the best chance of getting into West Point? Read the checklist at right.

When a student is accepted at West Point, his family and hometown are proud. The student himself is probably overwhelmed, because a West Point Cadet is not simply moving away from home to go to college. He or she is actually joining the Army.

The West Point experience begins long before the first day of classes in late August. It begins on Reception Day (or "R" Day) in late June or early July. As seen on page 529, Cadets report to campus that morning. After a parent/Cadet information meeting, they have ninety seconds to say goodbye to their parents. At the end of the day is an oath ceremony and review. Other photos on page 529 show some of what happens in between.

Each Cadet is awarded a full scholarship to pay for college tuition. Because they are members of the U.S. military, Cadets also receive a salary of more than $10,000 per year,

---

Checklist for Admission

___ Take hard courses throughout high school and make all A's and B's.

___ Be a leader in clubs and organizations.

___ Exercise and play demanding sports, such as cross-country running and swimming.

___ Score high on tests, especially the SAT or ACT (college entrance exams).

___ Apply to attend West Point's Summer Leaders Seminar the summer before your senior year of high school to learn what it's like to be a West Point Cadet.

___ Begin the rigorous application process long before high school graduation. Complete all paperwork. Send in test scores and transcripts.

___ Obtain a nomination (most Cadets are nominated by their senator or congressman).

___ Pass a medical exam.

___ Pass a Candidate Fitness Assessment.

Reception Day

Sir/Ma'am, New Cadet Doe reports to the Cadet in the Red Sash for the first time as ordered.

plus a place to live, meals, and medical and dental care. Out of the salary, a Cadet pays for expenses like a laptop, uniforms, textbooks, and laundry service. Life as a Cadet at West Point is life in the Army. They live in a room in a barracks with one or two other Cadets. They wear uniforms, are under the authority of officers, and eat in the Cadet mess hall.

Cadets choose a major course of study just like students at other universities do. West Point offers over forty choices of majors. During their years at West Point, students take ten courses in their major and thirty other required courses.

While at West Point, Cadets have the opportunity to attend church and Sunday school. Many professors are Sunday school teachers. West Point Cadets can get to know their professors well, since most professors and their families live at West Point.

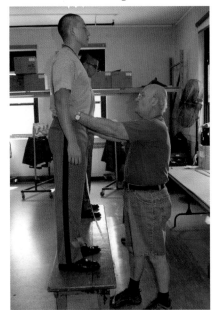

Uniform Fitting

Cadet Honor Code Reminder

West Point Cadets exit Cadet Chapel.

Cadets are expected to live according to high standards. The West Point Cadet honor code is, "A Cadet will not lie, cheat, steal, or tolerate those who do." Cadets adhere to a Cadet Honor System overseen by the Cadet Honor Committee. Members of the committee are elected by their fellow Cadets.

Cadets' minds work hard at West Point, and their bodies do, too. The Army needs officers who are strong and ready for action. Every Cadet takes physical education classes and participates in athletics. West Point competes with other universities in twenty-four sports, including baseball, football, rifle, soccer, swimming, and track. Cadet companies also compete against each other in eighteen sports.

Plebes and Yearlings

Each new Cadet is assigned to one of the thirty-two companies of Cadets. Each company has about 135 Cadets. After Reception Day, new Cadets leave for six and a half weeks of Cadet Basic Training (CBT) at nearby Camp Buckner. CBT includes basic soldier skills, courtesies, discipline, personal appearance, drill, ceremony, and physical fitness. At the end of CBT, Cadets participate in the March Back on Acceptance Day. On that day they become "plebes," the West Point term for freshmen. See photos at left.

In his second summer at West Point, a Cadet spends almost eight weeks in Cadet Field Training. Here Cadets learn how to function in an Army crew/squad and platoon. They also learn how to handle various weapons. They travel to Fort Knox, Kentucky, to learn about armor and equipment. A second year Cadet is a "yearling" (sophomore).

Cows and Firsties

In their third summer, Cadets spread out all over the world. Some are assigned to a regular Army unit in the U.S. or in another country so they can gain experience as platoon leaders. Others help train plebes and yearlings in Cadet Basic Training and Cadet Field Training. Third-year Cadets are called "cows."

Cadets in their fourth year at West Point are called "firsties." In late August, they receive West Point class rings at an annual Ring Ceremony. Firsties take command of plebes and yearlings during Cadet Basic Training and Cadet Field Training. This gives them practice in leadership, a skill essential to an Army officer. By the time Cadets graduate, they are soldiers ready to lead other soldiers. In their fourth year, Cadets find out which specialized field of the military they will enter when they graduate from West Point. Their assignments are based both on their preferences and what the Army needs.

Cadet Basic Training

March Back from Camp Buckner

Water Confidence Course During Cadet Field Training, 2010

A cow presents an award to a plebe after leading them in CBT.

A firstie and a staff sergeant deliver an American flag during a double stack parachute demonstration.

Following the Ring Ceremony

Family members are invited to participate in a bar-pinning ceremony after the graduation ceremony.

It takes forty-seven months of hard work to graduate from West Point. By the time Cadets enter the stadium on graduation day in the legendary "Long Gray Line," each has completed an extremely challenging set of academic, athletic, and military requirements. They have earned a Bachelor of Science degree and are now second lieutenants in the U.S. Army.

The United States has made a time-consuming and expensive investment in each graduate. In return, graduates must serve in the Army on active duty for at least five years, followed by three years of inactive duty. Each Cadet is the distinguished result of the West Point Mission: "To educate, train, and inspire the Corps of Cadets so that each graduate is a commissioned leader of character committed to the values of 'Duty, Honor, Country' and prepared for a career of professional excellence and service to the nation as an officer in the United States Army."

The wise will inherit honor, but fools display dishonor.

Proverbs 3:35

Lesson Activities

Thinking Biblically — Read 2 Chronicles 26:11-15 to learn about the training and equipment of Judah's army.

Vocabulary — Copy these words in your notebook, each on a separate line: rigorous, scholarship, tolerate, discipline, legendary. Look up each word in a dictionary. Next to each word, write what part of speech it is according to the way the word is used in this lesson.

Literature — Read "Remembering West Point Years" in *The Citizen's Handbook*, pages 86-88, and chapter 3 in *Basher Five-Two*.

Creative Writing — In your notebook, write a journal entry of at least two paragraphs as if you are a new West Point Cadet on Reception Day.

Find Out! — Find West Point, New York, on a map.

Student Workbook or Lesson Review — If you are using one of these optional books, complete the assignment for Lesson 78.

Three Days of Marine
BASIC TRAINING

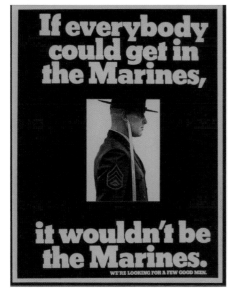
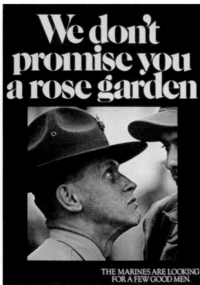
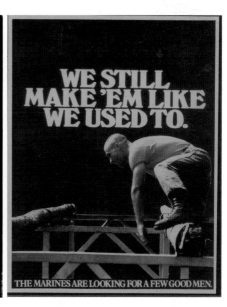

Vintage Marine Recruiting Posters

Reggie was ten years old when terrorists attacked America on September 11th, 2001. He began to have the desire to serve his country by defending our freedoms. After high school, Reggie attended a mini boot camp, like the one pictured below, to help him decide if he wanted to enlist. He did. Leaving his hometown in Illinois, Reggie flew to South Carolina.

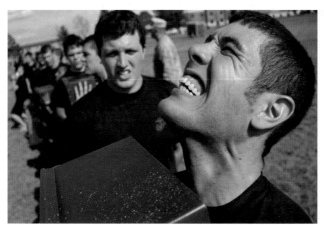

Young men participate in a mini boot camp in 2011. Campus such as this one help potential Marines decide whether they want to join the Marines, 2011.

Marine Corps Base Hawaii, Kaneohe Bay Chapel
Marines honor two of their own who died in battle, 2010.

Sinait, Philippines
Marines pray with a Navy chaplain, 2010.

After eleven weeks of intense training at the U.S. Marine Corps Recruit Depot in Parris Island, South Carolina, Reggie and his fellow recruits must face the final challenge of Basic Training—the Crucible. With the sound of reveille ringing in his ears, Reggie rolls out of his rack (bunk bed). It is 0200 hours (2:00 a.m.) on a Thursday morning.

Nawa District, Helmand Province, Afghanistan
U.S. Marines unload boxes of Meals, Ready-to-Eat, 2009. The meals were produced by AmeriQual Packaging in Evansville, Indiana, a private company which supplies food for the U.S. Department of Defense.

Marine History and Core Values

By this point in his training, Reggie has already endured eleven intense weeks. In addition to the physical discipline, Reggie has learned about the history of the United States Marine Corps, and he has studied the Core Values of honor, courage, and commitment. Though training has not been quite as hard as he anticipated, being away from his family has been a challenge. Reggie does not get alone time. He has been kept busy six days a week with a little time for rest on Sundays. Reggie has attended chapel weekly to help him stay grounded in his faith. See chapel and chaplain photos above. Most of the photos illustrating this lesson show Marines doing the things during their Marine careers that they learned in basic training.

On the March

At 0300 hours, Reggie and his fellow recruits are on the march. They have six miles to hike in the darkness carrying over fifty pounds of equipment and supplies. Reggie nearly falls asleep while he is walking, but he manages to keep trudging ahead. He starts to feel a little hungry. He has three MREs (Meals, Ready-to-Eat) in his pack, but he remembers that he has to make them last for more than two days. So instead of eating, he thinks about why he wanted to join the Marines. See cases of MREs on page 534.

Reggie's grandfather served as a Marine during World War II. He did not talk much about his experiences, but Reggie grew up having great respect for his grandfather's courage.

Drill Instructors

A Marine drill instructor met Reggie and several other recruits at the airport. Reggie learned to listen carefully to instructions and to do immediately what he was told. Even today the drill instructors are close by to keep Reggie and his fellow recruits on the move. Reggie's thoughts are interrupted as they reach the end of their early morning hike.

San Diego, California
Marine Basic Training Drill Instructor at the Marine Corps Recruit Depot, 2012

Obstacle Course

Reggie is assigned to a team of recruits who must carry water, ammunition, and MREs through an obstacle course of trenches, wire fences, and walls. Imagining that they are in a combat situation, they work together to accomplish their mission of bringing supplies across the battlefield.

Marines practice clearing a fence in an area where a possible Improvised Explosive Device has been seen, 2010.

Training Exercises

The obstacle course is followed by four training exercises. The recruits must cooperate to cross logs supported by cables, demonstrate hand-to-hand combat skills, climb over a log eight feet off the ground, and react to a simulated IED (Improvised Explosive Device). See photo at left.

The second event of the day is a three-hour session in which recruits must work as a team to solve a series of problems. One problem requires them to use three wooden boards to move from stump to stump without touching the ground. They must also cross a water hole using wooden boards and move a large container over a wall by hand.

During the next phase, the recruits practice rescuing wounded soldiers and taking them to safety. See photo at right. They also demonstrate their MCMAP (Marine Corps Martial Arts Program) abilities and listen to a presentation by a drill instructor on the core value of honor.

Marines participate in rescue training, 2011.

Reggie has been up for eighteen hours, but his day is still not over. He must hike another five miles in the darkness, and he has to do it in three hours. At midnight, Reggie and his fellow recruits are able to lie down for a brief rest. They are up again at 4:00 a.m.

Day Two

The early morning brings another obstacle course through which Reggie and his comrades must carry water, ammunition, and MREs. Then they must swing on ropes across an imaginary contaminated area and climb a ten-foot wall. The men have been taking turns being the leader in figuring out how to accomplish each objective. Reggie is selected as the leader for climbing the wall. Reggie suggests that they lift up two of the strongest men first. When they get to the top, they are able to stand on a platform and reach down to help others climb up after them. Reggie is the last one on the ground. No one is left to push him up, so he steps back and runs toward the wall. He jumps up and two fellow recruits grab his hands. They pull him up to join the rest.

After getting over the wall, the recruits must demonstrate their ability to read a map and plot coordinates on a grid (in the photo at left, Marines use a map in a dangerous situation). Reggie is glad when they get another short break to listen to a presentation on courage.

During the next round of challenges, the recruits must retrieve a wounded dummy located on top of an eighteen-foot tower,

Now Zad, Afghanistan
Marines read a map while clearing out enemies, 2009.

Marine trains by climbing a rock wall, 2010.

carry ammunition cans up a thirty-six-foot ladder system, walk across ropes while carrying ammunition and water, and go over and under a series of twenty-four logs carrying supplies. The Combat Endurance Course requires the recruits to simulate a patrol, collecting information about obstacles to report back to their officers.

The final daytime event involves a live fire exercise and another practice removing casualties from a danger area. But that is not the last event of the day. The recruits must carry supplies through the obstacle course again, but this time in darkness. Reggie is exhausted when midnight comes and he has the chance to close his eyes.

Day Three

Reveille soon rouses Reggie again at 3:00 a.m. It is time for the final test, a nine-mile hike back to the barracks. The men are worn out physically, mentally, and emotionally. They are hungry and sleepy. But they are determined to finish. One of Reggie's friends is falling behind the others. Reggie slows down to walk beside him. Reggie reminds him how far they have come and encourages him to keep going. After three hours of hiking, they arrive together back at the base.

Eagle, Globe, and Anchor Ceremony

The recruits form up for the Eagle, Globe, and Anchor Ceremony. One drill instructor says a few words about what the recruits have accomplished over the past three days and the past twelve weeks. Then the drill instructors move down the lines of recruits handing out their metal emblems. When the drill instructor steps in front of Reggie, Reggie extends his left hand to receive the emblem. With his right, he shakes the drill instructor's hand. The drill instructor calls Reggie a Marine for the first time.

Djibouti
*U.S. Marines participate in
a rope obstacle course and
a water obstacle course.*

After a quick clean up, the troops are ready for their first real meal in nearly three days. They enjoy all the steak, eggs, and potatoes that they can eat!

At right is a recruiting poster showing a brand new recruit on the left and the same man about half way through Marine basic training on the right. Below the poster are several men who have met the challenge of becoming a Marine.

In the process of becoming a Marine, many people realize that they are capable of accomplishing more than they dreamed was possible. Sometimes people look at themselves and think, "That's just how I am," but people can change. As we look to Christ, God is changing us.

But we all, with unveiled face, beholding as in a mirror the glory of the Lord, are being transformed into the same image from glory to glory, just as from the Lord, the Spirit.

2 Corinthians 3:18

Lesson Activities

Vocabulary — Write a paragraph using all of these words: intense, recruit, ammunition, retrieve, emblem. Consult a dictionary if you need help with their definitions.

Literature — Read "The Service Flag" in *The Citizen's Handbook,* page 89, and chapters 4-5 in *Basher Five-Two.*

Creative Writing — In your notebook, write a poem of at least twelve lines about an aspect of the armed forces.

Picture This! — Draw a picture of Reggie and other recruits doing an activity described in this lesson.

Student Workbook or Lesson Review — If you are using one of these optional books, complete the assignment for Lesson 79.

★ Remember to choose an American Holiday to study this week! ★

UNIT 17 – STATE GOVERNMENT

BOOKS USED IN UNIT 17

- The Citizen's Handbook
- Basher Five-Two
- Student Workbook (optional)
- Lesson Review (optional)

Speaker Matthew J. Ryan Legislative Office Building in Harrisburg, Pennsylvania

In the STATE CAPITAL

LESSON 81

Frankfort, Kentucky
Governor Steve Beshear Signs Bill, 2012.

Gainesboro, Tennessee
State Senator Burks speaks at an event honoring first responders, 2012.

Lincoln, Nebraska
Supreme Court Chamber in Capitol

The headquarters of a state's government is in the city called the state capital. Here the legislature meets and the Governor has his office. In most states, the state's supreme court holds its sessions there. Depending on the size of a state's government, many hundreds or thousands of workers in state government offices work in the capital city.

State capitals are great places to visit. As seen in the photo on the top of page 541, tourists visit state capitol buildings. They tour state museums to learn about state history. The capital city itself is important in each state's history, so tourists visit other local sites that are famous in state and even national history. In Little Rock, Arkansas, they visit Little Rock Central High School, the scene of a major event in the civil rights movement in the 1950s. A statue commemorating the event has been erected on the grounds of the capitol, as seen in the second photo on page 541.

Impact of Government on the Capital City

The work of state government provides many jobs and causes a great deal of money to be spent in the capital. For small capital cities, state government might be the city's largest employer. For example, in Montpelier, Vermont (population about 8,000), Pierre, South Dakota (population about 14,000), and Augusta, Maine (population about 20,000), state government is a big part of what goes on in these cities. When the legislature is in session, the city is alive with activity; but at other times of the year the city feels much like any other small town. For Phoenix, Arizona (population about 1.5 million), Indianapolis, Indiana (population about 830,000), and Austin, Texas (population about 820,000), a great deal of activity takes place there all the time. State government still has an impact in these larger capitals, but the impact is not as big a part of the overall life of the city.

Harrisburg, Pennsylvania
A tour group stands in the rotunda of the Pennsylvania State Capitol.

State capitals are also the scene of activity by other levels of government. Many state capitals have Federal district courts which meet there, and other Federal agencies have offices there, too. Each capital city has its own city government, with a city hall, fire department, police department, and other departments to serve the people of the city.

Every state capital, except one, is the county seat of the county in which it is located, so county government activity takes place in capital cities as well. Lansing, Michigan (population about 115,000), is the only state capital which is not also a county seat. The city of Mason (population about 8,000) twelve miles south of Lansing is the county seat of Ingham County. Charles Noble founded Mason in 1836 in the hope that the legislature would choose it to be state capital, but in 1847 the state government chose Lansing because water power was more available there. Thirty years later, the two cities agreed that Mason would remain county seat but that some county offices and courts would be moved to Lansing.

Little Rock, Arkansas
Statues of the "Little Rock Nine" on the Capitol Grounds.

Phoenix, Arizona
State Senate Chamber in the Arizona State Senate Building

Denver, Colorado
Capitol Quilt Show 2011 in the State Capitol

Sacramento, California
California State Assembly Chamber in the California State Capitol

541

Three Levels of Government in Trenton, Capital of New Jersey

Let's use government activity in Trenton, New Jersey, as an example. The first settlers in what would become Trenton were Quakers who moved to this site beside the Delaware River

1719 William Trent House Museum

in 1679 to escape persecution in England. The town adopted the name Trent-towne in 1719 (later shortened to Trenton), naming it for William Trent, a leading landowner. Trent's country estate, pictured at left and now known as the 1719 William Trent House Museum, is open for visitors. Trent-towne citizens built a courthouse and a jail in 1720. The town was part of Hunterdon County at the time and Trent-towne was the place where county officials, called Freeholders, met.

General George Washington led his Continental Army troops to their first victory at Trenton, after he and his troops made their famous crossing of the Delaware River. Barracks used by American troops during the Revolution are now part of the Old Barracks Museum in Trenton.

Trenton became the capital of New Jersey in 1790. The New Jersey State House was constructed in 1792. It is still in use, but it has had many additions.

The Delaware River is the border between New Jersey and Pennsylvania. The capitol cities of Trenton and Carson City, Nevada, are the only state capitals located along a border with another state. Juneau, Alaska, is on the border between Alaska and the Canadian province of British Columbia.

Trenton has a population of about 85,000. City, county, state, and Federal governments all have offices here. Various departments of those governments are listed in the chart on page 543.

Details of the Architecture of the Clarkson S. Fisher Federal Building & U.S. Courthouse in Trenton

The Old Barracks Museum, built in 1758, first housed English, Scot, and Irish soldiers.

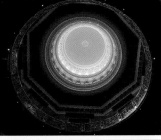

New Jersey State House

The City of Trenton has a mayor, a city council, and a city clerk. Trenton is now in Mercer County, which has a population of over 367,000. Trenton serves as its county seat. The county elects a county executive, a board of freeholders, a county clerk, a county surrogate (who is a judge in a court that handles certain kinds of cases), and a sheriff. Mercer County government has several boards and commissions made up of citizens who serve part-time or as volunteers. These include the park commission, the planning board, and the board of taxation.

The only state officials elected by all New Jersey voters are the Governor and Lieutenant Governor. All of the departments of New Jersey state government have their headquarters in Trenton. New Jersey has over seventy special boards, commissions, agencies, and other official government organizations. Examples include the Clean Air Council, the Motor Vehicle Commission, the New Jersey State Police, and the New Jersey Commission on Cancer Research.

Government activity is a big part of what goes on in Trenton, New Jersey!

Government Departments and Agencies with Offices in Trenton, New Jersey

City of Trenton

Finance
Fire
Health & Human Services
Housing & Economic Development
Inspections
Law
Municipal Court
Police
Recreation
Public Works*

Mercer County

Consumer Affairs
Corrections
Cultural and Heritage
Economic Development & Sustainability
Elections
Housing & Community Development
Human Services
Library System
Planning
Schools
Taxation
Public Safety & Emergency Management

State of New Jersey

Agriculture
Law and Public Safety
Banking and Finance
Children & Families
Community Affairs
Corrections
Education
Environmental Protection
Health
Human Services
Labor & Workforce Development
Military and Veterans Affairs
Transportation
Treasury

United States

District of New Jersey Federal Court
Secret Service
General Services Administration
Federal Aviation Administration

* Public works in Trenton includes water, sewer, solid waste, managing city-owned property, engineering, streets, traffic, and transportation.

State Government in Pierre, Capital of South Dakota

Pierre is near the center of South Dakota along the Missouri River. Arikara, Dakota, Lakota, and Nakota tribes lived, hunted, and traded in the area, before and after Pierre Chouteau Jr. built Fort Pierre Chouteau for John Jacob Astor's American Fur Company in 1832. Artist George Catlin visited the fort that year and said that "no site could have been selected more pleasing or advantageous than this."

The Black Hills of South Dakota became the scene of a gold rush in the late 1800s. In 1877 gold seekers settled across the river from Fort Pierre, becoming the first settlers in present-day Pierre. Soon businesses from Fort Pierre began to move to the new town across the river. The U.S. Congress divided Dakota territory into the states of North Dakota and South Dakota in 1889. By 1904 Pierre was the permanent state capital of South Dakota.

> **State Government Departments in Pierre, South Dakota**
>
> Agriculture
> Corrections
> Education
> Environment & Natural Resources
> Game, Fish, & Parks
> Economic Development
> Health
> Human Services
> Labor and Regulation
> Military
> Public Safety
> Revenue
> Social Services
> Tourism
> Transportation
> Tribal Relations
> Veterans Affairs

In addition to its role as state capital, Pierre has a city government, serves as the county seat of Hughes County, and has a U.S. District courthouse and other Federal agencies.

Let's learn about state government in Pierre. South Dakotans elect many more state officials than do the citizens of New Jersey. In South Dakota, voters select a Governor, a Lieutenant Governor, a secretary of state, an attorney general, a state auditor, a state treasurer, a school and public lands commissioner, and a public utilities commissioner. South Dakota state government has a Bureau of Administration, a Bureau of Finance and Management, a Bureau of Information and Telecommunications (which includes the public broadcasting system for the state), and a Bureau of Human Resources.

The departments of the executive branch of South Dakota are listed above. Notice that some are the same as in New Jersey, some have slightly different titles, and some address needs in South Dakota that are not found in New Jersey state government. South Dakota has several boards and commissions that deal with specific issues, but not as many as New Jersey. All of the state's elected officials and executive departments have offices and staffs in Pierre. With its small population, government activity is an even bigger part of life there than it is in Trenton. However, the actual number of government workers is much smaller in Pierre, since the South Dakota state government serves a state population of about 824,000, while the New Jersey state government serves a state population of about 8.8 million.

Pierre, South Dakota
View of the City with State Capitol, c. 1913

South Dakota State Capitol Today

God created rivers to provide water, food, transportation, and beauty. Cities benefit from rivers. The only capitals that are not beside a body of water are Carson City, Nevada; Helena, Montana; and Raleigh, North Carolina. Madison, Wisconsin; Salt Lake City, Utah; Juneau, Alaska; and Tallahassee, Florida, are beside lakes. Honolulu, Hawaii, is beside the Pacific Ocean; and Olympia, Washington, is beside Puget Sound. The rest of our state capitals are beside rivers, including, of course, Trenton and Pierre.

The Bible mentions rivers 150 times. John the Baptist spent time at the Jordan River. One day Jesus came to him there.

In those days Jesus came from Nazareth in Galilee and was baptized by John in the Jordan.

Mark 1:9

Lesson Activities

Literature — Read "A Civil War Letter from Nashville" in *The Citizen's Handbook*, pages 90-91, and chapters 6-7 in *Basher Five-Two*.

Vocabulary — In your notebook, write the vocabulary words and the letter of the definition that goes with each word: sustainability, workforce, advantageous, revenue, commissioner.

    a. beneficial

    b. one who is given responsibility for a certain task

    c. the state of being able to be maintained

    d. money that is earned or taken in

    e. the group of people who hold jobs or can hold jobs

Find Out! — What is the population of the capital in your state?

Picture This! — Draw a plan for an imaginary capital city. Include a state capitol building, plus other buildings for local, county, state, and Federal government. Include at least one historic site. Think of a name for your capital city and its state.

Student Workbook or Lesson Review — If you are using one of these optional books, complete the assignment for Lesson 81.

At the STATE CAPITOL

The heart of state government is the capitol building or state house. Every state has a state capitol, and the people of the state take great pride in it. A capitol building is a symbol of state government as well as a symbol of the state itself. Often building materials such as stone and wood from the state are used in its construction. Artwork in the capitol reflects state history.

Common features in state capitols are a central dome with a rotunda beneath it; a majestic lobby on the main floor; the chambers where the two houses of the legislature meet; murals that portray history; and portraits of former Governors and other important people in state and American history. See examples from the Pennsylvania State Capitol below.

State capitols appear to be permanent, but in fact they have gone through many changes. First, the city chosen to be the state capital has not always been the same. Many states moved their capital from one city to another at least once during the 1800s. Also, older capitol buildings have been replaced by newer structures.

In addition, the work that takes place in capitols changes. When most capitols were built, the people of that day assumed that the building would house all of state government that

Harrisburg, Pennsylvania
Art in the Pennsylvania State Capitol in Harrisburg, Pennsylvania

would take place in the capital city. However, state governments have grown just as the Federal government has. As a result, many state governments have had to purchase or build additional office space near their capitol for many departments of state government. State governments continue to grow, and old capitol buildings need remodeling and restoration. Construction in and around state capitols is common.

Activity in the Capitol

In most states, the legislature meets for only a few months in the spring. This is called the "session." In a few states, the legislature meets only every other year. When the legislature is in session, the capitol buzzes with activity. Legislators hurry to sessions or to committee meetings. Staff members answer calls, update websites, and relay messages.

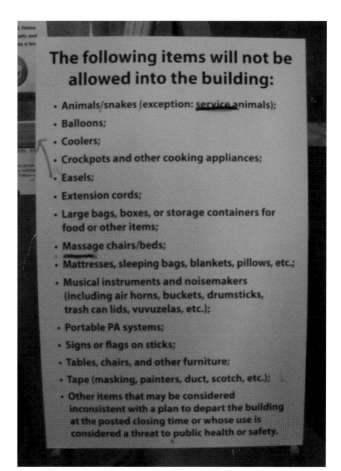

Madison, Wisconsin
Rules Posted at Entrance to the Wisconsin State Capitol

Citizens come to watch sessions of the legislature. Lobbyists try to influence legislators to vote in certain ways on bills being considered. The list of rules above are ones posted in the Wisconsin State Capitol. Their purpose is to keep protestors behaving appropriately.

The capitol is much more quiet when the legislature is not in session, but work still takes place. Legislators sometimes have committee meetings to attend. The state government offices that are located in the capitol are still open and conducting business. Guides continue to take tour groups through the capitol. As with all public buildings, security is important in the state capitol. At right is a capitol security guard.

Harrisburg, Pennsylvania
Senate Chamber Security Station

A Tour of the Iowa State Capitol

"Hello, and welcome to the Iowa State Capitol! A guided tour is just starting over there. Just come on through security. Do you have any keys or coins in your pockets? Sir, can you take your belt off please? Thank you. Okay. You can all go right on through.

Des Moines, Iowa

Iowa State Capitol

"Welcome! My name is Amanda, and I will be your guide through our beautiful state capitol. I am a native of Iowa, and I have been proud of our capitol ever since I first visited in 5th grade. Our capitol was built between 1871 and 1886. The structure is the only state capitol with five domes. If you looked up as you walked toward the building, you saw one dome in the center and one on each corner of the building. The central dome is made of brick and steel and is covered with 23-karat gold leaf. Yes! That was very expensive! At the top is a belvedere with a golden lantern. What's a belvedere? Good question. It's a structure built high on a building to take advantage of a fine view. The four smaller corner domes are covered in copper. Each is topped with a golden lantern. When you go back outside, be sure to notice them and their decorations that look like lines of braided gold.

"This area under the central dome is called the rotunda. Look up! The building is open all the way up to the dome. While we're here, notice the grand staircase. It has beautiful figurines on the support posts. These lanterns on the figurines were once gas-powered, but they have been converted to electricity. Look closely at the newel posts. They are made from twelve different kinds of marble! The wreaths are made from alabaster with carvings of ladybugs, snakes, fruit, and more. The stairs are granite.

Top of the Rotunda

*Newel Posts
of the Grand Staircase*

"Step back and look at this huge painting on the landing. This mural is entitled 'Westward,' painted by Edwin Blashfield of New York in 1905. It commemorates the settlement of Iowa. Can any one guess the size of the painting? It is fourteen feet high and forty feet wide!

"Westward" by Edwin Blashfield

"The corridors that extend from the rotunda in three directions lead to important offices. Follow me down the north corridor and please remember that people are hard at work! Here's the office of the Governor. And this one is the Lieutenant Governor. These offices belong to the state auditor, the state treasurer, and the secretary of state.

"Here is the original state supreme court chamber. We can walk inside this room. The state supreme court now meets in the Judicial Branch Building which is nearby. The beautiful justice bench is mahogany. This room is now used for legislative committee meetings. Okay, follow me back into the corridor. More offices to show you. These are the offices of the supreme court justices. These other rooms are for legislative committee meetings. No, I'm sorry. They are in use, so we can't go inside.

Chandelier Reflected in Mirrors in the Governor's Office

"Now that we're back in the rotunda, look at the floor. I forgot to mention it before.

Corridor

Bell from the USS Iowa Battleship

Notice the circle of glass tile. This circle was cut in 1915 to give light and ventilation to the basement. In 2010 the opening was covered with these glass tiles.

"Now come into the west corridor. This is a model of the battleship USS *Iowa*. It is 18 feet 7 inches long and weighs about 1,350 pounds. This bell over here is from the real USS *Iowa* battleship.

"Now follow me to the south corridor. These forty-three dolls are wearing miniature replicas of the inaugural gowns worn by 43 Iowa Governor's wives. The idea for the display came from Billie Ray, wife of former Governor Robert Ray, in celebration of America's 200th

First Lady Dolls

birthday in 1976. Notice that all the dolls have the same face. She was modeled after Mrs. Ray. That's right! We have to keep the cute dolls in a glass case so girls and their moms aren't tempted to pick them up!

"Okay, now we can climb the grand staircase. See the arched panels above the 'Westward' mural. They are mosaics of glass tiles, created in Venice, Italy by Frederick Dielman of New York. They were installed in 1908. The mosaics represent Defense, Charities, Education, and the executive, legislative, and judicial branches of government. See if you can figure out which is which.

"Now that we are on the second floor, look at the twelve statues surrounding the base of the dome. Their sculptor was S. Cottin and they were installed in 1885. Okay, follow along with me and don't get dizzy. They represent: History, Science, Law, Fame, Art, Industry, Peace, Commerce, Agriculture, Victory, Truth, and Justice. Those paintings with rounded tops on the walls between the statues are called lunettes. They were painted by Kenyon Cox in 1906. They represent Hunting, Herding, Agriculture, the Forge, Commerce, Education, Science, and Art. My favorite is the Forge.

"Look up to the top of the dome to see the beautiful painting of blue sky and white clouds on its interior surface. The banner suspended just under the dome reproduces the emblem of the Grand Army of the Republic, an organization of Union veterans that was formed after the Civil War. The banner is there to commemorate Iowa's part in preserving the Union. The original banner was put in place in the early 1920s. It was replaced during the restoration of the dome in 1998.

"This winding staircase from the second floor leads to the balcony of the dome. The view of the dome and the lower floors of the capitol is spectacular! Oh! I guess I shouldn't have told

Mosaics by Frederick Dielman

S. Cottin Statues and Cox Lunettes

you that, because with a group this large, we don't have time for you all to climb up and down. I'm sorry!

"Let's go look at the chambers of the state senate and state house of representatives, the main attractions of the second floor. No, they are not in session now. The legislature only meets for a maximum of one hundred days one year and 110 days the next year. These rooms and the state law library were the first rooms completed in the capitol. Come in and look at the senate chamber. These desks for the senate's fifty members are original. The chandeliers are original, too. They weigh 500 pounds each, so I guess they wouldn't want to replace them! Don't miss the beautifully painted ceiling. It's worth your while to look up every so often in our state capitol!

State Law Library

"Now let's look at the chamber of the state house of representatives, which has 100 members. Sadly, a fire in 1904 did a lot of damage to this room. The ceiling, stained glass, and chandeliers had to be replaced.

"Now you will get to climb a circular staircase! One circular staircase leads to the senate gallery and another to the house gallery. When the senate and house are in session, you can go there to watch the action. You'll have to come back sometime and see these rooms alive with state business! Take five minutes to check out the galleries, then meet me back here.

State Senate Chamber

"One more room to show you on the second floor. This is the state law library. Anyone care to guess how many books are on all five levels? 100,000! You see we have more circular staircases leading to those beautiful balconies. You're right, those railings are cast iron. This library is looking its best because it was renovated just a little while ago in 1997. Okay, please follow me back down the grand staircase.

Ceiling of State House Chamber

"Thank you for joining me on this tour! Don't hurry away. Look around on the capitol grounds at our numerous memorial statues and pieces of artillery used in past wars. We also have an interesting replica of the Liberty Bell and a downsized Statue of Liberty. They were donated in 1950.

"Thank you so much for visiting the Iowa state capitol! If you are from Iowa, I hope you're as proud of it as I am. If you're from another state, I encourage you to visit your state capitol, too. They are great places to visit! All in one building you can see beautiful art, inspiring architecture, reminders of history, the workings of government, and civics in action."

Soldiers and Sailors Monument on Capitol Grounds

Many of America's most beautiful state capitols are decorated with marble and gold. God created marble and gold and placed them in the ground for man to use. Both were valued in the times of the Bible, too. A Persian palace was described this way in the book of Esther.

There were hangings of fine white and violet linen held by cords of fine purple linen
on silver rings and marble columns, and couches of gold and silver
on a mosaic pavement of porphyry, marble, mother-of-pearl and precious stones.

Esther 1:6

Lesson Activities

Thinking Biblically — Copy Psalm 119:72 into your notebook. Think about the value of gold and precious stones and that which has far greater value.

Literature — Read "Kentucky's New State Capitol Building Dedicated at Frankfort" in *The Citizen's Handbook*, pages 92-93 and chapters 8-9 in *Basher Five-Two*.

Creative Writing — In your notebook, write 1-2 paragraphs about the purpose and value of paintings, statues, and other memorials that help us remember people and events from history.

Find Out! — When was the state capitol in your state built?

Student Workbook or Lesson Review — If you are using one of these optional books, complete the assignment for Lesson 82.

In the
GOVERNOR'S OFFICE

The chief executive in every state is called a Governor. Some of the ways that a Governor serves a state are similar to how the President serves the country, but a Governor's job is different in many ways also. The requirements to be Governor and the responsibilities that a Governor must perform are set out in each state's constitution. The role of a Governor is much the same in every state, but since the state constitutions are not exactly the same, the work that each state's Governor does is somewhat different in each state.

Who Can Be Governor

Each state constitution sets a minimum age for the state's Governor. The usual age is about thirty years, but few people have become Governor that young. The average Governor is in his late fifties. Most have served for several years in the state legislature or as mayors of large cities in the state. However, sometimes businessmen are elected Governor without serving in another government position first.

Madison, Wisconsin
Inauguration of Governor Scott Walker, 2011

State constitutions also have a minimum number of years that a person must have lived in the state before he or she can be elected Governor. This requirement is usually about five years. Many people who are elected Governor have lived in other states first. A Governor can also be a naturalized citizen and does not have to have been born in the United States. This is different from the requirements in the United States Constitution for one who serves as President.

The word gubernatorial is an adjective used to describe things related to a Governor. See a gubernatorial inauguration in Wisconsin above.

Terms of Office

In Vermont and New Hampshire, the Governor is elected every two years. In those states there is no limit to the number of times someone can be elected Governor. In the other forty-eight states, the Governor is elected for a term of four years. States have many different rules about how many times a person can be elected Governor. Some states have a limit of two terms for life, other states allow no more than two terms over twelve years, and a few states have no limit to the number of times a person can be elected to four-year terms as Governor.

Springfield, Illinois
Governor's Mansion

Overseeing State Workers and Making Appointments

As chief executive of a state, the Governor oversees the work of thousands of state employees in offices in the state capital and in many other places around the state. These jobs are organized like the work of the Federal government. States have various departments, and each department has a leader who is part of the Governor's cabinet. The Governor appoints the members of his cabinet and appoints many other citizens of the state to serve on various boards and commissions, such as the board of trustees that oversees a state's universities. In some states a Governor can appoint people to serve as judges in some kinds of state courts.

Cooperating with the State Legislature

A Governor usually works closely with the state legislature to pass laws that the Governor and legislature believe are good for the state. Usually a state Governor and a state legislature are not sharply opposed to each other the way that the President and Congress often are. Each year the Governor presents a state of the state address to the legislature (like the President's State of the Union speech). In this speech the Governor reviews the state's accomplishments for the past year and suggests new laws for the legislature to consider in the current year.

Every Governor has the authority to veto laws that the state legislature passes, the way the President can veto laws passed by Congress. However, the vote needed by the legislature to override a Governor's veto varies from state to state. One

Baltimore, Maryland
Maryland Governor Martin O'Malley congratulates Senator Norman Stone for fifty years of service.

Harrisburg, Pennsylvania
Pennsylvania State Capitol

state just requires a simple majority of the members of both houses of the legislature, while other states require a two-thirds majority. In some states, proposed laws can be placed on the ballot in an upcoming election for the people to vote on directly.

Preparing a Budget

One of the most important jobs for a Governor and his staff is to prepare the budget for the state government for the upcoming year. The legislature has to approve the budget before it can be used. Most states spend more money on public schools than on any other single area of activity.

Overseeing Federal Programs

The Federal government gives states money to spend on welfare programs, public education, road construction, and preparation for emergencies, but state governments have freedom to make some decisions about how the money is spent. A Governor has considerable responsibility in overseeing projects funded by the Federal government.

U.S. Agriculture Secretary Tom Vilsack welcomes Governor Dennis Daugaard of South Dakota to a meeting in Washington, D.C.

Commander in Chief

The Governor is commander in chief of the state's militia or National Guard. A Governor can call out the National Guard when the state faces an emergency such as a flood, tornado, or hurricane. The President can also call a state's National Guard into service. When this happens, the Governor hands over his authority for his state's Guard to the President. Many Governors have visited National Guardsmen from their states who are serving in foreign countries like Afghanistan.

Connecticut Governor Dan Malloy (left) and Delaware Governor Jack Markell (right) meet with General John R. Allen in Kabul, Afghanistan.

Pardons

A Governor has the authority to give pardons to people who are serving sentences in state prisons for crimes they have committed. Sometimes new evidence comes to light which shows that someone in prison for a crime is actually innocent. When this happens, the Governor can set the person free from prison.

Shaanxi, China
Minnesota Governor Mark Dayton (fourth from left on back row) visits China on a trade mission, 2012.

Encouraging Business

Governors often visit out of state to encourage businesses to build factories in their states. Sometimes a Governor will even visit a foreign country to try to bring business to his or her state. For instance, if an automaker from another country wants to build a new factory in the United States, states will try to get that company to locate there. A new factory means jobs for workers in a state and helps the state's economy in many ways.

Jackson, Wyoming
Wyoming Governor Matt Mead speaks at the National Elk Refuge Centennial Ceremony.

Timber Lakes, Utah
Utah Governor Gary Herbert attends the 2nd Annual Rocky Mountain Conservatives BBQ.

Making Personal Appearances

A state Governor spends a great deal of time traveling around the state, meeting people and making speeches. The Governor might appear at a weekend festival in a small town, at the dedication of a new school building, or when a major bridge is completed that will help traffic move more easily. He or she will give speeches at banquets for groups that are working to help the state improve its quality of life.

Varying Responsibilities

The responsibilities for a Governor depend to some degree on what is important in a particular state. For instance, a Governor of a state with a coastline and harbors will have different responsibilities from the Governor of a state with many mountains and mines. A state where many immigrants live will have issues that are different from those found in a state with a large number of retired persons.

Living in the Governor's Mansion

The Governor's family usually lives in the Governor's mansion, which is like a White House for the state. Many parties and receptions take place there. These receptions might honor someone from the state who is a famous author or musician, a hero who has returned from battle, or an important visitor from another country. The husband or wife of a Governor might have a favorite program that he or she encourages, such as improved reading skills or better health for the state's children.

Becoming a National Leader

A Governor can have influence on the national level. The Governor is considered the leader of his or her political party in the state. He or she can try to influence the state's Senators and Congressmen regarding ideas in Congress that would directly affect his state. Because of the wisdom and experience that they gain in overseeing government operations, many Governors go on to run for the U.S. Senate or are appointed to serve in a President's cabinet. Some Governors decide to run for President. Between 1977 and 2009, four former Governors—Jimmy Carter of Georgia, Ronald Reagan of California, Bill Clinton of Arkansas, and George W. Bush of Texas—served as President.

Charleston, West Virginia
Governor's Mansion

Jackson, Mississippi
Governor's Mansion

Honolulu, Hawaii
Governor's Mansion

Richmond, Virginia
Governor's Mansion

Cheyenne, Wyoming
Historic Governor's Mansion,
Formerly Used by Wyoming Governors

Lincoln, Nebraska
"First Dog" Snickers

Governors have a powerful opportunity to do good for the people of their states and for all of the citizens of the country. A key character trait that they need for this is integrity. In speaking of the way King David led the Israelites, the psalmist said:

So he shepherded them according to the integrity of his heart,

And guided them with his skillful hands.

Psalm 78:72

Lesson Activities

Thinking Biblically — In your notebook, list five ways that King David showed integrity and skill as a leader of the Israelite people.

Vocabulary — In your notebook, write your own definition for each of these words: gubernatorial, budget, pardon, reception, integrity. Look in the lesson for clues for the meaning of the words. When you are finished writing your definitions, look in a dictionary for comparison.

Literature — Read "Circular Letter to the State Governors" and "Proclamations by the Governor" in *The Citizen's Handbook*, pages 94-98.

Creative Writing — Imagine you are writing your state's constitution. In your notebook, make a list of what your requirements will be for the Governor's age, years as a resident, citizenship, term length, and term limits.

Find Out! — What is the name of your state's Governor?

Student Workbook or Lesson Review — If you are using one of these optional books, complete the assignment for Lesson 83.

Around the STATE

State government is headquartered in the capital city, but state government is busy all over the state! No resident has to go far to interact with state government. The purpose of state government is to keep things flowing smoothly for the state's residents. To do a good job of that, each state government has people and offices located in cities, towns, and rural locations around the state. State governments work hard to serve their citizens. Websites maintained by the state are a way for states to be as close as a computer for the state's citizens. These websites are packed with ways to find help and information.

In this lesson we will look at some of the ways state residents interact with their state outside of the state capital. Keep in mind that states vary in the way they handle different responsibilities. Some states hire private businesses to handle some of these responsibilities. This is called contracting. Even when a state contracts with a private business to perform a service, the state is still responsible for making sure it happens.

Licenses and License Plates

States require a variety of licenses. A license is an official paper or card that says, "The state hereby gives you permission to do _____." The state government tries to make it easy for residents to comply with the laws. Many state services are in county seats.

A state resident needs a driver's license to drive. Most states have offices scattered all over the state where a resident can fill out forms, have an eye examination, take a test of knowledge, take a test of driving skills, get his license, and be on his way. Some of the steps to getting a driver's license in Oregon are illustrated on this page and on page 560.

Oregon Driver Testing

Filling Out Forms

Eye Exam

Oregon Driver Testing

Photo ID

Driving Test

License Plates and Stickers

A couple who wants to get married is required to obtain a marriage license from the state. For these, state government cooperates with county government workers. Couples can go to the county clerk's office in their county seat, fill out forms, and get a marriage license.

State governments also require licenses for hunting and fishing. These can be purchased online, by phone, or in person at government offices and some stores. When a hunter or fisherman has paid for a license, he can tuck his license in his pocket and have fun in his state's great outdoors!

One distinctive feature of each state is its license plate. License plates are a way for states to show what they are proud of. When someone drives outside of his home state, the license plate on his car is a mini-billboard advertising the state where they live. License plates show everything from wildlife to native plants to scenery to state slogans. Keep an eye out for license plates as you ride around. Sometimes you'll spot a visitor from very far away.

How do car owners get license plates? Every vehicle must have one. States issue license plates through county offices or through businesses that they hire to issue them. States and counties have fees that must be paid for a car owner to get a license plate. See photos at left. In some states, license plates are manufactured by inmates at state correctional facilities (prisons). Other states make arrangements with private companies to manufacture their license plates.

Colleges and Universities

State governments operate community colleges, state colleges, and state universities around the state. These schools provide affordable higher education for residents of the state, and they also enroll students from other states. Wyoming has one state university, the University of Wyoming in Laramie, and seven community colleges in different parts of the state. Maine has the University of Maine in Orono (with campuses in several other towns), the Maine Maritime Academy in Castine, and seven community colleges. California, a state with a large population, operates California State University with 23 campuses, The University of California with 10 campuses, and more than one hundred community colleges. State universities provide much more than college education. They are homes to art and history museums, theaters, musical events, sports teams, and libraries that enrich their communities.

State Parks and Land Management

A great deal of land in each state is owned and maintained by the state in state park systems. This is an asset when your family wants to stay in a woodland cabin or go camping, hiking, biking, boating, or picnicking. State parks preserve beautiful or historic areas for the enjoyment of residents and out-of-state visitors. Roman Nose State Park in Oklahoma is named for a Cheyenne chief. It is one of Oklahoma's seven original state parks. Little Sahara State Park has over 1600 acres of sand dunes from twenty-five to seventy-five feet high. Visitors explore them on dune buggies or ATVs. Robbers Cave State Park is in the San Bois Mountains of southeast Oklahoma. A hideout used by outlaws Jesse James and Belle Starr is in the park.

West Virginia
Pricketts Fort State Park

South Dakota
Custer State Park

Oklahoma
Little Sahara State Park

North Dakota
Cross Ranch State Park

West Virginia has thirty-five state parks. Tu-Endie-Wei State Park preserves the site of the Battle of Point Pleasant fought on October 10, 1774 between frontiersmen and Native Americans led by Chief Cornstalk. "Tu-Endie-Wei" is a Wyandotte word that means "point between two waters." At Hawks Nest State Park, visitors can see hawks, turkey vultures, black vultures, bald eagles, golden eagles, and peregrine falcons along the New River. The Watters Smith Memorial State Park was given to the state by a descendant of Watters Smith so that the family's 1700s farm could be preserved for coming generations. It has a log cabin similar to the original and another Smith family home built around 1876.

These and the hundreds of other state parks scattered all across our country protect some of our most historic and beautiful places so that future generations of Americans can enjoy them. Check out what your state has to offer in its state parks!

In addition to state parks, states maintain thousands more acres of public lands. Some of this land is in state forests while other tracts are in wildlife management areas. Many of these tracts have valuable resources such as oil, minerals, and timber. Often a state makes a lease agreement with a private company that allows the company to obtain and sell the resources from state lands. States also allow farmers to lease land for grazing livestock and raising crops. Selling timber is another way for states to make money from their land. Some states sell Christmas trees grown in public forests. State-owned land is also used for hunting. Sportsmen appreciate a place to hunt and states appreciate hunters' help in managing the animal population.

As of 2010, 7.2% of Utah's 52.6 million acres were managed by the State of Utah. In Idaho, the Department of Lands manages over 2.6 million acres. Most of the money generated from these lands benefits Idaho's public schools. With a Recreational Mining Permit from the state, residents and tourists can pan for gold on some of Idaho's public rivers and streams!

Louisiana
Pearl River State Wildlife Management Area

Maryland
McKee-Beshers Wildlife Management Area

Transportation

The state government provides safe roads for their residents to get where they need to go for work and play! The Department of Transportation is busy in all corners of the state. They maintain roads, make maps, gather traffic information, provide weather-related driving information to travelers, study how to make certain sections of roads safer, and plan new roads and bike trails.

Maryland
Baltimore-Washington International Thurgood Marshall Airport

And the Department of Transportation has more than roads to take care of! It also oversees railroads and air travel. For example, in Maryland the Maryland Aviation Administration (part of the Department of Transportation) owns and operates the busy Baltimore/Washington International Thurgood Marshall Airport and Martin State Airport.

Supporting Business and Commerce

States want their businesses and farms to be successful. These provide jobs, boost the economy, generate tax money, and make the state a better place to live. State departments of agriculture help promote a state's farm products. States help people find and purchase locally grown produce and other farm products by listing Farmers' Markets on a state website. Maryland's department of agriculture has designated a Maryland's Best Ice Cream Trail. This trail includes seven dairy farms where visitors can get fresh ice cream right on the farm where it is made!

States also help farmers find markets for their products in other states and in other countries. Chef Justin Timineri represents the Florida Department of Agriculture and Consumer Services around the world as an ambassador for fresh Florida products. He creates new recipes that feature foods raised in Florida. He cooked and served Florida seafood for Olympians at the 2012 Olympics in London.

Tennessee
Farmers' Market

563

If your family goes on a camping trip to a state park, your dad drives there legally by carrying his state driver's license. Attached to your car is a state license plate. Your trip will likely take you on state highways with road signs approved by your state department of transportation. Along the way you may purchase apples advertised by your state department of agriculture. You may pass through a state forest or wildlife management area along the way. The park rangers you meet might have been educated at a state university. You see that you do not have to visit the state capitol in the state capital to touch your state government. It's all around you—even in your dad's billfold.

All of the beautiful lands in state parks and state forests are God's creations and all the animals that live there belong to Him.

> For every beast of the forest is Mine,
> The cattle on a thousand hills.
> Psalm 50:10

Lesson Activities

Thinking Biblically — Copy Psalm 50:10 in your notebook.

Vocabulary — Write five sentences in your notebook, using one of these words in each: interact, comply, affordable, timber, ambassador. Check in a dictionary if you need help with their definitions.

Literature — Read chapters 10-12 in *Basher Five-Two*.

Picture This! — Take a photograph or draw a picture of an example of state government's presence in your town or the area where you live.

Student Workbook or Lesson Review — If you are using one of these optional books, complete the assignment for Lesson 84.

★ Remember to choose an American Holiday to study this week! ★

UNIT 18 – LOCAL GOVERNMENT

BOOKS USED IN UNIT 18

- The Citizen's Handbook
- Misty of Chincoteague
- Student Workbook (optional)
- Lesson Review (optional)

City Hall, Athens, Georgia

At the County
COURTHOUSE

In the United States, the phrase local government usually means county and city governments. Local governments have been important in America since the first European settlers organized communities like Jamestown, Plymouth, and Massachusetts Bay.

Iron County, Missouri

Most of what we hear in the news media concerns what the Federal government does. We don't hear as much about local government in the media, but local government has a greater practical impact on most citizens day to day than the Federal government does.

We drive on local roads, visit our local library, and call our local 911 when we have an emergency. Most citizens can have the greatest impact for good at the local level. It is easier, for instance, to change a town's speed limits or to build a county park than it is to amend the U.S. Constitution. In this unit, we will look at government on the county and city levels.

County Government Serves State Government

In England, before the colonies in America were established, the English king had local officials who worked for him. They collected taxes and enforced laws. The local area in which he had authority from the king was called the county. When English settlers came to America, they set up county governments.

In a way similar to the English counties, county government in most states today is a kind of local extension of state government. State governments create county governments by acts of the state legislature. A county government can enact laws that are needed in that place, but county governments exist primarily to serve the purposes of the state government. When someone goes to a county government office to buy a hunting and fishing license or to obtain a marriage license, or when people register to vote at the election official's office, the county official is working not just for the county but on behalf of the state government.

Similar, but Different

Today just over three thousand counties exist in the fifty United States. Counties are called parishes in Louisiana and boroughs in Alaska. In most states, counties have governments; but in Connecticut and Rhode Island no separate county governments exist. Each of Alaska's boroughs has a government except the largest one which is called an unorganized borough. The unorganized borough of Alaska does not have any local governments, like towns or cities either. The Alaska legislature acts as the government for the unorganized borough.

Counties in the United States vary greatly in terms of size and population. Arlington County, Virginia, covers twenty-six square miles, while the North Slope Borough in Alaska covers 88,695 square miles. Loving County, Texas, has a population of less than one hundred residents, while Los Angeles County, California, is home to about ten million people. Seventy percent of the counties in the United States have a population under 50,000.

The United States Constitution gives few guidelines about how states are to set up local governments. Article IV, Section 4 of the Constitution says that, "The United States shall guarantee to every State in this Union a Republican Form of Government." This means that the Federal government guarantees that each state will have an elected government as opposed to a king or the rule of a few people who take power for themselves. The Constitution assumes that states will have three branches. Beyond that, states have freedom in how they organize state and local governments. As a result, states vary in the details of how they operate day to day and in how local governments are set up.

No two towns are exactly alike, and no two states are alike either. Think about how geography, history, and local interests affect what a local or state government does. Mackinac Island, Michigan, is in Lake Huron. The island does not allow cars or trucks on the island, though it does make an exception for ambulances, fire trucks, and the city's one police jeep. The city provides bicycle parking spaces beside streets. To avoid bicycle traffic jams, it limits the number of bicycles that companies can rent to tourists. It also limits the number of horse-drawn taxis and drays (delivery wagons) to avoid the extra expense of cleaning up after too many horses. See photo at right.

Mackinac Island, Michigan
Horse-drawn dray delivers freight.

St. Louis, Missouri
America's Center

Killington, Vermont
Ski Lift

Edmond, Washington
Washington State Ferry

Tourism is important to the economy in many places, including the City of St. Louis, St. Louis County, and the area around them. One local attraction is the St. Louis Rams professional football team. The State of Missouri has a regional organization called the St. Louis Convention & Visitors Commission (CVC), which is responsible for attracting visitors to the area. The CVC operates the America's Center Convention Complex, which includes the Edward Jones Dome where the Rams play football, Ferrara Theatre, meeting rooms, and exhibit halls for conventions. Members of the CVC include a chairman appointed by the Governor, five members appointed by the Mayor of St. Louis, and five appointed by the St. Louis County Executive.

Vermont has the geography and the weather for great snow skiing, so the Vermont Department of Labor has a Passenger Tramway Division which inspects each of Vermont's more than 175 ski lifts. The State of Washington has several inhabited islands and is close to the Canadian province of British Columbia, so its Department of Transportation has a Ferries Division. Washington State Ferries is the largest ferry system in the U.S. See photos at left.

Still, most of the differences that we find from state to state primarily involve such matters as the titles given to certain offices, whether some officials are elected or appointed, and what responsibilities are carried out by which agencies. There is a degree of variation; but since the states share a common heritage of government, local governments are quite similar all across America.

Types of County Government

Almost all county governments in the U.S. are one of three types. The first, used in just over half of American counties, is the *commission*. In this type of county government, people elect representatives from districts within the county. The governing body is usually called the county commission, the board of supervisors, or a similar name. Commissioners are elected for a term of two or four years. In this type of county government, there is no executive office.

The commission not only passes the county budget and enacts new laws like a legislature, but it also oversees the work of county government employees like an executive. The commission usually selects one of its members to serve as chairman of its meetings. In many places these meetings take place once per month.

The second common type of county government is the *commission-executive/mayor* form. Under this form, the people of the county elect a commission and also elect a county executive or county mayor to oversee county government. In some places this official is called the county judge. He or she is called this because county commissions were once called county courts. They had some responsibilities like those of a court as well as those of a legislative body. The county mayor is usually elected for a term of four years (two years in Arkansas). In most places, there is no limit on the number of terms a county mayor can serve.

Lenawee County, Michigan

The third type of county government in America is the *commission-administrator* form of county government. With this form, the people elect a commission, but then the commission hires a professional administrator to oversee the daily work of county government. The administrator can hire and fire county employees, but the commission can also fire the administrator. Some places have chosen this type of government because it is the way that many large companies are organized. Though the company is run by a board of directors, the board hires a chief executive officer (CEO) to operate the business day to day. Many citizens like to be able to have one person (either a county mayor or a county administrator) who is responsible for carrying out the work of the county, so that people know whom to call when they have a need or a problem.

Jackson County, Tennessee

Seal on County Vehicle

The County Courthouse

The county seat is the city or town where the county government is located. This town is usually located in the middle of the county. When counties were being formed, the goal was to have the seat of government within a half-day's wagon or buggy drive of all parts of the county. This allowed people to come to the county seat, take care of any business they had with the government, and get home in one day.

Courthouses

Park County, Wyoming

St. Bernard Parish, Louisiana

Decatur County, Indiana

Doddridge County, West Virginia

Colbert County, Alabama

The building that is the headquarters of county government is usually called the county courthouse. The courthouse once contained all of the offices of county government; but as county governments have grown, many counties have built or purchased additional buildings.

At the courthouse are many offices where government workers take care of a variety of jobs. Many citizens come and go as they pay taxes, request documents, apply for business licenses, talk to the county mayor about a concern, or take care of other matters. Notice the courthouses at left, especially the one in the center. It has a tree growing out of its tower and has since 1870!

County Departments

The most common elected official in county government is the county clerk. This official issues marriage licenses and automobile license plates and performs other official services that people need on a regular basis.

Other typical county officials include:

★ County treasurer or trustee, who collects taxes and fees and pays the bills and salaries that county government has to pay;

★ Property assessor, who decides the value of every piece of property in the county for the purpose of determining the property tax that the owner has to pay;

★ Road supervisor, who oversees road construction and maintenance in the county;

★ Zoning or planning official, who helps the county oversee how county land is used.

County government usually includes a sheriff's department for law enforcement and often also has an animal control office, a public library, a public health department, county parks, and many other services. See photos on page 571.

Everyone who lives in one of the fifty states also lives in a county or a parish or a borough, even if it is an unorganized one. County governments touch the lives of their citizens in practical ways every day. In the days when Jesus walked on the earth the government of Palestine had government areas that were bigger than a town, but smaller than a country, too. The name of one was Galilee.

Moore County, North Carolina

> Immediately the news about Him spread everywhere into all the surrounding district of Galilee.
>
> Mark 1:28

Lesson Activities

Cheatham County, Tennessee

Vocabulary — Copy these words in your notebook, each on a separate line: amend, county, resident, heritage, administrator. Look up each word in a dictionary. Next to each word, write what part of speech it is according to the way the word is used in the lesson.

Literature — Read "Changes and Improvements Made in Boston" in *The Citizen's Handbook,* pages 99-101, and chapters 1-2 in *Misty of Chincoteague.*

Franklin, Indiana
Johnson County Health Department

Find Out! — How is the government organized in your county?

Picture This! — Draw a picture or take a photograph of your county courthouse.

Student Workbook or Lesson Review — If you are using one of these optional books, complete the assignment for Lesson 86.

Franklin, Indiana

Around CITY HALL

Wytheville, Virginia

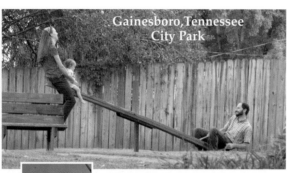

Gainesboro, Tennessee
City Park

Salt Lake City, Utah
City Hall at Sunrise

Oldenburg, Indiana

Gainesboro, Tennessee

Indianapolis, Indiana

For much of American history, most people lived in small towns and in rural areas. Over time more and more began living in larger towns and cities. In 1920 the U.S. Census showed for the first time that a majority of Americans lived in towns and cities of 2,500 or more. That trend has continued. Now seventy percent of Americans live in urban areas of 50,000 or more.

The purpose of a town or city government is to govern, protect, and provide services for the people who live there. With growing urban populations, city residents need and expect good government. Notice the town park, streetlight, and streets in the photos at left. These are services that towns and city governments provide.

New towns and cities are organized every year. Most are former rural areas beside a large city where many new houses have been built recently. As the population there grows, the residents usually want services that they cannot provide for themselves individually, such as police and fire protection; electricity, water, and sewer services; and parks and recreational opportunities. Citizens join together to ask their state for incorporation as a city.

Some rural communities, like Nameless pictured at right below, choose to stay unincorporated. However, even people who live in the country use the services cities provide when they travel there for various purposes.

Juneau, Alaska

Skagway, Alaska

Starting a City Government

When a city is organized, it receives a charter from the state government that gives it the legal right to exist. A charter is like a constitution for a city, except that, if the people want to change the charter, they usually have

Nameless, Tennessee

to ask the state government for permission to do so. Some cities are given home rule, which means that it can change the charter through a referendum or a vote by their city council. Although cities are chartered by the state government, they are not expected to carry out state government functions the way that county governments do.

Being incorporated as a city is a right that the residents of a place can enjoy. However, as we have mentioned before, with rights come responsibilities. State governments require cities to provide certain services to their residents. If a city grows to a population of 100,000 but the city government never gets around to providing water or sewer utilities or other basic services, living in that city would be difficult. Requirements for cities differ according to their population. Small towns (sometimes called villages or boroughs) have fewer responsibilities to fulfill than larger towns and cities.

Velva, North Dakota
Mayor meets with a manager from the U.S. Army Corps of Engineers.

South Carolina

Types of City Government

As we discussed in Lesson 26, the oldest kind of city government in the United States is the town meeting. At these sessions, usually once a year, all of the adult residents of a town meet to discuss ideas and vote on which ones they want to put into practice. This form is used only in a few small towns today, mostly in New England. Even there, citizens are usually elected as selectmen or aldermen to oversee city government between town meetings.

Cities in the United States generally have one of three different forms of government. Over half of U.S. cities use the *council-manager* system of government. In these cities, the people elect representatives to the city council. The council then hires a professional city manager to run the daily work of city government.

Cities with a council-manager government usually have a mayor also, but the mayor in this arrangement typically does not have much authority. In some places he is a council member whom other members choose to be chairman of their meetings. In others he is the council member who received the most votes in the election. The mayor in a council-manager government attends ceremonies, cuts the ribbon when a new business opens, and makes proclamations about local civic activities such as Neighborhood Watch Week.

Mount Airy, North Carolina
Hometown of Actor Andy Griffith

About forty percent of American cities use the *council-mayor* form of government. In this arrangement, a mayor is elected by all the people of a city, while council members are elected by districts within the city. The mayor is the chief executive of the city under this form of government. He oversees the city government, recommends a budget to the city council, and proposes new laws. This is the form of government used in most of our larger cities. In this system the mayor is responsible to the voters to lead well.

A few American cities use the *commission* form of government. In this system each person elected to the city commission has a certain government service to oversee, such as utilities, law enforcement, or street maintenance. This form of city government gives the legislative role and the executive role to the same group of people on the commission. It allows voters to know who is responsible for each area of city government. However, it can also create competition among the commissioners, each of whom probably will always want more money for his or her area of responsibility.

In a smaller town or city, the mayor and councilmen are often local businessmen and women who serve in government on a part-time basis. As the city becomes larger, the need for a full-time mayor becomes greater. Even when the job of mayor is full-time, the members of the city council usually still serve on a part-time basis.

Other Kinds of Local Government

We began this unit by noting that local government is usually understood to be county and city government. However, local government is not always quite that simple. There are several special kinds of local governments that carry out important responsibilities for many citizens on the local level.

About twenty states have townships, which are areas that are larger than a town but smaller than a county. Townships are typically led by a group of elected officials called selectmen or the board of supervisors or some similar title. This board hires full-time employees to carry out day to day responsibilities for the township. Township governments are often responsible for many of the jobs that cities and counties carry out, such as road maintenance, fire and rescue squads, building code and land use zoning enforcement, and sometimes providing public utilities.

In a few places in the United States, the county government and the city governments within the county have merged into one government, called consolidated or metropolitan government. These local governments are an attempt to provide government services with less expense for people in the county, since many activities had been provided by both the county and the city governments.

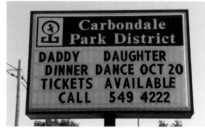

Virginia

A special district is not quite a city and not quite a county. It is usually created to provide one specific need, such as fire protection, library services, or schools. The district is often overseen by an elected board that might have the authority to raise and collect taxes on property owners, or the board might only be able to propose a tax rate to the city or county government. Small communities or rural areas might band together to create a special district to provide a service that they cannot provide individually. Over 35,000 special districts have been formed in the United States.

The largest single expense for many local governments is education, but the way that public schools are operated is different in different places. Many counties oversee all of the schools within the county, in some places cities have their own school district, and in other localities special school districts have been created. The board of education is usually made up of elected citizens, while the superintendent might be elected or he might be appointed by the board.

Urbana, Illinois
Urbana School District

At City Hall

The offices located in city hall often include the office that collects city business and property taxes, a city planning department, a city traffic court that handles any tickets or citations handed out to drivers, and offices for utilities operated by the city (like water, sewer, natural gas, and electric services).

Carbondale, Illinois
Park District

Morrilton, Arkansas
Ball Field

576

In small towns, fire and police departments are sometimes located at city hall. Many cities also have water departments and sewer treatment plants in other locations. Another facility might be set aside to keep city-owned vehicles in good repair, and yet another office might be in charge of parks and other recreational services.

As with county governments, you can see that city governments handle services that affect many aspects of everyday life. The people who work for the city are often long-time residents of the city, and local citizens can have a powerful voice in what happens in their community.

When it goes well with the righteous, the city rejoices,
And when the wicked perish, there is joyful shouting.
Proverbs 11:10

City Hall

New Orleans, Louisiana

Idaho City, Idaho

St. Augustine, Florida

Lesson Activities

Thinking Biblically — Copy Proverbs 11:10-11 in your notebook.

Literature — Read "Dedication of Weston Town-House" in *The Citizen's Handbook,* pages 102-103, and chapters 3-4 in *Misty of Chincoteague.*

Creative Writing — In your notebook, make a list of ten good things about the city or town where you live.

Find Out! — For what or for whom is your city named?

Picture This! — Draw a picture or take a photograph of one of your favorite places in your city or town.

Student Workbook or Lesson Review — If you are using one of these optional books, complete the assignment for Lesson 87.

Working Together for a STOP SIGN

Gainesboro, Tennessee

Nichols Road is a two-lane road that runs between Greenwood and Coopertown. About two miles outside of Greenwood, Shady Lane turns off to the right. A few years ago Jess Nichols, who owned a farm on Shady Lane, sold his property to a developer who wanted to build a subdivision on the land. Its beautiful location and its closeness to the growing town of Greenwood made Shady Lane Estates popular. Lots sold quickly, houses went up, and many families began to enjoy their lives there.

The families that moved to Shady Lane Estates included several children who enjoyed riding their bikes on the country roads and playing ball in the vacant lots. Nichols Road had been popular with runners and bikers for several years. The growth of Shady Lane Estates meant that both Shady Lane and Nichols Road started to have more traffic. Parents told their children to watch for cars. Runners and bikers grumbled about the changes.

Then problems began to develop. Drivers who were leaving Shady Lane Estates were frustrated by having to wait for children on bikes followed by their dogs. Turning left from Shady Lane onto Nichols Road toward Greenwood took longer and longer as the traffic got heavier. Drivers had to watch for children chasing balls from the fields. Runners and bikers often had no choice but to get off of the roadway as more and more cars passed them.

Citizens Get Involved

Residents of the subdivision decided they needed to fulfill their rights and responsibilities as parents and as citizens. They agreed to meet and discuss the situation. They invited people who lived close by, as well as the county mayor, the county road superintendent, and their representatives on the county commission. Road superintendent Nathan Lawrence and county commissioners John Elmwood and Greg Rich attended the meeting on March 13.

At the meeting, people shared their observations and experiences concerning the traffic. Many people made suggestions about what could be done. Everyone agreed that children should no longer play in the vacant lot at the intersection of Shady Lane and Nichols Road. This was something they could do as private citizens to keep the children safe. The majority of people in attendance agreed that the existing stop sign at the end of Shady Lane was not enough. They decided that Nichols Road needed stop signs, too, one for northbound traffic and one for southbound.

Superintendent Lawrence explained that stop signs would have to be authorized by the state department of transportation since Nichols Road was a state highway. He said the state would require a traffic study. Commissioner Rich noted that the cost of the signs would have to be paid by the county. Commissioner Elmwood said that the county budget was already stretched to the limit for this year, but that he would try to help all he could. Several people expressed concern that a serious accident might occur.

The citizens at the meeting decided to take action to make sure that the intersection was made safer. Several people offered to call and write letters to the county mayor, the other commissioners, and to the state highway department. One mother said that she would ask a reporter at the local television station to do a story about the problem. A civic club president who lived in the neighborhood said that he would

United States

Mexico

Canada

Thailand

Tennessee Department of Transportation Conducts Meeting with Property Owners

Citizen signs in at meeting.

TDOT employees explain intersection improvements to citizens.

TDOT employee shows project maps to citizens.

Citizens gather around maps.

bring it up at the next club meeting to see how the club might help. Commissioner Elmwood said that he would get the item put on the agenda for the next county commission meeting.

A Meeting of the County Commission

County Mayor Lee Elmwood (father of Commissioner John Elmwood) and the county commissioners began receiving phone calls and letters from Shady Lane residents and from members of the civic club. When the county commission met in the courtroom at the courthouse on April 22, there was standing room only. Mayor Elmwood invited several Shady Lane residents to speak. Afterwards Commissioner Rich made a motion that the county send an official request to the state department of transportation asking them to do the necessary study. Commissioner Elmwood seconded the motion. When Mayor Elmwood called for a vote of the commissioners, the vote was unanimous in favor.

Road superintendent Lawrence told the group that he had a supply of stop signs at the county highway department shop, but that they were all 24-inch signs. He said that it was his guess that the state would recommend 48-inch signs which he thought would cost about $150 each. Mr. Elmwood made a motion to appropriate the needed funds, and Mr. Rich seconded. Again the vote was unanimous.

Action Is Taken

Since many other traffic studies were already on the schedule at the state department of transportation, it was early August before the Nichols Road survey was completed. The department took another four weeks to review the information that was gathered. In September they held a community meeting at the school near Shady Lane Estates to get more citizen input.

Finally, in November the state transportation department approved putting up two 48-inch stop signs on Nichols Road at its intersection with Shady Lane. They also stated that the county must attach small All-Way signs to the post as well. Superintendent Lawrence ordered the necessary signs. They were delivered in early December. As soon as they arrived, he sent Ethan and Ryan, two members of his crew, to the intersection where they installed the signs.

Since so many stop signs are destroyed by vandalism, Nathan Lawrence's crew was experienced in putting them up. Before they left the shop, they put all their tools in the back of the county truck. They put road sign posts, their custom-made post pusher, a sledge hammer, street sign brackets, and, of course, the stop signs. See photos at right.

First, they installed the Galvanized U-Channel Sign Post beside the northbound lane of Nichols Road, making sure that it was six feet away from the pavement. Ryan held it in place while Ethan stood on the tailgate of the pickup truck and forced the post downward with the post pusher, first with his strength and then with a sledgehammer. Then Ryan stood on the tailgate to attach the bracket. Together they lifted the sign in place. Ethan secured the bolts. They repeated the process beside the southbound lane.

A History of Stop Signs

How does a driver know when traffic laws require him to stop? Residential streets and rural roads have stop signs. Busy intersections in towns and cities have traffic lights. When a traffic light is out of order, a policeman may stand at an intersection to direct traffic. At road construction sites, a construction worker may hold up a hand-held stop sign. When a school bus stops, the driver extends a stop sign from the side of the bus. However, drivers have not always had these helps.

In the era of horse-drawn transportation and in the early days of the automobile, there were no traffic control signs. As the number of automobiles grew, the situation became more and more dangerous. In 1915 Detroit (where many cars were manufactured) erected a two-foot by two-foot white metal

Posts

Custom-made Post Pusher

Sledgehammer

Bracket

Jarratt, Virginia

Rural Minnesota

Rural Kentucky

Franklin, Indiana

Hot Springs, Arkansas

sign with the word "STOP" painted in black letters at an intersection. Eight years later, the Mississippi Valley Association of State Highway Departments recommended that signs have shapes based on the seriousness of the sign's message. A circle would mean the highest danger. These would be used at railroad crossings. An octagonal (eight-sided) sign would mean the next highest danger, and this was the shape chosen for stop signs. Warning signs would be diamond-shaped.

In 1935, the American Association of State Highway Officials and the National Conference on Street and Highway Safety worked together to publish the Manual on Uniform Traffic Control Devices (MUTCD). The manual's first recommendation was for stop signs to be yellow with black lettering. When the manual was revised in 1954, it changed the design of stop signs to red with white letters because red was more commonly associated with stop.

The MUTCD standards became law in the United States in 1966. Today's stop signs must be at least 24 inches tall and 24 inches across, but most stop signs are 30 inches by 30 inches. Busier roads must have larger signs, which can be up to 48 inches by 48 inches.

Before 1971, stops signs were commonly two to three feet above the ground, but today the bottom of the sign should be seven feet above the ground. The post is to be located at least six feet from the edge of the pavement.

The MUTCD also sets standards for a sign's capacity to reflect light directly back with a minimum of light scattering. This capacity is called retroreflectivity and helps a sign be seen more clearly at night. Road and transportation departments for cities, counties, and states commonly receive bids from companies that manufacture signs so that governments can purchase the signs that they need at the lowest possible price.

How Does a Stop Sign Get Placed at the End of Your Road?

Putting up a stop sign or a traffic light is not something that an individual citizen or group of citizens can do on their own. This is a job for a government agency, but individuals and groups can and should be involved. Sometimes when a new road is built or new homes or businesses are constructed on an existing road, city planners know what traffic control signs and signals will be needed even before the work is completed. In other situations, like the one discussed in this lesson, changes in traffic patterns cause a need for new signs and signals where the need had not existed before. In these cases, many people work together to make driving, walking, jogging, and playing safer.

When you see signs as you travel along the roads and highways, think about the road superintendents, government workers, elected officials, private organizations, sign-making companies, and private citizens who worked together so those signs could mark your way.

In Proverbs God uses the idea of a highway to illustrate a lesson.

The way of the lazy is as a hedge of thorns, but the path of the upright is a highway.

Proverbs 15:19

Lesson Activities

Thinking Biblically — Copy Proverbs 16:19 in your notebook. Write 2 or 3 sentences about what you think the verse means.

Vocabulary — In your notebook, write which of the following words belongs in each sentence: subdivision, superintendent, intersection, civic, unanimous.

1. As _____ of schools, my uncle has a lot of phone calls from concerned parents.

2. On the way home, we passed through an _____ with a broken traffic light.

3. My grandfather thought it was his _____ duty to run for mayor.

4. I thought we would argue all night about what game to play, but the vote was _____ for charades.

5. The Jones live in a _____ on the edge of town, right beside a pasture with cows.

Literature — Read chapters 5-7 in *Misty of Chincoteague*.

Creative Writing — Imagine that a stop sign had thoughts about his life and what he sees in a given day. In your notebook, write at least 2 or 3 paragraphs as if a stop sign is talking.

Picture This! — Draw a picture or take a photograph of a road sign near your house.

Student Workbook or Lesson Review — If you are using one of these optional books, complete the assignment for Lesson 88.

Hometown CELEBRATIONS

Albuquerque, New Mexico
Balloon Festival

Warrens, Wisconsin
Cranberry Festival

Clay Junction, West Virginia
Golden Delicious Apple Festival

Agood citizen takes pride in his or her community, helps it to be better, and honors those to whom honor is due. What is special about the place where you live? Is it a place of exceptional beauty? Did someone prominent in history live there? Was it the scene of a memorable event? Is there a farm product or mineral the town is known for?

Communities can have many reasons for being proud of what they have. Welcome signs at the city limits might proudly inform visitors that a community is the home of a famous athlete, a well-known entertainer, or a former President of the United States. Neil Armstrong gave his hometown of Wapakoneta, Ohio, a reason to be proud in 1969 when he became the first man to walk on the moon. Tiny Dixon, Illinois, was proud to be the birthplace of Ronald Reagan when he was a famous actor and then even more proud when he became the fortieth President of the United States.

The reasons for civic pride can vary greatly from one community to another. A village in New England can be proud of its forests and hills, while a city in Arizona can be proud of its desert scenery. The people of Gettysburg, Pennsylvania, honor the history of the decisive battle of the Civil War which took place near their town; while residents of Portsmouth, New Hampshire, take pride in the fact that the peace treaty ending the Russo-Japanese War in 1905 was signed at the nearby Portsmouth Naval Shipyard.

Celebrating Our Heritage

Many communities in America honor their past, give thanks for their blessings, encourage people to learn about their town, and help the local economy by hosting one or more annual festivals. The themes of these festivals vary greatly. Local history is a common festival theme. In Lesson 101 you will read about the 911 Festival in Haleyville, Alabama, held every September, which commemorates the first-ever 911 emergency call made there in 1968. Valentine, Nebraska, hosts the annual Nebraska Cowboy Poetry Gathering and Old West Days every October. Mule Day, begun to remember the role of mules in Southern agriculture, is held every first Saturday in April in Columbia, Tennessee; while the Mule Days Celebration, honoring the role of mules as pack animals in mining and in the settlement of the West, takes place in Bishop, California, in the days before Memorial Day every year.

Local agriculture or industry can be a theme. Plant City, Florida, offers the Florida Strawberry Festival in February and March. In Lesson 118 you will learn about the West

Granville, Tennessee
John Notgrass performs "One Soldier's Story" at the Granville Fall Celebration.

Reno, Nevada
Reno River Festival

War Eagle, Arkansas
War Eagle Mill Craft & Culinary Fair

Oklahoma
Oklahoma Regatta Festival

Pella Tulip Time in Pella, Iowa

Texas Wind Festival in Roscoe, Texas, an event that began because wind-powered energy-producing turbines were built there and made the local economy blossom.

The ethnic or national identity of a group in a locality can provide the basis for a festival. For instance, the Basque (pronounced bask) people of northern Spain are a distinct ethnic group. Many Basques emigrated to the northwestern part of the United States and worked as sheepherders. To honor and preserve Basque culture, many communities in that part of the country hold Basque festivals, including Buffalo, Wyoming, and Boise, Idaho. Remember the lesson on Columbus Day in Part 1 of *Uncle Sam and You*? Cities where many people of Italian heritage live often plan a Columbus Day activity of some kind.

Communities hold festivals of the arts, which celebrate visual or performing arts, or crafts and hobbies such as quilting. Sometimes communities hold a fall festival or have a large Christmas event that offers the products of many local crafters. Natural resources can offer an appropriate theme. For instance, a place where many species of birds migrate might hold a birdwatching festival.

Sometimes the theme is unusual and just for fun. Metropolis is a small city in southern Illinois of about 6,500 residents. Since it shares the name of the hometown of the fictional comic book character Superman, Metropolis hosts the Superman Celebration every June.

Organizing a Festival

A local festival is a good example of how different elements of civic life work together for good. Local festivals don't just happen. A successful festival needs individuals taking initiative to help their town, groups working together to support a cause, and government involvement to make sure things go smoothly. A successful event requires a great deal of prayer, vision, organization, communication, cooperation, and hard work.

Bitterroot Scottish Irish Festival in Hamilton, Montana

Often an event begins through the ideas and efforts of one person who believes in his or her community, wants to make a difference, and is able to share the vision with others. However, even though one excited volunteer may have a clear idea of what he or she wants to accomplish, a successful festival requires the cooperation of many people.

Local officials must make preparations for a festival. They will need to make sure that there are enough law enforcement officers and emergency medical workers available during the event. They might need to help with traffic control and with the blocking off of certain streets.

Successful festival planners also involve local clubs and businesses. Clubs can provide volunteers, and the clubs may wish to have booths to let attendees know about what they do. Local businesses are often willing to provide financial help in exchange for advertising. Other groups that get involved in local festivals are the Chamber of Commerce and local and state convention and visitor bureaus. Many churches are willing to offer space for craft booths or for displaying quilts or artwork. Some churches will use a festival as a fundraiser by providing a pancake breakfast, a hamburger lunch, or a chili supper.

Look back and ahead at all of the festivals pictured in this lesson and think about the planning and working together—and think about how people are enjoying one another!

Festivals Around the Country

Morro Bay, California
Morrow Bay Kite Festival

Minot, North Dakota
Norsk Hostfest, Largest Scandinavian Festival in North America

Austin, Texas
The Pecan Street Festival

Arthur, Illinois
Illinois Amish Country Cheese Festival

Portland, Oregon
Portland Rose Festival

Santa Clarita, California
Santa Clarita Cowboy Festival

God gave the Israelites many opportunities throughout the year to have special festivals. They were meaningful spiritually to the Israelites, but they were also times to enjoy one another. An especially happy one was the Feast of Booths.

> You shall celebrate the Feast of Booths seven days
> after you have gathered in from your threshing floor
> and your wine vat; and you shall rejoice in your feast,
> you and your son and your daughter and your male
> and female servants and the Levite and the stranger
> and the orphan and the widow who are in your towns.
> Seven days you shall celebrate a feast to the Lord your God
> in the place which the Lord chooses, because the Lord
> your God will bless you in all your produce and in all
> the work of your hands, so that you will be altogether joyful.
> Deuteronomy 16:13-15

Morro Bay, California
Morro Bay Winter Bird Festival

Lesson Activities

Thinking Biblically — Read Deuteronomy 16:1-20.

Vocabulary — Look up each of these words in a dictionary and read their definitions: exceptional, commemorate, locality, vision, fundraiser.

Literature — Read chapters 8-10 in *Misty of Chincoteague*.

Creative Writing — Think of an idea for a festival that could take place in your town. In your notebook, write one page describing the festival.

Student Workbook or Lesson Review — If you are using one of these optional books, complete the assignment for Lesson 89.

★ Remember to choose an American Holiday to study this week! ★

UNIT 19 – NATIVE AMERICAN TRIBAL GOVERNMENT

BOOKS USED IN UNIT 19

- The Citizen's Handbook
- Misty of Chincoteague
- Student Workbook (optional)
- Lesson Review (optional)

Dan Akee, a World War II Veteran Navajo Code Talker, visits with members of the Dishchili Bikoh Apache Group at Grand Canyon National Park.

The Bureau of
INDIAN AFFAIRS

The original inhabitants of the land that became the United States of America were Native Americans, also called American Indians and Alaska Natives. As Europeans came to settle here, they began to make treaties with various tribes. When the colonies organized a Federal government just before the American Revolution, that government developed official relationships with tribes.

★ After the Continental Congress was formed, it created a Committee of Indian Affairs. Benjamin Franklin was its chairman.

★ When the U.S. Constitution was adopted, it mentioned tribes in Article I, Section 8, which gives Congress power "to regulate commerce with foreign nations, and among the several States, and with the Indian tribes."

★ In 1824, Secretary of War John C. Calhoun, pictured at right, established a bureau to oversee trade and treaty relationships between the United States and Indian tribes.

John C. Calhoun

★ In 1849 the Bureau of Indian Affairs was placed in the U.S. Department of Interior. At various times, it was called the Indian Office, the Indian Bureau, the Indian Department, and the Indian Service, before officially becoming the "Bureau of Indian Affairs" in 1947.

The Bureau of Indian Affairs (BIA) is one of the oldest agencies of the Federal government. As a part of the executive branch, it has been responsible for carrying out Federal laws which specifically concern Native Americans. Here are some examples of laws that the Bureau of Indian Affairs has implemented:

- ★ The General Allotment Act of 1887. This act allowed non-Indian settlers to move onto tribal lands west of the Mississippi River.

- ★ The Indian Citizenship Act of 1924. This act gave American Indians and Alaska Natives U.S. citizenship and the right to vote.

- ★ The Indian Reorganization Act of 1934. This act established the basis for how individual tribal governments work today.

The way that the BIA has handled relationships with Native Americans has changed dramatically through the years (in this lesson, we will use the term Native Americans when referring to both American Indians and Alaska Natives). At one time, many tribes were seen as enemies and the U.S. Army fought wars with them. At times the BIA tried to control Native Americans and force them to blend in with other Americans and become like them. For example, many Native American children were taken away from their families and sent to boarding schools, where they lost much of their native culture.

An Iroquois princess gives an invitation to presidential secretary Marvin McIntyre for President Roosevelt to attend the Six Nations Iroquois Grand Indian Council at the St. Regis Reservation, 1937.

Ignacio, Colorado
Boy's Dormitory at the Southern Ute Boarding School

Above: Members of the U.S. House of Representatives Indian Affairs Committee left Washington, D.C., on May 6, 1920, to inspect the conditions of Indians in Oklahoma and other states. The House and Senate continue to have committees related to Native Americans.

Mrs. Isabelle Haggett worked for the Bureau of Indian Affairs for thirty-three years before retiring in 1933 at age seventy. In retirement she enrolled at George Washington University.

Native Americans worked for improved civil rights in the 1960s and 1970s. In an effort to treat Native Americans more fairly, Congress passed the following laws that changed the way the Federal government handled its relations with them:

- ★ Indian Self-Determination and Education Assistance Act of 1975. This law gave tribes the authority to spend funds that the Federal government gave them instead of Federal agencies overseeing these funds.

★ Tribal Self-Governance Act of 1997. This law gave tribes even more authority over Federal funds they receive. It also encourages tribes to keep their distinct cultures.

Today the BIA words its mission statement like this:

The Bureau of Indian Affairs' mission is to enhance the quality of life, to promote economic opportunity, and to carry out the responsibility to protect and improve the trust assets of American Indians, Indian tribes, and Alaska Natives.

Fulfilling Obligations

The Continental Congress made the first treaty between the Federal government and a Native American tribe in 1778. The Federal government continued to make treaties with tribes until 1871. In many treaties, tribes agreed to transfer millions of acres of land to the Federal government in exchange for protection and for food and other supplies. The Bureau of Indian Affairs has the responsibility of making sure that the Federal government continues to fulfill its obligations to Native Americans.

Tulalip Reservation, Washington

On January 22, 1914, natives of the northwestern United States celebrated Treaty Day. The 1855 Treaty of Point Elliot established the boundaries of this reservation which created a permanent home for the Snohomish, Snoqualmie, Skagit, Suiattle, Samish, and Stillaguanish tribes and bands of natives living near them.

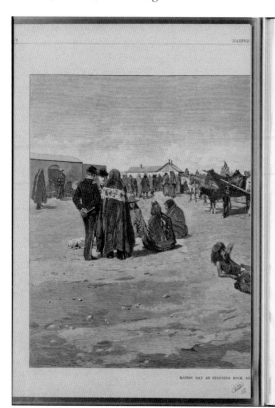

Standing Rock Sioux Indian Reservation, North and South Dakota

The Standing Rock Sioux tribe signed a treaty with the United States government on April 29, 1868. The July 28, 1883 issue of Harper's Weekly *included an illustration of tribesmen arriving at the Bureau of Indian Affairs Standing Rock Agency to*

Washington, D.C.
Above: Three Cheyennes and one Kiowa visit the White House in 1863. One is wearing a Thomas Jefferson Peace Medal brought to their tribe by Lewis and Clark.

Right: Pueblo leaders visit D.C. in 1923. They brought a cane given to them by President Lincoln, who promised that they would keep their lands permanently.

June 18, 1870 Harper's Weekly *Illustration of Leaders Coming to Meet Ely S. Parker*

Native Americans Involved in the BIA

More than fifty people have served as the head of the BIA since it began in 1824. Though many Native Americans cooperated with the Bureau and worked for it, the first Native American to head the Bureau was Ely S. Parker of the Seneca tribe, who served from 1869 to 1871. No Native American headed the Bureau again until 1966 when Oneida tribesman Robert L. Bennett assumed leadership. Since then, the BIA has almost always been led by a Native American.

Since 1849 the BIA has been part of the Department of the Interior. In 1977 Interior established a new position, called the Assistant Secretary-Indian Affairs, to aid the Secretary of the Interior. The chart at right gives the tribes of some of the people who have served as head of the BIA or as the Assistant Secretary-Indian Affairs. Notice that some who served were descendants of more than one tribe.

Today the majority of the people working for the BIA are American Indians and Alaska Natives. BIA employees across

Tribes of Individuals Who Have Served as Head of the Bureau of Indian Affairs and as Assistant Secretary-Indian Affairs for the Department of the Interior

Athabascan

Cherokee Nation

Chickasaw Nation

Lac Courte Oreilles Chippewa-Choctaw

Mandan-Hidatsa

Menominee

Mohawk-Oglala Sioux

Oglala Lakota Sioux Blackfeet

Oneida

Oneida Tribe of Wisconsin

Pawnee

Red Lake Chippewa

Sault Ste. Marie Chippewa

Seneca

Sioux

Tohono O'odham-Yaqui

Wasco

the country work with tribal governments to improve the quality of life in tribal communities. The BIA assists American Indian and Alaska Native tribes, villages, and groups through four offices, described in the box on page 597.

Indian Health Service

The Bureau of Indian Affairs once provided health care to American Indians and Alaska Natives, but since 1954 the Department of Health and Human Services has operated the Indian Health Service.

Bureau of Indian Education

Within the Bureau of Indian Affairs is the Bureau of Indian Education (BIE). The BIE directly operates almost sixty schools and assists in the operation of more than 100 other facilities. These facilities include elementary schools, high schools, boarding schools, and dormitories near other schools. It helps to educate more than 40,000 elementary and high school students on sixty-three reservations in twenty-three states. The BIE also helps more than twenty tribal colleges and universities which serve more than 25,000 students. The BIE directly operates two post-secondary (after high school) institutions: Haskell Indian Nations University in Lawrence, Kansas, and the Southwest Indian Polytechnic Institute in Albuquerque, New Mexico. It also offers scholarships to American Indians and Alaska Natives and provides job training. Since the Indian Reorganization Act of 1934 was passed, schools operated by the Bureau of Indian Affairs have included the teaching of Indian history and culture.

Lawrence, Kansas
*View from the Campus of
Haskell Indian Nations University*

Albuquerque, New Mexico
*Road Runner on the Campus of
Southwest Indian Polytechnic Institute*

The history of the relationship between the Federal government of the United States and Native Americans includes sad stories and promising ones. Both the Federal government and Native Americans have given a great deal—Native Americans gave their lands; the United States continues to give aid in many ways. It is important that the United States honor its word by honoring its treaties.

The Office of Indian Services

The Office of Indian Services helps Native American tribes with:

★ Issues involving the tribe's children.

★ Needs of the tribe's government.

★ Making their own decisions, called "self-determination."

★ Reservation roads and bridges (reservations are described in Lesson 92).

★ Improving housing.

The Office of Justice Services

The Office of Justice Services operates or pays for:

★ Tribal law enforcement.

★ Tribal courts.

★ Correctional facilities located on Federal Indian lands.

The Office of Trust Services

The Office of Trust Services helps tribes and individual Native Americans manage their:

★ Land.

★ Assets (what they own).

★ Natural resources, including underground mineral estates held in trust for Native Americans, who earned a total of $524 million in 2007 from these underground resources.

The Office of Field Operations

The Office of Field Operations oversees twelve regional offices and eighty-three agencies which work directly with tribes.

The practice of writing treaties is an ancient one. Israelite king Asa offered a treaty to the king of Damascus:

Let there be a treaty between you and me, as between my father and your father.

1 Kings 15:19

Lesson Activities

Vocabulary — Write five sentences in your notebook, using one of these words in each: enhance, asset, obligation, dormitory, tribal. Check in a dictionary if you need help with their definitions.

Literature — Read "Crow Tribe, United States and State of Montana Sign Historic Water Compact" in *The Citizen's Handbook*, pages 104-106, and chapters 11-12 in *Misty of Chincoteague*.

Creative Writing — In your notebook, write a paragraph about why the relationship between Native American tribes and the United States government has tensions and what you think should be done to improve it.

Picture This — Draw a picture that illustrates the mission statement of the Bureau of Indian Affairs.

Student Workbook or Lesson Review — If you are using one of these optional books, complete the assignment for Lesson 91.

Native American Tribes and RESERVATIONS

Window Rock, Arizona
Navajo Nation Veterans Day Memorial Service, 2011

Native Americans are American citizens. Many are very patriotic. A significant number show their patriotism by serving in the U.S. military. Two out of every one hundred members of the U.S. military are Native Americans. About half of those serve in the U.S. Navy and about twenty percent serve in the Marine Corps. See photo at left.

Native Americans live in each of the fifty United States. The state with the lowest number in 2010 was Vermont with 7,379. California had the largest population of Native Americans with almost one hundred times that many—723,225. Some live in rural areas and some live in cities. See the chart at right to find out which twelve U.S. cities have the highest number of Native Americans. In 2010 about 88 out of every 1,000 Native Americans lived in one of these twelve cities. You may be surprised by the thirteenth city—it is Philadelphia, Pennsylvania!

Some Native Americans celebrate their heritage every day by living their lives in much the same way as their tribal ancestors did. Others live their lives in a manner similar to the average American on most days, but they come together with other members of their tribes for special occasions.

Native Americans work in many kinds of careers. Again some of their jobs reflect their heritage and others do not. On page 599 is a sculpture that reflects the Blackfeet tribal heritage of the artist. The artist created these Blackfeet warriors on

---

Twelve Places with the Largest Number of Native Americans 2010

New York City, New York
Los Angeles, California
Phoenix, Arizona
Oklahoma City, Oklahoma
Anchorage, Alaska
Tulsa, Oklahoma
Albuquerque, New Mexico
Chicago, Illinois
Houston, Texas
San Antonio, Texas
Tucson, Arizona
San Diego, California

horseback by using recycled objects. The sandstone base is made of blocks which were once part of a Catholic mission. The horses and riders are metal car parts and bits of barbed wire. The statue stands on the Blackfeet reservation.

Native American Tribes

Many, but not all, American citizens who are descended from the original inhabitants of America continue to be part of tribes. The Federal government of the United States recognizes a total of 566 American Indian or Alaska Native tribes, villages, and groups.

Each of these has some form of tribal government and each of those governments has a government-to-government relationship with the United States. Each of the tribes has certain obligations to the United States government, and the United States has obligations to them. Each of these tribes, villages, and groups is eligible for assistance from the Bureau of Indian Affairs. The Secretary of the Interior is required to publish a list of all federally-recognized tribes in the Federal Register each year (the Federal Register is explained on page 231). The 566 federally-recognized tribes include about 1.9 million American Indians and Alaska Natives.

Not every person who is descended from an American Indian or Alaska Native is part of a recognized tribe. Groups of Native Americans continue to apply to the Federal government for recognition. Individual American citizens also apply to become part of a recognized tribe.

Native American Reservations

The land of the United States has a variety of owners, such as private individuals, companies, states, and the Federal government. Federal government land is divided into three types: military, public (such as national parks and national forests), and Indian. Indian lands are also called Indian land areas and sometimes "Indian Country." Though they include reservations, pueblos, rancherias, missions, villages, and communities, they are often referred to simply as reservations. The Federal government actually owns Indian lands, but keeps these lands set aside as permanent homelands for various tribes. In legal terms, the Federal government owns the title to the land while holding the land in trust for each tribe which has a reservation.

Blackfeet Reservation, Montana
Native American Jay Laber created this statue of Blackfeet warriors on horseback.

Navajo Nation Reservation

Dine Bikeyah or Navajoland, Home of the Navajo Nation

Indian lands cover more than fifty-six million acres of the United States. Some Native American reservations include portions of where a tribe once lived, but others are lands where the Federal government forcibly sent tribes at some point in the past. The largest reservation is the Navajo Nation Reservation in Arizona, New Mexico, and Utah. Navajoland covers sixteen million acres, or 27,000 square miles, making it larger than ten of the fifty states. The nation works together to provide a good living for its 250,000 people.

Navajo Tribal Government

Oil was discovered on Navajoland in the 1920s. In 1923 tribal leaders decided to form a tribal government so that the nation could negotiate with oil companies that wanted to drill there. The Navajo Nation chose Window Rock, Arizona, as its tribal capital. Window Rock is named for the redstone arch geological formation which is now in Window Rock Navajo Tribal Park and Veterans Memorial pictured on page 601.

Navajo tribal government was reorganized in 1991 into three branches: executive, legislative, and judicial. A president and vice president head the executive branch. The Navajo Nation is divided into 110 communities. These communities, also called chapters, send eighty-eight delegates to the Navajo Council in the nation's capital city. The council is the nation's legislative branch.

Navajo Nation Flag

During the Great Depression in the 1930s, the Federal government began many programs to help the U.S. economy recover. One program was the Works Progress Administration which conducted building projects across America. One of those projects was the Navajo Council Chambers, completed in 1935. The Chambers is an octagonal building, designed to look like a traditional Navajo dwelling, the hogan. Navajo artist Gerald Nailor decorated the interior with a mural, "The History and Progress of the Navajo Nation." The Navajo Nation Council Chamber, pictured below, was designated a National Historic Landmark in 2004.

The Navajo court system is the largest Indian court system in the United States. It includes trial courts and the Navajo Nation Supreme Court with a Chief Justice and two Associate justices. These courts handle 75,000 cases per year. Since the 1980s, Navajo courts have begun to revive historic Navajo methods of peacemaking. In addition to the courts, the nation also has almost two hundred and fifty peacemakers who have been certified by the nation.

Navajo Jay R. Degroat from New Mexico designed the Navajo Nation Flag which was officially adopted in 1968. It includes symbols of traditional and modern Navajo life. See above.

Window Rock, Arizona — Navajo Nation Capital City

The photos at left and above were taken in Window Rock Navajo Tribal Park and Veterans Memorial. Many brave Navajos have served in the U.S. military. During World War II, a group of Navajo Marines used the Navajo language to create a code that the Japanese never deciphered, greatly aiding the U.S. military. The statue honors the Navajo Code Talkers. This park is one of eight operated by the Navajo Nation.

At top left is the Navajo Council Chambers in Window Rock.

Many aspects of Navajo tribal government are similar to other governments in the United States. It has commissions related to taxes, telecommunications, and the nation's budget. The tribe has a division of public safety with a highway safety department, fire and rescue services, emergency medical services, a police department, and detention centers for people who violate the law. It has an office of broadcast services which operates a radio network and a television network. The office also works with filmmakers who wish to make movies or documentaries in their scenic homeland.

To protect their land and help their people economically, the nation's division of natural resources has departments related to agriculture, fish and wildlife, and water management. To help preserve its history, it has departments related to archaeology and historic preservation. The tribe operates a museum and has a tourism office to encourage people to visit the reservation.

The Navajo tribal government has a board of education, a superintendant of schools, and a library system. Its education system is expected to teach students:

★ To be competent in both the English and Navajo languages.

★ To learn to be good U.S. citizens and Navajo citizens.

★ To be knowledgable of American culture and Navajo culture.

From top right to lower left: 1) Navajo Code Talkers attend the Fourth Annual White House Tribal Nations Conference at the U.S. Department of Interior on December 5, 2012. 2) A member of the Navajo Pollen Trail Dancers performs the Eagle Dance at Grand Canyon National Park on September 21, 2010. The dance was part of a ceremony on the south rim of Grand Canyon National Park celebrating the official launch of the America the Beautiful Quarters® Program's Grand Canyon National Park quarter. 3) Navajo Girl in Navajoland 4) Navajo Woman in Wind Rock

At right are photographs of American Indians from other tribes.

And they sang a new song, saying,
"Worthy are You to take the book
and to break its seals; for You were slain,
and purchased for God with Your blood men
from every tribe and tongue
and people and nation.
Revelation 5:9

Lesson Activities

Thinking Biblically — Copy Revelation 5:9 into your notebook.

Vocabulary — In your notebook, write your own definition for each of these words: patriotism, publish, pueblo, forcibly, designate. Look in the lesson for clues for the meaning of the words. When you are finished writing your definitions, look in a dictionary for comparison.

Literature — Read chapters 13-14 in *Misty of Chincoteague*.

Find Out! — How many square miles are in your state? How does it compare to the size of Navajoland?

Student Workbook or Lesson Review — If you are using one of these optional books, complete the assignment for Lesson 92.

Neshoba County, Mississippi
Choctaw dancers perform at the Choctaw Indian Fair. A portion of the Mississippi Band of Choctaw Indians Reservation is in Neshoba County.

Leech Lake Reservation, Minnesota
A Leech Lake Band of Ojibwe youth tends a wild rice crop.

Las Vegas, Nevada
Secretary of Agriculture Tom Vilsack is wrapped in a blanket given to him from the Pine Ridge Reservation, home of the Oglala Sioux in South Dakota. With the Secretary are (from left to right) Kye Wientjes of the Cheyenne River Sioux, Nitara Cheykaychi of the Pueblo of Santo Domingo, and Jess Begave Oldham of the Navajo Nation, 2011.

San Carlos Apache Indian Reservation, Arizona

Native Americans and
THE STATES

Just as the Federal government has relations with Native Americans, the states do as well. The 566 federally-recognized tribes live in a total of thirty-three states. Each of these states also has at least one reservation. The numbers of federally-recognized tribes in each of these states are printed in red on the map below. Fourteen states recognize tribes that the Federal government does not. The numbers of state-recognized tribes in those states are printed in blue on the map below. Of those fourteen states, Delaware, Maryland, Vermont, and Virginia have no federally-recognized tribes. The pictures on page 605 were taken at ceremonies celebrating two tribes becoming officially recognized by the State of Maryland.

Number of Recognized Tribes in the United States

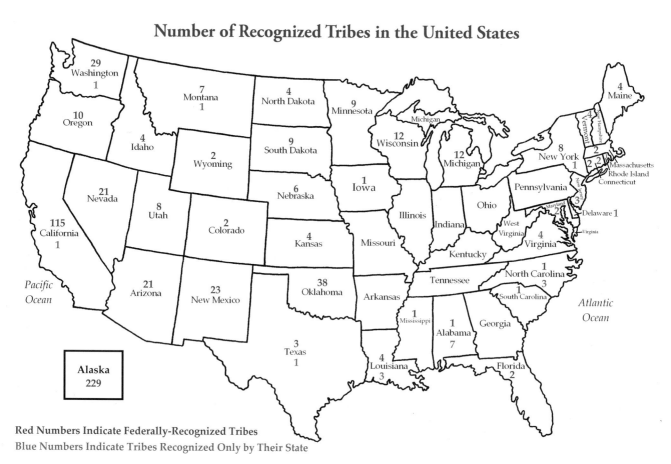

Red Numbers Indicate Federally-Recognized Tribes
Blue Numbers Indicate Tribes Recognized Only by Their State

The Piscataway Indian Nation and the Piscataway Conoy Tribes Receive Recognition

When the federally- and state-recognized tribes are added together, thirty-seven states have government-to-government relations with at least one tribe of American Indians or Alaska Natives and, as mentioned in Lesson 92, every state has Native American residents. In fact, every state except Delaware and Vermont have at least 10,000. Alaska, Arizona, California, Colorado, Florida, Illinois, Michigan, Minnesota, New Mexico, New York, North Carolina, Oklahoma, Oregon, Texas, and Washington have more than 100,000.

Exemption from State Laws

Native Americans must obey state laws with one exception. When a member of a tribe is on his or her own reservation, he does not have to obey the laws of the home state of the reservation. He must obey tribal laws and Federal laws there, but not state laws. However, if a member of that tribe breaks a state criminal law while on his reservation, his misdeed automatically becomes a Federal offense and he or she can be arrested and tried for breaking a Federal law (criminal laws are explained in Unit 22). Exemption from state laws sometimes

Seneca Falls, New York

results in conflict between Native and non-Native Americans. Look at the photo above to see an example. The owner of the business is complaining because his customers must pay certain taxes on gasoline, while the nearby Cayuga Nation can sell gasoline without the same taxes.

State-to-Tribe Relations

Some states and tribes have a history of conflict with one another; but in many states, this is changing for the better. About two-thirds of the states, including some who have no recognized tribes, have special commissions or councils that are devoted to Native American issues. Here are ways that Arizona and Wisconsin are reaching out to tribes.

Since 1953 the State of Arizona has had a Commission of Indian Affairs. Each year it sponsors an Indian Nations and Tribes Legislative Day to celebrate the Arizona tribes and to discuss issues that are of interest to both the tribes and the state.

Since 2005 the Wisconsin legislature has taken one day to welcome members of its Federally-recognized tribes to the state capitol. The legislature invites a leader of one of the tribes to give a State of the Tribes address to the legislature and to visitors in the gallery. In 2005 the speaker was Ray DePerry, chairman of the Red Cliff Chippewa tribe. The program began with a march of flags down the aisle of the Wisconsin assembly chamber. It was followed by the Pledge of Allegiance and a prayer spoken in a native language. According to a tradition of many Native American tribes, DePerry honored the elders in the audience. He said that elders remind us that deeds must be done in an honorable way without selfishness.

Before Chairman Mike Wiggins Jr. of the Bad River Band of Lake Superior Chippewa Indians spoke in 2011, members of Wisconsin tribes and others gathered outside the capitol to honor the state's Indian veterans. See photos on page 607. The ceremony included native singing and drum playing. The group then followed flag-bearers into the capitol before they walked down the assembly chamber aisle. At the time, the state was considering whether to allow a company to mine iron close to his tribe's reservation. During his address, Wiggins told the legislators that his tribe was concerned about the mine's effect on the environment. He also encouraged lawmakers to keep lines of communication open between the state and tribes. Wiggins thanked the legislature for ways they had responded to other tribal concerns.

Scenes Outside the Wisconsin State Capitol Before the 2011 State of the Tribes Speech

Native Pride Caps

T-Shirt

In the photo above, native musicians sing and play the drum.

Native Americans in Statuary Hall

Five states have donated statues of Native Americans to Statuary Hall in the U.S. Capitol. They are listed below in chronological order according to birth.

Po'pay—New Mexico. Po'pay was born around 1630 in what would become New Mexico. He was a member of the Pueblo people. Po'pay was a religious leader who organized a revolt against the harsh rule of the Spanish in 1680. The Spanish took refuge in the city of Santa Fe. The Pueblo besieged them, but the Spanish escaped and the Pueblo did not pursue them. As a result of the revolt, relations between the Pueblo and the Spanish were more positive; and the Pueblo culture was able to survive. Po'pay died around 1688. Cliff Fragua of the Jemez Pueblo created the statue. This statue, unveiled in 2005, is the first statue sculpted by a Native American to be placed in Statuary Hall.

Sequoyah—Oklahoma. Sequoyah (also spelled Sequoya) was born in Tennessee around 1770, the child of a Cherokee woman and an English man. Lame from childhood (his name means "lame one"), Sequoyah developed skills as a silversmith and blacksmith. Sequoyah believed that the Americans' ability to read and write what he called "talking leaves" helped them accomplish what they did. He worked for twelve years to develop a syllabary, a written language of 86 symbols for the sounds of the Cherokee language. The Cherokee adopted his syllabary in 1821 and its use spread quickly. Sequoyah moved to Oklahoma in 1828 and was greatly honored by his people. He died in 1843. Sequoyah was the first Native American to be honored in Statuary Hall.

Sakakawea—North Dakota. A young Shoshone girl was captured by the Hidatsa tribe around 1800. The Hidatsa gave her the name Sakakawea (also spelled Sacajawea). By 1804 she had become the wife of French Canadian hunter Pierre Charbonneau, who Lewis and Clark hired to be a translator on their expedition. Sakakawea also translated. She also helped the contact between the Americans and the Shoshone and Hidatsa nations to be peaceful. She gave birth to a son, Jean Baptiste, on February 11, 1805, while the expedition was in winter quarters at Fort Mandan in what is now North Dakota; and she continued with the expedition when it resumed in the spring. North Dakota honored her with a statue in Statuary Hall for being a "traveler, guide, translator, diplomat, wife,

and mother." Sakakawea is believed to have died in 1812.

Washakie—Wyoming. This Native American was born around 1800 among his father's Salish (Flathead) people, but he later joined the tribe of his mother, the Shoshone, and received the name Washakie. He was a famous warrior and united several bands of Shoshone. Washakie learned English and French and knew several Native American languages. Washakie negotiated with Americans to preserve about three million acres in the Wind River area of what is now Wyoming, which is still the home of the Shoshone today. He encouraged education for his people, and he gave land for Welsh missionary John Roberts to build a boarding school for Shoshone girls to learn language and traditional crafts. Washakie received full military honors at his funeral in 1900.

Sarah Winnemucca—Nevada. The daughter of Paiute Indian Chief Winnemucca, Sarah was born around 1844 in what became Nevada. It is not known when she took the name Sarah. She was skillful with languages and served as an interpreter and negotiator between the Paiute and the U.S. Army. In 1878 the Bannock Indians, who were holding her father's band captive, revolted against the Army. Sarah volunteered to lead her father's band to safety in a three-day

ride over 230 miles of difficult terrain with little food or rest. She gave over 300 speeches in defense of her people. She met President Rutherford B. Hayes and Interior Secretary Carl Schurz in 1880. Her 1883 autobiography was the first book written by a Native American woman. She started a school for Native American children and taught them in both their native language and in English. Sarah died in 1891.

Will Rogers—Oklahoma. Will Rogers was born in Indian Territory (what became Oklahoma) in 1879, the son of a Cherokee mother and a father of European descent. He became a ranch hand and circus entertainer, traveling around the world before he was 24. In 1905 he developed an act for live variety shows called vaudeville that were presented in theaters. Rogers would twirl a lasso, tell jokes, and offer commentary on life and politics. He became a movie star, radio broadcaster, newspaper columnist, and author. He was one of the most popular and influential people of his day. Privately, he gave generously to charity and disaster victims. Rogers died in a plane crash in Alaska in 1935.

Let no one seek his own good, but that of his neighbor.
1 Corinthians 10:24

Lesson Activities

Thinking Biblically — Think of three Biblical figures who were leaders and helpers for their people. Write one or two sentences summarizing what each one accomplished.

Literature — Read "To Fight for My Down-Trodden Race" in *The Citizen's Handbook*, page 107, and chapters 15-16 in *Misty of Chincoteague*.

Creative Writing — In your notebook, make a list of at least ten qualities that a person needs to be a good leader.

Find Out! — If your state has at least one Federally-recognized or state-recognized tribe, find out the name of the tribe, if the tribe has a reservation, and the name of the reservation.

Student Workbook or Lesson Review — If you are using one of these optional books, complete the assignment for Lesson 93.

Native American
HERITAGE MONTH

The Federal government of the United States sets aside many days to honor those who have had an impact on their fellow citizens. For example, we honor our founding fathers on Independence Day, George Washington on Washington's Birthday, and Martin Luther King Jr., on Martin Luther King Day. Early in the twentieth century, Dr. Arthur Caswell Parker began an effort to designate a special day to honor Native Americans. He was a Cattaraugus Seneca then serving as the director of the Rochester Museum in Rochester, New York (the museum is now the Rochester Museum of Arts and Sciences). Dr. Parker was the great nephew of the first Native American to serve as Commissioner of the Bureau of Indian Affairs, Ely S. Parker. Dr. Parker also worked to obtain American citizenship for Native Americans.

Another American Indian who advocated citizenship was minister Red Fox James (also known as Red Fox Skiukusha), whose tribe is unknown. In 1914 James traveled 4,000 miles to Washington, D.C., on horseback to request an Indian day. In 1915 he traveled to many states to meet with Governors and get their support for American Indian citizenship. In the last month of that year, he traveled to Washington to tell President Woodrow Wilson that he had won the support of twenty-four Governors. Red Fox James is pictured at right.

Red Fox James, 1915

At the same time, another American Indian minister, Sherman Coolidge of the Arapaho tribe, asked America to observe a day for Native Americans and to make them citizens. As mentioned in Lesson 91, American Indians did receive citizenship in 1924.

State American Indian Days

States began to set aside an American Indian day long before there was any kind of national observance. States often chose the fourth Friday of November. In 1919 the Illinois legislature made this its official day for honoring American Indians. Some states designated other days. One state that has historically seen the most violent conflict between Native and non-Native Americans is South Dakota. In 1989 its legislature declared 1990 as the "Year of Reconciliation." Its Governor named Columbus Day as South Dakota's American Indian Day.

National Days and Weeks to Honor Native Americans

When the United States celebrated its bicentennial in 1976, Congress passed a resolution which authorized President Gerald Ford to declare one week in October as "Native American Awareness Week." He issued his proclamation on October 8.

After President Ford, the next President to designate a special time to honor Native Americans was Ronald Reagan, who designated May 13, 1983, as the first national "American Indian Day." From 1986 to 1988, President Reagan proclaimed one week each fall to honor Native Americans. Twice it was "American Indian Week" in November. In 1988 it was "National American Indian Heritage Week" in September.

President George H. W. Bush designated a week in December as "National American Indian Heritage Week" in 1989.

A National Month to Honor Native Americans

In 1990 the U.S. Congress and President George H. W. Bush declared November 1990 as "National American Indian Heritage Month." The following year Congress authorized and requested the President to proclaim each November as "National American Indian Heritage Month."

The Year of the American Indian

As towns, states, and the nation prepared to celebrate the 500th anniversary of Christopher Columbus discovering America in 1492, Congress recognized that Native Americans had different feelings than those who planned to celebrate. In late 1991, Congress passed a joint resolution declaring 1992 the "Year of the American Indian." President George H. W. Bush signed it in December. Bush also proclaimed November as "National American Indian Heritage Month" that year. He did the same in 1993.

Presidents Bill Clinton and George W. Bush also proclaimed each November "National American Indian Heritage Month" throughout their presidencies. Beginning with the presidency of Barack Obama, the month came to be called "Native American Heritage Month."

Native American Heritage Day

In 2008 Congress passed a joint resolution designating the day after Thanksgiving that year as "Native American Heritage Day." The following year it passed the Native American Heritage Day Act of 2009. It designates the Friday following Thanksgiving Day of each year "Native American Heritage Day." The law was signed by President Obama.

Public Celebrations of Native American Heritage Month

Native American Heritage Month is celebrated by various Federal agencies. Enjoy photos of some of these below and on pages 614-615.

United States Department of Agriculture (USDA) Celebrations

Native Americans participate in Native American Heritage Month observances. 1) Arthur "Butch" Blazer, Deputy Under Secretary of the USDA, gives a keynote address at a 2011 USDA celebration. 2) Noller Herbert, a director in the Natural Resources Conservation Service, offers a blessing at a ceremony in 2011. 3) U.S. Air Force veteran John Egnew carries the U.S. flag as part of the Vietnam Era Veterans Intertribal Association color guard at the 2012 observance at the USDA office in Washington, D.C. 4) USDA Rural Development South Dakota Housing Specialist Ken Lynch of the Red Cliff Band of Chippewa Indians stands beside the 2012 Native American Heritage Month poster. 5) Casper College student Odessa Oldham speaks about her experience in Future Farmers of America at a 2011 USDA observance. 6) In honor of Native American Heritage Month, Ken Lynch's artwork is on display at a Wisconsin USDA office in 2012.

Fort Wainwright Army Base, Fairbanks, Alaska

Alaska Native Joy Shockley Huntington spoke to attendees of the Fort Wainwright Native American Heritage celebration at the Last Frontier Community Center in Fairbanks. The 9th Army Band Brass Quintet played the national anthem. Huntington read an original poem. The Pawa Inupiaq Dancers performed. Some members of the audience tried a dance, 2009.

Army Corps of Engineers, Norfolk Division

Chief Walter D. "Red Hawk" Brown III spoke about the history of his people and also performed a traditional tribal dance with other members of the Cheroenhaka (Nottoway) Tribe, 2009.

Grand Canyon National Park

*As part of the celebration of Native American Heritage Month in 2010, the Dishchi' Bikoh' Apache Group
from Cibecue, Arizona, performed the Apache Crown Dance at a special day of events at Grand Canyon National Park.
In attendance that day was Dan Akee, a World War II Veteran Navajo Code Talker.*

Be devoted to one another in brotherly love;

give preference to one another in honor.

Romans 12:10

Lesson Activities

Vocabulary - Find each of these words in a dictionary, then find the definition that corresponds to the way the word is used in this lesson: advocate, support, observe, bicentennial, authorize. Copy the words and definitions into your notebook.

Literature - Read chapters 17-18 in *Misty of Chincoteague*.

Creative Writing - Imagine that you are in charge of a program for a Native American Heritage Month celebration. Write a paragraph in your notebook of what you would say to begin the ceremony. Include thanks to participants and to the audience.

Picture This! - Draw a picture of one of the Native American headpieces or garments pictured in this lesson.

Student Workbook or Lesson Review — If you are using one of these optional books, complete the assignment for Lesson 94.

Lac du Flambeau, Wisconsin
This street sign is in the Lac du Flambeau Reservation.

★ Remember to choose an American Holiday to study this week! ★

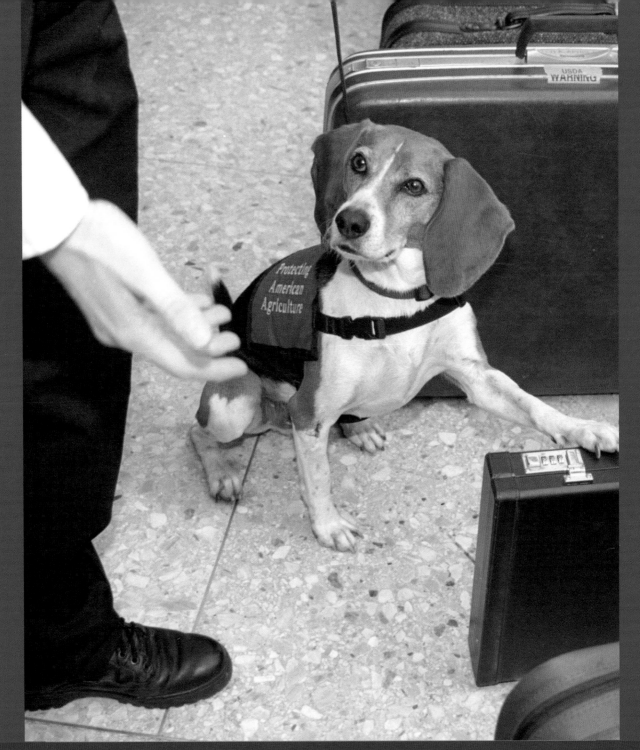

UNIT 20 — HOMELAND SECURITY

BOOKS USED IN UNIT 20

- The Citizen's Handbook
- Student Workbook (optional)
- Lesson Review (optional)

A member of the USDA Beagle Brigade signals that a piece of luggage contains contraband at Dulles International Airport, August 2012.

Helping Our COUNTRY BE SAFE

When your family goes to bed each night, your parents probably lock the outside doors of your house. They do so again when everyone is about to leave the house. Locking doors is a wise way to protect your home and family.

All three levels of government work together to protect our country, which is sometimes called our homeland. Sheriff and police departments help to prevent crime on the local level. State troopers or state policemen also work to keep citizens safe. The U.S. military helps to protect our country from people outside the country who might want to harm us.

Sometimes Americans need help when a natural event like a flood, hurricane, or tornado occurs. We can't prevent these things from happening, but we can be prepared for them. When they occur, government helpers respond to them and help people recover. Knowing that these helps are available if disaster strikes gives us additional feelings of security. Many other government agencies cooperate to keep Americans safe.

Though we appreciate all that government workers do to help us be safe, Christians know that our safety really comes from God's loving care and that our true security is in His Son, Jesus Christ.

U.S. Department of Homeland Security

Your parents check to make sure that the locks on your house work. If a lock on a window needs replacing, your dad will buy a new one at the hardware store. Your parents make sure that their bank account and credit card information cannot be stolen. They have installed smoke alarms in your house, and they replace the batteries when that needs to be done. When a snowstorm is predicted for your area, your mom might pick up a few extra items at the grocery store just in case you can't get out for a few days. Your parents take these steps to provide home security for your family.

Over the years, our government became aware of the need to take many different steps to provide security for our country. However, these steps were taken by several different departments of the Federal government. For instance, the Customs Service, which checked items brought into the United States, was part of the Treasury Department. The Immigration and Naturalization Service was in the Justice Department. The U.S. Coast Guard was part of the Department of Transportation (except in times of war when it became part of the military). One job of the Animal and Plant Health Inspection Service in the Department of Agriculture was to inspect animals and plants being brought into the country. The Federal Emergency Management Agency was an independent agency that was not part of any Cabinet department. The efforts of these various agencies were not always coordinated well.

A few days after our country was attacked by terrorists on September 11, 2001, President George W. Bush took steps to bring together the many Federal security efforts under one

leader. He created the Office of Homeland Security. The next year, Congress passed a law that created the Department of Homeland Security, making its Director part of the President's Cabinet. The new department officially began operations on March 1, 2003. It brought together twenty-two different departments and agencies to create a coordinated system of protection for our country.

The various components of the Department of Homeland Security work together. As illustrated in the photographs below, they also work with other Federal departments and with local and state officials. One of the most important ideas behind this department is coordination and cooperation. Here are some of the ways in which the Department of Homeland Security works to make our country safer.

A Federal Emergency Management Agency search and rescue team works at Ground Zero twelve days after September 11, 2001.

A California National Guardsman monitors the California coastline in 2010. The National Guard supports the efforts of the Customs and Border Protection and the Immigration and Customs Enforcement divisions of the Department of Homeland Security.

U.S. Department of Agriculture inspectors at a Florida Plant Inspection Station check to see if these flowers are free from pests and diseases that would hurt crops of U.S. farmers. This program is a joint effort between the USDA and the Department of Homeland Security, 2005.

Customs and Border Protection (CBP)

Near Columbus, New Mexico
The U.S. Border Patrol is part of Customs and Border Protection. The National Guard sometimes helps the Border Patrol.

The Customs and Border Protection agency enforces rules about who and what may enter the United States. The agency uses technologies such as sensors that detect certain objects that may be hidden in luggage or in cargo containers. They make use of radar. Border Protection agents travel in all-terrain vehicles, 4x4s, helicopters, planes, and even horses, while using their eyes and ears to find out what comes to our borders. They also use the sense of smell of trained dogs.

The agency helps our trade relationships with other countries by making sure that legal trade products get into our country and illegal products stay out. Since these problems always need to be taken care of in a local setting, Federal agents work closely with state and local law enforcement departments by sharing information with them and by providing training for government officials and for first responders. Read more about the CBP in Lesson 98.

U.S. Citizenship and Immigration Services (USCIS)

USCIS helps immigrants already in the U.S. or people who plan to come as legal residents. On a typical day, USCIS helps 3,000 immigrants become U.S. citizens, assists American parents in adopting 125 foreign-born children, and grants permanent resident status to 3,400 people.

Immigration and Customs Enforcement (ICE)

ICE deals with people who are in the United States illegally, especially those who have committed crimes. The photos on page 621 illustrate ICE agents cooperating with agents from other divisions of Homeland Security and with the Drug Enforcement Administration (DEA), which is part of the Department of Justice.

Transportation Security Administration Agents

Homeland Security Investigations (HSI) is a division of ICE. With 10,000 employees, including 6,700 special agents, HSI concentrates on watching out for the illegal movement of people and goods into, within, and out of the U.S.

Transportation Security Administration (TSA)

The TSA is a well-known Homeland Security agency, since it is responsible for checking all passengers and baggage in the nation's airports. In addition, TSA provides security for mass transit systems, seaports, and the moving of cargo by any type of transportation.

Federal Law Enforcement Officers Cooperate to Fight Crime

Fingerprinting

Dinosaur Skull Being Imported Illegally

Above: Finding Fake Licensed Merchandise

Below: Agents Return Stolen and Looted Art and Antiquities to Peru

In these pictures, find: ICE Agent from Immigration and Customs Enforcement, CBP Federal Officer from Customs and Border Protection, USCG Special Agent from the Coast Guard, HSI Special Agent from ICE's Homeland Security Investigations, and DEA Agent from the Drug Enforcement Administration.

Federal Emergency Management Agency (FEMA)

FEMA is the agency of the Federal government that helps when Americans experience a natural disaster or some other major crisis. Most of these are weather-related, such as floods, tornadoes, and hurricanes. FEMA also helps when areas are damaged by earthquakes and forest fires. The agency gives advice to state emergency agencies before and after a disaster. The Federal Emergency Management Agency helps to get methods of communication, such as telephones, radio, television, and Internet services, back in good working order. FEMA helps people get food and shelter after a disaster strikes. It also helps those who have been affected by disasters to obtain long-term assistance so that they can get back to their normal lives as soon as possible. For example, FEMA provides camping-style trailers for families to live in until they can repair or rebuild their homes. The agency educates and encourages families, communities, and states to be ready when disasters strike.

Joplin, Missouri
Left: Federal Emergency Management Administration (FEMA) modular home is delivered for victims of a tornado.
Center: U.S. Corps of Engineers temporary housing adviser and temporary
housing mission manager watch as FEMA modular homes are delivered.
Right: A private contractor working for FEMA levels the base for a modular home. All photos were taken in 2011.

Other Ways Homeland Security Protects

In this day of instant worldwide communication, people can talk, write, do business, obtain government services, and even control the utilities in their homes through the Internet. A great deal of information is available on the Internet. Unfortunately, criminals can obtain information and can engage in illegal activity through the Internet also. Homeland Security protects government websites and helps protect Americans from thieves who use the Internet illegally.

Homeland Security works worldwide. Its agents work in over seventy-five countries, gathering information and helping foreign governments. At the same time, the Department works on local and state levels in the U.S., training and sharing information with local authorities and giving grants to local safety agencies so that they can purchase needed equipment.

As Homeland Security works to protect us from harm, it also protects the freedom of Americans. Sometimes it is difficult to balance the need for protecting Americans with the rights and freedoms of Americans.

How Can Individual Citizens Be Involved?

The Department of Homeland Security coordinates and encourages several programs that help individual Americans play an important part in the safety and security of our communities and nation. For instance, its Community Emergency Response Team program teaches citizens how to help first responders, how to help victims of disasters, and how to organize volunteers in times of need. The Fire Corps teaches citizens ways that they can help fire departments. The Volunteers in Police Service program does the same for local police departments. The Medical Reserve Corps guides medical professionals and others in addressing public health needs and in helping with injuries in times of crisis.

Homeland Security also encourages Americans to be aware of the need for security when using the Internet and to report suspicious activity they see to law enforcement officials. At the ready.gov website, Homeland Security provides information to help Americans to know how to be prepared for and recover from natural disasters, home fires, and other events that require special actions.

You can rest assured knowing that your parents take the steps that are needed to keep you safe. Our nation is safer and our freedoms are more secure because of the people who work to protect us from harm.

In peace I will both lie down and sleep,

For You alone, O Lord, make me to dwell in safety.

Psalm 4:8

Lesson Activities

Thinking Biblically — Write a paragraph in your notebook answering the question, "Why is true safety and security found only in the Lord?"

Vocabulary — In your notebook, make a drawing for each of these words that illustrates what it means: disaster, security, install, inspection, assistance. Write the word under the drawing. Check in a dictionary if you need help with their definitions.

Literature — Read "The Horse Patrol: Running Neck and Neck with Technology" in *The Citizen's Handbook*, pages 108-110.

Picture This! — Take a photograph or draw a picture of something in your home that is there for safety or security.

Student Workbook or Lesson Review — If you are using one of these optional books, complete the assignment for Lesson 96.

The SECRET SERVICE

Secret Service agent holds limousine door for President Obama, 2011.

The United States Secret Service has two important responsibilities. It protects our nation's financial system; and it protects the President, other national leaders, and heads of state who visit our country (see photo at left). The Secret Service received both of these assignments as a result of times of crisis. Now, over a century later, the Secret Service still has these two responsibilities; but their work has expanded to include more areas of our financial system and now they protect more people.

Protecting Our Nation's Financial System

Before the Civil War, the United States government issued only coins. State banks printed their own paper certificates that were used as money, and these were often counterfeited. Counterfeiting is printing fake money. The number of different kinds of bills in circulation made it hard to tell what was counterfeit and what was real. During the Civil War, the U.S. government began to print paper money.

With paper money becoming more important in the U.S., people decided to take advantage of the situation and print their own. Some historians estimate that one-third to one-half of the nation's currency was counterfeit. Currency is paper money. The Federal government began working to catch counterfeiters and bring them to trial. On April 14, 1865, President Abraham Lincoln authorized the formation of the

The five men in front are identified as Chief Telegraph Operator, Indian Scout, and three Secret Service Men, c. 1865.

Secret Service Agents at Work, October 1938

Secret Service as the government agency that would be responsible for stopping counterfeiters. That evening, Lincoln was assassinated at Ford's Theater in Washington. Almost two months later, on July 5, 1865, the Secret Service was officially created as part of the Treasury Department (see photo of early agents on page 624).

The Secret Service was the first agency of the Federal government specifically created to investigate crime. Over the years, it has worked to solve many different kinds of violations of Federal law. These crimes have included smuggling illegal goods into the United States, the robbing of United States mail, the illegal production of alcoholic beverages ("moonshining"), fake sales of land, the production of counterfeit postage stamps, and spying activities against the United States. In 1908 President Theodore Roosevelt moved some Secret Service agents into the Department of Justice. This was the beginning of what became the Federal Bureau of Investigation (FBI). See examples of Secret Service agents at work above.

Today the Secret Service investigates the crimes of making counterfeit U.S. currency, foreign currency (when it is counterfeited within the United States), and coins. In 1984 Congress passed a law that made using credit and debit cards illegally a Federal crime. The law gave the Secret Service authority to investigate these crimes. The Secret Service also investigates the crime of printing fake identification documents. A 1990 law gave the Secret Service the authority to investigate crimes against any bank that is Federally insured. When people put money into a Federally-insured bank, the Federal government guarantees that if that bank goes bankrupt, the Federal government will pay the people who had deposits in the bank the money they had deposited.

With new technologies, people can commit money-related crimes in many more ways than printing counterfeit money. Therefore, the authority of the Secret Service has increased. It now investigates:

★ Telemarketing fraud. Fraud is deceiving for the purpose of gaining something, like money. Telemarketing fraud is using telephones to cheat people.

★ Identity theft. When criminals steal a person's Social Security number, credit card number, and other personal information so they can use it to pose to be that person, they have committed identity theft.

★ The spreading of computer viruses and malware (software that causes harm to computers on purpose), and other computer-based crime.

★ EBT (electronic benefit transfer) fraud. An EBT card is like a debit card, except that the money available for a debit card is money the debit card owner has in a bank, savings and loan, credit union, or other financial institution. The money available for an EBT is government money supplied to people who need financial assistance from the government.

★ Advance fee fraud. Advance fee fraud is the sending of spam e-mail that says something like, "Congratulations! You have received 4.6 million dollars from the government of Nigeria. You must reply today to receive the money that is legally due you. You will need to send $1,500 to pay for legal processing before you can receive your money."

Protecting the President and Other Officials

The Secret Service provided informal, part-time protection for President Grover Cleveland beginning in 1894. After William McKinley was assassinated in 1901, the Secret Service began to provide full-time protection for President Theodore Roosevelt. See photo at right.

Over the years, Congress has expanded the number of people whom the Secret Service protects:

★ In 1913 the Secret Service became permanently responsible for protecting the President and the President-elect (between Election Day and Inauguration Day). See photo from 1914 on page 627.

Oyster Bay, New York
*Secret Service Agents
at Roosevelt Home, 1908*

* In 1917 the Secret Service became responsible for protecting the President's immediate family.

* In 1922 President Warren G. Harding requested that the White House Police Force be created. Eight years later the force was placed under the supervision of the Secret Service.

* In 1951 the Secret Service became responsible for protecting the Vice President if he wanted this protection.

* In 1961 the Secret Service became responsible for protecting former Presidents for a reasonable period of time.

* In 1962 the Secret Service became responsible for protecting the Vice President and Vice President-elect.

* In 1963, following the assassination of John F. Kennedy, Congress authorized the Secret Service to protect Mrs. Kennedy and her children for two years.

Secret Service Agent Thomas J. Callaghan, 1914

* In 1965 the Secret Service became responsible for protecting former Presidents, their spouses, and their children until the children reached age 16.

* In 1968 Congress authorized the Secret Service to be responsible for protecting major presidential and vice presidential candidates and nominees.

* The Secret Service also became responsible for protecting the widows of Presidents until the widow died or remarried.

* In 1970 the White House Police Force was renamed the Executive Protective Service. It was given responsibility for protecting diplomatic missions in the Washington, D.C., area.

* In 1971 Congress authorized the Secret Service to protect visiting heads of state and other official guests.

* In 1975 the Secret Service was given responsibility for protecting foreign diplomatic missions throughout the United States and in its five territories.

* In 1977 the Executive Protective Service was renamed the Secret Service Uniformed Division.

* In 1986 the Secret Service was made responsible for protecting the spouses of visiting foreign leaders.

★ In 1997 Congress passed a law stating that Presidents elected after that year would receive protection for no more than ten years after leaving office. Presidents elected before then would continue to receive lifetime protection. In 1985 former President Richard Nixon had voluntarily given up Secret Service protection, the only former President who has ever done so. It saved the American people an estimated three million dollars per year.

★ In 2000 the Secret Service was given the responsibility to help provide security for "special events of national significance," as determined by the President.

★ In 2003 the Secret Service was transferred to the Department of Homeland Security.

Madison, Wisconsin
Secret Service agents at the Air National Guard Base scan for danger as Air Force One lands bringing President Obama for a speaking engagement at a middle school, 2009.

Washington, D.C.
Secret Service Motorcycle Unit participates in a motorcade transporting President and Mrs. George W. Bush to visit with former First Lady Betty Ford, 2007.

How the Secret Service Works

Secret Service agents must complete a difficult training program and stay in good physical shape to carry out their many responsibilities. Agents do much more than just surround a protected person with bodyguards. The Secret Service works with the military and with local, state, and Federal agencies to coordinate protection efforts. The Secret Service Uniformed Division, the Metropolitan Police Department of Washington, D.C., and the U.S. Park Service continually patrol the area around the White House. When the President or another protected person travels, the Secret Service works with local and state law enforcement officials to provide the needed security.

The Secret Service has two divisions. The Uniformed Division provides protection for the White House, the Vice President's residence, and about 170 foreign embassies in Washington. The Special Agent Division is in charge of protection for a protected person's travel. It also has agents who investigate possible financial crime activity.

The Secret Service offers three ways young people can work for the service on a temporary basis. The Student Temporary Employment Program (STEP) offers paid positions with the

Secret Service Vehicles

Secret Service to students enrolled at least half-time in an accredited high school; a vocational, technical, two-year or four-year college or university; or graduate or professional school. The Student Career Experience Program is a two-year work-study program that combines classroom studies and work experience. This program is a non-paid internship that offers a work assignment for at least twelve hours per week for at least one semester, two quarters, or a summer.

The people who are guarded by the Secret Service are grateful for this protection. For the person who trusts in God, His protection is sure.

> In You, O Lord, I have taken refuge;
> Let me never be ashamed;
> In Your righteousness deliver me.
> Incline your ear to me, rescue me quickly;
> Be to me a rock of strength, a stronghold to save me.
> Psalm 31:1-2

Lesson Activities

Vocabulary — In your notebook, write the vocabulary words and the letter of the definition that goes with each word: counterfeit, currency, smuggle, fraud, spouse.

a. to import or export in an illegal manner

b. a husband or wife

c. produced to appear like something else with the intention of deception

d. paper money

e. trickery, falsehood or bending truth to gain something

Literature — Read "Thirty-Six Years in the White House" in *The Citizen's Handbook*, pages 111-112.

Creative Writing — Write a short story of at least one page about a Secret Service member.

Find Out! — Ask your parents if they have ever received an e-mail that was probably an attempt at advance fee fraud.

Student Workbook or Lesson Review — If you are using one of these optional books, complete the assignment for Lesson 97.

Protecting
AMERICA'S BORDERS

All around the clock, people and things are entering the United States. We are a welcoming country. We welcome grandparents from Paraguay coming for a visit with their family members who live in the United States. We welcome shortbread made in Scotland to be sold in our grocery stores. We welcome American families returning from a safari vacation in Africa. We welcome antiques purchased in France and brought to the United States to sell in specialty stores. We welcome immigrants from Iraq who want to move to our country permanently. We welcome shea butter from Africa destined for beauty products manufactured in the United States. We welcome couples from Canada who drive over the border on a day trip to Minnesota or Maine. We welcome people and things that make our country a better place to live.

The government has rules about who and what can enter. When people and the things they carry with them are in accordance with the rules, they are welcome in the United States. Some people try to break the rules. That's why America needs the Customs and Border Protection agency of the Department of Homeland Security we introduced in Lesson 96.

Customs and Border Protection

Customs and Border Protection (CBP) is the guard at our nation's borders. We have land and sea borders. Airports where international flights enter the country are another kind of border. Any place people and things enter the United States from another country is called a "port of entry." At hundreds of ports of entry, officers of CBP perform thousands of checks every day. They check by asking questions: "Why are you visiting the United States?"; "Did you bring any foreign currency?"; "Did

Why, Arizona
Breaking Ground for New Ajo U.S. Border Patrol Station in the Town of Why, Arizona

you bring anything with you from another country?"; "How long do you plan to stay?"; "How long were you away from the United States?"; "What is in this container?"; "Who is traveling with you?"; "What is the value of the goods you are bringing?"

CBP also performs checks at America's borders through investigations. Agents investigate passports and other official documents carried by Americans returning home. They also investigate the passports and documents people from other countries bring, whether they are coming for a visit or are hoping to make America their new home. Agents check shipping containers, suitcases, and car trunks for items such as illegal drugs that are not allowed to enter the country. They check hiding places such as behind hubcaps and inside shoes. They inspect products raised on international farms to make sure they don't have bugs or diseases that could spread to American farms. They keep an eye out for criminals who may be trying to enter the country. They make sure that businesses that bring goods to sell in the U.S. have paid what they owe in tariffs (a tariff is a tax for bringing items for sale into the country). Most people follow the rules. For the safety of America, CBP has to be on constant watch for the people who don't.

Jobs in CBP

CBP needs experts in many different fields to fulfill its mission of protecting our nation's borders successfully.

Bisbee, Arizona
Naco U.S. Border Patrol Station

★ Customs and Border Protection officers screen passengers and cargo at ports of entry.

★ The U.S. Border Patrol, one part of CBP, serves on the Canadian and Mexican borders between ports of entry to catch people trying to enter illegally and to stop the smuggling of illegal goods. See pictures on page 630 and above.

★ Air and Marine Interdiction agents use their special skills and high-tech equipment to stop people and forbidden goods from entering the United States illegally by air or water.

★ Agriculture specialists know how to recognize pests and diseases on plants and livestock coming from other countries.

★ Import specialists judge the value of goods entering the U.S. Most international shipping is done in large metal sea containers, which are about the size of a semi trailer. Each year CBP processes 11 million containers shipped by sea, 11 million shipped by truck, and 2.7 million shipped by rail.

People who work in the CBP revenue department collect $30 billion every year in taxes and tariffs. Agents who work as guards and who interact with people and goods entering the country depend on a large team of supporting CBP staff. These CBP employees repair equipment, hire personnel, manage offices, purchase supplies, and provide legal support to help CBP accomplish its responsibilities.

CBP Canine Program

Canine is another word for dog. The CBP Canine Program has over 1,500 teams, making it the largest canine law enforcement program in the country. CBP trains dogs to detect illegal drugs, large amounts of U.S. currency, firearms, and people who are hiding. In addition to training the dogs, CBP trains people to be their expert handlers. The people/dog teams learn how to communicate with each other and how to investigate vehicles, aircraft, freight, luggage, mail, passengers and large areas. They learn how to search in special environments such as snow, desert, pine forests, and mountains. Canine teams are one of the best tools CBP has to protect America's borders.

CBP has a program that raises puppies to make sure they have enough dogs for their teams. Puppies take their final test to become CBP trainees when they are between seven and fourteen months of age. If they pass, puppies enter formal training at CBP training facilities in either El Paso, Texas, or Front Royal, Virginia, near Washington, D.C. The dogs that CBP uses to help inspect agricultural products are trained at the U.S. Department of Agriculture's facility in Atlanta, Georgia. See photo on page 617.

A Typical Day for CBP

The following statistics illustrate the work of the U.S. Customs and Border Protection's staff on a typical day in 2011. The number of staff members working that day was 60,079.

- ★ CBP guarded 329 air, sea, and land ports of entry into the United States.

- ★ They processed almost one million passengers and pedestrians at the ports of entry, including:

  - 259,191 travelers and airline crew members who arrived by air.

  - 48,073 travelers and crew members who arrived by ship.

  - 621,874 travelers who came across the borders between the U.S. and Mexico or Canada.

- ★ CBP processed 64,483 trucks, railcars, and sea containers that arrived at U.S. ports of entry.

★ They refused to allow 470 people to enter the U.S.

★ CBP arrested 61 criminals who arrived at U.S. ports of entry.

★ They used 26,875 vehicles that travel on land.

★ CBP used 269 aircraft.

★ They used 228 ships and boats.

★ A total of 334 CBP horse patrol agents patrolled on horseback.

★ A total of 1,576 CBP dog teams searched for illegal items coming into our ports of entry.

★ CBP protected:

  • 5,000 miles of border with Canada.

  • 1,900 miles of border with Mexico.

  • 95,000 miles of U.S. shoreline.

On the border between the United States and Canada is the Peace Arch, pictured at top right. It commemorates the signing of the Treaty of Ghent, which established the U.S.-Canadian border west of Lake Superior. On the American side, it reads, "Children of a Common Mother"; and on the Canadian side, "Brethren Dwelling Together in Unity." An international group of volunteers used privately-donated funds to construct the Arch, which was dedicated in 1921. The arch is in Peace Arch Park which is managed as a state park by the State of Washington and as a provincial park by the Canadian province of British Columbia. Beside the park, CBP manages Peace Arch Port of Entry, pictured at lower right.

The United States Coast Guard

The United States Coast Guard has many responsibilities, including working as a partner with Customs and Border Protection to protect America's coastlines. In time of peace, the Coast Guard functions as an agency of the Department of

Peace Arch

Peace Arch

Peace Arch Park

Peace Arch Port of Entry

"Amazing Grace" is played at a ceremony at Peace Arch Park honoring victims of the September 11, 2001 terrorist attacks.

Scenes from the Work of the U.S. Coast Guard

U.S. Coast Guard Helicopter

A barge carries the retired Space Shuttle Enterprise, while a U.S. Coast Guard crew enforces a safety zone around it.

U.S. Coast Guard Motor Lifeboat

U.S. Coast Guard Seaplane

U.S. Coast Guard Auxiliary teaches boat safety.

Duluth, Minnesota
Lake Superior Maritime Museum

San Diego, California
U.S. Coast Guard Patrol Boat

Galveston, Texas
U.S. Coast Guard Boat

Homeland Security. In time of war, or at the President's command, the Coast Guard becomes part of the United States Navy.

Coast Guard history began in 1790 when President Washington signed an act designating ten ships to enforce U.S. tariff and trade laws and to prevent smuggling. This agency was later called the Revenue Cutter Service. In 1915 Congress merged the Revenue Cutter Service with the U.S. Lifesaving Service, an agency which protected ships coming into America's harbors. Together they became the U.S. Coast Guard. In 1939 President Franklin D. Roosevelt made the Lighthouse Service, which operated U.S. lighthouses, a part of the Coast Guard.

Coast Guard at the Portland Rose Festival

Portland, Oregon
U.S. Coast Guard cutter arrives for the annual Fleet Week held during the Portland Rose Festival on the waterfront of the Willamette River.

The Coast Guard's mission is to protect people on the sea, protect America from danger from the sea, and to protect the environment of the sea. When a vessel in America's waters is in danger, the Coast Guard responds to rescue the crew and save the vessel if possible. They inspect vessels to make sure they are safe for sea travel. On an average day, members of the Coast Guard check or repair over one hundred buoys used to mark places near our shores. In 2011 the Coast Guard visited 1,150 boat manufacturers to provide education and ensure the manufacturers were following safety regulations. The Coast Guard develops rules, procedures, and aids to help people navigate more safely on the sea.

The Coast Guard stops many ships with illegal goods or illegal immigrants before they arrive at U.S. ports. They check to make sure the crew and passengers on inbound ships have the proper documents. They work with the U.S. Navy to provide national defense. As of 2011, the Coast Guard had over 43,000 members on active duty, over 7,800 members on reserve duty, 8,300 civilian employees, and 33,000 volunteer members.

To protect the sea environment, the Coast Guard conducts research, checks ships to make sure they are not harming the environment, and responds to incidents of pollution at sea. They check to make sure fishermen are obeying laws about how much fish can be caught.

The Coast Guard uses many different types of boats to perform its work. It has boats as small as twelve feet long and as long as 400 feet. The Coast Guard has special icebreaker ships that work in Arctic and Antarctic regions. These ships are used to conduct scientific research and to bring supplies to remote stations. The Coast Guard also uses over 200 aircraft, both fixed-wing and helicopters.

The motto of the Coast Guard is "Always Ready." Since dangers from the sea and to the sea can occur at anytime, the Coast Guard must be trained, equipped, and prepared. They have a long history of vital service to the United States.

Those who go down to the sea in ships,
Who do business on great waters;
They have seen the works of the Lord,
And His wonders in the deep.
Psalm 107:23-24

Lesson Activities

Thinking Biblically — Copy Psalm 107:23-24 in the center of a piece of paper. Decorate around the verse with fish, boats, and other things from the sea.

Vocabulary — In your notebook, write a paragraph that uses all of these words: document, hubcap, tariff, firearm, pedestrian. Consult a dictionary if you need help with their definitions.

Literature — Read "Record-Breaking Career Ends for San Francisco CBP Canine" in *The Citizen's Handbook,* page 113.

Find Out! — Ask your parents if they have ever crossed the U.S. border with Canada or Mexico, and if they remember anything interesting about the experience.

Picture This! — Take a photograph of draw a picture of something in your house that was imported from another country.

Student Workbook or Lesson Review — If you are using one of these optional books, complete the assignment for Lesson 98.

When an Immigrant BECOMES A CITIZEN

America gains new citizens every year from every corner of the world. Our country is a better place because people have come ready to work and raise families and participate in democracy in the United States as their adopted home country.

To keep America safer, the United States has immigration laws about who may come, how long they may stay, how they may be employed, and how they can become U.S. citizens. U.S. Citizenship and Immigration Services is the agency of the Department of Homeland Security that helps people follow the rules about immigration and citizenship. The USCIS has about 18,000 people working at 250 offices around the world.

It is an exciting time for America and for immigrants when they join our nation. The photographs in this lesson are of real people becoming American citizens. Look at them as you read this imagined story about one such immigrant. Stories like this have been lived by millions of immigrants since America was founded. This story is about a Vietnamese immigrant. After the Vietnam War, America welcomed many immigrants like Quang from Vietnam, from Cambodia, from Laos, and from Thailand. Again and again America has generously welcomed people from around

President Barack Obama salutes a sailor who has just become a U.S. citizen at a naturalization ceremony at the White House, where twenty-four members of the military became citizens.

Painting of an Immigrant Scene at the U.S. Department of Justice

637

the world. We have been true to the words engraved on a plaque inside the pedestal of the Statue of Liberty, "Give me your tired, your poor, your huddled masses yearning to breathe free."

Charles Maggio was an immigrant who settled in Shreveport, LA.
He founded the Santa Maria Produce company in 1927.
This sign expresses his appreciation for his adopted country.

Introducing Quang

It is 8:00 a.m. on a Wednesday morning. Quang, age thirty-eight, waits with almost 6,000 other immigrants at the Los Angeles Convention Center. They have arrived at a naturalization ceremony to become citizens of the United States of America. Each of them has received an invitation to attend this particular ceremony. Quang presents his invitation to a government official and turns in his Green Card, which shows that he has been living in the United States legally as a permanent resident.

Immigrants from dozens of countries file through processing, too. They have come from Chile, Ethiopia, Russia, Sao Tome, and dozens of other countries. Small American flags and booklets about citizenship wait for them in their seats.

The crowd rises when a Federal judge is introduced to preside over the ceremony. They then are seated. An official from the U.S. Citizenship and Immigration Services says a few words about the significance of becoming a U.S. citizen. Then Quang and his fellow immigrants stand to take the Oath of Allegiance. The judge reads a few words at a time and the crowd repeats:

I hereby declare, on oath, that I absolutely and entirely renounce and abjure all allegiance and fidelity to any foreign prince, potentate, state or sovereignty, of whom or which I have heretofore been a subject or citizen; that I will support and defend the Constitution and laws of the United States of America against all enemies, foreign and domestic; that

I will bear true faith and allegiance to the same; that I will bear arms on behalf of the United States when required by the law; that I will perform noncombatant service in the armed forces of the United States when required by the law; that I will perform work of national importance under civilian direction when required by the law; and that I take this obligation freely without any mental reservation or purpose of evasion; so help me God.

The judge announces that the immigrants have now become citizens, and the crowd erupts in cheers, waving their flags enthusiastically. They watch a video recording of the President welcoming them as citizens of the U.S. The new citizens recite the Pledge of Allegiance to the Flag and listen to "The Star-Spangled Banner." Quang then waits in line with the others to receive his Certificate of Naturalization.

After Quang receives his certificate, he finds his wife and children for a joyful hug. Tears form in his eyes as he thinks about the long journey that has led to this point.

Coming to America

Quang was born during the war between North Vietnam and South Vietnam in the 1970s. His father was an American soldier sent to fight against North Vietnam; his mother was Vietnamese. Quang's father went back to the U.S. after the war, and Quang never saw him again. His mother took care of him until she died when Quang was a teenager.

The U.S. Congress passed a law in 1988 called the American Homecoming Act. This allowed many people from Vietnam like Quang, who had an American parent, to move to the United States more easily. Quang moved to California, where his uncle lived. Moving to the United States did not automatically make Quang a citizen of the United States, however.

In Vietnam, many people had treated Quang unkindly because he looked different. In the United States, he received more

Naturalization Ceremony in Arlington, Virginia

In September of 2012, 400 people became U.S. citizens at a naturalization ceremony at Kenmore Middle School. In the second photo from the top, President Obama welcomes them as new citizens by video.

639

Soldiers Become Naturalized Citizens While Serving Abroad

Bagram Airfield, Afghanistan
Spc. Paul Velchez of the Tennessee National Guard examines his certificate of U.S. citizenship, February 14, 2012.

Soldier holds his citizenship certificate after becoming a naturalized U.S. citizen at a ceremony in Afghanistan.

Twenty soldiers become naturalized citizens at Bagram Airfield in Afghanistan, February 14, 2012.

Subic Bay, Philippines
Sailors take the oath of allegiance during a naturalization ceremony aboard the USS Essex, *2011.*

New citizens Aboard the USS Essex.

Al-Faw Palace, Baghdad, Iraq
More than 250 members of the U.S. military from more than sixty countries, including ten from Iraq, become citizens, 2009.

Camp Liberty, Iraq
Iraqi-born soldier, serving in the U.S. Army as an interpreter, becomes a naturalized U.S. citizen along with 236 other members of the military from more than fifty countries. Shaking his hand is Vice President Joe Biden.

acceptance, but still some people looked down on him. He worked hard at different jobs and after several years was able to start his own business, a restaurant that specializes in Vietnamese food. Quang married Nhu, who is also from Vietnam, and they have three children.

Quang and his family speak Vietnamese at home, and many of his customers speak Vietnamese. However, Quang's children learned English at school, and Quang picked up some from them. He took ESL (English as a Second Language) classes from a church in his community to improve his skill.

Living in America has given Quang many opportunities. He decided that he wanted to become a citizen so that he could have all of the rights that citizens have, including the right to vote.

Becoming a Citizen

Naturalization Ceremony at the Statue of Liberty

Top: Marine Lance Corporal Tomas Roginski examines his citizenship paperwork after he became a naturalized U.S. citizen at a ceremony held at the Statue of Liberty in October, 2011. Roginski emigrated from Poland to Brooklyn, New York, when he was a child. Bottom: Two babies sleep at the ceremony at the Statue of Liberty in October of 2012.

In order to become a citizen of the United States, a person from another country must follow certain rules. He must be a permanent resident of the United States for a certain period of time, usually at least five years. He must have good moral character, which means not having committed certain criminal acts. The candidate for citizenship must be able to read, write, and speak basic English. He must also pass a test showing a basic understanding of U.S. history and government. Finally he must take the Oath of Allegiance declaring his loyalty to the Constitution.

Immigrants who serve honorably in the U.S. military are eligible to apply for citizenship sooner than other immigrants. Also, children under age eighteen may automatically become citizens if one of their parents becomes a U.S. citizen.

Approximately 700,000 immigrants become U.S. citizens each year. In 2009 California, New York, Florida, Texas, and New Jersey were the five states in which the most immigrants became citizens. The top countries from which they came were Mexico, India, the Philippines, China, and Vietnam.

After the Ceremony

Gerda Weissman Klein (center) was born in Poland and survived terrible treatment by the Nazis during World War II. She married an American soldier who had immigrated to the United States from Germany when he was seventeen. Mrs. Klein founded Citizenship Counts to help Americans appreciate the blessings of our country. In 2011 she received the Outstanding American by Choice award.

Before he leaves the convention center, Quang registers to vote. Representatives from political parties have displays of information encouraging new citizens to join their party. Growing up in Vietnam, Quang only knew about one political party, the Communist Party of Vietnam. In the next election, Quang looks forward to being able to choose the candidate he feels best represents his values and interests.

When he returns home, Quang signs his Certificate of Naturalization to make it official. Tomorrow he will apply for a passport and report his citizenship to the Social Security Administration. But now after a quick lunch, Quang must return to work at his restaurant, proud to be an American.

The stranger who resides with you shall be to you as the native among you,

and you shall love him as yourself, for you were aliens in the land of Egypt;

I am the Lord your God.

Leviticus 19:34

Lesson Activities

Literature — Read "Civics Questions for the Naturalization Test" in *The Citizen's Handbook*, pages 114-118.

Creative Writing — In your notebook, write a letter to a new citizen of the United States.

Find Out! — Ask your parents if they know anyone who has become a naturalized citizen of the United States.

Picture This! — Draw several people from other countries holding American flags.

Student Workbook or Lesson Review — If you are using one of these optional books, complete the assignment for Lesson 99.

★ Remember to choose an American Holiday to study this week! ★

UNIT 21 – HOMETOWN SECURITY

BOOKS USED IN UNIT 21

- The Citizen's Handbook
- Student Workbook (optional)
- Lesson Review (optional)

Tennessee Highway Patrol Honor Guard in Gainesboro, Tennessee, at a service to honor first responders who gave their lives in New York City on 9-11 and also local first responders, September 2012.

Call 9-1-1

New York City, New York
*Police Department Telephone
Operators, 1909*

Perhaps the first telephone number you ever learned was 9-1-1. For most citizens of the United States, 9-1-1 is the number they use to call for help during an emergency. The first telephone call ever completed was an emergency call. On March 10, 1876, telephone inventor Alexander Graham Bell was working in his laboratory. His assistant, Thomas A. Watson, was working in the next room when Bell accidentally spilled a chemical and needed help. The lab notebook Bell was using that day is in the collection of the Library of Congress.

In his notebook, Bell wrote, "I then shouted into M [his symbol for the telephone mouthpiece] the following sentence: 'Mr. Watson—come here—I want to see you.' To my delight he came and declared that he had heard and understood what I said."

Using Telephones in an Emergency

After the invention of the telephone, Americans could use their voices to communicate with someone in a different location instantly. Naturally, they started using telephones to call for help in emergencies. Sometimes they called their families, friends, or neighbors, while at other times they called the sheriff, the police, the fire department, or ambulance services. The various emergency workers they needed to call had different telephone numbers. See police department telephone operators above.

In this day of cell phones that can be used almost anywhere, it is hard to imagine what it was like before these were invented. Early telephone users simply picked up their telephone and told a telephone operator who they wanted to call. The operator connected their two phones by moving wires on a switchboard, like the one pictured on page 645. In that era, the telephone operator connected an emergency caller with the appropriate emergency workers. Eventually each telephone was assigned a telephone number and the role of the operator changed.

644

Aberdeen, Maryland
Telephone Operator, 1941

Until the 1970s, all telephones were connected to wires and stayed in one location in a home or business. Some homes had a telephone nook built into the wall of a hallway. These nooks had two shelves, one for the telephone and another for the telephone book. Some families had a special telephone table. These also had a drawer or a shelf for the telephone book. Some telephone tables had an attached seat so that people could sit down to talk on the phone. People used telephone books printed by their telephone company to find phone numbers of homes and businesses in the local community. Though emergency numbers were printed in the telephone book, people often kept a list of emergency phone numbers beside the phone. Businesses and civic organizations sometimes printed cards with these important phone numbers. The cards provided a service and also advertised the business or organization. When away from home, people used coin-operated phones to make calls. Emergency numbers were posted on pay phones. Few pay phones are still operating in the U.S., but some are, such as the one in the photo below.

After telephones were assigned numbers, telephone companies continued to hire operators. Operators had access to phone numbers across the country and could be called to look up a phone number. They also assisted callers who wished to make a long distance call to a telephone outside of their local community or city. Telephone operators could be reached by dialing a zero. Emergency callers sometimes dialed zero and told an operator their need and the operator called the appropriate agency. However, operators had many other responsibilities. This method was not fast enough for many emergencies.

The Idea Behind 9-1-1

In 1937 the island of Great Britain began to use one simple telephone number that its citizens could use to call the police, to report a fire, or to get medical help. They used the numbers 9-9-9. American soldiers learned about the 9-9-9 emergency number while they were stationed there during World War II. In the 1950s, all U.S. military bases began using one emergency telephone number.

Santa Monica, California
Pay Phone, February 2012

In 1957 the National Association of Fire Chiefs recommended that America adopt one emergency number for all U.S. citizens. In 1967 two presidential commissions involved in law enforcement recommended this also. In 1968 the American Telephone & Telegraph (AT&T) company announced that it would set aside the numbers 9-1-1 as the emergency telephone number all across the nation. You will learn more about AT&T in Lesson 122.

9-1-1 Service Begins and Spreads Across the Country

The Alabama Telephone Company worked quickly to beat AT&T and become the first telephone company to install an emergency telephone system using 9-1-1. At 2:00 p.m. on Friday, February 16, 1968, Alabama state legislator Rankin Fite placed the first 9-1-1 call from Haleyville City Hall. Tom Bevill, a U.S. Congressman from Alabama, answered the call at the Haleyville police station. Haleyville, Alabama, celebrates their role in 9-1-1 history and also honors police, fire, rescue, and emergency workers in its annual 9-1-1 Festival.

AT&T began to install 9-1-1 telephone systems in some cities around the country. In 1975 Bell Labs, AT&T's research division, received a patent for technology that would allow emergency dispatchers to know the telephone number an emergency caller was using. Emergency dispatcher is the job title for people who answer emergency phone calls. In 1980 AT&T began to test Enhanced 9-1-1 systems. An Enhanced 9-1-1 system allows the dispatcher to know both the caller's telephone number and his address. This is very important during an emergency, since the caller may not be able to answer questions.

The government agency that is responsible for making sure that telephone companies obey Federal laws is the Federal Communication Commission (FCC). In 1996 the FCC began to require all cell phone companies to provide Phase 1 Wireless 9-1-1 service. This service gives dispatchers the cell phone number of the caller and the location of the cell phone tower being used for the call. The first Phase 1 9-1-1 call in the United States was made in Indiana in 1998. The FCC also required cellular companies to provide Phase 2 9-1-1 service to dispatchers in localities that requested them to provide this service. Phase 2 service provides dispatchers with the longitude and latitude where the cell phone call is made. The first Phase 2 9-1-1 call in the United States was made in Illinois in 2001.

Since the late 1960s, local governments across the United States have installed 9-1-1 systems for their police, fire, and ambulance services. Installing these systems costs a great deal of money, so state governments raise money through various methods including placing a tax on telephone service. Today

646

almost all Americans live in areas where they can call 9-1-1 in an emergency situation. Some places are now experimenting with texting 9-1-1 messages.

An Emergency Dispatcher's Job

Emergency dispatchers, also called emergency telecommunicators, answer 9-1-1 calls at a Public Safety Answering Point (PSAP). Various public facilities, such as a police station, can serve as a PSAP. Small PSAPs may have only one dispatcher working at any given time and may receive only a few dozen calls per month. Many communities have a 9-1-1 center (sometimes called an emergency communications center). Large centers have several stations where a team of dispatchers answers thousands of calls each day. Read about Utah's largest emergency communication center below.

Civics at West Valley City, Utah

When residents of Salt Lake City, Utah, and the surrounding area call 9-1-1, their calls are answered at the Valley Emergency Communications Center (VECC) in West Valley City, Utah. The VECC is completely self-sufficient in case of an emergency; dispatchers can continue working even during an earthquake or other major disaster. The VECC's 25,000 square foot facility is also home to the state headquarters of the Utah Communications Agency Network (UCAN). See its 100-foot communication tower and its call center below.

Private companies design and build most public buildings in the United States, including the VECC/ UCAN facility. One of the VECC/UCAN designers was AECOM, one of the largest companies in America. AECOM employs architects, designers, engineers, managers, planners, and scientists. AECOM serves clients in more than 130 countries. AECOM was chosen to create the master plan for the London Olympic Games of 2012 and the Rio de Janeiro Games of 2016. AECOM has received many awards, including one for being one of the most ethical companies in the world.

Because emergencies can happen at any time, 9-1-1 centers are open twenty-four hours a day, seven days a week, including all holidays. When emergency dispatchers answer calls, they determine the type of emergency and its location. They decide on appropriate actions based on procedures that are already in place. They notify the appropriate emergency or non-emergency workers who are needed. For example, they may need to send police cars, fire trucks, and an ambulance to one emergency and just one policeman on a motorcycle to another. Dispatchers sometimes give first aid instructions over the phone so that the caller can assist someone until help arrives. They keep track of where the various emergency workers are while they are on their way to or from an emergency. Dispatchers must stay calm, think quickly, and make difficult decisions, while helping callers stay calm. They must keep detailed records about calls they receive.

What to Do if You Need to Call 9-1-1

Winston-Salem, North Carolina
Phone Numbers on Police Car

People should call 9-1-1 only in an emergency. Police departments, fire departments, and ambulance services have other telephone numbers that should be used if someone wants to ask a question like, "Can we come and tour your facility for a field trip?" or "Would it be okay if we brought you some cookies to say, 'Thank you'?"

Citizens should call 9-1-1 when they need help immediately, such as to report a fire, a serious car accident, a crime that is currently being committed, or a person who needs medical help right away.

Pictured on page 649 is a small child learning how to use 9-1-1. Many children have saved the lives of people they love by knowing how to call 9-1-1. If you are ever in an emergency situation and no adult is available to make the call, this is what you should do:

★ Enter the numbers 9-1-1 on a home phone or a cell phone.

★ Quickly tell the dispatcher what the problem is and then wait for him or her to ask you questions.

★ Answer the questions quickly. You may need to tell the dispatcher your phone number and the address where the emergency is happening. You may also need to answer questions about the emergency.

★ Do not hang up. Stay on the phone until the dispatcher tells you to hang up. Many times the dispatcher can tell you things to do and may even stay on the phone with you until policemen, fire fighters, and/or other emergency workers arrive.

★ Never call 9-1-1 as a joke. Taking the time of a dispatcher unnecessarily may keep him from being able to help someone who is truly in need. If you ever call 9-1-1 accidentally, do not hang up until you have talked to a dispatcher and apologized. If you hang up before the dispatcher answers, he or she may send emergency workers to where you are, tying up workers who may be needed for a real emergency.

Many other nations have also implemented nationwide emergency phone systems, using different number combinations. If you are ever instructed to call 9-1-1, remember to be a faithful messenger.

Chicago, Illinois
Child Learns about Calling 9-1-1
at Chicago Children's Museum

> Like the cold of snow in the time of harvest
> is a faithful messenger to those who send him,
> for he refreshes the soul of his masters.
> Proverbs 25:13

Lesson Activities

Vocabulary — Find each of these words in a dictionary, then find the definition that corresponds to the way the word is used in this lesson: operator, dispatcher, self-sufficient, ethical, implement. Copy the words and definitions into your notebook.

Creative Writing — In your notebook, write a short story of at least one page about a 9-1-1 call.

Find Out! — Look in your local phone book for the non-emergency numbers for your local police and fire departments.

Picture This! — Take photographs or draw pictures of all the telephones in your house.

Student Workbook or Lesson Review — If you are using one of these optional books, complete the assignment for Lesson 101.

Fighting Fires, SAVING LIVES

LESSON 102

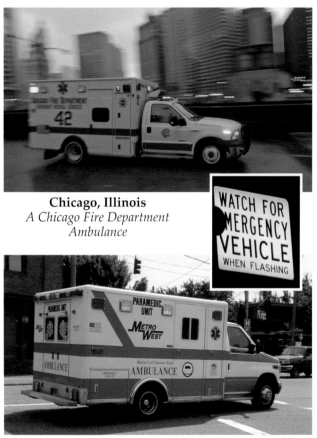

Chicago, Illinois
A Chicago Fire Department Ambulance

WATCH FOR EMERGENCY VEHICLE WHEN FLASHING

Washington County, Oregon
Metro West Ambulance, a Privately-Owned Provider of Emergency Services

Beatty, Nevada
Volunteer Ambulance Service in Unincorporated Town

When you hear a siren, you know first responders in your town are on the way to an emergency. Police cars, fire engines, and ambulances have their own special sirens, just as they each carry first responders with their own special responsibilities. In this lesson, we will learn about emergency medical responders and firefighters.

EMTs and Paramedics

When someone calls 9-1-1 to report an accident or an emergency medical situation, the dispatcher sends an ambulance to the scene. Inside the ambulance are emergency medical technicians (EMTs) and/or paramedics. An EMT receives about 150 hours of training in life-saving skills. EMTs can also receive more training and advance to EMT intermediate and advanced levels. Medical first responders with the most training and skills are paramedics. Paramedics train for about 1,200 hours, which can take up to 2 years. EMTs and paramedics can take additional training to become certified to drive an ambulance. States require EMTs and paramedics to have licenses.

When medical first responders arrive at the scene of an accident or emergency, they check the victim to decide what treatment is needed. They perform first aid such as bandaging wounds and, if necessary, CPR (which stands for cardiopulmonary resuscitation). Medical first responders often use backboards, head braces, and other restraints to secure a patient for transport to the hospital. One or more EMTs or paramedics stay with the patient in the back of the ambulance for the ride to the hospital, while another drives. Once at the hospital, they explain to the doctors what happened and what treatment was given to the patient.

Ambulances and Equipment

An ambulance is like a mini-hospital. It has the supplies needed for emergency care in many different medical situations. A typical ambulance has supplies to help patients with breathing and heart trouble. It has a stretcher, bracing equipment, and a cot on wheels that

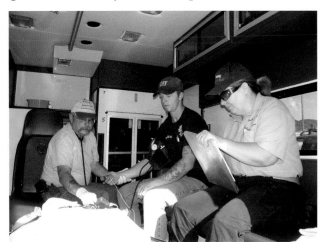

Beatty, Nevada
Volunteer Ambulance Service EMTs check blood pressure of firefighter.

can go from the ambulance to the scene of an emergency, back into the ambulance, and then out of the ambulance into the hospital. An ambulance has bandages, a thermometer, cold packs, a stethoscope, sheets, blankets, and towels. Also onboard are supplies to prevent germs from transferring from the patient to the first responder and from the EMT or paramedic to the patient. These include gloves, clothing covers, goggles, and masks. An ambulance has supplies used to deliver babies. Ambulances have communication equipment so that 9-1-1 dispatchers, EMTs, paramedics, and hospital staffs can communicate with one another about what the patient needs. All equipment is stored so that they can find what they need instantly. After an ambulance has answered a call, they must restock the ambulance with needed supplies. Ambulances and all their medical equipment are checked frequently to make sure everything works.

Nye County, Nevada

Serving the Community

Medical first responders work indoors and outdoors in all kinds of weather. They must be physically fit, alert, and well-trained. They must work well as a team with their fellow EMTs and paramedics, other first responders, and doctors. A good medical first responder knows how to remain calm, compassionate, and reassuring in a frightening situation. They are skilled and ready to serve people at their time of greatest need.

The Big Red Fire Engine

From the time you were very young, you probably learned about firefighters. Firefighters are a favorite subject for children's books, movies, and television because their jobs are exciting. They wear special uniforms, jump onto big fire trucks, race to put out fires, and save lives. Firefighters do have an exciting job, but not all parts are exciting. They work their way through many hours of specialized training, check and maintain equipment, and keep irregular schedules, often with little sleep. Firefighters must also be ready to face danger.

Governments must provide safe, effective fire trucks. This is a large purchase, and sometimes a fire department in a small town has to wait a long time before a new or additional truck can fit into the budget. Fire departments have many different types of fire trucks to choose from, such as pumpers that pump water, aerials with attached aerial ladders, tankers that carry water, rescue trucks, and trucks designed for off-road use.

Pumper Truck

Tanker Truck

Aerial Truck with Aerial Ladder

Several American companies make fire trucks. Pierce Manufacturing in Appleton, Wisconsin, is one. The company was founded by Humphrey and Dudley Pierce in 1913. They began building fire trucks in 1940. In addition to selling trucks to cities and counties, Pierce sells to other organizations that fight fires, including the U.S. military, the FBI, and the governments of foreign countries. Over the decades, Pierce has continually made improvements in its designs to build safer and better fire trucks.

Firefighters

Firefighters must be trained before they are hired, and they never stop training throughout their careers. They must be trustworthy. They must pass written and physical tests. They must know how to handle and maintain expensive and specialized equipment, be in top physical condition, and know the latest, most effective fire fighting and emergency medical procedures. Most firefighters are required to be certified as EMTs and are dispatched to more medical emergencies than fires. They are often the first emergency personnel at the scene of an accident.

Many firefighters work 24-hour shifts. Fire stations have beds, bathrooms with showers, exercise equipment, kitchens, lounge areas, classrooms, and offices, in addition to the areas where trucks and other equipment are stored. For 24 hours, they eat, sleep, train, study, practice, and work out at the station, all while being on call to respond to a fire, accident, or medical emergency. Because of long hours spent together at the fire station and the way firefighters depend on one another in emergencies, they become like a second family.

Fire departments serve their communities in many ways beyond emergency situations. They inspect buildings for fire safety, check that fire hydrants are working, and educate citizens about fire safety.

Training

The sizes of fire departments vary depending on the number of people and the size of the area they serve. The Cedar City, Utah, fire department has two stations. They serve about 30,000 people. The famous Fire Department of New York (FDNY) in New York City serves a population of eight million with more than 200 fire stations and over 10,000 firefighters.

Some communities are too small to maintain a full-time team of firefighters, so they organize volunteer fire departments, like the one in Mayflower, Arkansas, pictured below. Volunteer firefighters receive much of the same training and must meet many of the same requirements as full-time firefighters. Volunteer firefighters do not receive a salary, but sometimes they are reimbursed for the time they spend on the job. Many communities have junior volunteer fire fighter programs that give teenagers training and experience.

Franklin, Indiana

Mayflower, Arkansas

The Firefighter's Uniform

During their shift, firefighters wear basic, comfortable clothing such as a cotton T-shirt and fitted fire resistant slacks. Their clothing must fit well under firefighting gear. When called to a fire, a firefighter puts on the gear that is always waiting and ready. A firefighter's trousers are called turnout pants because they are "turned out" around heavy steel-toed boots. The firefighter can step into the boots and pull up the pants right-side out, easily secured by Velcro, snaps, and suspenders. The pants and jacket are made of several layers of heavy, fire-resistant material. Both have reflective stripes and large pockets for equipment. A firefighter must sometimes put on a self-contained breathing apparatus with a face mask so he can breathe fresh air while exposed to smoke and toxic gases in a burning building. The firefighter's helmet protects his head and also indicates his rank, fire department, and company. The last part of the firefighter's uniform is a pair of heat-resistant protective gloves. When fully dressed, a firefighter has added about fifty pounds to his weight.

Being a firefighter is a demanding job, but it is a job that dedicated men and women are proud to do. They train well, stay prepared, and keep learning. Firefighters serve the people of their community when they need help immediately.

Cornelia, Georgia
*Chenocetah Memorial Tower,
Fire Tower Built in the 1930s.*

Smokejumper in Alaska

Avery, Idaho
*Smokey Bear and
Forest Service Personnel*

*Helicopter picks up water from a
creek to use to fight a fire.*

Fighting Wildfires

Some firefighters are trained to fight forest and brush fires. The first step is to spot the fire, either by air or from a fire tower, like the one pictured at left. Some firefighters fight wildfires on the ground and others from helicopters. They sometimes vacuum water into a helicopter from a stream, creek, or lake. Smokejumpers parachute into forests to fight the spread of wildfires. See photos at left.

Since 1944 Smokey Bear has been encouraging people to prevent forest fires.

A Fire Station Tour in Ashland City, Tennessee

The photographs on this page and on page 656 were taken when the authors took an impromptu evening tour of Charlene's hometown fire department in Ashland City, Tennessee, 2010 population, 4,539. Our guide was Dustin Shadowens, age 26, pictured on page 655. Dustin was enthusiastic about his job. He had already been fighting fires for twelve years, beginning as a junior firefighter volunteer when he was fourteen years old.

Enjoying a Cookout Behind the Fire Station

This fireman is an EMT. The patch honors those who died on 9/11.

Sparky, the Fire Dog Costume

Firefighter Collectibles in the Chief's Office

Many firemen bring a sleeping bag to put on the bunk.

Firemen hat to give to children.

Two-Way Radios

Uniform Shirt

The marker board in the office reminds firefighters to get fuel for all trucks at a local gas station.

A Fire Station Tour in Ashland City, Tennessee

Dustin Shadowens, Who Just Arrived and Has Not Yet Changed into His Uniform

Chief's Helmet

Dustin's Locker Notice the photo of his child on the inside of the door.

Turnout Pants

Probationary Firefighters' Helmets

Firefighters' Helmets

Fire Hydrant Model Showing Interior

Chaplain's Helmet

When you hear a siren and see a fire truck, ambulance, or other first responder vehicle rushing past, say a prayer for the people they are going to help and also for the first responders and their families. In this way you will be helping all of these fellow citizens at a time when they need help immediately. Jesus is our example of praying often.

But Jesus Himself would often slip away to the wilderness and pray.
Luke 5:16

Lesson Activities

Thinking Biblically — EMTs help people they don't know with their most basic needs. Read about the Good Samaritan who did this in Luke 10:25-37.

Literature — Read "Presidential Proclamation — Fire Prevention Week" in *The Citizen's Handbook*, pages 119-120.

Creative Writing — In your notebook, make a list of 5 skills each that you think EMTs and firefighters should receive in their training.

Picture This! — Take a photograph or draw a picture of an ambulance or a firetruck.

Student Workbook or Lesson Review — If you are using one of these optional books, complete the assignment for Lesson 102.

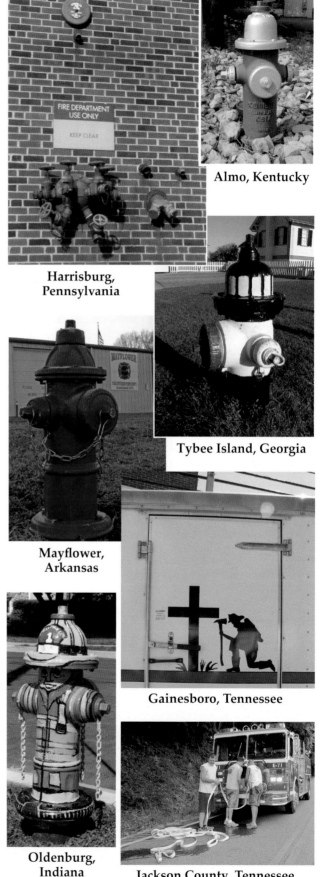

Almo, Kentucky

Harrisburg, Pennsylvania

Tybee Island, Georgia

Mayflower, Arkansas

Gainesboro, Tennessee

Oldenburg, Indiana

Jackson County, Tennessee
Volunteers extinguish a small brush fire beside a road during a drought.

657

Friends and PROTECTORS

Charlotte, North Carolina
*Policemen on Duty for the 2012
Democratic National Convention*

The phrase on the side of the police cars in a small Tennessee city said it well. They called themselves "Friends and Protectors." This is the role that law enforcement personnel have in a community. They are good guys; they are on the side of right, order, justice, and peace. They are citizens who help other citizens live with safety and security.

What Does a Law Enforcement Officer Do?

The work of a law enforcement officer is not what people see on television. It's not a comedy like "The Andy Griffith Show." It's not a drama like a crime show. Law enforcement officers are human beings who are dedicated to their work and to the community they serve. They help people; they sacrifice time and energy; they protect and they serve.

Law enforcement officers enforce the law. They protect people and property. They respond to calls for help. They work to prevent problems, and they stop those who are causing problems.

When necessary, they issue citations for traffic violations and arrest those who are breaking the law. Detectives and criminal investigators collect evidence, interview witnesses, and make arrests. Law enforcement personnel must write out detailed records of what happens, and they often have to appear in court to tell what they know.

Uniformed officers are easily recognized by the public. They have the responsibility to patrol regular areas of a city or county, respond to emergency calls, investigate complaints, and enforce traffic laws. Some police officers work on particular kinds of problems. Some officers in cities walk a regular beat (or route), drive a police car, ride a bicycle or motorcycle or horse, or patrol a harbor on a boat. Some officers work on the campus of

Mounted Police

Albuquerque, New Mexico

New York City, New York
Mounted police gather after a ticker tape parade in honor of the New York Giants football team.

Helping People Drive Safely

Waco, Texas
This City of Waco traffic vehicle helped mark a parade route for the Baylor University Homecoming Parade, the oldest homecoming parade in the country..

Washington, D. C.
Mrs. L. O. King directs traffic, 1918.

Winston-Salem, North Carolina
A law enforcement officer helps vendors leave the loading dock after a homeschool convention at the convention center.

659

a public university, get to know students as resource officers in public schools, or patrol a mass transit system. Some law enforcement jobs are specialized—detectives, dispatchers, officers who work with trained police dogs, researchers in crime labs, and those who work in jails and prisons.

Sheriffs and deputy sheriffs generally do the same kind of law enforcement work on the county level that police do on the city level. In many places voters elect the

Officers Involved with Students

Mount Berry, Georgia
Berry College Police

Washington, D.C.
Metropolitan Police Truancy/Curfew Department

Waco, Texas
Baylor University Police

Virginia Beach, Virginia
School Crossing Guard

sheriff. In communities with a large police force, the county sheriff might just be in charge of the county jail, deliver legal documents, and work with the local court system.

State police officers are sometimes called state troopers or the highway patrol. They spend a great deal of time enforcing a state's traffic laws. They also assist law enforcement agencies

Transportation Police

Federal   **Virginia**   **New Jersey**

Boston,
Massachusetts
and Maine

Tennessee

New York and
New Jersey

Special Police Roles

Virginia Beach, Virginia

in rural areas and small towns. Fish and game wardens enforce fishing, hunting, and boating laws; conduct rescue operations; and educate the public about safety and the environment.

Law Enforcement Tools

Officers have available to them weapons to stop suspects and equipment, such as bullet proof vests, to protect themselves. Some officers wear helmets. They carry tools to gain entry into locked or damaged vehicles. They carry flares and cones to mark disabled vehicles or ones that have run out of gas. They carry first aid kits to help those who are hurt. Law enforcers have long relied on two-way radios to communicate with their headquarters and with other officers. Cell phones have increased their ability to communicate with others. Police and sheriff cars have computers for checking and sharing information they gather (such as automobile registrations). Their vehicles have radar guns to check the speed of vehicles. They have video cameras that record what suspects do and what the officers themselves do.

Technology has enabled law enforcement to make great progress in solving crimes. For instance, officers are able to take fingerprints of suspects at the scene and transmit the image of the prints around the world to help identify a suspect. They also gather DNA evidence.

St. Paul, Minnesota
Police officers guard a street near the Republican National Convention, 2008.

The FBI

Agents of the Federal Bureau of Investigation (FBI) are the Federal government's principal investigators of violations of Federal law. It was formed as part of the Department of Justice in 1908. At first the Bureau investigated crimes related to banking, bankruptcy, naturalization, and fraudulent land sales. Over the years, the Bureau's work expanded as the Federal government made laws about other aspects of life. The FBI investigated foreign spies in the United States during World War I and II. They investigated illegal activities of Communist agents during the Cold War (1950s-1980s). They investigated violations of civil rights laws and organized crime. The Bureau set up field offices in many cities around the country. In 1932 the Bureau built a crime investigation lab. Since then it has used the most advanced technology available to investigate and fight crime. The most

FBI Mobile Command Center

famous director of the FBI was J. Edgar Hoover, who was appointed to be the director of the Bureau in 1924. Hoover continued in this role for almost 48 years, until his death in 1972.

Federal Marshals

Your grandparents probably think of United States Marshals as the law enforcement officials of the Old West, since that is what they saw on television westerns made in the 1950s and 1960s. This is only part of their story, however. The U.S. Marshals Service was created by the Judiciary Act of 1789. Their job was to help Federal courts and to carry out orders given by Federal judges, Congress, and the President. Marshals delivered arrest warrants and summonses to appear in court. They made sure that witnesses were present at trials. It was their responsibility to inform people that they needed to be on a jury. They represented the Federal government on the local level across the country. Through 1870 Federal marshals had the responsibility to gather census information every ten years. They also collected information on commerce and manufacturing.

U.S. Marshals are still called upon to enforce Federal court orders. In 1962 they came to Oxford, Mississippi, to help James Meredith become the first African American to enroll at the University of Mississippi. In 1989 they enforced Federal court orders during a coal miners' strike in West Virginia and Virginia. Today Federal Air Marshals provide security for U.S. passenger aircraft.

Texas Rangers

One of the best known law enforcement organizations on the state level is the Texas Rangers. In 1823, when Texas was still part of Mexico, Stephen F. Austin received permission from the Mexican government to organize a group to defend settlers from attack by Native Americans. The group was called the Texas Rangers. The Rangers helped their fellow Texians (as the settlers were called)

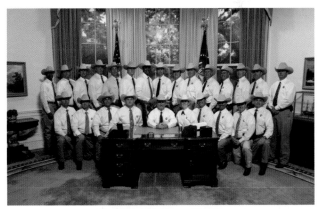

College Station, Texas
Texas Rangers at the George H. W. Bush Library

gain their independence from Mexico. They fought in the Mexican War. These men enforced the law when Texas became part of the United States, and they continue to enforce the law in the State of Texas today. The Texas Rangers are part of the Texas Department of Public Safety.

Historic & Modern City, County, & State Law Enforcement Patches

Alabama

North Pole, Alaska

Lapaz County, Arizona

Arkansas

California

Colorado

New Milford, Connecticut

Bethany Beach, Delaware

Florida

Georgia

Hawaii

Idaho

Chicago, Illinois

Allen County, Indiana

Davenport, Iowa

Dodge City, Kansas

Kentucky

Louisiana

Bar Harbor, Maine

Greenbelt, Maryland

Northampton, Massachusetts

Warren, Michigan

Minnesota

Mississippi

Missouri

Historic & Modern City, County, & State Law Enforcement Patches

Montana

Nebraska

Nevada

New Hampshire

Franklin, New Jersey

New Mexico

New York City, New York

Greensboro, North Carolina

North Dakota

Columbus, Ohio

Muskogee, Oklahoma

Rockaway Beach, Oregon

Philadelphia, Pennsylvania

Rhode Island

South Carolina

South Dakota

Tennessee

San Antonio, Texas

Utah

Vermont

Virginia

Washington

West Virginia

Two Rivers, Wisconsin

Laramie, Wyoming

Law enforcement officers face difficult situations. Like firefighters, they must be in good physical shape to perform the rigorous work they do, both when they begin their careers and when they take physical tests from time to time during their careers. Many colleges now offer degrees in law enforcement or criminal justice. Officers are also usually expected to complete a course of study at a police training academy and they must participate in continuing education through the years.

Most importantly, law enforcement officials must have the character, honesty, and dedication to do their jobs with integrity. The American people must be able to trust the men and women who enforce the laws. Two Presidents have been involved in law enforcement. Grover Cleveland was once a sheriff and Theodore Roosevelt served as a police commissioner for the City of New York.

Have you thanked an officer lately for the work they do? Have you said a prayer for their safety? Law enforcement is difficult because officers are trying to protect people who do right from people who do wrong.

. . . law is not made for a righteous person, but for those who are lawless and rebellious,

for the ungodly and sinners . . . .

1 Timothy 1:9

Lesson Activities

Thinking Biblically — Write a paragraph in your notebook about how a Christian law enforcement officer could use his or her position to be a light for Jesus.

Vocabulary — In your notebook, write the vocabulary words and the letter of the definition that goes with each word: justice, arrest, patrol, flare, criminal.

a. capture and keep in custody

b. a device that gives off a blaze of light as a signal

c. one who breaks the law

d. to travel an area for the purpose of maintaining security

e. just dealing, fairness, impartiality

Literature — Read "A Marine's Grade-School Dream is Realized" in *The Citizen's Handbook*, pages 121-122.

Find Out! — How many people are part of your local law enforcement department?

Student Workbook or Lesson Review — If you are using one of these optional books, complete the assignment for Lesson 103.

Ready for the WEATHER

Arizona
Grand Canyon National Park Winter Storm, February 20, 2011

The weather affects farming, business, travel, our health, how we dress, and many other aspects of our daily lives. Knowing the weather can sometimes help us to be safe and to avoid a dangerous situation. People have observed the weather since ancient times. Jesus used an illustration based on observing the weather in Matthew 16:2-3:

> . . . *When it is evening, you say, "It will be fair weather, for the sky is red." And in the morning, "There will be a storm today, for the sky is red and threatening." Do you know how to discern the appearance of the sky, but cannot discern the signs of the times?*

Weather Observation History

The use of precise measurements in observing weather developed in the 1600s. The Italian physicist Evangelista Torricelli invented the barometer to measure atmospheric pressure in 1643. In 1664 Italian Francesco Folli invented the first practical hygrometer to measure humidity. German Daniel Fahrenheit developed the mercury thermometer in 1714.

John Campanius Holm (sometimes called John Campanius) is considered to be the first weatherman in North America. Holm was a Swedish Lutheran minister who came to New Sweden in 1643 and settled near present-day Wilmington, Delaware. He evangelized the Lenape Native Americans who lived in that area, and while doing so he learned their language. Holm eventually translated Luther's Shorter Catechism into the Lenape language. In 1644 and 1645, Holm recorded the weather at New Sweden twice per day. In 1646 he consecrated the first Lutheran church building in the New World, a log building on Tinicum Island south of what is now Philadelphia. Holm returned to Sweden in 1648 and died in 1683.

Weather observations were important in the American colonies. Since just about everyone in the colonies was a farmer or in a farming family, almost everyone was concerned about having accurate weather information. George Washington, Thomas Jefferson, and Benjamin Franklin recorded their observations of the weather. Jefferson kept almost daily records for about forty years. He also recruited people to be volunteer weather observers throughout Virginia.

Bear Lake, Alaska
Aurora Borealis, January 29, 2011

Arches National Park, Utah
Storm over the Park

J. Clark Salyer National Wildlife Refuge, North Dakota
November Sunset, 2005

Death Valley National Park, California
Wind Patterns on the Sands of Death Valley

History of the National Weather Service

In 1870 President Ulysses S. Grant signed a joint resolution of Congress that authorized the Secretary of War to create a "Division of Telegrams and Reports for the Benefit of Commerce" with the purpose of gathering weather information. The job was assigned to the War Department because weather is important for military activity and because military discipline could help regular, accurate weather information to be recorded. The Division was transferred to the Department of Agriculture in 1891 and renamed the U.S. Weather Bureau. Weather information was sent to ships at sea

Norman, Oklahoma
*Mobile Doppler Radar on Display
at National Weather Center Festival*

by wireless telegraphy for the first time in 1902. In 1910 the Weather Bureau began publishing weekly weather forecasts to help farmers. The Bureau was transferred to the Commerce Department in 1940 because of its importance to air travel and thus to the nation's economy. As seen at left below, airports came to be a common point of weather data collection.

In the late 1940s, the military gave the Bureau twenty-five surplus radar units. Meteorologists still depend on radar today. Weather radar is often described as Doppler radar. See photo above. This kind of radar produces information based on the Doppler effect, a principle of physics proposed by Austrian physicist Christian Doppler in 1842. Doppler radar sends a microwave signal toward a storm. When it bounces off precipitation and returns to the point of origin, a computer can determine where the rain or snow is and how fast it is moving. Computer graphics can represent this information on a television screen.

The increasing use of computer technology since the 1950s has enabled experts to develop weather models or estimates of the movement of weather systems that provide more accurate forecasts. The use of weather satellites began in the 1960s and provided global information about and eventually photographs of weather patterns. See the satellite receiver at right below and a satellite image from the National Aeronautics and Space Administration (NASA) on page 669.

In 1970 the Bureau's name was changed to the National Weather Service (NWS), and it became part of the National Oceanic and Atmospheric Administration (NOAA) .

Washington, D.C.
*Weather Station at the
National Airport, 1943*

New Mexico
*National Weather Service employee
aims Direcway Satellite Dish.*

Global Weather, Local Impact

Weather happens everywhere, and the National Weather Service provides information about weather all over the country. However, the impact of weather is always felt on the local level. When a storm, hurricane, or tornado strikes a community, people all over the country are concerned and might be affected indirectly; but the people in that community are most directly impacted.

Knowing about the weather is important. Before a snowfall, street and road departments must prepare road surfaces with salt, sand, or a mixture of salt and a juice by-product of beet processing. After the snow falls, they must remove it. See photos at right and below. Utility companies must repair equipment after a power outage. In hot weather, electric departments handle power overloads. Communities must prepare and operate shelters if people must leave their homes.

Many communities have sirens that sound when severe weather is approaching. In extreme cases, first responders go from house to house to warn citizens of approaching flood waters or other emergencies. Reverse 911 calls

Hurricane Irene off the East Coast, August 2011

Oregon Department of Transportation
Top: Plowing Snow; Lower: Snowplow Operator;
Inset: Keeping Signs in Good Repair

Chicago, Illinois

669

are sometimes placed by the local 9-1-1 center to all telephone subscribers to inform them of an emergency. Industries that use large amounts of water use weather information to prepare for severe drought conditions.

Flight Park State Recreation Area, Utah
Glider pilots enjoying the park depend on NOAA's aviation services, which include soaring forecasts.

The National Weather Service works with individual citizens and with local community governments and first responders to provide accurate forecasts and to help communities to be prepared for severe weather events and to respond effectively when they occur. NWS information is available on the Internet and on mobile device apps and is used in preparing commercial radio and television weather broadcasts.

The NWS provides weather information for American citizens through the NOAA Weather Radio All Hazards service which has one thousand transmitters spread throughout all fifty states, Puerto Rico, the Virgin Islands, and our Pacific territories. Seven days a week, twenty-four hours per day, these stations continuously broadcast current local weather conditions and local forecasts. The service also broadcasts warnings about earthquakes, avalanches, oil spills, chemical spills, and public safety announcements such as AMBER alerts and problems with 9-1-1 telephone systems. Citizens must have a special receiver called a "weather radio" to hear the broadcasts, since they are not broadcast on typical AM or FM stations. This is a way in which every home can be in touch with the government's National Weather Service.

Special weather events are usually announced by a local NWS office as either advisories, watches, or warnings. An advisory is announced for an event that will likely have only a little impact, such as an early frost or a light snowfall. A watch means that conditions are favorable for severe weather but no severe storm has been identified. A warning is issued when a severe weather event is about to happen or is already happening.

Weather Volunteers

The National Weather Service depends on a team of about 12,000 Americans who volunteer as Cooperative Weather Observers. Each day they collect temperature and precipitation information at their homes with equipment provided by the NWS and send the information to the NWS. The Service honors people who have been outstanding weather observers and those who have served for long periods of time. The Thomas Jefferson Award is the highest honor given to outstanding volunteer observers. Other awards include:

- ★ The John Campanius Holm Award presented to as many as twenty-five volunteer observers each year.

- ★ The Earl Stewart Award given for seventy-five years of continuous observation service. Mr. Stewart lived in Cottage Grove, Oregon and achieved seventy-five years of service in 1992.

- ★ The Ruby Stufft Award presented for 70 years of service. Mrs. Stufft lived in Elsmere, Nebraska and rendered 70 years of service as a cooperative weather observer.

- ★ The Albert J. Meyer Award is given for 65 years of service. Meyer was the first head of the "The Division of Telegrams and Reports for the Benefit of Commerce."

- ★ The Helmut E. Landsberg Award is presented to observers who complete 60 years of service. Dr. Landsberg was a widely respected meteorologist of the twentieth century.

- ★ The Benjamin Franklin Award is given for fifty-five years of service.

- ★ The Edward H. Stoll Award is given for fifty years of service. Mr. Stoll of Arapahoe, Nebraska, took weather observations for 76 years, which at the time of this writing is the longest service anyone has given in voluntary weather observations.

San Benito County, California
In 2010 Cooperative Weather Observer Clorene Akers received the Benjamin Franklin Award from Dave Reynolds, Meteorologist-in-Charge at the NWS office in Monterey, California. Mrs. Akers had just turned ninety-three and was still managing eighty-five head of cattle on the ranch where she had lived since 1933.

About 290,000 Americans have been trained to be SKYWARN® Severe Weather Spotters. These volunteers include police and fire personnel, dispatchers, emergency medical service personnel, public utility workers, ham radio (amateur shortwave radio) operators, and others. Spotters are trained to know how a thunderstorm develops, to identify severe weather features, and to know what information to report and how to report it to the NWS.

The StormReady® Community Preparedness Program began in Tulsa, Oklahoma, in 1999. Through the program the National Weather Service helps communities of any size be ready for severe weather and its effects. See photo above. To qualify for this status, a community must establish a 24-hour warning point and emergency operations center, have more than one

**Harrisburg,
Pennsylvania**
*Thermometer in
State Capitol*

way to receive severe weather warnings and alert the public, create a system to monitor local weather conditions, hold community seminars to help local citizens be more aware and prepared, and develop a formal hazardous weather plan, which includes training spotters and conducting emergency exercises. Improving communication and safety skills in this manner helps protect lives and property in a community.

We can't stop the weather, but government and citizens working together can help lessen the impact of severe weather on our communities.

He said to them, "Why are you afraid, you men of little faith?"
Then He got up and rebuked the winds and the sea, and it became
perfectly calm. The men were amazed, and said,
"What kind of a man is this, that even the winds and the sea obey Him?"
Matthew 8:26-27

Lesson Activities

Thinking Biblically — In your notebook, draw a picture of a Bible story related to weather, such as the creation of the sky, the flood of Noah, the famine in Egypt, or Jesus calming the storm.

Vocabulary — Look up each of these words in a dictionary and read their definitions: mercury, forecast, data, surplus, transmitter.

Literature — Read "Rain in Summer" in *The Citizen's Handbook*, page 123.

Creative Writing — In your notebook, write at least two paragraphs about a memory you have related to weather.

Find Out! — Where do your parents get their information about the weather?

Picture This! — Take a photograph or draw a picture of the weather at your house today or another day this week.

Student Workbook or Lesson Review — If you are using one of these optional books, complete the assignment for Lesson 104.

Anchorage, Alaska
A moose discovers NWS weather equipment.

★ Remember to choose an American Holiday to study this week! ★

UNIT 22 – THE AMERICAN JUSTICE SYSTEM

BOOKS USED IN UNIT 22

- The Citizen's Handbook
- The Long Winter
- Student Workbook (optional)
- Lesson Review (optional)

Entrance to the United States Supreme Court

Justice
FOR ALL

Chautauqua, New York

Danville, Kentucky

Wise parents make rules for their children. They enforce those rules and discipline their children when they break them. When loving parents use kind discipline to teach their children, they are following God's example. Hebrews 12:9-11 teaches us about the discipline of earthly fathers and the discipline we receive from our heavenly Father:

> *Furthermore, we had earthly fathers to discipline us, and we respected them . . . For they disciplined us for a short time as seemed best to them, but He disciplines us for our good, so that we may share His holiness. All discipline for the moment seems not to be joyful, but sorrowful; yet to those who have been trained by it, afterwards it yields the peaceful fruit of righteousness.*

Countries develop a system of rules called laws. In the United States, laws are passed by the legislative branches of our local, state, and Federal governments. The photos on these pages illustrate some of the many laws that young people must remember. You probably wish that everyone in America would obey all laws and live as they should. Unfortunately,

Franklin, Indiana

Jackson County, Tennessee

Duluth, Minnesota
Along the Skywalk Connecting Downtown Buildings

674

not everyone lives this way. This is why America and other countries must have a legal system.

The purposes of the American legal system are to:

★ Enforce what is accepted behavior;

★ Protect the community and its citizens from those who break the law;

★ Punish, teach, and reform law breakers; and

★ Resolve major disagreements between two parties.

Danville, Kentucky

Justice

Everyone wants to be treated fairly. In other words, everyone wants to be treated with justice. The definition of justice is "the quality of being fair and reasonable." Justice is important when someone has been accused of breaking a law. Just because someone has been accused does not mean he is guilty. Even if he is guilty, he should be treated fairly. On the other hand, the victim of a crime deserves justice, too. Also, people who commit a crime often commit similar crimes in the future; and citizens need to be protected from their wrong actions.

Justice is important to God. The word justice is used 138 times in the New American Standard Bible translation. The first time is in Genesis 18:19 when God said this about Abraham:

> *For I have chosen him, so that he may command his children and his household after him to keep the way of the Lord by doing righteousness and justice . . .*

Many American and English laws are based on the Law of Moses, which God gave to Abraham's descendants. Let's look at a brief history from Abraham to Moses. God blessed Abraham with a son, Isaac. Isaac's son Jacob had twelve sons. After his sons' births, God gave Jacob a new name—Israel. Most of Jacob's sons were jealous of one brother, Joseph. One day they sold him as a slave. Joseph ended up in Egypt and through God's providence was later able to bring his father Jacob and all of his family to Egypt to save them from a famine. The descendants of Jacob's twelve sons became the twelve tribes of Israel.

The descendants of these first Israelites later became slaves in Egypt. After the Israelites lived there 430 years, God chose Moses to lead them back to the land He had promised to give to Abraham's descendants. While they were on their journey, God gave them laws to obey. These laws became known as the Law of Moses. Copies of the portion of the Law of Moses called the Ten Commandments have been erected in many public places across America, as illustrated on page 676.

Memphis, Tennessee
*Ten Commandment Monument
Erected in Confederate Park
by the Memphis Jaycee Civic
Organization in 1952*

Beckley, West Virginia
*Justice Mural in the Robert C. Byrd
U. S. Courthouse
and Federal Building*

Sandra Day O'Connor takes the oath of office to become an Associate Justice of the U.S. Supreme Court. Chief Justice Warren Burger (left) administers the oath while Mr. O'Connor looks on, September, 1981.

Examine the mural at left below. The use of a female figure to represent justice began in Greek and Roman mythology. Over the centuries, a scale was added to represent weighing the opposing sides; the blindfold means that justice is blind to status or wealth. This figure of "Justice" holds a book of law.

Judges

Sometimes people cannot settle their disagreements without help. God provided the Israelites with judges to help in those times, and He gave rules for how they should act in Deuteronomy 16:18-20.

> *You shall appoint for yourself judges and officers in all your towns which the Lord your God is giving you, according to your tribes, and they shall judge the people with righteous judgment. You shall not distort justice; you shall not be partial, and you shall not take a bribe, for a bribe blinds the eyes of the wise and perverts the words of the righteous. Justice, and only justice, you shall pursue, that you may live and possess the land which the Lord your God is giving you.*

The United States has judges who serve in either the Federal judicial branch or one of the fifty state judicial branches of government. The ways that judges are chosen in the fifty states varies. Some are elected and others are appointed. Federal judges are appointed by the President and confirmed by the U.S. Senate. They take the following oath of office:

> *I _____, do solemnly swear (or affirm) that I will administer justice without respect to persons, and do equal right to the poor and to the rich, and that I will faithfully and impartially discharge and perform all the duties incumbent upon me as _____ under the Constitution and laws of the United States. So help me God.*

When taking the oath, the judge (or justice) fills in the second blank with the title of the position he or she is about to fill (for example, United States District Judge or Associate Justice of the Supreme Court). Notice that judges who serve on the U.S. Supreme Court or a state supreme court are called justices.

Oxford, Mississippi
Lafayette County Courthouse

Hilo, Hawaii
Federal Building and U.S. Courthouse

Detroit, Michigan
Theodore Levin U.S. Courthouse

Judges and Courtrooms

Judges preside over a court of law which meets in a courtroom in a courthouse. The U.S. has many kinds of courthouses—county courthouses, district courthouses operated by states, Federal district courthouses, and the Supreme Court Building, to name a few. See a county and two Federal courthouses above and at right.

When a judge sits on the bench in a courtroom, he is in charge of all that happens there. A bench is a seat on a raised platform. See bench in the Theodore Levin courtroom at right. As seen in the photo of Associate Justice Sandra Day O'Connor on page 676, judges and justices wear business clothing covered by a black robe. The people in a courtroom are told to rise when a judge approaches the bench and when he or she leaves. Everyone addresses the judge as "Your Honor." The people in a courtroom, even observers who are not participating in the official business, must show respect to the judge by how they dress, what they say, and how they act. People who do not show respect can be held in contempt of court and be required to pay a fine. Read the rules of one courtroom above.

Ashland City, Tennessee
Rules on the Door of General Sessions Courtroom

677

People in a Courtroom

Attorneys - Lawyers (also called counsel or members of the bar) who represent a defendant or a plaintiff.

Clerk - A court employee who assists the judge and who is responsible for all documents involved in a trial and all objects used as evidence. The clerk administers the oath to witnesses.

Court Reporter - A court employee who keeps official records of every word spoken in a trial.

Defendant (civil case) - The party being sued. The defendant in a civil case does not always attend the trial.

Defendant (criminal case) - The person accused of committing a crime has a constitutional right to attend his trial.

Judge - If the trial is a jury trial, the judge gives jury members instructions about how the law applies in the case. If the trial is a bench trial, the judge will make the same sorts of decisions that a jury makes. In criminal trials, the judge decides on the punishment of a defendant who is found guilty.

Jury - Citizens who are chosen by the judge and approved by the attorneys to decide on a defendant's guilt or innocence in a criminal case and decide whether the plaintiff in a civil case deserves to receive what he is requesting. The number of jurors is often twelve. They sit in a jury box.

Jury Foreman - One jury member chosen by the other jurors to serve as their chairman and spokesman.

Court Security Officer(s) - Law enforcement officer(s) who guard criminal defendants and keep people in the courtroom safe.

Plaintiff - The party who has sued another party in a civil case. The plaintiff does not always attend the trial.

Prosecuting Attorney - An attorney who represents the State in a criminal case (also called a District Attorney or DA).

Witnesses - People that the defendant, plaintiff, and their attorneys ask to come to court to tell what they know about the case being tried.

Places in a Courtroom

Defendant sits behind the bar on the front row on this side.   Plaintiff sits behind the bar on the front row on this side.

Behind the row where the defendant and plaintiff sit are more rows of seats for observers.

The courtroom above is in the William O. Douglas Federal Building in Yakima, Washington.

Chattanooga, Tennessee
Courtroom in the Joel W. Solomon Federal Building and U.S. Courthouse

Federal Courts Try Cases Involving:

More Than One State
Laws Passed by Congress
Copyrights and Patents
Other Countries
Certain Crimes Committed on Federal Property
Disputes Between States
Bankruptcy*

State Courts Try Cases Involving:

Laws Passed by a State Legislature
Family Law
Real Estate
Inheritance
Personal Injuries
Violations of Traffic Laws and Motor Vehicle Registrations
Contracts Between Two Parties
Regulation of Doctors, Dentists, Lawyers, and Other Professions

*Bankruptcy involves the inability to pay money that is owed. People, companies, and even governments can go bankrupt.

United States Judicial System

The Federal judicial branch operates a system of district courts that handle Federal cases. Almost 700 judges hear cases in ninety-four Federal court districts. At left is a Federal courtroom in the Eastern District of Tennessee.

Each of the fifty state judicial branches operates a system of state courts that handle state cases. Most cases in the U.S. are tried in these courts. Read the chart at left to learn about some differences between Federal court cases and state cases.

Each state has courts of appeal and a state supreme court where people can appeal a decision made in a lower state court. These courts are considered "higher courts." States have various names for their state supreme courts.

The Federal court system has thirteen Circuit Courts of Appeal and a Supreme Court. Learn about the United States Supreme Court in Lesson 109. In most lower courts, one judge at a time oversees a trial, but in higher courts three or more justices often hear a case together.

The purpose of a court of law is to decide if a party has broken a law and, if so, what kind of punishment the party will receive (a party is a person or entity involved in a legal case; a case is a conflict to be decided with the help of the judicial branch). The American justice system also has courts that handle specific kinds of cases. Examples are courts that handle tax questions, traffic violations, or cases involving juveniles who have been accused of breaking the law.

Civil Law and Criminal Law

Laws are divided into two types: criminal law and civil law. Civil law involves the rights of private citizens. Civil cases involve two or more parties and are tried in

a civil court. The following is an example of a problem between two private citizens that might be decided by a civil court. If Mr. Jones paid a painter to paint his house and the painter caused expensive damage to the Jones home, Mr. Jones could sue the painter to try to force him to pay for the damages. Other citizens are not endangered by such a disagreement, but the situation has to be resolved by an authority that does not favor either side.

Summons for Jury Duty

Miami, Florida
Jury Assembly Room in the James L. King Federal Justice Building

Cleveland, Ohio
Jury Room Door in the Howard M. Metzenbaum U.S. Courthouse

Criminal law involves those actions that are considered harmful to society. This includes serious crimes such as bank robbery and intentionally harming others. Criminal cases are tried in a criminal court. Criminal cases involve the government (called the State) and a defendant (the person accused of committing a crime).

In addition to laws that various legislatures have passed, courts also consider whether people have violated a "common law." Common law is what has generally been accepted as wrong or harmful behavior in the past and how past courts have decided such cases for the last several centuries. Precedent is the term used for what past courts have decided. Courts take common law into account in both criminal and civil cases.

Citizens Involved in the Justice System

Citizens who are not accused of a crime or involved in a civil dispute may still become involved in a case. Sometimes a citizen is required to be a witness in a trial and tell what he knows. A more common way is serving on a jury. The jury is an important part of the American justice system.

From time to time, government officials gather names of adult citizens to create a pool of possible jurors. These people are required to be available to serve on a jury unless they have an extreme hardship, such as physical disability or not being able to get off from work. Judges notify citizens when they are needed for jury duty, often by mail, as seen in the photo at left above. Serving on a jury can be inconvenient, but American citizens should be willing to serve on a jury to make sure the system continues and works well.

When a trial is to be held, potential jurors gather at a courthouse. See photos on page 680. Attorneys on both sides of a case question potential jurors to see if they can listen to both sides of the case fairly. The judge chooses from the pool of potential jurors people who are acceptable to both sides in the case to serve as jurors.

The members of a trial jury sit in the jury box and listen to what is said in a trial. The judge then explains the applicable law to them and dismisses them to the jury room to make their decision. A door into a jury room is pictured on page 680.

Jury decisions must be unanimous. In a criminal trial, each member of the jury must believe that the accused person is guilty beyond a reasonable doubt or the defendant will be declared not guilty. In any trial, the judge and the jury have difficult decisions to make. In a criminal trial, they must remember that a person is not necessarily guilty just because he has been accused. He may be completely innocent. Our Savior was accused even though He was innocent. Jesus endured an unfair trial, and then He was punished by death on a cross.

Now when the centurion saw what had happened, he began praising God, saying,
"Certainly this man was innocent."
Luke 23:47

Lesson Activities

Thinking Biblically — In your notebook, make a list of what God commanded the Israelite officers and judges to do, based on Deuteronomy 16:18-20.

Literature — Read "Mr. Chief Justice" in *The Citizen's Handbook*, pages 124-129.

Student Workbook or Lesson Review — If you are using one of these optional books, complete the assignment for Lesson 106.

Crime and
PUNISHMENT

New Mexico has one of the toughest DWI (driving while intoxicated) laws in the United States. Imagine what might have happened one month after the state legislature passed a DWI bill and the Governor signed it into law. Dan Drinker got drunk and drove west on Interstate 40 doing 110 miles per hour. In the car Suzy Followthecrowd held a beer can out the window. Citizen Joe Soberandsmart spotted Dan and Suzy. Joe knew about New Mexico's ENDWI program. ENDWI stands for "end driving while intoxicated." The program makes it easy for good drivers to report other drivers that they suspect might be drinking and driving. Joe decided to be a "Drunk Buster" and called 1-877-DWI-HALT.

ENDWI is a joint program of the New Mexico State Police, the New Mexico Department of Transportation, the Governor's Office, and local and county law enforcement officers. ENDWI notified a New Mexico State Police officer who was sitting in his patrol car in the I-40 median. The officer turned on his lights and siren; he followed Dan, caught up with him, and pulled him over. The officer asked for Dan's driver's license and gave Dan a breath alcohol test. His breath alcohol content was .17%. Dan's driver's license was taken away from him immediately and he was taken to jail.

Dan had to appear in court the following day. The judge required Dan to post bail because he doubted that Dan would come back to court for his trial. Dan did not have the bail money he needed, so he had to stay in jail until his trial. While in jail, Dan received a visit from public defender Ian D. Fence. A public defender is a lawyer who represents people who cannot pay for an attorney.

On Dan's court date, Judge Fairness presided over a jury trial. Jurors listened to the case against Dan. They heard the state police officer tell of Dan's speed, the reckless way he was driving, and his breath alcohol level. The judge told them that a level of .16%

New Mexico
State Police Vehicle

was considered an aggravated DWI. The judge dismissed the jurors to the jury room. They discussed the case and returned with a verdict of guilty.

Judge Fairness sentenced Dan to ninety days in jail, but he counted the time Dan had already served toward the ninety days. He required Dan to pay $500, the maximum fine for a first offense. He charged Dan with $200 in court costs and required him to participate in a DWI educational program.

Dan completed his ninety-day jail sentence. He borrowed money from his grandmother to pay for his fine and court costs. For six months after his release, he had to meet with a parole officer once a month (see photo of parole office at right). Dan attended his DWI program. By the end of six months, he was able to make his final payment to his grandmother. In six more months, Dan got back his driver's license. Dan felt confident that he would not drink and drive ever again, but he also knew that his conviction for drunk driving would remain on his driving record for fifty-five years.

Government Offices, Including a Parole Office

Rights of the Accused

The Bill of Rights guarantees that each American citizen who is accused of breaking a law has a right to be treated fairly. An officer must have a good reason to suspect wrongdoing before he can search someone's home or vehicle or take his belongings for evidence. A person who has been arrested is protected against harsh questioning by police.

In America a person is considered to be innocent until it has been proven beyond a reasonable doubt that he is guilty. An accused person cannot be forced to testify against himself. The Bill of Rights guarantees a speedy, public trial by an impartial jury for all criminal cases.

When a citizen is accused of committing a serious crime, an attorney working for the state justice department or the U.S. Department of Justice prosecutes him or her. The Bill of Rights guarantees that every person accused of a crime is given the opportunity to have an attorney. He may hire an attorney or he may use a public defender or another attorney that a court appoints to defend him. In a small number of instances, the accused person chooses to defend himself and does not have an attorney.

People accused of a crime are guaranteed due process of law. Due process means that all accepted legal procedures are followed when a case is being tried. The Fourteenth Amendment to the Constitution guarantees equal protection under the law. This means that no one is to receive unfair treatment and no one is to be treated with favoritism.

Posting Bail

When someone is arrested and charged with a crime, a magistrate (a legal authority like a judge) determines how much money the accused person will have to post as bail in order to get out of jail until the trial. A bond is a guarantee that the accused person will not run away. Some defendants pay a bail bond business a percentage of the bail in exchange for the bail bond company promising to pay the bail money if the defendant does not appear in court when he is supposed to do so. A bail bond business is pictured above. Bail bond businesses have long-term relationships of trust with local judges. When a defendant does not show up, the bail bond company may send their own private investigator to find him or her.

Grand Jury

A grand jury might have to decide if enough evidence can be found to justify a trial. A grand jury is a group of citizens chosen in a way similar to a regular jury. A prosecutor presents evidence to the grand jury and they decide if there is enough evidence to hold a trial.

Beyond a Reasonable Doubt

In a criminal case like Dan's, the state has the job of proving to every member of the jury that the accused person is guilty beyond a reasonable doubt. The state prosecutor does this by showing evidence (called the introduction of evidence) and by having witnesses answer questions about what they know (called giving personal testimony).

The defendant's attorney (called the defense attorney) tries to show that the state has not proved beyond a reasonable doubt that the accused is guilty. The defense attorney might raise questions about the state's evidence or about the testimony of witnesses, or he might introduce additional evidence and testimony in favor of the accused. The judge makes sure that the trial proceeds fairly, and the jury (or the judge in a bench trial) determines whether the accused person is guilty or not.

Cases Settled Out of Court

A trial is a formal event held in a courtroom for the purpose of deciding whether the accused person is innocent or guilty in a criminal trial and whether a plaintiff deserves what he is requesting in a civil trial. Deciding a case in a trial in a court is called trying a case. Most cases are not tried in a court, but instead they are settled before the case comes to trial. Both civil and criminal cases can be settled out of court.

Two parties involved in a civil case can agree to a settlement. Some civil cases are resolved by mediation, in which the two parties in conflict meet with a mediator to try to resolve their differences without having to go through the time and expense of a trial. Consider the case of Mr. Jones versus the painter (see Lesson 106). Mr. Jones may have originally asked for $10,000. If the painter agrees to give him $7,500 in an out-of-court settlement, Mr. Jones may decide that $7500 in hand is better than risking going to court where a jury may decide that he deserves only $5,000 or even no payment at all. A settlement can benefit both Mr. Jones and the painter because each one may be able to save money on court costs and lawyer's fees.

In a criminal case, the state and the defendant may enter into a plea bargain, which is a sort of compromise. When a defendant has been accused of several crimes, he is often willing to plead guilty to one or more crimes in exchange for having the other charges against him dropped (or dismissed). A plea bargain can benefit the state as well. Plea bargains take less time than trials. Taking less time is less expensive. Sometimes a prosecutor believes that the defendant is guilty but knows that there is not enough evidence to convince a jury. If a defendant is willing to agree to a plea bargain, the community will be safer. Plea bargains are often easier on the victims of a crime, because they do not have to go through the trauma of a trial.

Justice and Punishment

Justice sometimes requires that people be punished for the things that they do wrong. In Luke 23:41, one of the thieves who died on a cross beside Jesus said this to the other thief:

> *And we indeed are suffering justly, for we are receiving what we deserve for our deeds; but this man has done nothing wrong.*

Romans 13:1-4 teaches about governments punishing those who do wrong:

> *Every person is to be in subjection to the governing authorities. For there is no authority except from God, and those which exist are established by God. Therefore whoever resists authority has opposed the ordinance of God; and they who have opposed will receive condemnation upon themselves. For rulers are not a cause of fear for good behavior, but for evil. Do you want to have no fear of authority? Do what is good and you will have praise from the same; for it is a minister of God to you for good. But if you do what is evil, be afraid; for it does not bear the sword for nothing; for it is a minister of God, an avenger who brings wrath on the one who practices evil.*

The Bill of Rights gives Americans the assurance that they will not suffer "cruel and unusual punishment." Judges are sometimes given some freedom in deciding what the punishment will be when someone is found guilty of a crime. However, he must obey laws that give guidelines for what punishments are to be given for particular crimes.

Punishment for breaking laws in the United States varies greatly, depending on the circumstances. Here are examples.

Fines — A fine is money paid as a penalty for breaking a law. Fines can vary from a few dollars for a violation of a parking regulation to fines of billions of dollars. For example, on

July 2, 2012, *The New York Times* reported that a British drug company would have to pay the U. S. government $3 billion in fines for illegal activities.

Restitution — Restitution also involves paying money. A fine is simply a punishment for wrongdoing, but restitution is paid to the victim of a crime to reimburse them for stolen property or to help pay medical bills or something of that nature. If, for example, someone is convicted of stealing from the government, he may have to pay both restitution and a fine.

Community Service — Sometimes a judge will require an offender to perform acts of service to his community.

Incarceration — Sometimes a citizen who is convicted of a crime receives a sentence, requiring him or her to spend time in a corrections facility. Whether the corrections facility is a local jail, a state penitentiary, or a Federal penitentiary depends on the offense the person committed. The length of time that a person is incarcerated varies depending on the seriousness of the offense and also the number of offenses for which he or she has been found guilty.

Suspended Sentences — Sometimes when a person is convicted of a crime, the judge sentences him and then suspends the sentence. The convicted person does not have to serve time in jail, but his conviction remains a part of the public record. When a judge chooses to suspend the sentence of someone who has been convicted, the citizen returns to the community but is on probation. This means that he has limited freedom and has certain rules that he must obey. The rules vary depending on the crime committed. He must meet regularly with a probation officer who works for the courts. If a convicted citizen violates the rules of his probation, he will have to serve his sentence. The purposes of probation are to help the offender become a law-abiding citizen, to protect the people he hurt when he committed his crime, and to protect the rest of the general public. Judges often choose probation for people who have never been convicted before or who do not seem likely to commit the crime again.

Death Penalty — Some crimes are considered to be so horrible that persons convicted of those crimes receive the sentence of a death penalty.

Rights of Victims

People who are hurt physically, emotionally, or financially by a crime are called victims. The Federal government and many states and communities have programs to help them. Victims of crimes have the right to be protected from the people accused of the crime, to know what is happening in the court system concerning the person accused of hurting them, and the right to restitution.

For the report of your obedience has reached to all; therefore I am rejoicing over you,

but I want you to be wise in what is good and innocent in what is evil.

Romans 16:19

Lesson Activities

Thinking Biblically — Write a paragraph in your notebook answering the question, "How are government authorities a minister of God to you for good?" (see Romans 13:1-4).

Vocabulary — In your notebook, write your own definition for each of these words: bail, reckless, verdict, parole, impartial. Look in the lesson for clues for the meaning of the words. When you are finished writing your definitions, look in a dictionary for comparison.

Literature — Read chapters "Make Hay While the Sun Shines," "An Errand to Town," and "Fall of the Year" in *The Long Winter*.

Creative Writing — In your notebook, make a list of ten minor offenses (such as parking in a no-parking zone) and what you think the fine should be for each offense.

Find Out! — When was your county courthouse built?

Picture This! — Draw a design for decorations on the wall behind a judges bench.

Student Workbook or Lesson Review — If you are using one of these optional books, complete the assignment for Lesson 107.

Chuck Colson and
PRISON FELLOWSHIP

Law enforcement officials, courts, and prisons exist because people break the law. Crime involves human beings hurting other human beings. Real people with names violate the law, and, if they are found guilty by a court, they receive punishment. Real people with names are victims of crime. The ultimate answer to crime is not just more policemen, more judges, or harsher penalties. The real answer involves changed hearts through Jesus Christ so that fewer people commit crime and so that those who have committed crimes do not do so again.

Many Christians try to help people who are in jail or prison. One of them was Chuck Colson, who was born in 1931 and died on April 12, 2012.

Chuck Colson, 2009

The President's Man

When Republican Richard Nixon was President, some of his staff members tried to hurt the reputations of people who disagreed with Nixon's ideas. The President himself knew about some of the things his aides were doing.

Chuck Colson was one of those aides. Colson, pictured above, was an attorney and a former Marine. He served as a Special Counsel to the President. He gave advice to Nixon and carried out various jobs that were meant to help him. Sometimes Colson did and said things that were hurtful to the President's opponents. Many people saw Colson as cold and ruthless in his willingness to do anything to help Nixon.

One of the people that Chuck Colson hurt was Daniel Ellsberg, who opposed the President's policies about the Vietnam War. In 1971 Colson tried to hurt Daniel Ellsberg by giving secret information about him to the press. Ellsberg is pictured on page 689.

The following year, people working for President Nixon's re-election committee paid men to break into offices the Democratic Party had rented in the Watergate office and hotel complex in Washington, D.C. The burglars were caught and arrested. Chuck Colson was not involved in the break-in at the Watergate, but many people suspected that he was.

Daniel Ellsberg

God's Man

In 1973 Chuck Colson resigned his job in the White House to work as a lawyer in the private sector. Around that time, a friend gave him a copy of *Mere Christianity* by C. S. Lewis. Colson read the book and thought about its message. He thought about his friend's faith. He felt sorry about things he had done during the time he worked for President Nixon. Colson made a decision to give his life to Christ.

However, Colson was still suspected of being involved in the Watergate scandal. In 1974 he was arrested for trying to hide (or cover up) what others had done to prepare for the break-in. Colson believed he was innocent regarding Watergate, but he agreed to plead guilty to a charge of obstructing justice regarding Daniel Ellsberg (obstructing justice is taking actions that keep someone from receiving justice). Colson was sentenced to serve one to three years in prison. He entered prison in July of 1974. One month later, Nixon resigned as President. In January of 1975, Colson was granted an early release.

While in prison, Colson became concerned that the American prison system did not do more to try to change prisoners' lives for the better. In 1976 he founded Prison Fellowship to share the good news of Jesus with prisoners.

Prison Fellowship volunteers began going into prisons to share the gospel. Many prisoners came to believe in Jesus. The volunteers began to disciple the new believers and to help them learn how to bring other prisoners to Christ.

Prison Fence

Helping Prisoners, Families, and Communities

Families are devastated when a family member has to go to jail. Communities are hurt. A high percentage of those who leave prison commit crimes again and end up back in prison.

The stated mission of Prison Fellowship is "to seek the transformation of prisoners and their reconciliation to God, family, and community through the power and truth of Jesus Christ." Prison Fellowship staff and volunteers meet with prisoners in regular training classes and in one-on-one mentoring relationships. Hundreds of thousands of prisoners have received this training, and tens of thousands of volunteers have participated. The following are some of the programs of Prison Fellowship.

Operation Starting Line

Operation Starting Line brings special events such as concerts and special speakers to prisons. The good news of Christ and the hope of changed lives and healed relationships are shared with prisoners at these events, which help many prisoners see for the first time that a different way of life is possible.

InnerChange Freedom

The InnerChange Freedom Initiative offers intensive training to inmates who volunteer for it. Those who work with inmates in this program help them grow spiritually while they advance in their education, learn skills for good vocations, and improve their living skills. The program helps prisoners use the teachings of Jesus to prepare to earn an honest living.

Out4Life

Out4Life trains local churches, community groups, and individuals how to help ex-prisoners make the difficult change from prison life to a life of freedom. Released prisoners often do not know how to make good decisions and where to turn for help. At the same time,

Moundsville, West Virginia
Former West Virginia Penitentiary

Carthage, North Carolina
Moore County Detention Center

Represa, California
Folsom State Prison

Carthage, North Carolina
Another View of the Moore County Detention Center

many people in society are suspicious of someone who has served time in prison, even if that ex-convict sincerely wants to live differently. Out4Life seminars teach people how to offer released men and women spiritual as well as practical help, such as housing, jobs, transportation, and relationships.

Angel Tree

In 1982, another ex-convict, Mary Kay Beard, organized Angel Tree, which provides Christmas gifts to the children of adults who are in prison. Today this part of Prison Fellowship touches the lives of over 400,000 American children every year with gifts and, even more importantly, with the love of Christ.

Hillsboro, Texas
The Hill County Cell Block Museum served as the Hill County Jail from 1893 to 1983.

Justice Fellowship

Justice Fellowship was formed as a part of Prison Fellowship in 1983. Its purpose is "to promote Biblical standards of justice in our nation's justice system." This group has helped states:

★ Pass victims' rights legislation,

★ Create programs to bring reconciliation between victims and the criminals who hurt them, and

★ Provide punishments other than imprisonment for criminals who have not been violent.

Prison Fellowship International

In 1979 Prison Fellowship and Christian groups from England, Australia, Canada, New Zealand, and the Bahamas, which were also working to help prisoners, joined together to form Prison Fellowship International. By 2012 Prison Fellowship International was serving in more than 115 countries.

A New Start

Chuck Colson made some huge mistakes in his life, but God brought about huge changes in him. God used Colson to help thousands of other people who had made huge mistakes change the way they live. Prison Fellowship offers those who have failed in their civic responsibilities to re-enter communities in a positive way. It also teaches responsible citizens how to help those who have made such big mistakes that they had to go to jail. When individuals are able to grow and change through the power of Christ while they are in prison, prisoners themselves and America as a whole are better off.

Danville, Kentucky
Sign by Reconstructed Log Jail

"I am the Lord, I have called You in righteousness,

I will also hold You by the hand and watch over You,

And I will appoint You as a covenant to the people,

As a light to the nations,

To open blind eyes,

To bring out prisoners from the dungeon

And those who dwell in darkness from the prison.

Isaiah 42:6-8

Lesson Activities

Thinking Biblically — Imagine that a person in prison asked you who Jesus is and what difference he makes. In your notebook, write one or two paragraphs telling how you would answer.

Vocabulary — In your notebook, write which of the following words belongs in each sentence: violate, transformation, inmate, suspicious, legislation.

1. Paula was _____ because the customer came out of a closed check-out lane with bulging pockets.
2. My dad has been meeting weekly for a Bible study with a former _____.
3. There are consequences for people who _____ the law.
4. We hope that the new _____ will make it simpler to file our taxes.
5. Jesus is the only way to real _____ in a person's life.

Literature — Read chapters "October Blizzard," "After the Storm," and "Indian Summer" in *The Long Winter*.

Creative Writing — In your notebook, make a list of at least ten ways that churches and communities can help former inmates after they leave prison.

Find Out! — Is there a way to give to Angel Tree in your community?

Student Workbook or Lesson Review — If you are using one of these optional books, complete the assignment for Lesson 108.

The SUPREME COURT

Each October the highest court in the land begins its annual session in the beautiful Supreme Court Building, which stands near the Capitol and the Library of Congress in Washington, D.C. The Court has been meeting here since 1935. See photo at right.

Like the legislative and executive branches of the Federal government, the judicial branch met first in New York City, then in Philadelphia, and finally in Washington, D.C. In New York City, the Supreme Court met in the Royal Exchange. In Philadelphia, it met first in Independence Hall and then in the building now called Old City Hall.

When the Federal government moved to Washington, D.C., the Capitol was constructed for the use of Congress and the White House was built for the President, but the Supreme Court had no building to call its own. Congress loaned the Court space to meet in the Capitol. It used various rooms before the British burned the Capitol in 1814. The Court met for a few years in a private home before returning to the Capitol in 1819, where it met in a basement room. Visitors to the Capitol can see this room today. The chamber, now restored as the Old Supreme Court Chamber, is pictured at right. Notice its umbrella-vaulted ceiling. When construction of a new Senate Chamber was completed in 1860, the Supreme Court moved into the old Senate Chamber, pictured at right, where it remained until the Supreme Court Building was completed in 1935.

U.S. Supreme Court Building

Old Supreme Court Chamber

Old Senate Chamber

Cass Gilbert and Cass Gilbert Jr.

Only one President has served on the Supreme Court. In 1921 President Warren G. Harding appointed former President William Howard Taft to be Chief Justice of the Supreme Court. At left is Harding's letter to the Senate nominating Taft. In 1929, shortly before he retired from the Court, Chief Justice Taft convinced Congress that the Supreme Court needed its own home. Architect Cass Gilbert was chosen as the designer.

Gilbert oversaw construction until his death in 1934. His son, Cass Gilbert Jr., who had been involved in the work, continued with the project until it was completed. The building opened for the beginning of the Court's October session in 1935.

The Building's Exterior

Thousands of tons of American marble were used in the construction of the Supreme Court Building, including marble from Vermont, Alabama, and Georgia.

The Supreme Court building has many carvings that illustrate law. On the two sides of the steps leading up to the main west entrance are statues carved by James Earle Fraser. "Contemplation of Justice" is a seated female figure. Her left arm rests on a book of law. In her right hand is a blindfolded figure of Justice holding scales. "Authority of Law" is a male figure holding a tablet inscribed with the word LEX (the Latin word for law). Behind the tablet is a sword in a sheath, symbolizing enforcement of the law. See photos at left.

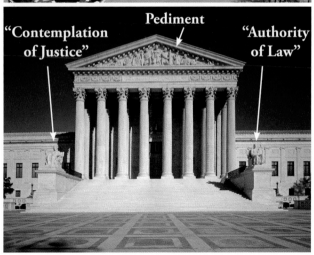

Washington, D.C.
U.S. Supreme Court Building

The main west entrance faces the U.S. Capitol. Above its columns is the phrase "Equal Justice Under Law." Above the phrase is a triangular pediment with figures carved by Robert Aitken, who also designed the statues outside of the National Archives building (see Lesson 6). He included Chief Justice Taft as a youth, Chief Justice John Marshall as a youth, Chief Justice Charles Evans Hughes, Secretary of State Elihu Root, architect Cass Gilbert, and himself. The pediment at the east entrance includes Moses, the Chinese philosopher Confucius, and Solon, a lawmaker from ancient Athens.

The Supreme Court Chamber

Supreme Court Chamber Showing Close-Up of Spanish Marble Column and Italian and African Marble Floor

The main corridor of the Supreme Court Building is the Great Hall. Along its walls are busts of all former Chief Justices. At the end of the corridor, oak doors open into the Supreme Court Chamber, pictured at right.

The Chamber is 82 by 91 feet and its ceiling is forty-four feet high. The walls of the Court Chamber are Ivory Vein marble from Spain and its twenty-four columns are light Siena marble from Italy. Carvings on the chamber's walls are described below.

Carvings in the Supreme Court Chamber

High on the chamber's walls are marble friezes. Each frieze is forty feet long and seven feet, two inches tall. The friezes were designed by Adolph A. Weinman.

East Frieze — Carvings illustrate the Bill of Rights, the majesty of law, the power of government, wisdom, human rights, and safeguarding liberties.

South Frieze — Carvings illustrate ancient lawgivers: the Egyptian Pharaoh Menes; the Babylonian King Hammurabi; Israelite leaders Moses and King Solomon; Greek lawgivers Lycurgus of Sparta, Solon of Athens and Draco of Athens; Chinese philosopher Confucius; and Roman Emperor Caesar Augustus. It also has carvings representing fame, authority, history, and the light of wisdom.

North Frieze — Carvings illustrate more lawgivers: Justinian, Muhammad, the Frankish or French King Charlemagne, King John of England, Louis IX of France, the Dutch legal scholar Hugo Grotius, the English law professor Sir William Blackstone, U.S. Chief Justice John Marshall, and the French emperor Napoleon. It also has carvings representing liberty and peace, rights of man, equity, and philosophy.

West Frieze — Carvings illustrate the battle of good versus evil. At the center are carvings representing justice, divine inspiration, wisdom, and truth. On one side are the powers of good: security, harmony, peace, charity, and defense of virtue. To the right are the powers of evil: vice and crime, corruption, slander, deception, and despotic power (power held by an oppressive ruler).

Inside the Building

The Supreme Court Building has four stories plus a basement. It has offices for the justices and other Court officials, a library, a dining room, a museum, a public cafeteria, and a gift shop. On the top floor, above the Court Chamber, is a basketball court where justices, law clerks, and other employees play basketball games for exercise. This room has been called the "highest court in the land."

Judicial Review

After a Federal trial, a defendant may have a question about how his case was handled. He may even believe that the law on which the case was based is illegal because it is not in keeping with the U.S. Constitution. When this happens, the defendant can appeal to the U.S. Circuit Court of Appeals. If the defendant still has a question after the Court of Appeals gives its decision, he may then try to have the case reviewed by the U.S. Supreme Court. The practice of a higher court examining a case that was already decided in a lower court is called judicial review. When a case is brought before the Supreme Court, the justices on the Court seek to answer these questions:

★ Does the Constitution permit the Federal government to do what a particular law attempts to do?

★ Does the Constitution forbid the government from doing what a law attempts to do?

If there were no way to decide whether a law conforms to the Constitution, the Constitution would have no authority over the laws passed by Congress and the states. Who would decide whether a law kept to or violated the Constitution? An early Supreme Court Chief Justice, John Marshall, wrote in 1803, "It is, emphatically, the province and duty of the judicial department, to say what the law is."

Questions about whether a law is constitutional are often not obvious. Let's look at an example. If Congress passes a law that puts a limit on the amount of money that a corporation can contribute to a political candidate's campaign, the Court could be asked to decide whether that law violates the First Amendment, which assures Americans of free speech. This is the kind of question that the Supreme Court is asked to decide.

Choosing Cases

After the annual session of the Supreme Court begins on the first Monday in October each year, it continues until the following summer. The Supreme Court receives about 10,000 requests to review cases each year, but the Court only accepts about eighty or ninety of these. The Court selects cases that deal with major constitutional issues. Often these are controversial issues of the day. The Court is more likely to accept a case if different Circuit Courts of Appeals have ruled differently in similar cases and some clarification is needed. Four of the nine Supreme Court justices must agree to review a case for the Court to accept it.

Hearing Cases

When the Supreme Court agrees to hear a case, all of the records of the case are sent to the Court. Each side also submits a summary or brief of its position. These briefs are primarily references to other cases in which (the attorney believes) those decisions support that side's position. In addition, other individuals or groups can submit briefs pointing out cases that they think prove their point. After the justices review all of this material, the Court schedules a time for oral arguments in the case.

Supreme Court Chamber Bench

Oral arguments are heard in the Supreme Court Chamber during two-week periods on Monday, Tuesday, and Wednesday mornings. Justices sit at the chamber's mahogany bench, a portion of which is pictured at right.

The Court usually hears two or three cases each of these days and gives one hour to each. An attorney has one half-hour to present his case, and then the other side's attorney has a half-hour. The justices can ask questions at any time during an attorney's half-hour presentation to the Court. Additional afternoon sessions are scheduled from time to time as needed.

Let's use a case about political contributions as an example. During oral arguments, the attorney representing the corporation might say: 1) that the Constitution protects free speech; 2) that restricting the amount a corporation can contribute restricts free speech; and 3) that previous Court decisions have held that making political contributions is a form of speech.

On the other hand, the solicitor general (the attorney in the U.S. Department of Justice who argues cases on behalf of the government before the Supreme Court) might argue that the limitation is constitutional because: 1) the limitation makes it more possible for everyday citizens to have an influence on elections; 2) previous Courts have imposed some reasonable limitations on speech; and 3) the Constitution protects equal justice under the law.

Deciding Cases and Writing Opinions

Soon after the oral arguments take place, the justices meet to discuss the case, usually on a Friday. The Chief Justice begins the discussion. When a vote is taken, the justice that has been on the Court the shortest time votes first to avoid being influenced by the justices who have been on the Court longer. For the Court to reach a decision, at least five of the nine justices must vote in favor of one side or the other.

In many cases, the Supreme Court will issue a written majority opinion. The Chief Justice may choose to write it himself or he may assign the writing to another justice. If the Chief Justice is in the minority, the writing of the majority opinion is usually assigned to the justice that has been on the Court the longest who is in the majority. The justices who are in the minority on a decision also write an opinion. Before majority and minority opinions are announced, the justices discuss the rough drafts of these opinions and may make changes. Justices use the last two weeks of a month to write opinions.

In the majority opinion, the Court majority explains why it believes a law is or is not constitutional. Sometimes only one part of a law is ruled unconstitutional while the rest of the law is allowed to stand. The minority opinion gives the opposing viewpoint. A minority opinion might influence future decisions, but it has no impact on the law that is being considered.

As the justices consider a law and the wording of the Constitution, three principles guide them. First is the tendency to let a previous decision stand. Only rarely does the Court overturn a previous decision. Second is the reluctance of the Court to become involved in political issues and the politics of laws passed by Congress or by state legislatures. A third principle is the Court's tendency to take a firm stand to protect personal freedom and individual conscience.

It is important to remember that, for the Court to issue an opinion on a law, a case has to be brought to it. The Court cannot just decide to issue an opinion on a law if no case has been heard in a lower court and appealed to the Supreme Court. In the example of the campaign contribution law, a corporation would have to be prevented from making a contribution or fined for making such a contribution. The case would have to be brought to trial in a Federal district court, and then to the U.S. Court of Appeals, and finally to the Supreme Court.

The decisions of the Court are the final word on the laws of the land. A Court decision cannot be changed by an act of Congress and it cannot be vetoed by the President. The only way that a decision of the Court can be changed is if a later Court reverses the decision or if the Constitution is amended. The Supreme Court's role in deciding whether a law is constitutional is part of the checks and balances between the three branches of the U.S. government (see Lesson 12).

Original Jurisdiction

In addition to its judicial review responsibilities, the Supreme Court is responsible for all cases involving Ambassadors and consuls; cases in which the defendant and the plaintiff are two states; and cases in which the defendant and the plaintiff are one state and the Federal government. These cases were assigned to the Supreme Court in the Constitution. The Court's responsibility for these cases is called original jurisdiction.

Justices and Traditions

Since 1789 more than 12,000 people have served in the U.S. Congress. As of 2012, 112 persons had served as justices on the Supreme Court, including seventeen who had been Chief Justice. Justices serve until they retire or die or are removed from office in an impeachment trial. Only one associate justice, Samuel Chase, has ever been impeached. He was tried by the Senate in 1804 but was not removed from office.

U.S. Supreme Court Building

Throughout American history, justices have served for an average of about sixteen years. A vacancy has occurred on average about every two years. However, since 1970,

Chief Justice William Howard Taft and Other Justices Call on President Calvin Coolidge at the White House, 1924

the average time a justice has served has been about twenty-five years, so vacancies have occurred less often. The average age of a modern Supreme Court justice is about 67 years old.

The Court has several traditions. The justices exchange a "conference handshake" in private before every public session and also before their Friday conferences. Each justice shakes hands with every other justice. This demonstrates that they are working together for the same purpose even with their differing viewpoints. The conference handshake has been used for over a century.

White quill pens are placed on the attorneys' tables in the oral argument sessions, just as they have been since the early days of the Court. Many attorneys take these pens as souvenirs of their appearance before the Court.

As the public session begins, the Marshal of the Court announces, "The Honorable, the Chief Justice and the Associate Justices of the Supreme Court of the United States. Oyez! Oyez! Oyez! All persons having business before the Honorable, the Supreme Court of the United States, are admonished to draw near and give their attention, for the Court is now sitting. God save the United States and this Honorable Court." The Marshal is an officer of the Court who maintains order, records the audio of public sessions, and watches the time of the attorneys' presentations so that they do not go over their half-hour limit. "Oyez" is an Old English word that means "Hear ye."

When William Howard Taft became Chief Justice of the Supreme Court, he ascended to a position he had wanted for many years. In fact he wanted to be Chief Justice much more than he wanted to be President. Like Taft, many Presidents have been attorneys and many have been involved in the judicial system in other ways on the local, state, and/or Federal levels. See box at right.

The American government, as we discussed in Lesson 19, is founded on such principles as freedom, justice, truth, and equality before the law. Our country endures as its people uphold these principles. The Supreme Court is intended to defend these principles for all Americans, and the Supreme Court building symbolizes this purpose. Even more enduring, however, is the Word of God.

The grass withers, the flower fades,

But the word of our God stands forever.

Isaiah 40:8

Lesson Activities

Vocabulary — In your notebook, make a drawing for each of these words that illustrates what it means: chamber, contemplation, sheath, frieze, defendant. Write the word under the drawing. Check in a dictionary if you need help with their definitions.

Literature — Read "Lighter Side of Life at the United States Supreme Court" in *The Citizen's Handbook*, pages 130-133, and chapters "Indian Warning" and "Settled in Town" in *The Long Winter*.

Picture This! — Take a photograph or draw a picture of a handshake.

Student Workbook or Lesson Review — If you are using one of these optional books, complete the assignment for Lesson 109.

★ Remember to choose an American Holiday to study this week! ★

Using Talents to Serve: Judicial and Law Enforcement Positions Held Before Becoming President

Andrew Jackson was a judge in Tennessee.

Martin Van Buren served as the Attorney General of New York (a state attorney general represents the state in legal matters).

Rutherford B. Hayes served as the city solicitor of Cincinnati, Ohio (a city solicitor does for a city what an attorney general does for a state or country).

Grover Cleveland served as assistant district attorney for Erie County, New York, and was later elected as its sheriff.

Benjamin Harrison was a court reporter for the Supreme Court of Indiana.

William McKinley was the prosecuting attorney for Stark County, Ohio.

William Howard Taft was an assistant prosecutor in Cincinnati, Judge of the Ohio Superior Court, Solicitor General of the U.S. (third highest position in the U.S. Department of Justice), and Judge of the U.S. Court of Appeals for the Sixth Circuit.

Bill Clinton was the Attorney General of Arkansas.

UNIT 23 – MAKING MONEY

BOOKS USED IN UNIT 23

- The Citizen's Handbook
- The Long Winter
- Student Workbook (optional)
- Lesson Review (optional)

U.S. Currency

America's FREE ECONOMY

Monroe, Wisconsin
Alp and Dell Cheese Factory

Ryan is a manufacturing engineer at a factory that makes cheese. The new assembly lines that Ryan designed and helped to build at the factory enable the company to make twenty percent more cheese this year than they did last year. Even with all of the rapid work that takes place, the lines are set up in such a way that the employees will be safe around the large machines and the quality of their cheese is even better than before.

Some of the equipment used to make the cheese was made in Switzerland because Ryan's company made an agreement with the Swiss government. The equipment was shipped by ocean freight to the East Coast and then a trucking company brought it to the factory. The cheese that Ryan's company makes is just one of several brands that Americans can buy, so his company must work hard to stay competitive. The company where Ryan works has decided to compete by having better tasting cheese than by trying to have the lowest price.

Ryan works five eight-hour days each week and gets his paycheck on Friday. His employer, Moo Cheese, has already taken income tax, Social Security tax, and Medicare out of his paycheck. They will send this money to the Federal government. Ryan has also arranged for money to be taken out of his paycheck for a retirement fund. Moo Cheese sends this money to an investment company. Power Investments uses this money to invest in other companies so that they can buy new machinery and increase their production.

On his way home from work, Ryan stops by his bank to get cash for the weekend. That night Ryan and his family go to a restaurant for supper. He pays for the meal with his debit card that takes money from his bank automatically and uses cash for tip.

Saturday morning is the time when Ryan pays his bills. Ryan makes the monthly mortgage payment on his family's house, and he also pays the electricity and telephone utility bills. He uses an online service that lets him transfer some of his money to a savings account for their upcoming vacation to Canada, and he transfers other money to another savings account for his children's college fund.

That afternoon, the young man who mows Ryan's yard comes over and works for a couple of hours. Ryan pays him with a check. Later that afternoon, Ryan takes his children to Electronics 4 U. The children use their allowance to buy one new Christian music CD each. Meanwhile, Ryan's wife goes to the shoe store and selects a new pair of dress shoes for the fall. With each of these purchases, they pay sales tax. Before going home, the family stops at the grocery store and buys paper towels, two cookie sheets, and food for the church fellowship meal on Sunday. Unlike some states, Ryan's state has no sales tax on food, but they do have to pay sales tax on the paper towels and cookie sheets.

At church on Sunday, Ryan puts his weekly contribution check in the collection plate. An announcement is made about a family in the community who lost their home in a fire. Ryan and several other people write additional checks to help that family.

Notice the photos of cheese companies in Wisconsin and Oregon at right and on page 702.

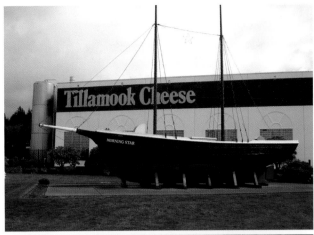

Tillamook, Oregon
Tillamook Cheese Factory

Buying and Selling

This story shows several ways that Ryan, his family, and all other Americans are involved in the economy. Economics is the study of making, distributing, and using goods and services. The cheese company, the company that makes CDs, the shoe company, and the farmers and grocery store are all involved with producing and distributing goods, which are items that people buy. Mowing a lawn is a service that people pay for. A restaurant provides goods (food) but it also provides the service of cooking and serving the food and cleaning up after the meal. The photos at right illustrate goods and services. Distribution is getting goods from one place to another, such as getting cheese from a factory to a store that sells them. See photos below.

Goods

Jersey City, New Jersey
Jewelry at Craft Fair
North Dakota
Vegetables For Sale
Ripley, West Virginia
Pottery at the West Virginia State Arts and Crafts Fair

Distribution

A train transports goods across Kansas.

Duluth, Minnesota
A Busy Freight Port

Galveston, Texas
Del Monte Sea Containers

Trucks haul sea containers on highways.

Philadelphia, Pennsylvania
Philadelphia Food Distribution Center

Services

Savannah, Georgia
Hotel & Sign Hanging

Tennessee
Above: Moving; Right: Barn Painting

704

Free Markets

The American economy is described as free market. Individuals are free to start companies that make and offer goods and services. These people and companies compete with each other for customers in the market. A market is anywhere goods and services are bought and sold. A market can be a Saturday morning farmers' market or businesses on the Internet. In our story, individuals and companies competed in the cheese market, the shoe market, the electronics market, the restaurant market, the lawn care market, and the grocery market. Ryan and his family made choices in several markets to buy goods and services.

Greenwood, Indiana
Two homeschool dads involved in private business attend the Indiana Association of Home Educators Convention, 2012.

Banks

Banks provide people with a safe place to keep their money. Money that is deposited in a savings account at a bank earns interest. The bank uses money that people deposit to make loans to other people who want to buy a house or start a business. People who take out a loan pay a higher interest rate on the money they borrow than the interest rate the bank gives to people who deposit their money. This is one way that a bank makes a profit.

The story also shows how people in an economy are interconnected with each other and how their decisions and actions affect others. Ryan's company sells cheese to thousands of Americans. These Americans work at other jobs (for example, in restaurants, grocery stores, and electronics stores) where they earn money to buy cheese and other goods and services. The purchases that Ryan and his family make help pay the salaries of these workers, who then buy the cheese that Ryan gets paid for helping to make.

Hillsboro, Texas
A Night Deposit Box for a Local Bank

Planned Economies

In a planned economy, sometimes called socialism, the government tells everyone what they are to make or do. Every worker in a factory is a government worker. Government workers decide how many shoes, lawn mowers, and how much cheese will be made in a given year. A planned economy gives control to government leaders, but this kind of economy usually does not work well. People do not have the motivation

Savannah, Georgia
Barber Shop

to do a good job. Government planners who work in offices in the capital cannot know how farmers far away are doing or if a motorcycle factory runs out of parts.

In a free market economy, people and companies can produce more goods and services and thus make more money. They can start new businesses. Competition between companies helps to make goods and services cheaper and encourages companies to develop new products.

Government Involvement in a Free Market

However, a free market will still have some degree of involvement by the government. Generally speaking, the more the government is involved in economic activity, the more expensive it is for companies to operate. This raises the prices of goods and services for the people who pay for them. Taxes reduce the amount of money people have for goods and services.

However, the purposes of government regulations are to make workplaces safer, to make banks safe places for depositing money, to protect Americans against unhealthy food being sold in the marketplace, and to protect American citizens in other ways. Federal laws make sure that products sold in the United States are really what they are advertised as being. Regulations help the economy if the benefit of a regulation is greater than the cost of enforcing the regulation.

Taxes that the government collects pay for roads, the military, meat inspectors, park rangers, veterans hospitals, and other workers who provide services that the American people want and need. Some taxes also pay for government programs that help the poor and the elderly.

Making Money

The government prints paper money and mints coins for people to use in buying and selling. The use of money helps buying and selling to go more smoothly than if people only exchanged goods or services. The exchange of goods and services is called barter. A barter economy can work, but it is sometimes difficult to know how many chickens have the same value as mowing a lawn. The use of money allows people to set prices for chickens, cheese, lawn mowing, and other goods and services. When people earn money from their work, they can buy whatever they want and need without being concerned whether the gas station owner will be willing to sell them gasoline if they only have oats or corn to pay for it. The U.S. Department of the Treasury oversees the money that the government collects and spends.

Jesus spoke often about money. He talked about wages of workers. In the Old Testament, God gave the Israelites laws about how to treat people fairly in their economic system. The book of Ruth is an example of the economic system of ancient Israel. Boaz was an employer who was concerned about the poor widow Ruth. He told her:

Oregon
Loggers haul wood, an important material used for making goods.

> May the Lord reward your work,
> and your wages be full from the Lord,
> the God of Israel, under whose wings
> you have come to seek refuge.
>
> Ruth 2:12

Lesson Activities

Thinking Biblically — Jesus used money as an example in his teaching. Read Luke 7:40-50.

Vocabulary — Write five sentences in your notebook, using one of these words in each: freight, competitive, retirement, fictional, distribution. Check in a dictionary if you need help with their definitions.

Literature — Read "Plain Bob and a Job" in *The Citizen's Handbook* pages 134-135, and chapters "Cap Garland," "Three Days' Blizzard," and "Pa Goes to Volga" in *The Long Winter*.

Find Out! — Ask your parents to name all the paying jobs they have had. Write down the list in your notebook.

Picture This! — Take a photograph or draw a picture of your mom and/or dad at work.

Student Workbook or Lesson Review — If you are using one of these optional books, complete the assignment for Lesson 111.

The Life of
DOLLAR BILL

Today's lesson is a biography. Let us introduce you to its subject. You have probably met some of his friends. His name is Dollar Bill.

Birth Announcement

Federal Reserve One Dollar Note serial number K55841820B, nicknamed Dollar Bill, was born on December 21, 2009. He rolled off the press at the United States Bureau of Engraving and Printing (BEP) production facility in Fort Worth, Texas. The BEP is part of the Department of the Treasury. The Fort Worth facility was one of two places that Dollar Bill could have been born. The other is in Washington, D.C., which is also home to the headquarters of the Bureau of Engraving and Printing.

Dollar Bill was printed on a large sheet of paper. He was one of thirty-two Dollar Bills printed on that sheet. Like his siblings on that sheet, and like all his other siblings, Dollar Bill was made of 75% cotton and 25% linen. His sheet was first inspected and then cut into individual bills. Dollar Bill was 6.14 inches long and 2.61 inches high at birth and he weighed one gram. The cost to produce Dollar Bill was about five cents.

Dollar Bill arrived in a big bundle of brothers. Over sixteen million other dollar bills were produced the same day. About forty-five percent of the currency produced by the BEP are one dollar bills. Dollar Bill was born into a large family. The Treasury Department estimates that about four billion one dollar bills are in circulation on any given day.

Family Likeness

Dollar Bill and all his brothers that arrived that day looked exactly alike except for two

Washington, D.C.
Two pitchers for the Los Angeles Dodgers baseball team, Ted Lilly (second from left) and Clayton Kershaw (second from right), see a demonstration of how bills are made at the Bureau of Engraving and Printing, 2011.

characteristics: the unique serial number on each one, and the seal and numbers that indicated to which Federal Reserve Bank they were to be sent. Get a dollar bill to look at while we describe Dollar Bill to you.

The front or obverse of the one dollar U.S. Federal Reserve Note has a reproduction of a portrait of George Washington that was painted by Gilbert Stuart. To the left of the portrait is a seal showing the Federal Reserve Bank for which each bill is intended. The United States has twelve Federal Reserve Banks. See the Federal Reserve Bank of Richmond below.

Richmond, Virginia
At left is the Federal Reserve Bank of Richmond. In the photo above it is seen from the Richmond Riverfront. At far left is the lobby. At top left is a display about how the value of money changes due to conditions in the economy.

Each Federal Reserve Bank has its own letter and number. They are listed at right. Our Dollar Bill was printed for the Federal Reserve Bank in Dallas, Texas, so its seal has a letter K. The letter for the Dallas Federal Reserve Bank is K. Since K is the eleventh letter of the alphabet, Dollar Bill's number is 11. The number 11 was printed in each of the

Regional Federal Reserve Letters & Numbers

Boston, MA—A 1	Chicago, IL—G 7
New York City, NY—B 2	St. Louis, MO—H 8
Philadelphia, PA—C 3	Minneapolis, MN—I 9
Cleveland, OH—D 4	Kansas City, MO—J 10
Richmond, VA—E 5	Dallas, TX—K 11
Atlanta, GA—F 6	San Francisco, CA—L 12

Treasurer of the United States Rosie Rios signs her name in order for her signature to be printed on U.S. currency, 2009.

Treasurer of the United States Rosie Rios describes her job to 9th grade students and shows them her signature on a $1 bill.

four corners of Dollar Bill's white central panel on the obverse. The seal of the U.S. Department of the Treasury is to the right of Washington. The outside border of the obverse is decorated with olive branches.

The signatures of the current Treasurer of the United States and the current Secretary of the Treasury are to the left and right of Washington respectively. See photos at left. The Treasury Secretary is a member of the President's Cabinet. The Treasurer of the United States works in the Treasury Department. She is an advisor to the U.S. Mint, the Bureau of Engraving and Printing, and the Treasury Secretary. The U.S. Mint makes U.S. coins. In addition to printing paper money (called currency), the Bureau of Engraving and Printing also prints award certificates, invitations, many types of identification cards, and other documents used by the Federal government.

In 1949 President Harry Truman appointed a woman to be Treasurer of the United States. Since then every Treasurer has been female. The series number that is printed next to the Treasury Secretary's signature on U.S. currency changes when either the Treasurer of the United States or the Secretary of the Treasury retires or resigns.

The reverse of the one dollar bill features both sides of the Great Seal of the United States and the national motto, "In God We Trust." The national motto was first printed on U.S. currency in 1955 during the presidency of Dwight D. Eisenhower, who worked to make that change. Also on the reverse of the bill are strings of thirteen pearls.

The current design of the one dollar bill came into use in 1969. Dollar Bill's bigger brothers, the $5, $10, $20, $50, and $100 bills, have been redesigned in recent years to make counterfeiting more difficult. At left is a photo of the unveiling of a new $100 bill in 2010. Few people try to make counterfeit one dollar bills since they are not worth the effort and risk, so there are no plans to redesign the one dollar bill.

Bill's Journey

After Dollar Bill was printed, the Bureau of Engraving and Printing sent him to the Treasury Department office. The Treasury Department sent him to the Federal Reserve Bank

Treasurer of the United States Rosie Rios unveils new $100 bill, 2010.

of Dallas, which bundled him with other dollar bills and sent him to a local bank, First National Bank of Dallas. Dollar Bill spent several days in the vault at this bank, and then was put into the cash drawer of one of the bank's tellers.

Jack Gold gets paid at work by the direct deposit of his check into the family checking account at First National Bank. After his paycheck was deposited on January 4, 2010, his wife Penny Gold cashed a check for $250 at the bank the next day for the cash the family would need for the month. Dollar Bill was

Dodger pitchers walk up to $1 million in ten dollar bills at the Washington D.C. Bureau of Engraving and Printing.

included in that cash, along with four other identical one dollar bills and several of his bigger brothers. That evening, Mom gave Dollar Bill to their son Jimmy as part of his allowance. Jimmy put Dollar Bill in the box where he keeps his money.

A few days later, Jimmy used Dollar Bill to buy a bottle of spring water from a vending machine. The next week, Hank Means, a worker for the vending machine company, removed the cash that was in the machine, including Dollar Bill, and took him to the company's office in a cloth pouch. The secretary of the company, Betty Buck, prepared the cash to be deposited in the company account at Prairie National Bank. She made the deposit later that day, carrying Dollar Bill and the other money to the bank in a leather pouch.

After Dollar Bill spent a few days in the vault at Prairie National Bank, Rebecca McCoin, the manager of the Dallas Dollar Delites store, came in to get money for the cash registers at the store. Dollar Bill was among the currency she received. The next day, Dollar Bill was put into the cash drawer. Later that day, Sally Green came into the store to buy snacks for the Green family's annual skiing trip in Colorado and received Dollar Bill in her change.

On their way to the mountains, the Green family stopped for supper at El Taco in Lubbock, which is a family tradition. Mike Green left a tip for server, Judy Rich. Dollar Bill was part of the tip. Judy used Dollar Bill and some of her other tip money to buy some sopapillas at the restaurant to take home to her daughter Rachel. That same day, truck driver Bobby Buck paid cash for his meal at the restaurant and received Dollar Bill in his change. Bobby stuck Dollar Bill in the pocket of his sun visor in case he ever needed to use him to pay a toll.

Two months later, Bobby looked up and noticed Dollar Bill on his visor. He was getting out of his truck at George and Abe's Truck Stop in Huntington, West Virginia, so he grabbed

Dollar Bill and used him to buy some snacks. The truck stop manager, Ben Bread, included Dollar Bill in the deposit that he took that afternoon to Mountain Region Bank.

The next day, Melissa Fortune stopped by the bank to cash a check. Her son Tommy had lost a tooth, and Melissa wanted to put a dollar under his pillow that night. She was given Dollar Bill in her cash. When Tommy woke up the next morning, he was excited to find Dollar Bill. He put him in the bank that he kept in the bottom of his closet, and there he stayed for over a year. Tommy got his bank out every Saturday to count his money. He folded Dollar Bill carefully, but every time he folded him the creases got a little deeper. Once he accidentally tore Dollar Bill's upper right corner.

In May of 2011, the Fortune family was headed for a vacation to Washington, D.C. Along the way, they planned to stop in Richmond, Virginia, to see some friends and to go to a Richmond Flying Squirrels minor league baseball game. Tommy got out his bank and put most of his money into his billfold. This trip was what he had been saving for.

At the game, Tommy went to the souvenir stand and counted out ten one dollar bills, including Dollar Bill, to buy a Flying Squirrels T-shirt. The souvenir stand operator, Susie Money, deposited Dollar Bill and the other money she received that night in the company account at Richmond Federal Bank.

Dollar Bill Becomes a Souvenir

When banks receive currency, bank employees go through the bills and take out those that are too wrinkled, torn, or soiled to stay in circulation. These bills are bundled and sent to a Federal Reserve Bank, where they are exchanged for new bills that are sent to the local bank. The average useful life of a dollar bill is about eighteen to twenty-four months. Fives and tens last a little shorter time, while twenties and fifties last longer.

In late May of 2011, Dollar Bill was withdrawn from circulation by Richmond Federal Bank and sent to the Federal Reserve Bank in Richmond for exchange. Dollar Bill, along with other currency that was withdrawn that day, was shredded. A portion of the shredded money, including Dollar Bill, was placed in a small bag that contained about one hundred dollars in shredded currency. In June, the Sterling family that was attending the homeschooling convention in Richmond visited the Federal Reserve Bank and received the package as a souvenir. See photo at right. They took it home, and daughter Clara placed it in the back of her drawer where she keeps souvenirs from her trips. She covered it with her socks.

People earn money. They save money. They borrow money. They steal money. During the last week Jesus lived on earth before His crucifixion, He observed what one woman did with the only money she had.

> And He sat down opposite the treasury, and began
> observing how the people were putting money into the
> treasury; and many rich people were putting in large sums.
> A poor widow came and put in two small copper coins,
> which amount to a cent. Calling His disciples to Him,
> He said to them, "Truly I say to you, this poor widow
> put in more than all the contributors to the treasury;
> for they all put in out of their surplus, but she, out of her
> poverty, put in all she owned, all she had to live on."
> Mark 12:41-44

Lesson Activities

Thinking Biblically — Copy 1 Timothy 6:10 in your notebook.

Literature — Read "The Real Riches" in *The Citizen's Handbook* page 136, and chapters "Alone," "We'll Weather the Blast," and "One Bright Day" in *The Long Winter*.

Creative Writing — In your notebook, write out a timeline of the life of Dollar Bill, including at least ten highlights.

Find Out! — Look at ten different bills of currency. Find out to which Federal Reserve Bank they were originally sent.

Student Workbook or Lesson Review — If you are using one of these optional books, complete the assignment for Lesson 112.

From Kernel TO COOKIE

Greenville, South Carolina
Stossner's Bakery

Wheat is one of America's most popular foods. After it is ground into flour, we use it to make cookies, pizza crusts, hamburger and hot dog buns, donuts, crackers, pretzels, cakes, and pie crusts, not to mention bread! Wheat is a valuable American product. In this lesson, we will learn more about how the American economy works by following wheat from the time it lands in the soil to the time it lands in a happy person's mouth as part of a warm chocolate chip cookie!

It Begins in the Dirt

The story of our kernel of wheat begins on a large field in Kansas. The wheat has just been harvested, and it's already time to prepare the fields for next year's crop. After the harvest, the stubble of wheat stalks remains in the field. The farmer plows the ground to chop up the stubble and any weeds that have popped up, mixing them with the soil. This step will preserve the soil's moisture for next year's crop. The farmer checks the soil's nutrient levels and adds any nutrients and fertilizer he thinks the soil needs.

Centreville, Maryland
*A wheat field nearby
has recently been cut.*

When September rolls around, it's wheat-planting time in Kansas. The farmer uses his tractor to prepare his fields for planting. He turns the soil, breaking it into fine particles. The farmer buys seed wheat from his local farmers' co-op. The farmer loads seed into a drill, which he has attached to his tractor. The drill makes furrows (ridges in the soil), drops a line of seed into the furrow, and then covers the furrow with a thin layer of soil.

During the fall, the kernels sprout and grow to about six inches tall; but when winter's cold hits Kansas, the wheat goes dormant to wait out the season. During the winter, the farmer keeps a close eye on the crop to make sure it stays healthy and is not damaged by insects, weeds, or diseases.

The wheat begins to grow again in the spring and continues until it is two to four feet tall. Let's look closely at one stalk of wheat. See the stem with several long leaves that look like ribbons. At the top is a head with about twelve to fourteen spikelets, each with a "beard" that looks like a single hair. Each spikelet contains two to four kernels. One of those tiny kernels, about six millimeters long, is the one we'll be watching through the rest of its life.

Wheat Heads with Spikelets and Beards

Harvest Time

The wheat field's millions of stalks turn from green to golden, rippling in the wind under vast prairie skies. By harvest time in June or July, the wheat stalks are dead and drying. The stalks must be dry so that they can be cut easily and so that they can be stored without spoiling. The heads of wheat "nod" (bend over) when they are ready to be harvested. As soon as the wheat is ready, it's a race to gather it before wind, rain, hail, or fire can ruin the ripe wheat field.

Heads of wheat have nodded.

The farmer uses a combine to harvest his crop. At its front is a large reel that pushes the heads of the wheat stalk into a sickle. The sickle cuts off the heads, which are then pulled into the combine. The combine shakes and beats the heads to make the kernels come out. There's our kernel, vibrating out of its dry, protective covering. The combine moves our kernel and the others into a grain tank while the other plant material is blown out the back of the combine and across the field. On average, an acre of wheat produces about thirty-seven bushels. A bushel weighs about sixty pounds and has about one million kernels. Combines can harvest about 1,000 bushels per hour.

A farmer uses a combine to harvest wheat.

To the Prairie Skyscraper

Our kernel of wheat and the rest of the load is dumped from the combine into a truck. The truck heads to the local grain elevator, the skyscraper of a small Kansas town. First, the entire truck is weighed on a huge scale. Then the driver pulls the truck into the grain elevator and parks the back of the truck in front of a huge grate. Elevator workers open panels on the back of the truck. The truck tilts its load back to empty the truck. Our kernel slides over the edge of the truck bed and down into darkness below the grate. The empty truck pulls back over to the scale so it can be weighed empty. In this way, they determine the weight of that load of wheat. Then the driver heads back to the farm to pick up the next load.

The combine dumps the wheat into a truck.

Meanwhile, the wheat has taken a slide down a concrete slope into the "boot pit." The grain elevator, just as the name suggests, mechanically raises the grain from the bottom to the top. With large scoops, funnels, and conveyor belts, the wheat is raised and channeled into storage areas to await being sold. In a dark corner of the grain elevator, our kernel

A Kansas Grain Elevator

is kept cool and dry and protected from bugs. Before long, the wheat is shipped from the "country elevator" to a larger terminal elevator. There our kernel is cleaned, dried, tested, and mixed with wheat grown on other farms. Scientists check wheat for quality and assign grades. Factors like protein content and moisture will impact the way baked goods look and taste. The bin that holds our kernel has passed inspection for purchase by King Arthur Flour, a company that buys only the highest grade of wheat and follows the highest standards in the flour industry.

A North Dakota Grain Elevator

Cleaned and Beaten

Our kernel and its fellows will be ground right in Kansas, which leads the nation not only in wheat production but also in flour milling. Trucks transport wheat from the elevator to the mill. Before it can be ground, the wheat must be cleaned,

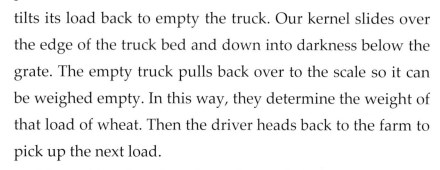

cleaned, and cleaned again. At first glance, a bin of wheat kernels looks like a bin of only wheat kernels. However, since wheat kernels are extracted from much larger plants, come out of a dirty field, and spend a long time in storage, a bin of wheat actually contains a lot of small, even microscopic unwanted material that can't end up with the flour in the flour bag. First the grain goes through a vibrating screen called a separator and next to an aspirator which blows away dust and tiny, lightweight impurities. Then the wheat goes through a magnetic separator which removes miniscule iron and steel particles. After the magnetic separator, the wheat enters a disc separator that divides wheat kernels from any larger or smaller particles. Next the wheat passes through a stoner that removes tiny stones, sand, and hard clumps of dirt. The cleaning process is almost done! A scourer rubs, scrubs and buffs each kernel. Finally! The wheat is just wheat—clean enough to become flour. Our kernel has taken quite a beating, but it's nothing to what is coming!

The cleaned grain goes into a tempering bin. Water is added to the bin to raise the moisture level of the wheat to make it easier to grind. When the moisture level is just right, the kernels pass through an impact machine to remove inferior wheat kernels (whew! our kernel passed!). The wheat kernels are broken by the mill's wheels several times and sifted in between. For white flour, the coarse, brown parts of the flour, called bran, are removed. For whole wheat flour, all parts of the wheat kernel end up in the finished flour. Since our kernel is destined to be white flour, it gives up its bran in the sifting process. Wheat bran is a valuable and nutritious by-product of milling white flour. It is sold in grocery stores and is used in making cereal, pet foods, and feed for farm animals. Removing the bran takes nutrition from the flour, so the final step in making white flour is to mix niacin, iron, thiamine, riboflavin, and folic acid back in to add nutritional value.

Bran (left) and Whole Wheat Flour

King Arthur Flour

At the end of the line at the mill, paper bags with the King Arthur Flour logo stand waiting to be filled with high-quality flour. The King Arthur Flour Company is America's oldest flour company. In 1790 Henry Wood began importing flour from Europe to Boston. In 1896 the company introduced a new flour at the Boston Food Fair. The company called their new U.S.-grown flour King Arthur Flour. In 1984 the company moved from Massachusetts to Norwich, Vermont. King Arthur Flour's consistently high-quality product is trusted

Norwich, Vermont
King Arthur Store and Baking Education Center

St. Paul, Minnesota
Two Former Flour Mills

by home bakers, professional bakers, cooking schools, and people who write cookbooks. The company encourages people to do more and better baking (with King Arthur Flour, of course). They have a website with recipes and baking advice. They sell baking supplies online and by catalog. They publish cookbooks and a baking magazine called *The Baking Sheet*. They also provide a baker's hotline that people can call with baking questions. In Vermont they have a baker's store, a bakery, and a school where people can learn to bake. They have taught 120,000 fourth through seventh graders in schools around the country how to bake through their Life Skills Bread Baking Program. King Arthur Flour proudly provides 100% U.S.-grown and U.S.-milled flour and the tools and skills needed to use it.

From Mill to Grocery Store

Our kernel of wheat is now pulverized powder, and it's dumped with another nineteen cups of flour into a bag. A machine folds the bag's top down and glues it closed. Most bags of flour that you see in grocery stores hold five pounds of flour. A bushel of wheat makes about forty-two pounds of white flour (just over eight bags) or about sixty pounds of whole wheat flour (twelve bags). The flour bags are boxed and stacked on a pallet. The pallets are loaded onto tractor trailer trucks and driven to the warehouses of grocery distribution companies. Individual grocery stores and grocery store chains order their groceries from these distributors. King Arthur Flour makes its way into supermarkets in every state.

Charles, grocery manager at the Happy Food Store in Elko, Nevada, places an order for non-perishables with his store's grocery distributor. In a couple of days, a truck arrives with everything from bathroom cleaner to animal crackers. Among many boxes stacked on pallets in the truck is a case of Unbleached All-Purpose Flour in the red and white King Arthur Flour bag. The truck driver unloads the pallets into the back storeroom of the Happy Food Store. Late that evening, Charles works stocking the shelves with groceries. He replenishes the baking aisle with a fresh supply of several different brands of flour. On the front of the shelf is our kernel-now-flour in its bag.

A couple of days later, Marsha goes to the store to do her grocery shopping. A week before, she had seen a King Arthur Flour advertisement in a magazine. The advertisement said that King Arthur makes the finest flour. While in the store, she recognized the logo on the King Arthur Flour bag from the advertisement and decided to give it a try. She picked up the bag on the front of the shelf and put it in her shopping cart.

Time to Make Cookies

That evening, Marsha decided to make chocolate chip cookies for her husband and children. She scooped 2 1/4 cups of flour into a mixing bowl. Our kernel-now-flour was near the top of the bag, so it landed right in the mixing bowl. Marsha added salt, baking soda, butter, sugar, brown sugar, vanilla, eggs, and chocolate chips. Her children helped her drop the dough onto baking sheets. While Marsha washed the dishes, the baking cookies deliciously perfumed the

kitchen. As soon as the oven timer beeped, her children came trooping back into the kitchen and waited impatiently for the cookies to cool off enough to gobble up. Mark used a spatula to lift the cookie with our little kernel. He held the hot cookie with the tips of his fingers, blew on it, and took the first delicious bite.

The Cookie Army

It takes many people to go from kernel to cookie. Each of these people has his own special set of skills. The step-by-step cooperation of skillful and creative people makes our economy work. The farmer's expertise is to raise and harvest a field of wheat. He depends on manufacturers of farm equipment, a supply of gasoline to run it, the store where he buys his seed wheat, and the workers at his local grain elevator. Scientists test and measure wheat to provide a consistent, predictable product. Trucks, their drivers, and the roads they travel are essential parts of the process at several steps. The skills of millers and the people who design and build cleaning and milling machines are necessary for wheat to become flour.

Artists design King Arthur Flour bags and their advertisements for magazines. Marketers decide where to advertise, and they convince grocery distributors to stock King Arthur Flour. Grocery store owners and managers order the flour. Truck drivers bring it to the stores. Stockers take it to the shelf. Marsha bought the car she uses for grocery shopping from a local dealer and uses a shopping cart made in an American factory. She and her husband work for small business owners in their town. This provides the income for them to buy their family's groceries. All the ingredients and equipment in Marsha's kitchen came from farms and factories in the United States and other countries. Her children had fun helping make and especially eating the cookies, not realizing they were helped by hundreds of others. God created the wheat plant, the soil it grows in, the weather that nurtures it, and the intelligent people who know what to do with it.

Truly, truly, I say to you, unless a grain of wheat falls into the earth and dies,

it remains alone; but if it dies, it bears much fruit.

John 12:24

Lesson Activities

Thinking Biblically — Jesus used wheat to tell a parable. Read Matthew 13:24-30 and 36-43.

Vocabulary — Find each of these words in a dictionary, then find the definition that corresponds to the way the word is used in this lesson: stubble, bushel, conveyor, microscopic, pallet. Copy the words and definitions into your notebook.

Literature — Read chapters "No Trains," "Fair Weather," and "Seed Wheat" in *The Long Winter*.

Creative Writing — In your notebook, write a poem of at least ten lines about the journey of wheat from kernel to cookie.

Find Out! — What brands of flour are in the kitchen in your house?

Picture This! — Take a photograph or draw a picture of three things made from wheat.

Student Workbook or Lesson Review — If you are using one of these optional books, complete the assignment for Lesson 113.

How We Pay for GOVERNMENT

It takes a great deal of money to run a business. The owner must buy or rent a place to conduct business. He must buy materials for making products to sell to customers. He must buy machinery to turn the materials into finished products. He must pay workers who make the products that his company sells. He must purchase insurance for the building, machinery, and goods that he has on hand. He must spend time and money to advertise his product so that people

Machine Which Makes Vinyl Signs

will know about it and want to buy it. After paying for all of that and all his other expenses, he hopes to make a profit, which is the money he has left after all of his expenses are paid. If he makes a profit, he can grow his business and hire more workers in the future.

The machine pictured above illustrates several aspects of business. The owner of this sign-making company had to purchase this machine, pay a worker to operate it, pay for the electricity to run it, order and pay for the vinyl to make the signs, and purchase or rent the building where he runs his business. Another company is paying the sign maker to print these vinyl signs so that it can use them to advertise products.

So how does a business owner pay for all of these expenses? He pays for his business expenses by selling the products that his company makes at a price that is more than it cost to make them. If he doesn't make enough from the sale of his products, he will have to borrow the money he needs to pay the workers, pay for insurance, and pay all his other expenses. But if he borrows money, he will have the extra expense of paying it back along with the interest that he owes the bank for borrowing the money.

The Cost of Government

It takes a great deal of money to run a government. Think about all the things we want government to do that cost money, lots of money. The Federal government must pay for all of the equipment that the military uses. It must pay for the office buildings that Federal workers use. The Federal government must pay the salaries of all of the people in the military and the salaries of all of the Federal workers.

A state government must pay its workers and also pay for the buildings and vehicles it uses, the education and medical services it provides, and voting machines used in elections. A local government must pay the salaries of police and fire fighters, the people who work in

Dale County, Alabama
Fort Rucker

Montana
Glacier National Park Boat Tour

USS Enterprise

Togus, Maine
Veterans Affairs Maine Healthcare System

Kingston, Tennessee

The Federal government must pay for this aircraft carrier, the fuel to run it, the planes that take off and land there and their fuel, the salaries of those who operate them, and even for the American flag. It must pay for boats in national parks like the one at left. It must pay for veterans hospitals like the one at right, for the doctors and nurses who work there, and for the medical tests and prescriptions veterans need. It must even pay for Sparky the Fire Dog costumes. State governments must buy patches for all of their state troopers. Local governments must purchase signs.

the offices of the local government, and the people who clean the streets and pick up trash and teach schoolchildren. Local government must pay for the equipment used to keep the city parks looking nice and the gasoline to run city vehicles. See examples on page 722.

The Federal government and state and local governments have these expenses and thousands more. So how does the government get the money to pay for all of these? The government does not make products that people buy. It does not charge people the actual cost of many of its services, such as the medical care it provides to people even when they cannot afford it, or the costs of putting out fires, maintaining parks, or paving roads.

Governments do collect fees for some services. For instance, hunters and fishermen have to purchase licenses for these activities from the state government. Visitors to national parks pay entrance fees. See photos at right. People who return library books late must pay fines. However, these fees and fines pay for only a small portion of the expenses that governments have. Governments charge private companies for the right to take and sell natural resources such as minerals and trees from government land, but again this cannot pay for all government expenses. So if government spends money and therefore needs money, but it doesn't make goods for sale and gets only a little from fees, how does government pay for all that it does?

The answer is primarily one word: TAXES. Taxes are charges made by government when certain things happen (such as when a sale is made in a store) or on the value of certain items that are owned or sold. Governments decide what are taxable events and what things ought to be taxed. The purpose of

Kalispell, Montana
Secretary of the Interior Ken Salazar and U.S. Fish and Wildlife Service Director Daniel Ashe purchase fishing licenses, 2011.

Arizona
East Entrance Station to Grand Canyon National Park

The National Park Service sells America the Beautiful National Parks and Federal Recreational Land passes. These members of the military received a new military version free at the Grand Canyon on Armed Forces Day, May 19, 2012, the day this program began.

taxes is to provide income for the government to carry out its responsibilities. Money that is paid to a government in taxes and fees and things like lease payments for government lands is called government revenue.

Revenue for the Federal Government

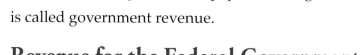

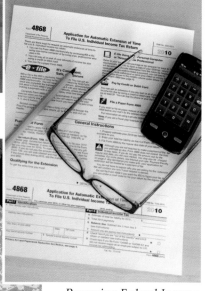

*Collection Box
for Kansas State Taxes*

*Preparing Federal Income
Tax Return*

*Opening of a Tax Center for U.S.
Service Personnel Serving in Europe*

Just over half of the revenue that the Federal government receives comes from taxes on income, which is money that people or corporations earn. Forty-seven percent of Federal revenue in 2011 came from personal income tax, and 8% was from taxes on the profits of corporations. Taxes paid by working individuals for Social Security and Medicare (sometimes called payroll taxes) amounted to another 36% of Federal revenue. Customs, which are taxes paid on items brought into the country, added up to 6% of Federal revenue. Federal taxes called excise taxes on the sale of certain items such as gasoline, tobacco, jewelry, and guns accounted for 3%. Taxes on gifts and money inherited through wills added less than 1%.

In 2011 these taxes accounted for about $2.5 trillion in revenue for the government. However, the Federal government spent about $3.5 trillion in 2011. The Federal government borrowed over $1 trillion to pay for its expenses that year. Many Americans are concerned about the amount of money that the Federal government borrows and owes. David Walker, a former

U.S. Comptroller General, organized a "$10 Million a Minute" bus tour through twenty-seven states in the fall of 2012. His purpose was to educate people about the increasing Federal debt and to suggest ways that the trend of greater Federal debt might be reversed. The name of the tour came from the fact that Federal debt grows by about ten million dollars every minute. Notice the photo at right.

Revenue for State Governments

States have two main sources of revenue. One source is state income taxes. As of 2012, forty-one states require its citizens to pay taxes on their regular earned income. People pay a smaller percentage of their income in state income taxes than they do in Federal income tax. The other main source of state revenue is sales taxes. These are taxes paid when people buy things. Business owners collect the sales tax and send it in to the state treasury on a regular basis, usually every month or every three months.

States add excise taxes to the price of gasoline and charge fees for registering cars and obtaining license plates. States also place taxes on amusement park admissions, the price of hotel rooms, and other sales. Another popular form of revenue for states is a state lottery or legalized gambling.

Many state constitutions require that the state government cannot spend more than it takes in through revenue. Some states do not have this restriction, and these states often borrow money to pay for what their governments spend.

Revenue for Local Governments

The most important source of revenue for county governments is the property tax. The value of property, such as land, houses, and business buildings, is determined by an official called the property assessor or a similar title. The county commission sets the property tax rate, and property owners pay the amount determined by multiplying the value of their property times the property tax rate.

Cities use a variety of revenue sources. These include fees, sales taxes, property taxes, and other means of revenue. State and local governments get a large amount of the money they spend from the Federal government. Much of the money that the Federal government spends goes to state and local governments to pay for programs such as health care and education.

Presidents and Government Spending

Many people blame the President for the high cost of the Federal government and for the debt that it owes. It is true that the President suggests a Federal budget each year for Congress to pass, but it is Congress who has the responsibility to pass each budget. Many Presidents have served in Congress prior to becoming President, and some have worked in other levels or branches of government where they had financial responsibilities. Read about these in the box on page 726.

Do We Have to Pay Taxes?

If we want to have government, we must provide a way for the government to have the money it needs. This money is provided primarily by citizens paying taxes. People complain that taxes are too high. Citizens have different ideas about what programs the government should have. Through elections and communication with elected officials, we have the opportunity and responsibility to help decide what government does, how much we pay in taxes, and how government spends the taxes we pay.

What we give to the government in the form of taxes is important, but it is not as important as what we give to God in the form of ourselves.

And Jesus said to them, "Render to Caesar the things that are Caesar's,
and to God the things that are God's." And they were amazed at Him.

Mark 12:17

Lesson Activities

Vocabulary — Copy these words in your notebook, each on a separate line: insurance, payroll, lottery, assessor, efficient. Look up each word in a dictionary. Next to each word, write what part of speech it is according to the way the word is used in this lesson.

Literature — Read "Supporting the Library" in *The Citizen's Handbook* pages 137-138, and chapters "Merry Christmas," "Where There's a Will," and "Antelope!" in *The Long Winter*.

Creative Writing — In your notebook, make a list of fifteen things that government pays for in your town.

Picture This! — Take a photograph or draw a picture of someone in your family making a purchase that includes sales tax.

Student Workbook or Lesson Review — If you are using one of these optional books, complete the assignment for Lesson 114.

★ Remember to choose an American Holiday to study this week! ★

UNIT 24 – USING THE RESOURCES GOD CREATED

BOOKS USED IN UNIT 24

- The Citizen's Handbook
- The Long Winter
- Student Workbook (optional)
- Lesson Review (optional)

*Electric Power Line Between Honey Creek
and Middletown, Indiana
(Photo by Homeschooling Father Sam Schlagel)*

America's God-Given RESOURCES

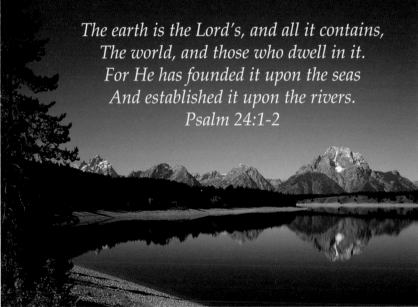

The earth is the Lord's, and all it contains,
The world, and those who dwell in it.
For He has founded it upon the seas
And established it upon the rivers.
Psalm 24:1-2

Natural resources are things God created in our environment that we can use for our needs. Among His many creations are plants, water, wildlife, minerals, air, and sunlight. Some of God's resources are rare. All are useful; many are beautiful. Examples on page 728 include (clockwise from top left): Multnomah Falls in Oregon; a whooping crane in a national wildlife refuge in Texas; Hat Rock State Park in Oregon; a muskrat in Lake Pepin in Wisconsin; copper ore outside the Arizona Sonora Desert Museum near Tucson, Arizona; Elephant Rocks State Park in Missouri; and the Grand Teton Mountains beside Jackson Lake in Wyoming.

We must use natural resources carefully. Renewable ones, such as trees, wind, and sunlight, God gives to us in abundance over and over again. Non-renewable resources such as minerals are those that God has provided in abundance, but that we can use up.

Removing resources from the places where God put them is called extraction. God wants people to use resources, but He also wants us to be good stewards or caretakers of them. It is irresponsible to extract resources without thinking about what might be available for future generations. It is also irresponsible to extract them in a way that harms other resources around them.

Nashville, Tennessee
Percy Warner Park

A Day in the Management of Our Resources

4:25 a.m. Wildlife Resources. A Maine father and son eagerly step into the darkness on the first day of hunting season. This is the day the young man has been waiting for. He is finally old enough to go hunting with his dad.

In earlier times, our country's supply of game and fish provided a direct source of food for many people. Hunting and fishing still play a role in feeding people, but they are also popular sports that keep the animal population at a healthy level. Today the Maine Department of Inland Fisheries and Wildlife oversees the issuing of hunting and fishing licenses. In addition to the standard licenses for hunting wild birds and wild animals, Maine issues a limited number of moose hunting permits each year. The bag limit is one moose per permit holder, per year.

10:00 a.m. Water Resources. At Hoover Dam on the border between Arizona and Nevada, civil engineers keep an eye on the immense water pressure against the dam from Lake Mead.

Minnesota
Governor Mark Dayton (blue hat) ice fishes with State Representative John Ward (red hat), January 22, 2011.

Madison, Wisconsin
The badger is the state animal of Wisconsin. This decoration is in the state capitol.

Clockwise Beginning at Top Left: Hoover Dam on the Nevada-Arizona Border, Photographed by Ansel Adams; Water Towers in Central Illinois; Tuscumbia, Alabama; Carthage, North Carolina; and West End, North Carolina; Water Meter Covers in Nashville, Tennessee. Center: Water Utility Payment Box in Wellington, Florida

Electrical engineers regulate the production of hydroelectricity from the water of the Colorado River rushing over the turbines at 85 miles per hour.

Water is a precious resource because it is essential to living. We get water from many sources: oceans, rivers, streams, lakes, springs, and wells. We need water to drink, we need it for cleaning, and we use it in industry. For example, mining companies use water to extract certain minerals from ore rock.

We need lots of water! Americans use over 400 billion gallons every day. Keeping our water supply clean and plentiful is an important priority for our country.

Hoover Dam is one project designed to make use of water resources. The dam was built in the Black Canyon of the Colorado River between 1931 and 1935 by a group of six private companies. It was turned over to the Federal government in 1936. The dam provides water for irrigation on over one million acres of farmland. Its water-powered turbines produce electricity for over one million customers in the southwestern United States. The United States sells the electricity generated by Hoover Dam to utility companies. Over the years these fees paid for the completion of the dam and still pays for its maintenance.

1:00 p.m. Minerals. Another long line of coal cars rumbles along the tracks heading out of Wyoming. God placed an abundance of coal beneath the state's wind-swept prairies. Coal lies under more than half of the state's land area. See photos at right. How much coal did God put there? Coal is mined in Wyoming at the amazing rate of twelve tons per second. Almost all of Wyoming's coal goes to fuel power plants in a total of nineteen states. Those power plants produce electricity that powers homes, businesses, and factories.

The United States has one of the largest reserves of coal in the world. Coal is mined in twenty-five of our fifty states. Wyoming is the top coal producer. About 40% of the electricity generated in the United States in 2011 was generated with coal as a fuel. After coal has been mined from an area, mining companies hire specialists to reseed land that has been harmed and to repair habitats for native animals.

Surely there is a mine for silver
And a place where they refine gold.
Iron is taken from the dust,
And copper is smelted from rock.
Job 28:1-2

While some locomotives pull coal cars out of Wyoming, others pull tankers filled with oil out of North Dakota. North Dakota has immense deposits of oil and natural gas. These minerals are in a large shale and dolomite

Mining and Quarrying Rocks and Minerals

Wyoming
Black Thunder Mine
Sign and Truck

Mt. Airy, North Carolina
Granite Quarry

Near Center Point, West Virginia
Equipment Used in Extracting Natural Gas

A Swedish Business that Helps Mining Companies

731

A North Dakota Oil Rig

Williston, North Dakota
Scenes at an Oil Rig

rock formation called the Bakken formation. The Bakken spreads out underground in North Dakota, Montana, and Canada. People have been extracting small amounts of oil from this area since the 1950s, but in recent years technology has made extracting the oil much cheaper. Through a process called hydraulic fracturing (also called fracking), workers pour large amounts of water mixed with sand and chemicals to make cracks in the shale. This allows them to extract more oil and natural gas than before. The western part of North Dakota has experienced a tremendous boom in the production of oil and gas. Oil production has increased from less than 100,000 barrels per day in 2005 to more than 600,000 barrels per day in 2012, making North Dakota the second-largest oil-producing state in America behind Texas.

Thousands of Americans have moved to sparsely-populated North Dakota to work in the oil industry, making huge changes in this rural region. The state economy has become stronger, and Americans are able to use more American oil and less oil from other countries.

3:00 p.m. Solar Power. In Albuquerque, New Mexico, a contractor finishes putting his tools in his truck, shakes hands with the homeowner, looks up to admire his work once more, and drives off. The homeowner and his wife go inside their home and smile at the thermostat regulating the central air system in their home. They are no longer buying electricity from the power company. Now that they have a solar panel system on the roof of their home, they will be generating all of the electricity they need. In some months they will even be able to sell excess electricity to the power company!

The abundance of sunshine (and therefore heat) in New Mexico—usually about 280 to 300 days per year—has sometimes been seen as a problem, but the New Mexico state government, utility companies, and private businesses have been working to change all that sunshine into a practical power source. The state legislature has set targets for the amount of energy to be produced by renewable sources by a certain year, and those working in the energy industry have worked to meet those targets. See solar energy photos at right.

6:00 p.m. Trees. An Arkansas sawmill is silent after another day of production. The variety of trees and the large number of acres available has made the lumber industry a major part of the state's economy since around 1900. Over half of the state is commercial timberland. Because businessmen and scientists learned early in the twentieth century the importance of replanting after cutting, the industry has been able to flourish and to provide plenty of jobs. See lumber below.

Trees are a renewable resource that serve many functions. They replenish our oxygen supply by taking in carbon dioxide and giving off oxygen. The water vapor that trees produce helps to cool the area around the trees. They provide a habitat for many wild animals. Trees provide wood for producing energy, wood for construction, and wood for making products, such as notebook paper, paper plates and napkins, and cardboard boxes. This valuable resource must be managed well so that it will continue to be a source for materials, jobs, and health-giving benefits.

Solar Energy in Oregon

Installing Solar Panels to Be Used by the Oregon Department of Transportation for Solar Highways

Representatives of the Korea Institute of Technology visit the site of the Oregon Department of Transportation Solar Highway.

Sheridan, Arkansas
Truck Carrying Lumber

Government's Role in Using and Preserving Natural Resources

Governments on the local, state, and Federal levels provide information for people as they use natural resources. The United States Geological Survey (USGS) studies our land, water, mineral resources, wildlife resources, and other natural resources. This Federal agency, established in 1879, helps the government and the American people understand our environment and the opportunities and challenges we face in using and protecting natural resources. Knowing what we have and how we are doing in managing our resources helps us to plan more intelligently and responsibly for the future.

Highest Point in Arkansas
U.S. Geological Survey Marker

Governments also take action and make regulations to help citizens be safe and healthy as they use natural resources. For example, governments check the quality of water to make sure that it is not contaminated by substances that are harmful to people. Agencies treat waste water so that it can be returned to the environment and used again. Federal and state governments set up safety guidelines for miners and make regulations about how mines may affect the environment. The Federal government enforces rules about transporting oil safely by ocean-going tankers, river barges, rail cars, and tanker trucks. Rules for hunters and fishermen protect animal populations from too much hunting and help animal populations stay at a healthy level for humans, the environment, and the animals themselves. As seen in the pictures from the Oregon Department of Transportation on page 733, governments encourage the use of solar power and other energy sources that do not harm the environment. Federal and state government oversee logging on public land by private companies (public land is land owned by the Federal government or by a state or local government).

Nashville, Tennessee
Drain Reads: "DUMP NO WASTE DRAINS TO RIVER"

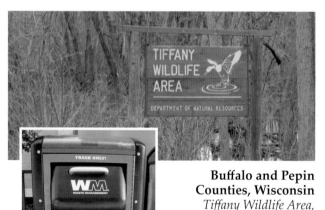

Buffalo and Pepin Counties, Wisconsin
Tiffany Wildlife Area, Wisconsin Department of Natural Resources

Winston-Salem, North Carolina
Solar Powered Trash Compactor

Two members of the President's Cabinet lead agencies that work with America's resources, the Secretary of the Interior and the Administrator of the Environmental Protection Agency (EPA). The U.S. Department of the Interior is responsible for protecting the country's natural resources and helping us have the energy we need. The EPA works to protect our health and the environment through education and enforcing Federal regulations.

Many Presidents have devoted time to protecting our natural resources. President Theodore Roosevelt was especially passionate about the environment. Presidents Herbert Hoover, George H. W. Bush, and George W. Bush were involved in extracting natural resources before being elected President. Hoover was a mining engineer and the Bushes were both involved in the oil industry.

When God created Adam and Eve, he told them, "Be fruitful and multiply, and fill the earth, and subdue it; and rule over the fish of the sea and over the birds of the sky and over every living thing that moves on the earth" (Genesis 1:28). With this position of ruling over and subduing the earth comes the responsibility of caring for the earth in order to bless people and to give the glory to God.

The heavens are Yours, the earth also is Yours;
The world and all it contains, You have founded them.
Psalm 89:11

Lesson Activities

Thinking Biblically — Write a paragraph in your notebook answering the question, "What is the Christian's responsibility in taking care of the earth?"

Vocabulary — Look up each of these words in a dictionary and read their definitions: renewable, extract, hydroelectricity, irrigation, contaminated.

Literature — Read "Rich Gold Strike Made Below Douglas" in *The Citizen's Handbook*, page 139, and chapters "The Hard Winter," "Cold and Dark," and "The Wheat in the Wall" in *The Long Winter*.

Find Out! — What minerals are extracted in your state?

Picture This! — Draw pictures of five different natural resources God placed in your state.

Student Workbook or Lesson Review — If you are using one of these optional books, complete the assignment for Lesson 116.

Power to RUN AMERICA

Massachusetts
Assabet River

Portland, Oregon
*This restored steam-powered
locomotive is used to carry
passengers on holiday rides.*

In the earliest years of America, people used renewable energy sources. Native Americans burned wood in fires for their heating and cooking. They used the sun to dry clothes and meat. Europeans sailed to the New World on wind-powered ships. Once in America, colonists used wood for their fires and utilized the drying power of the sun. Candles and oil lamps provided artificial lighting. People and animals powered farm machinery. Textile mills and grain mills used flowing water for power. The Assabet River in Massachusetts, pictured at left, provided power for mills from the mid-1700s to the mid-1900s. When settlers moved to the Great Plains, they used windmills to power their water wells.

Changes in Energy Use

Sources of energy and ways that energy was used in the United States changed in the first half of the 1800s. The first successful steamboat began service in 1807. Its steam engine was powered by burning wood. Soon steam locomotives powered by wood began to pull railroad cars carrying people and goods. See photo at left. In the mid-1800s, kerosene, which is distilled from petroleum, became a common fuel for lights.

Around the middle of the 1800s, coal became a major source of energy for America. Many Americans used coal to heat their homes. As railroads were constructed in the Midwest, railroad companies had to find a new fuel for locomotives because wood was not as commonly available in that region as it had been in the East. They began using coal and found that it worked better than wood. Companies that made the iron and steel used to build locomotives and railroad tracks found that coal worked well for that industry. Large steamships used coal to produce the steam that

powered them around the world. American manufacturers used coal to run their factories. Because of these many uses of coal, coal mining became an important business in the United States. See memorial at right.

Trinidad, Colorado
Southern Colorado
Coal Miners Memorial

After Thomas Edison discovered and invented ways to use and produce electricity, coal helped make electricity available for many people. In 1882 Edison built the first coal-fired generating plant. It made electricity for New York City. In the 1880s and 1890s, Americans learned how to transmit electricity over long distances. For many years electricity was available almost nowhere except in cities. During the 1930s, the Federal government began a Rural Electrification program, which brought electricity to rural areas of the country.

America is greatly dependent on electricity, but we should remember that electricity for homes and businesses is actually produced by other fuels. The electricity that is used in homes, offices, and factories in America today comes from a number of sources: coal (45%), natural gas (23%), nuclear energy (20%), hydroelectric dams (7%), renewable sources such as solar power and geothermal energy (4%), and petroleum (1%).

Minneapolis, Minnesota
General Electric Company
Meter Readers, 1918

During the second half of the 1800s, Americans built more and more factories. These factories used machines. For the first time in American history, most work was done by machines instead of by people and animals. Therefore America had to produce more energy. The use of energy in the U.S. increased four times between 1880 and 1918. See meter readers at right.

As more and more people began driving automobiles, governments began to build more and better roads. With more automobiles and more roads on which to drive them, America needed more gasoline, which is made from petroleum (the words oil and petroleum are often used interchangeably).

By the years after World War II, Americans were using more petroleum than coal. We continued to find more uses for

Hershey, Pennsylvania
Electric Street Lights Shaped
Like Kisses, One Chocolate
and One Wrapped in Foil

Trans-Alaska Pipeline

petroleum. As our use of petroleum products grew, we began to import more and more petroleum from other countries. This trend has continued to today. However, as mentioned in Lesson 116, several U.S. states have oil as a natural resource. One of those states is Alaska. To transport oil from Alaska to the lower forty-eight states, the State of Alaska agreed to the construction of the Trans-Alaska Pipeline, pictured at left. The state has earned billions of dollars in profits from the oil business. It has even put billions in its Alaska Permanent Fund, a savings account for future generations of Alaskans.

Natural gas is an important source for heat in the U.S. In some communities, underground natural gas lines bring the fuel to homes and businesses, but many also use a form of natural gas that has been processed into a liquid fuel called propane. Propane companies transport propane to homes and businesses using tanker trucks. They put propane in tanks that the homes and businesses own or rent. Underground pipes carry the propane into the buildings' heating systems.

Trucking companies have found that diesel fuel made from petroleum works well for tractor-trailer trucks. Many railroad companies also use it for train locomotives. Some locomotives (especially city commuter trains) have been powered by electricity, either by batteries, electric lines, or electrified rails.

At one time, individual homeowners and business owners had to get the fuel they needed, usually wood or coal, on their own. A major change occurred when they began purchasing electricity and natural gas that was produced away from their home and when they began to purchase fuels to use for transportation.

Private Ownership and Government Regulation

Private companies produce and deliver most of the electricity, natural gas, and propane used by American citizens today. Since these private utility companies must spend a lot of money to build transmission lines for electricity and gas lines for natural gas, the companies often have a monopoly in a given location. Such a situation is called a natural monopoly, since it is most natural for one company to provide the service instead of many companies competing with each other. Imagine three or four electricity utilities stringing their own separate wires above the streets. However, in such monopoly situations the government makes rules about what the utility company does. Without the government providing regulation for the good of the entire community, the utility might charge high rates or serve only certain portions of a city. The goal of government regulation is to insure that utilities are safe, that they are provided at reasonable rates, and that all residents are treated the same.

In some parts of the country, public companies provide utility service. These include the Tennessee Valley Authority (TVA) and utility companies operated by cities. TVA was begun by the Federal government during the 1930s to provide electricity for rural regions of portions of the South that did not yet have electricity. TVA produces electricity and then sells it to local utility companies or city-owned utilities. Some rural areas have cooperative utilities. These are companies that are owned by the customers who receive the services that the company provides.

Being Good Stewards of Energy

Workers take a test as they seek jobs with TVA, Mid-20th Century.

The United States uses more energy than any other country in the world. Americans need to be good citizens in how they use energy and in how much energy they use. We must consider the impact on the environment in the U.S. and the world. Several issues are involved in using energy responsibly.

Affordable Energy. One goal is to keep energy costs at a level where the majority of people can obtain the energy they need at a price they can afford. When energy prices go up, people must make decisions about how much energy they can afford. For example, when the price of gasoline rises, they must decide how often they will drive their cars. When energy prices increase, the cost of goods and services we purchase increases because it is more expensive to make products and to transport them from where they are made to where a customer lives. Being able to obtain and use the oil, coal, and natural gas God has placed in America helps us keep energy affordable.

Dependence on Energy from Other Countries. When we purchase oil from other countries, we pay people in other countries for their oil instead of using oil that we could extract from within the U.S. When we do this, our money flows out of the country. Using foreign oil also means that we depend on those countries to have stable governments. We also depend on the oil producers in those countries to charge what we can afford. We cannot control these factors, so being dependent on foreign oil means that we are dependent on what other people and other countries do. What those others do is not always reliable.

Fuel Efficiency. For many years, Americans were not concerned about the amount of energy we used. Coal and petroleum were cheap and plentiful. For example, homes were not always well insulated and cars did not get many miles per gallon of gasoline. However, as the cost of fuel has increased and as we have become more dependent on foreign sources of fuel, we have become more aware of the need to use less energy. As a result, Americans have become more aware of the need to conserve energy. Cars, homes, and factories have become more energy efficient. Being a good citizen now includes being good stewards of our energy sources.

Environmental Pollution. For many years, Americans were not worried about what using energy did to the environment. In some places mining companies practiced strip mining. In this process, large machines stripped away the soil to get to the coal underneath. This resulted in large tracts of land that were destroyed and unusable. Companies that practiced strip mining were not good citizens in those areas. In addition, factories polluted streams, rivers, lakes, and the air. Cars spewed exhaust into the air. Congress eventually passed laws that made strip mining illegal and that limited the amount of pollution that factories and cars could produce. This made life more healthy for Americans.

Alternative Sources of Energy. Coal and petroleum are called fossils fuels because scientists believe that they formed from fossils underground. When they are taken from the earth and used for energy, they are not replenished. These fuels will become more and more scarce, which means that energy created by using them will become more and more expensive. Burning these fuels also creates pollution. Americans have been working to develop ways to use renewable sources of energy that cause less pollution. Alternative energy sources include:

★ Solar-powered and wind-powered electricity (which in a way returns to the original sources of energy used in America!).

★ Biomass energy generation that uses plants and other organic materials.

★ Geothermal energy that uses the heat found far below the earth's surface.

★ Nuclear energy which is produced by dividing atoms. Nuclear energy is available in almost limitless supply; but it can be very expensive, and there is always the possibility of an accident that would cause radiation to escape into the environment.

★ Rechargeable electric batteries to power cars. Auto manufacturers have begun making cars that use rechargeable electric batteries, sometimes in addition to gasoline and sometimes instead of gasoline. Energy must be used to make the batteries and to recharge the batteries, but it is generally believed that affordable and dependable battery-powered cars will make us depend less on foreign oil.

We need energy every day, but using it always has consequences. As the residents of Mackinac Island know (see 567), even using horses for work and transportation has an impact on the environment! The challenge facing the citizens of America today is to be able to have the energy we need at a price we can afford, without being dependent on unreliable sources, in a way that will preserve the environment. We also need to do all we can to be sure that future generations of American citizens will have the energy they need. As Christians we must also be careful that we use energy for godly purposes, whether we are using electricity for entertainment or gasoline to go somewhere.

In His parable about the ten virgins, Jesus used the need for energy to teach a lesson about being prepared.

Ashland City, Tennessee
Electric Car Charging Station

For when the foolish took their lamps,
they took no oil with them,
but the prudent took oil in flasks along with their lamps.
Matthew 25:3-4

Lesson Activities

Literature — Read "Change Your Life with Electricity" in *The Citizen's Handbook*, pages 140-143, and chapters "Not Really Hungry," "Free and Independent," and "Breathing Spell" in *The Long Winter*.

Creative Writing — Write an energy timeline of your day. What do you do every day that uses energy, such as using a water heater when you take a shower, reading by the light of a lamp, or using a computer? List at least ten different activities.

Find Out! — How is your home heated (natural gas, electricity, wood, or propane)?

Picture This! — Take a photograph or draw a picture of someone using energy in your home.

Student Workbook or Lesson Review — If you are using one of these optional books, complete the assignment for Lesson 117.

Roscoe WIND FARM

People have used the power of wind since ancient times. Perhaps the first use of wind power was by sailing ships. Wind provided the power for large ships for centuries, including those that brought the first European explorers and settlers to America. Around 1300 A.D., people in Europe began building windmills to pump water, to mill lumber, and to grind grains, spices, and ingredients like chalk which were used to make paint.

Pella, Iowa, home of the Tulip Time Festival, pictured on pages 586-587, has a working Dutch windmill. Locals claim that it is the tallest working Dutch-style windmill in the U.S. Pella

Pepin, Wisconsin
Windmill Near the Birthplace of Laura Ingalls Wilder

was founded by Dutch immigrants who left the Netherlands in 1847 to seek religious freedom in America.

Pella, Iowa
Vermeer Windmill

Most European countries switched from traditional windmills to steam power after 1800. However, windmills, like the one pictured on page 742, were important in the American West throughout the nineteenth century and into the twentieth century. They pumped water for farms and railroads and for the towns that grew up beside railroads.

Scientists have experimented with windmills which could be used to produce electricity since the late 1800s. Modern windmills that produce electricity are called wind turbines. The Central Vermont Public Service Corporation was the first electric company to receive power from a wind turbine when one began operating in Castleton, Vermont, in 1941. The National Aeronautics and Space Administration began research in wind energy in the 1970s. The world's first wind farm began operating in New Hampshire in 1980. Today there are thousands of wind farms around the world.

Central Illinois
Modern Wind Farm Set Among Corn and Soybean Fields

Wind Turbines of the Lake Benton 1 Wind Farm in Minnesota are in the background at left. In both photos are blades lying on the ground. Find author Charlene Notgrass to get an idea of the size of the blades.

West Texas

In West Texas, you can drive for miles and miles and see nothing but miles and miles—huge, flat, dry prairies where farmers plant mostly cotton and wheat. The wind blows almost constantly because there are no hills or trees to stop it. America's prairielands have a certain kind of beauty, especially their vast expanses of sky. But West Texas farm country is not the sort of place where many tourists go or the kind of place that attracts many new businesses for its sparse population.

One Man Had an Idea

The little town of Roscoe, Texas, population 1,300, lies fifty miles west of Abilene and two hundred miles west of Fort Worth. In the early years of the twenty-first century, Cliff Etheredge was a cotton farmer in his sixties. Mr. Etheredge has only one arm; he lost the other one in a farming accident involving a cotton harvester. Cliff saw his town of Roscoe dying as children grew up and moved away and businesses closed their doors. Then he had an idea.

Cliff heard about giant wind-powered turbines that generate electricity. He saw some going up not far from Roscoe. He began to think about the possibility of some being located near his hometown. Cliff did some research, formed a company, and began making calls and writing letters. He looked for companies that would be willing to invest the money to build a wind farm in the Roscoe area. In 2007 Cliff's dreams came true. Financial companies decided to invest the money needed for the wind farm and another company was willing to build the turbines. The Roscoe Wind Farm was born.

The entire Wind Farm now has 627 turbines spread over 100,000 acres of land, an area almost seven times the size of Manhattan Island in New York City. The turbines range between 350 to 415 feet tall and stand about 900 feet apart. Each blade on a turbine is about 120-150 feet long. In 2010 Roscoe Wind Farm was the largest land-based wind farm in the world. It generated enough electricity to provide power for more than 250,000 homes.

Impact on the Community

The Roscoe Wind Farm is a community endeavor. About four hundred landowners in four counties rent land to the company that runs the system. The landowners also get payments called royalties for the energy that the turbines on their property generate.

Many permanent jobs have been created by the project, but the building of the turbines produced much more economic activity than that. The total amount invested in building the project was about one billion dollars. Construction companies, companies that make the turbines, trucking companies, and other related businesses all benefited from the project. Engineers and meteorologists determined the best way to position the turbines to get the maximum benefit from the wind. Local businesses grew or were created to serve the workers. New residents moved to Roscoe. This increased the home construction business there. The company operating the turbines pays taxes to the local governments; and this helps pay for schools, roads, and other government services.

Government policies encouraged the development of the Roscoe Wind Farm and other similar projects. Several years before it was built, the Texas state government passed a law requiring power companies that operate in the state to start using renewable energy as part of the way they supply electricity to customers. In addition, the Federal government gives tax credits to companies that invest in wind power. These government policies have helped Texas, perhaps best known for producing oil and natural gas, to become the leading state in the nation for producing wind power.

Roscoe, Texas
Old Meets New

The Wind Council and the Wind Festival

The Roscoe Wind Council is a non-profit organization which was created to promote wind energy and "civic and educational improvement in Roscoe, Texas, and other rural communities in West Texas." The Council sponsors the West Texas Wind Festival in Roscoe every year in mid-October. The festival features food and craft vendors, a barbecue cook-off, entertainment and fireworks, and helicopter rides above the wind farm. Measurements have indicated that the wind blows at an almost constant seventeen miles per hour in Roscoe. Before the wind farm was built, wind was generally seen as a problem. The wind dried up the land and killed the crops. Now the people of Roscoe see the wind as a blessing. Income from the wind farm is more constant than income from farming. The people there still grow cotton and wheat; after all, they still have all that land between the towering turbines.

The Roscoe Wind Farm is an example of how people can work together to benefit a community. Local businesses; investment and energy companies that are involved in several countries; workers; landowners; and government on the local, state, and national levels have all contributed to making the project a success. Wind energy helps the United States use less fuel that harms the environment when it is burned. It helps our country be less dependent on oil that comes from other countries. And the town that was dying has come back to life.

All because one person decided to make a difference in his community by using the wind provided by God.

He caused the east wind to blow in the heavens
And by His power he directed the south wind.

Psalm 78:26

Lesson Activities

Vocabulary — In your notebook, write which of the following words belongs in each sentence: expanse, invest, endeavor, meteorologist, vendor.

1. I suppose painting the barn by myself is an unrealistic _____.
2. Dad is going to _____ in my uncle's new restaurant.
3. The _____ at our local TV station came and spoke at our co-op about the weather.
4. The stage seemed like a vast _____ when I had to walk across it to get my diploma.
5. Kelly bought a hot dog and soda from a _____ standing on the corner.

Literature — Read chapters "For Daily Bread," "Four Days' Blizzard," "The Last Mile," and "It Can't Beat Us" in *The Long Winter*.

Creative Writing — Write a poem of at least ten lines about the wind.

Picture This! — Draw a picture that involves the wind.

Student Workbook or Lesson Review — If you are using one of these optional books, complete the assignment for Lesson 118.

Government and AGRICULTURE

America depends on what our farmers raise. In the early years of our nation, almost all families grew their own food and some grew cotton and flax for clothing. Many raised animals to provide meat, milk, eggs, and wool for their families. As more people began to work in specialized jobs such as in factories, they began buying these necessities in stores. With improved farming methods American farmers became able to provide enough for more people than just their own families. Now very few families grow all of their own food, and almost all Americas are dependent to some degree on what American farmers produce.

All business owners must be brave and take risks, but this is especially true for farmers. They must spend a great deal of time and money before their work produces anything to sell to others. Prices for farm products can vary greatly from one year to another. Farmers have no control over the weather. Their crops can be seriously affected by floods, droughts, and unusually hot or cold temperatures. Sometimes farmers in other countries send their products to the

Montana
Wheat Field

Acton, Massachusetts
Farmers' Market

West Tennessee
Cotton Bales

Maryland
Dairy Farm

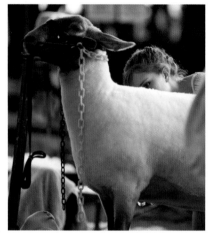

New Hampshire
4-H Sheep Grooming Competition

Bells, Tennessee
Pictsweet Frozen Vegetable Company
Family-Owned and -Run for Four
Generations

Oklahoma
Irrigation

United States to compete with what is grown here. One irony about farming is that if farmers do a good job and produce abundant crops, the supply of food can be so great that prices fall and farmers' income goes down.

Before the Great Depression of the 1930s, the United States government was not directly involved in American agriculture. During the 1920s, American farmers began to suffer from falling food prices and harsh weather conditions. The Depression only made matters worse. The New Deal under President Franklin D. Roosevelt set up assistance programs to help farmers. Government assistance for farmers continues today.

Helping Farmers Get Good Prices

One goal of the government's farm policies is to make sure that plenty of food is available to the American people at a reasonable cost. Low food prices help food buyers but hurt farmers. High food prices help farmers but hurt food buyers. The Federal government tries to keep food prices at a fair level to help both farmers and consumers.

The Federal government has tried many different programs to help farmers get good prices for their crops. One way is called *price supports*. The government establishes what experts believe is a fair price for farm products. This fair price is called *parity*. When prices for farm products fall below parity, the Federal government pays farmers the difference. For instance, if the parity price for a bushel of wheat is $2.00 but wheat is only selling for $1.75 per bushel, the government pays wheat farmers twenty-five cents for every bushel of wheat they sell.

The Federal government has helped farmers by buying and storing *surplus* farm products. It does this when farmers produce so much that prices naturally go down. Purchasing surpluses limits the food on the market that is available for American citizens to buy, making prices go up. Sometimes surpluses are made available for consumers to buy later and sometimes they are used in government assistance programs.

The *acreage set-aside* program is another Federal agriculture program. Farmers do not always know how much of a crop they should grow. If they plant a smaller amount, hoping that increased demand will cause prices to go up, they might not make much money. However, if they plant a larger amount, the greater supply available might cause prices to go down. Again the farmer's income goes down. In the set-aside program, the government puts a limit on how many acres of a certain crop a farmer can plant. Land that the farmer owns that he could use is set aside and not used to grow the crop. The government pays the farmer a certain amount for not growing the crop on that land, so that his income can remain at a reasonable figure. Set-aside programs make farmers able to have a good income without having to go through the work of planting and harvesting the land and then receiving a parity price support. It also limits the amount of pesticides used to kill insects that infest crops, and this helps the environment.

Saunderstown, Rhode Island
Coastal Growers' Market

The Federal government also uses *subsidies* to help farmers. A subsidy is a payment to a farmer for a particular crop. For instance, ethanol made from corn is often blended with gasoline to make fuel. The Federal government supports the use of this fuel because of two beliefs: that ethanol causes less

Rhode Island Red Chicken

air pollution than regular gasoline and that by using ethanol America will be less dependent on buying oil from other countries. However, ethanol is expensive to produce. To keep the price of ethanol down and to encourage people to use it, fuel companies pay corn farmers only a portion of the price of corn and the government pays the farmers an additional amount or a subsidy.

Some people who would like to see less government involvement in our everyday lives believe that these programs make farmers too dependent on government assistance. They also think that government involvement causes food prices to be higher. Usually, government involvement in an area of the economy causes prices for those products or services to rise.

Citizens have different ideas about how to help family farms stay in business. Many Americans want to help farmers against risks such as low prices and crop failure caused by weather. However, most agriculture in the United States today does not take place on

Arkansas Agriculture

Stuttgart, Arkansas
Rice and Duck Capitol of the World

Peanut Harvest

Sorghum

Grading Eggs

traditional family farms but on farms owned by corporations. Government farm assistance programs help family farmers, but they also help large farming corporations.

Purchasing Food

Some government programs help farmers in other ways. For instance, the Supplemental Nutrition Assistance Program (SNAP) provides money for people with low income to buy groceries. This program does not pay money directly to farmers, but it helps people buy food they might not otherwise be able to afford. This creates a bigger market for the food that American farmers grow.

Another indirect help comes in the form of school breakfast and lunch programs. The government provides meals free or almost free for children from low-income families. This program buys groceries that might not otherwise be bought and provides meals to children who often come to school hungry because their family cannot afford to buy as much food as they would like.

A third government program that offers food is the commodities program that helps low-income families. The government purchases surplus supplies of food and then makes the food available to families who meet certain requirements.

Protecting the Food Supply

The government has several programs that are designed to make sure that our food supply is safe. Government meat and poultry inspectors check meat processing plants to make sure the food is safe and the plants are clean. These requirements cause a small increase in the price of food since farmers and food processing companies must be more careful, but the regulations also help the food we eat to be safe. A food processing company is one that takes food that farmers grow and turns it into a convenient food product such as a box of macaroni or a bag of frozen green beans.

The Federal government has regulations about the kind and amount of herbicides (weed killers) and pesticides (bug killers) that farmers use. A certain pesticide, for instance, might do a great job of getting rid of insects; but it might also harm the environment and cause the food treated with it to be unhealthy. The Federal government also has regulations about how much and what kind of chemicals are added to processed foods.

Helping in Other Ways

Many other programs have encouraged farming and helped farmers. For instance, the Homestead Act of 1862 made it possible for thousands of families to purchase land inexpensively and to grow crops on it. Roads, canals, and railroads that the government has built or encouraged to be built have helped farmers get their products to market. Programs that made electrical service available to rural areas made life easier for farm families.

Government trade policies with other nations are also designed to help American farmers. The ultimate goal of American trade policy is free trade around the world, but this is not easy to accomplish. The governments of many other countries give their farmers large subsidies. This means that food from those countries can be brought to the United States and sold for lower prices than prices for the same food grown in America. American trade policies try to protect American farmers from

Colorado
Cattle Ranch with Rockies in Distance

Flat Rock, North Carolina
A portion of Mrs. Carl Sandburg's goat dairy is now part of the Carl Sandburg Home National Historic Site.

competition from cheap foreign food. At the same time, other countries might charge tariffs or taxes on food that American farmers export. The Federal government works to keep foreign tariffs and subsidies low. It also tries to keep out foreign foods that are contaminated by chemicals, bacteria, or other unhealthy substances.

Several Presidents have been involved in agriculture. Presidents Washington, John Adams, Jefferson, Jackson, and Pierce were gentlemen farmers. President Truman worked on his father's farm in Missouri. President Carter operated his father's peanut farm in Georgia after his father died. President Theodore Roosevelt owned ranches in the Dakota Territory. President Hoover managed the U.S. food supply during World War I so that enough food would be available for American soldiers.

Pennsylvania
Corn

Government involvement in agriculture is intended to help American farmers continue to be able to produce an abundance of food to feed our own citizens as well as many people in other countries. No government programs, however, can remove the need for farm workers to go into the fields to sow, water, and reap. Jesus spoke of a plentiful harvest that occurs when the seed of His Word is planted in the good soil of hearts that are open to receiving it.

And the one on whom seed was sown on the good soil,

this is the man who hears the word and understands it;

who indeed bears fruit and brings forth,

some a hundredfold, some sixty, and some thirty.

Matthew 13:23

Lesson Activities

Thinking Biblically — Read the Parable of the Sower in Matthew 13:1-9 and 18-23.

Vocabulary — In your notebook, write a paragraph that uses all of these words: specialized, dependent, parity, acreage, pesticide. Consult a dictionary if you need help with their definitions.

Literature — Read "When the Cows Come Home" in *The Citizen's Handbook*, page 144, and chapters "Waiting for the Train," "The Christmas Barrel," and "Christmas in May" in *The Long Winter*.

Find Out! — What agricultural products are produced in your area?

Picture This! — Take a photograph or draw a picture of an American farm.

Student Workbook or Lesson Review — If you are using one of these optional books, complete the assignment for Lesson 119.

★ Remember to choose an American Holiday to study this week! ★

UNIT 25 – TECHNOLOGY & COMMUNICATION

BOOKS USED IN UNIT 25

- The Citizen's Handbook
- The Wright Brothers: How They Invented the Airplane
- Student Workbook (optional)
- Lesson Review (optional)

New York Public Library, New York City

American TECHNOLOGY

America is a world leader in science and technology. Science is the study of *how* and *why* things happen. Technology uses the knowledge learned in science to make things happen. Americans like to make things happen.

On this page and the next is a timeline of many American inventions. Because America is free, inventors can turn those inventions into businesses that manufacture and sell to thousands or millions of people. Scottish immigrant Alexander Graham Bell did just that with the telephone, as did Orville and Wilbur Wright with the airplane, Bill Gates with computer software, and the list goes on.

Timeline of American Inventors and Technology

Philadelphia, Pennsylvania
Fairmount Water Works

Harrisburg, Pennsylvania
Telegraph Device in State Capitol

1752 – *Among Benjamin Franklin's many inventions was the lightning rod.*

1776 – *David Bushnell of Connecticut invented the first practical submarine, calling it the Turtle.*

1794 – *Eli Whitney of Connecticut patented a cotton gin, which made producing cotton much faster.*

1801 – *The Fairmount Water Works began using steam power to provide Philadelphia city water.*

1807 – *Robert Fulton's steamboat the* **Clermont** *traveled from New York to Albany at five miles per hour.*

1814 – *John Jethro Woods of Poplar Ridge, New York, created a cast-iron plow tip that improved farming.*

1831 – *Cyrus McCormick invented the McCormick reaper. By 1871 his company sold 10,000 per year.*

1836 – *Samuel Colt developed the Colt revolver when he was twenty-two.*

1844 – *Samuel F. B. Morse demonstrated the telegraph in the U.S. Capitol with the words, "What hath God wrought." His telegraph method made it possible to communicate quickly over long distances.*

1850 – *Isaac Singer improved Elias Howe's sewing machine. By 1880 yearly worldwide sales reached 500,000.*

1853 – *Elisha Otis of Vermont demonstrated his safety elevator at the Crystal Palace Exposition in New York.*

1859 – *Edwin Drake struck oil by drilling 69.5 feet into the ground at Titusville, Pennsylvania, beginning an oil boom.*

1863 – *James Plimpton of Massachusetts invented the first practical roller skates with four wheels.*

1876 – *Alexander Graham Bell made the first telephone call to his assistant Thomas Watson. Two years later a telephone was installed in the White House. In 1882 the Scottish-born inventor became a U.S. citizen.*

1877 – *Thomas Edison invented a machine that recorded the human voice.*

1879 – *Thomas Edison perfected the incandescent light bulb.*

1891 – *Thomas Edison and William Dickson perfected an early type of movie projector called a kinetoscope.*

1893 – *Whitcomb L. Judston introduced his clasp-locker at the World's Columbian Exposition in Chicago. It was later renamed the zipper.*

1902 – *Willis H. Carrier invented air conditioning. He later began the Carrier Corporation.*

Fort Myers, Florida
Thomas Edison's Laboratory at His Summer Home

1903 – *Orville and Wilbur Wright fly the "Flyer I" at Kitty Hawk, North Carolina.*

1908 – *Henry Ford introduced the Model T automobile.*

1920 – *The first regular radio broadcast began at KDKA in Pittsburgh, Pennsylvania, when the station announced the results of the 1920 presidential election.*

1927 – *Philo Farnsworth demonstrated the first television. The first television image was a dollar sign.*

1937 – *Engineers from the Union Pacific Railroad built the first ski lift. It was used at Sun Valley, Idaho.*

1948 – *Leo Fender began to sell electric guitars.*

1951 – *The U.S. Census Bureau purchased the first commercial computer, called the UNIVAC 1, from the Eckert and Mauchly Computer Co. of Philadelphia.*

1960 – *Theodore H. Maiman created the first laser.*

1962 – *On July 23, the Telstar satellite, invented by AT&T and launched by the National Aeronautics and Space Administration (NASA), beamed the first live video images from America to Europe and from Europe to America.*

1965 – *The Digital Equipment Company introduced the first computer with integrated circuit technology.*

1969 – *American astronaut Neil Armstrong became the first human to walk on the moon.*

1970 – *Corning Glass created an effective optical fiber which used light to send information.*

1973 – *Dr. Martin Cooper and his team at Motorola invented the first portable mobile phone.*

1974 – *American stores began to use barcodes. Checkout stands use laser technology to read them.*

1975 – *High school friends Bill Gates and Paul Allen formed Microsoft, which produces computer software.*

1976 – *Steve Jobs, Steve Wozniak, and Ronald Wayne began to sell Apple computer kits.*

1977 – *Two thousand customers in Chicago began testing cell phones. These phones came to be called cell phones because geographic areas are divided into "cells." Each cell has its own cell phone tower. A cell phone works by transmitting radio waves to the nearest tower.*

1981 – *NASA launched and landed the first Space Shuttle.*

1983 – *Each year* Time Magazine *names someone the "man of the year." In 1983 the magazine named the personal computer "machine of the year" instead.*

1996 – *Stanford University grad students Larry Page and Sergey Brin began working on an Internet search engine. The following year they named it Google.*

2001 – *Apple Inc. released the iPod.*

2007 – *Apple Inc. released the iPhone.*

The State of Utah donated this statue of Philo Farnsworth to U.S. Capitol's Statuary Hall.

Created in the Image of God

The Christian worldview encourages the development of technology. Christianity recognizes that God created human beings in His image (Genesis 1:26). God created people with minds that can think, investigate, research, learn, and compile information. We have technology because we have minds. You will not see or hear about rat technology or mosquito technology because those creatures do not have the minds necessary to develop it. Christians believe that God commanded humans to "fill the earth, and subdue it" (Genesis 1:28). Obeying this command involves a belief that the world makes sense, that we can understand it, and that we can use it. We must be good stewards of the physical world that God placed in our care. We can use it to live well and to bless others. Christianity honors work (Colossians 3:23). Christians are willing to work to honor God, to provide for ourselves, and to help others. We believe that what we do can make a difference in the world, so we work for that purpose.

Free to Work and Create

The freedom that we enjoy in America enables people to pursue their interests with energy and enthusiasm. If someone has an idea for an invention or a business, he or she can work to fulfill that dream without the need to get approval from a government official. The United States has always valued education. A good education trains the minds that produce technological advances.

Our country has abundant natural resources and a large workforce, but these alone do not guarantee the development of technology. Americans have always believed that it is important to be productive. Productivity involves to what degree workers are able to use abilities and resources to produce goods and services.

Because we have freedom of speech, we can communicate freely. When we learn history, we learn what past Americans have communicated about what they did. Having this knowledge helps us build on what past generations have learned. New technology builds on the technology produced in the past.

Government and Technology

Government plays a role in encouraging technology. America has benefited from a stable government. Stability helps people develop new ideas and inventions. It is hard to do research and invent new products when people live in constant fear of war, revolution, government corruption, and economic uncertainty. American government has also provided copyright and patent protection to people who develop new products. See patent office on page 757. When a book is copyrighted, others can not legally copy it. When an invention is patented, others cannot legally make something exactly like it. A lack of copyrights and patents would discourage people from inventing because an inventor would not be able to receive the profit he deserved from manufacturing and selling what he has produced from his own creativity. The most important way that our government encourages the development of technology is by staying out of the way of individuals and private businesses and protecting their freedoms.

Washington, D.C.
Stored Patents and Patent Office Employees, 1940

Technology for All

The way that technology has the greatest impact is when individuals use it to serve the greatest number of people. A person can make a profit by developing technology to produce better yachts and limousines for the wealthy. However, more Americans have made more income and have helped to raise the standard of living for a greater part of the American public by developing technology that helps many people. For instance, when the telephone and the automobile were first invented, they were seen as merely playthings for the wealthy. It was when Americans figured out a way to make these products available at a reasonable cost that millions were helped by them, and American life was improved overall. Jobs were created, too, which helped even more people and the American economy as a whole.

Communication Technology

Communication is sharing ideas and information. Communication technology helps us to share information. It also helps us share ideas faster and with more people. American technology has created or improved many means of communication (various types of communication are often called media). Samuel F. B. Morse developed a successful telegraph that transmitted information quickly over long

Message from President Lincoln which was telegraphed to General Grant

distances. At right is a message President Lincoln wrote, which was sent by telegraph to General Ulysses S. Grant during the Civil War. It reads: "I have seen your dispatch expressing your unwillingness to break your hold where you are. Neither am I willing. Hold on with a bulldog grip, and chew and chop, as much as possible." Alexander Graham Bell invented the telephone, which made it possible to use electricity to send speech. Thomas Edison invented the phonograph, which gave people a way to record and preserve sounds, including voices and music. Americans developed the first commercially successful typewriter, allowing people to communicate their ideas faster. The first author to have a manuscript typed was American Samuel Clemens, known better by his pen name Mark Twain. Italian Guglielmo Marconi invented the radio; but the radio had its greatest early success in the United States. Television was successful in the United States first as well.

North Pole, Alaska
The letters of the KJNP FM Radio Station stand for King Jesus North Pole.

American company AT&T created the first communication satellite that made it possible for people to send television video around the world. American computer and Internet technology have enabled people to send and receive enormous amounts of information quickly in almost all parts of the globe. Cell phones have helped people to stay in touch and have helped many people who were experiencing an emergency.

Technology and Civics

Technology impacts civic life. For example, technology helps Americans learn about candidates and elections. Inventors have used it to create voting machines. Technology allows Americans to file their income tax returns electronically. Technology allows first responders to help citizens faster. Television technology makes possible C-SPAN, the cable and satellite television service that broadcasts meetings of Congress. Through C-SPAN almost every American can see more of what actually goes on in Washington. Commercial radio and television stations also use technology to keep Americans informed about their government. See photo at right. The Internet allows information about city, county, and state governments to be widely available so

Washington, D.C.
Television cameras are ready to film news at the U.S. Supreme Court.

that we know what services are offered and what office we should contact if we have a particular need.

Technology and the Christian

Technology, especially communication technology, puts people in contact with new ideas. Some of those ideas are good and some are evil. Wise Christians are diligent to protect their own hearts and minds and those of their children by being careful what technology brings into their lives and minds.

St. Thomas, U.S. Virgin Islands
Using a Library Computer

Technology has given Christians the opportunity to share the good news of Jesus with more and more people around the world. Christians have produced television programs, radio programs, and websites that teach about Jesus. Christian missionaries do not have to feel as lonely and isolated as they once did because they can keep up with their loved ones with cell phones and video chatting over the Internet.

. . . faith comes from hearing, and hearing by the word of Christ.

Romans 10:17

Lesson Activities

Thinking Biblically — In your notebook, make a list of ten ways people have used technology to share the message of the gospel.

Literature — Read "Aim for the Stars" in *The Citizen's Handbook* pages 145-147.

Find Out! — Ask your parents when they got their first computer.

Picture This! — Take a photograph or draw a picture of three kinds of technology your family uses regularly.

Student Workbook or Lesson Review — If you are using one of these optional books, complete the assignment for Lesson 121.

From Tin Cans to SMART PHONES

Duluth, Minnesota
Lighthouse on Lake Superior

NEWSPAPER CORRESPONDENTS

NEWSPAPERS

Harrisburg, Pennsylvania
Office for Newspaper Reporters and a Slot in an Office Door for Newspaper Deliveries at the State Capitol

God created people with the ability to communicate. We have eyes to see and ears to hear, the ability to speak and write, and a mind that can process information and consider ideas. We can communicate with each other through speech, written words and symbols, a touch of the hand, an expression on one's face, and what we call body language. The importance of communication is shown by the fact that, when God wanted to communicate His love for us, He sent His message in the form of His Son, whom John 1:1 calls the Word.

Communication is essential in civics. Monuments and memorials communicate respect for the people and events of the past. Signs communicate laws and instructions that help our civic life run smoothly. First responders turn on sirens to communicate that drivers should move their vehicles out of the way. Lighthouses, like the one pictured at left above, flash lights and sound horns to signal information to ships. Political candidates communicate their beliefs and goals to voters. Government officials make public announcements in both print and online editions of newspapers.

The story of the invention and development of the telephone is an example of technology. This story weaves together our desire to communicate, the use of technology, and the impact of communication technology on our personal lives and on our civic life.

The Waves That God Made

What is a telephone? Perhaps the simplest kind is just two tin cans or paper cups and a piece of string. This telephone works because sound travels in waves. This is how it works:

★ Bob and Jane's parents punch a hole in the bottoms of two tin cans. The children connect the cans by placing a long piece of string through the holes.

★ Each child takes one can and they walk several feet away from one another.

★ Jane puts her can to her mouth while Bob puts his can to his ear.

★ When Jane speaks, the sound vibrates her can, which vibrates the string, which vibrates Bob's can. Bob hears Jane's voice.

God created many kinds of waves. Light rays, radio waves, X-rays, and other rays are part of the electromagnetic spectrum. God also created sound waves, which are not a part of the spectrum. Inventors have used both sound waves and waves of the electromagnetic spectrum to create telephones.

On and Off

"Yes" or "no" is the simplest form of communication. The simplest form of electronic communication is also yes or no. An electrical circuit is either complete or incomplete, on or off, connected or disconnected. This binary (two-way) system is a simple form of technology. It is how electronic communication began, and it is still used today.

When Samuel F. B. Morse perfected the electromagnetic telegraph in 1838, it used the on-or-off pattern of electrical impulses to send signals across a wire. Morse developed a code of signals for the alphabet that enabled messages to be sent by telegraph wires over long distances.

From the Telegraph to AT&T

A generation later, Alexander Graham Bell was a teacher of people who were deaf. He followed in the footsteps of his father and grandfather who had developed a system of symbols that gave deaf persons a way to communicate with others. Bell experimented with sound and speech and became interested in transmitting speech with electricity in a way similar to the signals sent by a telegraph. Telegraphs could only send one message at a time. Bell thought that different signals could be sent at the same time, just as people hear different notes at the same time when they listen to music. While researching ways to do this, he learned how to send the sound of a human voice through a wire. When Bell spoke through an experimental device to his assistant Thomas Watson on March 10, 1876, the telephone was born.

Alexander Graham Bell received a U.S. patent for his invention that year. Bell was able to communicate the news of his invention to people from many countries when he demonstrated it at the Centennial Exposition in Philadelphia later that year. In 1877 he formed the Bell Telephone Company with Thomas Watson serving as its manager. Pictured at right are some of Bell's first inventions, which he personally donated to the Smithsonian Institution. By the end of 1880, over 47,000 telephones were in use. Word got around! Bell's original company eventually became the American Telephone & Telegraph Company (AT&T).

Alexander Graham Bell's daughters and great-grandson, also named Alexander Graham Bell, along with scientists, examine Bell's donations to the Smithsonian, 1937.

Operators and Exchanges

For almost one hundred years, AT&T leased telephones to their customers. At first, they were leased to customers in pairs. A businessman, for instance, might have one telephone in his office and another in his home. Calls could only be made between those two telephones.

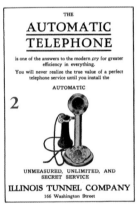

Rotary Dial Desk Telephone, 1920s

Desk Telephone, c. 1905

In 1878 the first public telephone exchange was established in New Haven, Connecticut. A customer would signal his desire to place a call by picking up his ear piece. See phones 1 and 3 at right. An operator at the exchange would respond and connect the caller to the telephone he wanted to reach. The exchange could handle sixty-four customers; but only two conversations could take place at the same time.

Wall Telephone, 1920s

Almon Strowger, an undertaker in Kansas City, Missouri, invented an automatic switchboard in 1889. The telephones in this system had a button on them that the caller could push to produce a series of pulses that signaled what telephone he wanted to reach. A system of switches (again using the on-

Princess Telephone with Rotary Dial, c. 1961

and-off principle) connected the caller to that telephone.

As telephone use began to spread across the country, AT&T set up telephone poles along the nation's highways and streets and strung telephone wire on them. AT&T hired telephone operators to operate switchboards. See U.S. Capitol switchboard operators at right.

Miss Harriot Daley, Chief Switchboard Operator for the U.S. Capitol standing with other operators in 1937. Miss Daley was appointed in 1898.

Rotary Dials and Touch Tone

In 1896 Almon Strowger and his associates developed a telephone with a rotary dial. See photos 2 and 4. Customers could turn the circular dial to a series of numbers to reach a telephone that had been assigned that "telephone number." After the invention of the rotary dial telephone, the human telephone operator was only needed to connect calls to other exchanges (these calls were called long-distance calls) and to look up telephone numbers when a telephone user did not know the telephone number of someone he wished to call. Telephone systems also began to use a dial tone that customers heard when they picked up the receiver. This tone let customers know that they could place a call.

Photos 5 and 6 illustrate phone numbers, the dial tone, and an exchange, in this case, the "Windsor" exchange. Notice that W and I are capitalized. The numbers 2 through 9 on a phone dial had letters printed above them. When someone called the phone number in illustration 5, they dialed W which stood for 9, I which stood for 4, and then the numbers 0-2577.

Bell Labs, the research division of the Bell Telephone System, developed a touch-tone system of placing calls in 1941. This telephone used push buttons that sent tones to an automatic switching system which connected the call. Touch-tone service was offered to the public beginning in 1963 for an extra fee, but most people continued to use rotary dial telephones until the 1980s. Phone number 7 is a 1993 version.

Color Photos on Pages 762-763 by Mark Mathosian

These phone cards could be placed in the center of the rotary dial. The lower card is an advertisement for the Triangle Cab Co. Notice the emergency numbers.

Touch Tone Princess Phone, 1993

763

Cordless Phones and Cell Phones

Scientists developed radio technology during the twentieth century, and radio and telephone technology sometimes merged. During the 1930s, a person on land could make a radio-telephone call to a ship at sea for seven dollars per minute. In the 1960s, cordless telephones were developed that used radio signals sent between a handset and a telephone base, which was connected to the wired telephone system. These became available to the public in the 1980s.

A major advance occurred when communication companies began to transmit sound digitally. Sounds could be converted to digital signals, which were basically on-or-off electronic pulses that could be sent or stored. This allowed for greatly improved cordless telephone sound quality, but it also created the possibility of another kind of telephone signal.

The first mobile phones were used in cars, especially police cars. In 1947 Bell Lab scientists proposed a system of phones capable of broadcasting digital signals to towers that would each cover a certain area called a cell. The towers could transmit signals to other towers, so that the call could go as far as the tower network extended. A plan for such a system was developed in the 1970s. Motorola developed the first handheld mobile phone in 1973. It weighed 2 1/2 pounds, was nine inches long, and could be used for thirty minutes after charging for ten hours. Continued development of cell phone technology resulted in much smaller and much more powerful phones.

Communications antennae have been placed on a silo in Burlington, Vermont, a fire tower in Moriah, New York, a water tower in South Burlington, Vermont, and a church steeple in Bloomsburg, Pennsylvania.

Phones, Data, and the Internet

The fact that voice signals could be converted to digital form meant that other kinds of data could be transmitted in digital form also. Alexander Graham Bell's invention was designed to carry the sound of the human voice, but today people also use their phones for sending written information. One way is by text messaging. The first person-to-person text message was sent in 1993.

The network of computer networks called the Internet uses telephone lines, fiber optic cables, and satellites to send digital information signals between computers around the world.

The line between telephone companies and Internet provider companies has blurred. Now telephone companies offer Internet service, Internet providers offer telephone service, and Voice over Internet Protocol (VoIP) phones use the Internet for making calls.

International Business Machines (IBM) invented a personal communicator called Simon in 1992. It was a combination cell phone, pager, fax machine, calculator, calendar, clock, and computer. Since it cost $899, few people could buy it. However, companies continued to work on smart phone technology that would be affordable. In 2007 the Apple computer company introduced the iPhone. In addition to making calls, the iPhone allowed users to access the Internet for e-mail, web browsing, and other applications. Today the iPhone and other smartphones are often used as much for receiving data from the Internet as for receiving calls.

The Break-Up of AT&T

Though a few businessmen formed small telephone companies, especially in rural areas, AT&T had very little competition during its first century. Late in the twentieth century, the Federal Communications Commission (FCC) and Federal courts forced AT&T to break apart into smaller regional companies.

Chesapeake and Potomac Telephone Company "Telephone Girls," 1914

Telephones and Civics

Telephones play an important role in the civic life of a community. We expect government workers on the local, state, and national levels to have telephones in their offices; and citizens expect to be able to contact them by phone. A quick way to get an answer or to register a complaint is to call the government office responsible for the matter. Sometimes the offices of elected representatives get flooded with calls about a piece of proposed legislation, and these calls can make a difference. A quick round of calls can turn out a large group at a city council meeting. Some political candidates pay for automated calls shortly before Election Day that

Nashville, Tennessee
AT&T Building with Ryman Auditorium Roof

play a recorded message urging voters to support them. Many people debate whether these "robocalls" are effective or simply annoying. The placement of cell towers in a way that does not detract from area scenery or interfere with community life is a continuing issue. Some churches have agreed to let cell towers be placed in their steeples or bell towers.

The most famous government telephone was the "hotline" that was installed between the White House and the Kremlin, the headquarters of the Russian government in Moscow, during the Cold War period of tension between the U.S. and the Communist Soviet Union. In 1962 the two governments had a tense showdown over Soviet missiles being put in Cuba. Communication between Washington and Moscow was difficult and slow. The next year, the two governments established a special line that made communication quicker in the event of an emergency. The first hotline was actually not a telephone but was a teletype machine. The machine sent typed messages that could be translated for the receiving officials. The hotline was often portrayed as a red telephone in the President's Oval Office. A telephone line using a red phone was installed in 1971. The President and the Soviet leader did contact each other a few times on the hotline, often about events in the Middle East. Satellite communication lines were added in later years.

President Dwight Eisenhower was an intelligent person and an able leader, but during his military career and as President he did not have to place telephone calls himself. Whenever he wanted to call someone, he simply picked up a phone and a switchboard operator completed the call for him. When Eisenhower retired from the presidency in 1961 and moved to his home in Gettysburg, Pennsylvania, he did not know how to use a rotary phone and didn't know what a dial tone was. A Secret Service agent instructed the former President and five-star general on how to use the device. Eisenhower spent the next hour happily calling friends and experiencing the delight of making telephone calls.

Telephone Etiquette

The development and use of telephones created new rules of polite society. One early issue involved what to say when you answered a call. Alexander Graham Bell suggested that a person receiving a call say, "Ahoy!" as a ship would say to another approaching ship. Thomas Edison, who also developed telephone technology, suggested the more simple "Hello?" For many years wealthy people and people in positions of power did not make or answer calls themselves. These were jobs for servants or office staff to do. The master or executive got on the phone only after the connection was established.

In the days when telephones were relatively rare and not used often, local phone systems offered party lines to subscribers. The advantage was that the cost to be on a party line was less than having a private line. A party line allowed up to eight homes to use the same line, and each home had a telephone and a distinctive ring pattern to indicate when the call was for them. The local operator would send the call to the desired party, and all parties on the line would know for whom the call was intended by the distinctive ring. It was possible for people in the other homes on the party line to pick up their receivers and listen to the call, but it was considered impolite to do so.

Today people commonly make and receive calls and texts on their cell phones in group settings that are often disrupted by the activity. It is not uncommon to see two or more people at a table in a restaurant not talking to each other, but instead talking to or texting people who are not present. As with every new stage in the history of the telephone, new capabilities mean that people have to make decisions about how they will use them.

The fact that telephones are everywhere has changed how life in our communities is lived. Even though the telephone was invented many years ago, two things are still basic: the binary, on-off nature of digital signals, and the need for people to communicate with each other.

When there are many words,

transgression is unavoidable,

But he who restrains his lips is wise.

Proverbs 10:19

Dallas/Fort Worth International Airport

Lesson Activities

Thinking Biblically — Copy Proverbs 10:19 into your notebook.

Vocabulary — In your notebook, write your own definition for each of these words: symbol, vibrate, undertaker, interfere, distinctive. Look in the lesson for clues for the meaning of the words. When you are finished writing your definitions, look in a dictionary for comparison.

Literature — Read "The First Long Distance Telephone Call" in *The Citizen's Handbook* pages 148-149, and chapters 1-2 in *The Wright Brothers: How They Invented the Airplane*.

Find Out! — Ask your parents when they got their first cell phone.

Picture This! — Take a photograph or draw a picture of someone using a telephone or cell phone.

Student Workbook or Lesson Review — If you are using one of these optional books, complete the assignment for Lesson 122.

The Travels of a
PIECE OF MAIL

Dear Ellen,

How are you? We are all fine. Our new baby is so pretty. I hope you like the picture I've included. I think she looks like Mama. Matt scored 10 points at the basketball game. It snowed last night. Matt and I have been sledding. Dad has fixed the back fence. Now the dog next door can't dig in our garden this summer! I have to finish up because it's time for co-op. Write soon. I miss you.

Love,
Laura

Laura put the letter and picture into an envelope and sealed it. In the middle of the front, she wrote Ellen's address:

Ellen Mitchell
904 Sunset Lane
Waskash, WA 98997

In the upper left corner, Laura wrote her return address:

Laura Stamford
111 Highway 12
Bingham, GA 31678

In the upper right corner, Laura placed a stamp. She put the letter in her family's mailbox and put up the red flag that indicated to the mail carrier that an outgoing letter was there to be picked up. That afternoon, when carrier Paula drove up to the Stamfords' mailbox, she took out Laura's letter, put in the Stamfords' mail for the day, and placed Laura's letter in the container that held outgoing mail. When Paula returned to the post office, she put the outgoing mail in the large mailbag that held the day's outgoing mail from all the local delivery routes.

The Birth of the Postal System

The U.S. Post Office began in 1775, when the Second Continental Congress appointed Benjamin Franklin to be the first Postmaster General. The Post Office Department was created in 1792. The Postmaster General became an official member of the President's Cabinet in 1872. In 1971 the Post Office became an independent agency called the United States Postal Service (USPS). The Postmaster General was no longer a member of the Cabinet. See historic photos below.

Transferring Mail Between Train and Truck

"Christmas Post Office" Truck and "Santa Claus" in Washington, D.C., December 10, 1921

Senator Ernest Lundeen and members of the National Federation of Post Office Clerks carry a four by six foot postcard they mailed to the Capitol to request sick leave and vacations for substitute post office employees, 1939. Notice the number of stamps used to mail it.

Rural Mail Carrier near Jackson, Kentucky, c. 1940

On May 15, 1918, President Wilson attended ceremonies at Polo Field to watch as a Post Office truck delivered the first mail to be sent by airplane. Pictured above are pilots in attendance that day.

Above: Mailman with Motorcycle At Left: Mailman with Mail Truck

At Right: Taking Mail Off the Morning Train in Montrose, Colorado, 1940

769

From Bingham to Nunbush to Savannah

At the end of the business day, mail truck driver David put all of the outgoing mail from the Bingham post office into his small mail truck. It included what Paula and the other carriers had picked up as well as what was gathered from the mail drop at the post office and the collection boxes around town. David drove to other nearby small post offices and picked up their mail, too. He carried it all to the larger post office in Nunbush. Henry, a USPS worker in Nunbush, put Laura's letter and all the other mail that had been brought there on a large mail truck, which carried it to a mail distribution center in Savannah.

Mail Trucks

There postal workers sent Laura's letter and all other mail through a machine that sorts mail by shape and separates letters from larger envelopes and packages. This is called the culling operation. Laura's letter went through a machine that arranges all letters so that the address side on each one is facing up and turned the same way. A machine printed a postmark in the upper right corner. The postmark included the date and the city where the distribution center is located. It also printed cancellation lines across the stamp so that it cannot be used again.

R2D2 mail collection box. In 2007 the USPS issued stamps based on the Star Wars movie. R2D2 was a robot in those movies.

A machine printed an identification code of fluorescent bars on the back of each letter. An optical character reader (OCR) reads the address on the front of each letter. The OCR can read printed addresses as well as handwritten ones. Postal workers send letters that have addresses that cannot be read by the OCR to another center where postal workers sort letters by hand. Since Laura wrote legibly, postal workers put her letter and all the other sorted letters on trays and took them to the next machine to have a barcode printed on them. This barcode, which represents Ellen's delivery address, will guide all further handling of Laura's letter. A postal worker put Laura's letter into a tray for a particular range of ZIP Codes. See photos of distribution center activities on page 771.

Processing Letters and Packages at the USPS Processing and Distribution Center, Merrifield, Virginia

Small Parcel Bundle Sorter

Typing ZIP Codes by Hand

Dumping Small Parcels

Loaded Flat Mail Cart

Flat Mail Sorting Machine

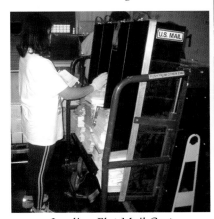

Loading Flat Mail Cart

Presorted Carts for Specific Locations

Mail Handler

*Distribution Center
Photos by ClintJCL*

Small Parcel Bundle Sorter

Flat Mail Sorting Machine

Postal workers are not the only people who work for American citizens at postal distribution centers. In the photo at right, U.S. Fish and Wildlife employees inspect a package to make sure it does not contain substances that are illegal to ship into the U.S.

Elizabeth, New Jersey
U.S. Fish and Wildlife Service employees inspect package.

ZIP Codes

The U.S. Post Office began using ZIP Codes in 1963. ZIP stands for Zone Improvement Plan. Previously, delivery addresses were simply name, street address, and city and state. Addresses in large cities also included a zone to indicate which post office in that city was to handle the letter. For instance, a letter addressed to "Chicago 6, Illinois" went to Chicago's post office number six. The ZIP Code system divided the country into ten regions, numbered 0 through 9. The first digit of a ZIP code indicates the region. The next two digits represent the sectional center facility that processes mail for an area within the region. The last two digits indicate

When ZIP Codes were first used, the Post Office used signs like this one to encourage people to use them.

the specific post office that will deliver the mail to the customer. The ZIP + 4 system, which was introduced in 1983, adds an additional four digits to indicate the particular street or route on which the recipient lives.

On to Seattle

Laura's letter left the Savannah processing plant in a large tractor trailer truck. Laura's letter was taken to the Atlanta distribution center, where it was placed with other first-class letters on an airplane bound for Seattle. Today the U.S. Postal Service rents space on regular passenger airplanes to send mail quickly to different parts of the country.

International Mail and Military Mail

If Laura had written to someone in another country, the handling of her letter would have been guided by the Universal Postal Union (UPU). The UPU was founded in 1874 and is now part of the United Nations. Nations that are members of the UPU agree to accept and deliver mail from other member countries and to send mail to those other countries. Each country keeps the money it collects from international postage in return for sending and delivering mail from other countries. Countries pay fees to each other depending on the difference in the total weight of the mail sent and received between them.

Top Left: **Osan Air Base Post Office, Korea**
Airman 1st Class Eden Meadows mails packages on December 22, 2009. During the Christmas holidays, this post office receives more than 2,000 packages and 4,000 letters a day.
Above: **Singapore**
Sailors and Marines sort mail aboard the USS Makin Island. *The ship received more than 5,000 pounds of mail during a stop in Singapore.*
Left: **Kuwait**
An American soldier writes a letter home.

Together the USPS and the Department of Defense operate a system to deliver mail to active duty military personnel and their families. Mail for these individuals is sent to APO (Army and Air Force Post Office) addresses and FPO (Fleet Post Office for Navy, Marine, and Coast Guard) addresses.

From Seattle to Ellen's Mailbox

When the plane carrying Laura's letter landed in Seattle, postal worker Al put the tray carrying Laura's letter in his truck and took it to another mail distribution center. At the facility, a barcode sorter separated Laura's letter for the specific ZIP Code where Ellen lives. The final sorting was done by a delivery sorter that identified the particular carrier who would carry the letter. This sorter even arranges the carrier's letters into the order they will deliver them.

Trucks carry letters and packages from mail distribution centers to individual post offices. There each postal carrier loads trays of mail into his or her postal service truck or personal vehicle. In a city neighborhood, the carrier parks his truck and then walks to deliver mail to

Key West, Florida

one neighborhood and then drives the truck to another part of his route, parks it again, and then delivers mail in that neighborhood. Where there are many delivery addresses in a small area, such as when there are several apartment complexes near each other, postal service personnel deliver sacks of mail to secure mail relay boxes for the carrier to pick up during his or her work day so the carrier does not have to carry all of the mail for his route.

The primary job of mail carriers is delivering mail, but they often serve citizens in other ways. Because carriers are in the same neighborhood every day, they notice when something seems not to be quite right. Many times a carrier is the first person who sees a crisis and is able to help immediately before other help arrives. Carriers are important in the lives of people who are lonely because the carrier may be the only person they see every day. The National Association of Letter Carriers gives Heroes of the Year awards to those who have performed heroic acts to benefit their fellow citizens.

In the case of Laura's letter, Ellen's address is on a rural route outside of a small town. Carrier Vic put the letter along with the other mail he must deliver in his car. The car has a special steering wheel and accelerator and brake pedals on the right side so that he can drive up to the mailboxes along the road and reach out easily to deliver the mail. The car also has a flashing light mounted on top to show that it makes frequent stops.

Soon after Vic put Laura's letter in the Mitchells' mailbox, Ellen took the mail from the mailbox and ran inside the house. She opened and read Laura's letter, smiled at the baby's picture, showed it to her family, put the stamp in her stamp collection, and sat down to write a reply. The next day, Ellen put her letter to Laura in her family's mailbox, put up the red flag, and the entire process began again.

Postage Stamps

The first official postage stamps issued by the Federal government went on sale in 1847. The five-cent stamp had a picture of first Postmaster General Benjamin Franklin, and the ten-cent stamp had a picture of first

President George Washington. In 1856 the Post Office Department issued a five-cent stamp honoring President Thomas Jefferson and in 1863 a two-cent stamp honoring President Andrew Jackson. Pictured below are commemorative stamps with photographs NASA has taken from space. The first U.S. commemorative stamps were produced in 1893. They honored the 1893 World's Columbian Exposition.

Letters are an ancient form of communication. King David wrote a letter to his military commander in 2 Samuel 11:14. Elected officials write letters to people they represent. Presidents write letters. Theodore Roosevelt wrote at least 150,000 letters in his lifetime, and that is just the number of Teddy's letters that have been kept!

E-mails, text messaging, and posts on social media sites on the Internet have reduced the number of letters that people write, but there is something very special about a handwritten letter from a loved one. A letter is a gift. Most of the New Testament books are letters. The first Christians cherished them. Paul told Christians at Thessalonica:

So then, brethren, stand firm and hold to the traditions which you were taught,

whether by word of mouth or by letter from us.

2 Thessalonians 2:15

Lesson Activities

Vocabulary — In your notebook, make a drawing for each of these words that illustrates what it means: cull, fluorescent, optical, legibly, barcode. Write the word under the drawing. Check in a dictionary if you need help with their definitions.

Literature — Read chapter 3 in *The Wright Brothers: How They Invented the Airplane.*

Creative Writing — In your notebook, write a short story of at least one page about a mail carrier who performs an heroic act for his community.

Find Out! — Where is the post office nearest to your home? What are the days and times it is open?

Student Workbook or Lesson Review — If you are using one of these optional books, complete the assignment for Lesson 123.

Voice of
AMERICA

1942

This is a voice speaking from America. The voice from America at war. Our voices are coming to you from New York across the Atlantic Ocean to London, from where they are relayed to you in Germany. Today America has been at war for seventy-nine days. Daily at this time we shall speak to you about America and the war. The news may be good or bad. We shall tell you the truth.

Thirteen-year-old Hans heard these words on his shortwave radio in his hometown of Berlin, Germany, early in 1942. His country had been at war for over two years. Germany had declared war on the United States following the Japanese attack on Pearl Harbor on December 7, 1941. Hans had looked forward to the day when he would be old enough to join the German army and become a soldier, but he also dreaded going into battle. Anything might happen. The message he heard made him think again about the country he was wanting to fight.

The words that Hans heard were broadcast from the United States but spoken in his own German language by a series of speakers. The leaders of the United States government knew that in the war against Germany, Italy, and Japan, one of the strongest weapons we had was truth. The Nazi government did not always tell the truth to the German people. They often told the German people lies about America. The U.S. government wanted them to know the truth about the Nazi government and its army. They also wanted the Germans to know that the United States stood for and practiced democracy and freedom. Americans could not send newspapers or pamphlets into Germany, but our nation could reach the minds of the German people by means of shortwave radio.

Berlin, Germany

What Hans heard was the first broadcast of the service that came to be known as Voice of America (VOA). As the war continued, other American broadcasts reached into other countries in Europe as well as countries in Asia, Africa, and Latin America. Before the end of the war, the United States government was broadcasting hundreds of hours of radio programs each week. Two dozen transmitters sent out programs in over forty languages.

This 1936 model Philco radio could receive both shortwave and AM radio signals.

1962

The year was 1962. Karl listened to Voice of America broadcasts from his home in Leipzig, Germany. World War II had been over for many years. Karl was too young to remember it. Now, however, he lived with another crisis. After the war, the Communist army from the Soviet Union had taken over the eastern part of Germany. The Communists carefully guarded the border between East Germany, where Karl's city was located, and West Germany, which was controlled by the English, the French, and the Americans. Hans' hometown of Berlin was also divided. The Communists had even built a wall down the middle of the city to keep people from escaping into the part of Berlin that was controlled by the Americans. Karl knew that the Communists ruled his country by force. He wanted to be free, and VOA helped him believe that one day he could be free.

This period of history is known as the Cold War era. The Cold War was a constant confrontation between the Soviet Union and the United States. The armies of the two nations did not go into battle against each other. Though there was always a danger that a war would be fought, the real battle was for influence over people. The Soviet Union used

Leipzig, Germany
Thomas Church

military force to control its citizens. It also controlled them by lying about Communism and about the United States. The United States again used truth as a weapon. Our government broadcast this truth on Voice of America radio. Voice of America told people who were controlled by the Communists the news of the world and the truth about what life was like in the United States.

However, in 1962 (and for many years before and after 1962) the Communists who controlled East Germany and other countries in Eastern Europe were not willing for people to hear the truth from the United States. The Communists usually interfered with the VOA broadcasts by an action called jamming. Jamming is broadcasting radio interference that keeps people from being able to hear radio broadcasts. Sometimes, though, the broadcasts got through; and Karl and millions

Washington, D.C.
Zofia Korbonska (right) worked as a senior news editor for the Polish Service division of Voice of America. Mrs. Korbonska began working for VOA in 1948. This photo was taken in 1974.

of others behind the Iron Curtain were able to hear the truth from America. One of the countries in Eastern Europe that suffered under a Communist government was Poland. Pictured above is a Polish immigrant who worked in the Polish Service division of Voice of America.

Later in the 1960s, VOA gave the world a place to hear coverage of Martin Luther King Jr.'s 1963 "I Have a Dream" speech about civil rights in Washington, D.C. It provided coverage of the American landing on the moon in 1969. In the 1970s, VOA honestly and openly told the world the story about two difficult issues for the United States, the Vietnam War and the Watergate scandal that involved President Richard Nixon. Years later, within minutes after the terrorist attacks on September 11, 2001, Voice of America was telling the world what happened that day.

Sharing the English Language and American Culture

To attract listeners, Voice of America does more than broadcast news about America and the world. It also helps its listeners understand what life is like in America. One way is by playing American music. Many people in other parts of the world like to listen to VOA because they are fascinated with America and want to learn all they can about our country. VOA broadcasts some programs in simple and slow-paced English to help people in foreign countries learn the English language. Since the English language is used all over the world in business, science, and entertainment, people in other countries know that if they can learn English they have a better chance of getting a good job and being successful. They eagerly listen to the English broadcasts on VOA to help them learn it.

Changing Technology

Voice of America has changed and grown with changes in the world and in technology. It now broadcasts shortwave, AM, and FM radio programs plus television programs. From its headquarters in Washington, D.C., Voice of America broadcasts to over 120 million listeners and viewers around the world. It also shares news on a website.

Washington, D.C.
VOA Headquarters is in the Wilbur J. Cohen Building.

The Voice of America Charter

The Voice of America Charter states its purposes and goals:

★ VOA will serve as a consistently reliable and authoritative source of news. VOA news will be accurate, objective, and comprehensive.

★ VOA will represent America, not any single segment of American society, and will therefore present a balanced and comprehensive projection of significant American thought and institutions.

★ VOA will present the policies of the United States clearly and effectively, and will also present responsible discussions and opinion on these policies.

Today

Today, Bong-Hwa in North Korea, Abbas in Iran, and Arghavan in Afghanistan can listen to VOA broadcasts if they get through the jamming by those countries' governments. People in countries that allow access to the Internet can go to the VOA website. They can learn about the United States, their own countries, and other places in the world. Unfortunately, there are still governments that don't tell the truth to their people. In addition, some countries lack the money

Bethany, Ohio
This former Voice of America relay station is now the National Voice of America Museum of Broadcasting.

to have good sources of information and reliable media to communicate information to their citizens. Voice of America is one way that the United States is a good citizen of the world, and it enables people in other countries to have greater access to things that we Americans hold dear: truth and freedom.

Audio Tapes of Commercials Advertising Voice of America Programs

> Therefore, laying aside falsehood,
> speak truth each one of you with his neighbor,
> for we are members of one another.
> Ephesians 4:25

Lesson Activities

Thinking Biblically — Copy Proverbs 21:28 into your notebook.

Vocabulary — In your notebook, write the vocabulary words and the letter of the definition that goes with each word: relay, pamphlet, confrontation, reliable, objective.

   a. a conflict; a clash of powers or ideas

   b. dependable, performs consistently

   c. to transmit or pass along

   d. undistorted by personal feelings or opinions

   e. brochure, small booklet of information

Literature — Read chapter 4 in *The Wright Brothers: How They Invented the Airplane*.

Creative Writing — In your notebook, write one or two paragraphs explaining one aspect of American culture as if you were writing an item to be broadcast on Voice of America to people in other countries.

Picture This! — Draw a picture of a family in another country listening to Voice of America on the radio.

Student Workbook or Lesson Review — If you are using one of these optional books, complete the assignment for Lesson 124.

★ Remember to choose an American Holiday to study this week! ★

UNIT 26 — GETTING FROM HERE TO THERE

BOOKS USED IN UNIT 26

- The Citizen's Handbook
- The Wright Brothers: How They Invented the Airplane
- Student Workbook (optional)
- Lesson Review (optional)

Tunnel in Georgia

Americans
ON THE MOVE

In the United States we enjoy the freedom to travel to any state or city. We can visit any local, state, or national park. Americans can pack up their belongings and move to a new place. We can send and receive goods to and from anywhere in the country and just about anywhere in the world. We have freedom of transportation. This freedom has helped our country expand. It has helped our economy grow.

Private companies, such as automobile manufacturers, airplane and ship builders, road construction companies, railroad companies, and trucking and delivery companies, meet many of our transportation needs. These companies are free to build what the public wants and to compete with each other to provide new and better means of transportation.

At the same time, government plays an important role in our transportation system. The Federal government sets regulations for the safety of vehicles, how the air transportation system works, and what comes into our ports from other countries. A good transportation system requires that private citizens, private companies, and government on all three levels work together to keep our transportation system safe, up to date, and able to help us accomplish our goals.

Let's travel across America and see Americans on the move in the daytime and nighttime, in summer and winter, at work and at play.

On Bikeways and Footpaths

We take walks on sidewalks and hike on trails. We ride bicycles to work and around the neighborhood. We do it for fun and to stay in shape.

Waco, Texas
Waco Suspension Bridge

Chautauqua, New York
Walking Path and Bridge

Ashland City, Tennessee
Pedestrian Crossing

Savannah, Georgia
Pedestrian Bridge

West Virginia
Trail by the New River Gorge Bridge

Portland, Oregon
Bicyclists in Portland have special green bike lanes and special signals.

On Rivers, Lakes, and Seas

We glide across lakes and harbors and board cruise ships for the Bahamas, the Caribbean, Europe, and our own states of Alaska and Hawaii. We build ships. We do commercial fishing. We pilot barges full of coal and grain down the Mississippi, the Ohio, and other great rivers. We take off across the Atlantic and the Pacific carrying sea containers filled with American-made goods (called exports) to distant shores. We pilot ships on the St. Lawrence Seaway and the Great Lakes. And we receive ships bringing imports from other lands. We pass close to the eastern and southern coastlines in tow boats, barges, and pleasure boats on the 3,000-mile Intracoastal Waterway, a series of inlets, rivers, bays, sounds, and man-made canals along the Atlantic and Gulf coasts. We drive vehicles onto ferries to cross rivers, bays, and harbors.

Delaware
Lewes and Rehoboth Canal

Galveston, Texas
Odfjell Shechem, a Tanker from a Norwegian Company

Georgetown, South Carolina
Shrimp Boats

Key West, Florida
Marker for the Southernmost Point in the Continental United States

Alaska
Cruise Ship from Mount Roberts

Savannah, Georgia
Container Ship Sailing Under the Flag of Liberia

Mobile, Alabama
Shipyard

Richmond, Virginia
Great Shiplock Canal Park

Wisconsin
Island Queen *Ferry on Lake Superior Between Madeline Island and Bayfield*

Rhode Island
Yacht

Montana
Two Medicine Lake Tour

Kentucky
*Turkey Neck Bend Ferry
Across the Cumberland River*

San Diego, California
Port of San Diego

Bayfield, Wisconsin
Island Queen *Ferry*

Vadez, Alaska
Ferry Terminal

Mobile Bay, Alabama
Mobile Bay Lighthouse

Narragansett, Rhode Island
*The Port of Galilee is a New England
fishing village within the city
of Narragansett.*

Galveston, Texas
Entrance to Ferry

785

On Streets and Highways

We travel the highways and byways in vehicles powered by gasoline, diesel, ethanol, or electricity, and in hybrids that use more than one kind of fuel. We cross bridges, climb mountains, weave through city streets, and find places to park. On a given day, many of us are making deliveries, many are traveling for work, and others are traveling for pleasure. Some of our fellow citizens are working to make these trips possible for the rest of us.

Portland, Oregon
Replacing Lights on the Freemont Bridge

Oregon
Using a level while constructing Bailey Bridge.

Prospect, Maine
When the Waldo-Hancock Bridge (left) needed to be replaced, engineers designed the Penobscot Narrows Bridge (right). Atop one of the bridge towers (or pylons) is the world's tallest public bridge-observatory. Tourists can see one hundred miles.

California
Humboldt Redwoods State Park

Oregon
Fog rises below the bridge across the Hood River.

Wisconsin
Motorcyclists on the Great River Road.

Savannah, Georgia
Talmadge Memorial Bridge

Gainesboro, Tennessee
A private company delivers beams for a bridge across Roaring River.

San Diego, California
Street Division

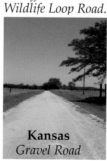

Columbus, Ohio
Mile Marker for the Cumberland Road, Authorized During the Presidency of Thomas Jefferson

South Dakota
Buffalo crosses Wildlife Loop Road.

Kansas
Gravel Road

Louisiana
Construction of Bridge Across Lake Pontchartrain

Portland Oregon
Installing Interstate Signs

New York
Delivering Interstate Signs

Portland, Oregon
Installing Interstate Signs

**Jamestown,
New York**
Parking Sign

PARKING
discover downtown

South Dakota
*Gray Line Tour Bus
on Needles Highway*

**Jamestown,
New York**
Parking Meter

Cornelia, Georgia

Tennessee
Delivering State Highway Signs

Maine

**Winston-Salem,
North Carolina**
Bus Terminal

SPEED LIMIT
12 MPH
ALL ROADS

**Chautauqua,
New York**

ADDITIONAL
PARKING
AT
CITY HALL

**Wellington,
Florida**

HISTORIC
CALIFORNIA
US 101
ROUTE

Oregon
Crew Who Built Bailey Bridge

Salem, Oregon
Interstate 5

Kentucky

On Trains and on Airplanes

In 1869 American railroad workers along with thousands of Chinese immigrants completed the Transcontinental Railroad. American brothers Orville and Wilbur Wright worked for years to perfect flying. After their historic flight on December 17, 1903, they became successful airplane entrepreneurs, making flight possible for many. In 1916 German immigrant Wilhelm "Bill" Boeing founded an airplane manufacturing company. By 1930 Boeing Air Transport, Inc. was offering flights for passengers in planes complete with stewardesses, many windows so that passengers could enjoy the view, and individual temperature controls for each seat.

Today trains cross America on 160,000 miles of track. Most carry freight, but some still carry passengers. American skies are filled with airplanes carrying people and goods. In 2011, the U.S. had 19,782 airports. Railroads and the air transportation industries are examples of individuals, companies, communities, and the Federal government working together.

Charleston, West Virginia
FEMA supplies are shipped from the Yeager Airport.

Commercial Airliner Temperature and Light Controls

Dallas/Fort Worth International Airport

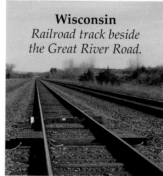

Washington, D.C.
Ronald Reagan National Airport

Jackson, Tennessee
Chessie System Caboose at the N.C. & St. L. Depot and Railroad Museum

Wisconsin
Railroad track beside the Great River Road.

Honolulu, Hawaii
Hawaii's state department of transportation owns Honolulu International Airport. Its 12,000-foot Reef Runway is the world's first major runway built entirely offshore.

God taught Israelite parents to teach His commands to their children throughout their everyday lives including when they were traveling from one place to another.

Hear, O Israel! The Lord is our God, the Lord is one! You shall love the Lord your God with all your heart and with all your soul and with all your might.

These words, which I am commanding you today, shall be on your heart. You shall teach them diligently to your sons and shall talk of them when you sit in your house and when you walk by the way and when you lie down and when you rise up.

Deuteronomy 6:4-7

Lesson Activities

Thinking Biblically — Jesus used roads as a teaching example. Copy Matthew 7:13-14 into your notebook.

Literature — Read "The House by the Side of the Road" in *The Citizen's Handbook* pages 150, and chapter 5 in *The Wright Brothers: How They Invented the Airplane*.

Creative Writing — In your notebook, write a short story of at least one page about a journey in America. Involve as many methods of transportation as you would like.

Picture This! — Take a photograph or draw a picture of the road on which you live.

Student Workbook or Lesson Review — If you are using one of these optional books, complete the assignment for Lesson 126.

Amtrak train crosses the Niagara River.

How to BUILD A ROAD

Millions of cars travel on country roads, city streets, state highways, and Interstates every day and night across America. Each mile was once a field of wildflowers, a forest of trees, a marsh of cattails, a sandy desert, a pebbly beach, a grassy prairie. How did they become roads? Civic leaders, people in different levels of government, and private businesses work together to build them.

Missouri

The Need for a New Road

The city of Flugleville grew after the construction of an Interstate one mile from town. New businesses opened and people moved to Flugleville from the large city thirty miles away. Growth was welcome, but all the new traffic was frustrating. State Highway 12, which was built through the center of town in the 1920s, was getting very crowded. People involved in the city and county governments, the regional planning office, and the Flugleville/Flugle County Chamber of Commerce all expressed a desire to build a Highway 12 bypass around the city. This would ease traffic in town and open up an area for more growth.

Planning the Road

Leaders held an open meeting to present the idea to the community. Those in attendance supported the idea but also raised some questions. The route that the regional planning office proposed would cut through property held by several local citizens. The route passed close to Lake Flugle. Some people expressed concerns that the road, the noise, and the exhaust fumes might damage the lake environment. The road pavement, plus any new businesses, parking lots, and homes would affect how the soil in the area could absorb rain and snowfall.

Since the road would begin and end within the city limits but also extend into the county, both city and county governments would have to be involved. The city council began to look into annexing into Flugleville the land along the entire route.

City and county officials applied to the state department of transportation for the bypass to be considered. The department agreed to consider the proposal as part of its long-range road construction plan for the state. It conducted an official survey of traffic to determine if a new road was needed. The results of the survey would help to determine where this bypass would be placed on the state department of transportation's list of priorities.

Archaeologists studied the route to see if any historic sites might be affected. Soil experts studied the soil to see if it could support a road. Utility companies checked on whether their supply lines would need to be moved. Planners studied how the road might impact present and future land use. Traffic planners estimated how many cars and how many large trucks might be expected to use the bypass on a daily basis. Four years after the city and county submitted the original proposal to the state, the department of transportation approved the construction of a four-lane bypass with a central median.

Designing the Road

Civil engineers who worked for the state department of transportation began the design process. Throughout the process, the city, county, and state governments held public meetings so that citizens could hear about the progress being made and make suggestions about the project.

The engineers took into account soil quality, geographic features, and land availability to determine an exact route. They

Oregon
An Oregon Department of Transportation engineer helps middle school students with a gum drop bridge model they have made during National Engineers Month, February 2012.

designed an overpass for where the bypass crossed the railroad track that ran from Flugleville to Nickel City. They designed bridges over the Flugle River and Salt Lick Creek. They studied water runoff in the area to determine the best drainage system for the road.

Engineers designed the road to be slightly higher in the center to help with water runoff. Since the bypass would have limited access, they designed the lanes to be twelve feet wide, the same width as a lane on an Interstate. Limited access means that drivers use entrance and exit ramps. Engineers planned the ramps and all of the road's curves with certain degrees of embankment so that drivers could maintain control of their cars while driving at the maximum speed limit for the bypass. They planned for an outside shoulder ten feet wide and an inner shoulder four feet wide. The state hired a private landscape architect to design landscaping for the median and the areas beside entrance and exit ramps.

Photos from the Oregon Department of Transportation

Preparing Ground for Construction

First Steps

The year after the designs were completed, the state legislature approved funding for the road. The department of transportation put it on the construction schedule. The state announced the project and began the long process of purchasing land from the citizens who owned land in the area where the road would be constructed.

Private road building companies submitted bids to do the work. The state chose the company that submitted the lowest bid. As of 2012, the cost of building one mile of one lane of road is often three or four million dollars or more. The "Big Dig" construction project in Boston, Massachusetts, in the early 21st century cost over one billion dollars per mile.

With Mt. Hood in the distance, an ODOT worker stacks sand at a maintenance yard.

Laying a Firm Foundation

With the land purchased, the road planned, and the company hired, construction began. First, the construction company cleared the route of trees, rocks, buildings, fences, older roads, and other obstructions. They began to prepare the roadbed. They brought in dirt to elevate it above the nearby land to avoid flooding on the road. They smoothed the dirt with a heavy rolling machine and packed it firmly. They added several layers of sand, rock, and gravel, packing down each layer and allowing it to settle.

Finishing the Road

As illustrated in the photos on page 793, the road construction crew poured the asphalt paving material on the road (1, 2), spread it out (3, 4), tested its temperature (5), and rolled it to make it smooth (6). Asphalt paving material is a combination of stone, sand, gravel, and asphalt (sometimes called bitumen). Asphalt is made from petroleum and is the glue that holds all the materials together. After the road surface cured or became hard, the crew tested it to make sure that it did not cause vehicles to vibrate. The crew cleaned the surface of loose materials (7) and painted center and outside lines (8). They put guardrails in place and erected signs. They also attached raised parallel rumble strips and raised reflective markers on center lines to make the road safer.

Meanwhile the city council and the county commission considered what to call the bypass. The two bodies created a committee to consider names. All citizens were welcome to submit ideas. The committee received many. Some proposed the names of historic national, state, and local figures. A few suggested the names of prominent city and county officials. A high school girl made the suggestion of naming the road after Dalton Jennings, a young man from Flugleville who had given his life while serving in Afghanistan. The committee recommended this choice to the city council and county commission. Both votes were unanimous. The two governing bodies also voted to place a memorial marker along the bypass to help future generations remember the young man's sacrifice for his country.

Photos from the Oregon Department of Transportation

The city council and county commission set a date for an opening ceremony. The city manager and county mayor sent written invitations to the Governor, the U.S. Congressman who represented their district, and the Jennings family. Members of the county manager's staff and the city mayor's staff planned a ceremony. They advertised it on the city and county websites and in the local daily newspaper. They also placed public service announcements on the local radio station. The Congressman and the Jennings family accepted their invitations. The Governor sent his regrets, but he promised to send a representative.

Finally the Sergeant Dalton Jennings Memorial Bypass was ready to open for traffic. Early on the morning of the ceremony, city transportation department employees put construction barrels across the bypass. They attached a long red ribbon to the barrels. They set up a portable stage, a podium, and a few rows of chairs. At 9:00 a.m. before the ceremony began, city policemen arrived. At 9:30 the high school bugle corps arrived and found their places beside the stage. At 9:40 the Jennings family arrived. The sheriff invited them to sit on the front row. Several citizens came and sat in the rows behind them. A newspaper reporter and a photographer arrived and stood in the back.

A few minutes before the ceremony began, Lieutenant Governor Clark, Congressman Elliott, Mayor Farmer, County Manager Peck, and Secretary Hendley of the state department of transportation arrived and climbed onto the stage. Mayor Farmer welcomed everyone. The county commission chaplain led a prayer of invocation. Sergeant Jennings' younger brother led the Pledge of Allegiance. The bugle corps played "The Star-Spangled Banner." Each of the dignitaries made a few brief remarks. They joined the Jennings family for photographs behind the ribbon. The photographer took some pictures. Mr. Jennings cut the ribbon and the photographer took more pictures. Dignitaries and the family exchanged greetings, as did members of the audience. A police car escorted the Jennings family as they drove the first private vehicle down the entire length of the bypass.

A Continuing Job

The road was finished, but work will continue. Cracks can develop in a road surface for a number of reasons. The earth underneath the roadbed can shift or wash away; heavy trucks can damage the road; and water can seep into small cracks, freeze and expand, and create larger cracks. These cracks will be repaired. Road signs will be replaced when they are damaged by weather, accidents, or vandals. Speed limits might be adjusted if the current limits are found to be dangerous or frustrating.

Oregon
Road Crew

The Infrastructure

State and Federal gasoline taxes pay for most road construction. Some states have toll roads, where state workers collect fees from drivers who use the roads. The thinking behind toll roads is that those who drive on the roads should be the ones who pay for them.

Roads are part of the system of structures that help a country operate. This system is called the infrastructure. The infrastructure also includes bridges, dams, power systems, airports, hospitals, and schools. As the population grows and as greater demand is placed on the facilities that society uses, it is a continual challenge for government to keep the infrastructure secure, up to date, and in good working order.

Naming a road for someone is a way to honor him or her. A few days before Jesus died on the cross, people honored Him as He walked along a road.

Most of the crowd spread their coats in the road,

and others were cutting branches from the trees and spreading them in the road.

The crowds going ahead of Him, and those who followed, were shouting,

"Hosanna to the Son of David;

Blessed is He who comes in the name of the Lord; Hosanna in the highest."

Matthew 21:8-9

Lesson Activities

Vocabulary — Write five sentences in your notebook, using one of these words in each: absorb, annex, median, vandal, infrastructure. Check in a dictionary if you need help with their definitions.

Literature — Read chapters 6-7 in *The Wright Brothers: How They Invented the Airplane*.

Find Out! — For what or for whom is your road named?

Picture This! — Draw an imaginary "before and after" picture of an area where a new road was built.

Student Workbook or Lesson Review — If you are using one of these optional books, complete the assignment for Lesson 127.

Traveling Together on MASS TRANSIT

Los Angeles, California
Department of Transportation

Madeline Island, Wisconsin
Island Queen

New York City
MTA New York City Subway

Perhaps because we love freedom, Americans like to travel by car. We enjoy the freedom of driving where we want to go, when we want to go, and stopping where we want to stop along the way. Just think about all of the places we can "drive thru"—the bank, the pharmacy, the fast food restaurant. Many Americans go somewhere in a car every day. However, many who live in large cities and the suburbs that surround them travel mainly by mass transit.

The term "mass transit" is used for buses, subways, and elevated trains which transport large groups of people. Mass transit, also called public transit or public transportation, is an important part of the American transportation system. Mass transit allows people to travel long distances quickly. It helps people who cannot or who choose not to drive and those who do not own a car. It also reduces the number of cars on the road. This is especially important in cities with crowded roads and limited parking facilities.

People who use mass transit enjoy different kinds of freedom. They do not have to worry about where to park. They are free to read, use their phones, daydream, or talk to other passengers while traveling where they need to go. Those who do not own vehicles are free from buying license plates, shopping for gasoline, or paying for car repairs.

Using mass transit takes planning. Passengers have to travel on a pre-set schedule and a set route. After all, you cannot have a subway pick you up at your front door!

Ferryboats

By the early 1850s, ferries were transporting passengers across the Hudson River between Manhattan, New York, and Jersey City, New Jersey, every fifteen minutes.

Virginia
Ferryboat on the James River, 1860s

Key West, Florida
Ferryboat, 1938

Before the Civil War, passengers were traveling by ferry across the Delaware River between Philadelphia, Pennsylvania, and Camden, New Jersey; across the Ohio River between Cincinnati, Ohio, and Newport, Kentucky; and across the Allegheny River between Pittsburgh and Allegheny City, Pennsylvania. See ferries above.

Omnibuses, Horsecars, Trains, Cable Cars, and Streetcars

Around 1830 entrepreneurs in some large cities began businesses to provide overland transportation for large numbers of people. Some operated large horse-drawn coaches called omnibuses which traveled on roads. Others operated horsecars which horses pulled along iron rails. Both began first in New York City. Private ominbus and horsecar companies made arrangements with local governments which allowed them to operate their vehicles on specific routes. See omnibuses in the illustration below.

Some people who lived in small towns used trains to travel to their workplaces in large cities. In New York City, entrepreneurs started elevated railways after the Civil War. The elevated trains were powered first by steam and later by electricity. Elevated train service began in other large cities, too. One of the best known "el" railways was the one that started in Chicago in 1892. See photo on page 799.

Philadelphia, Pennsylvania
Drawing of Horse-Drawn Omnibuses in Front of the Merchant's Exchange, 1838

Immigrant Andrew Hallidie invented the first cable car system. Hallidie's father was the first person in Great Britain to file a patent for rope made of wire. After Andrew immigrated to the U.S., he used wire ropes in California's gold mining industry. After he witnessed the difficulty horses had pulling horsecars in the hilly city of San Francisco, he decided to work on a cable car railway system. Steam-powered machines in a powerhouse pulled a loop of wire cables underneath the street. The cable cars were attached to the wire cables which pulled them along rails. See photo at right. New York City and other cities also built cable car systems.

In 1889 electric streetcars, also called "trolleys," began operating in Richmond, Virginia. The streetcars also traveled on rails. Trolleys quickly became popular in other cities. See photos below.

New Orleans still operates the St. Charles Streetcar Line which started in 1893. It is one of the oldest continuously operated electric streetcar lines in the world and was placed on the National Register of Historic Places in 1973. Most cities dismantled their lines in the second half of the twentieth century. A few cities have rebuilt them in recent years.

San Francisco, California
Cable Car

Oklahoma City, Oklahoma
Famed photographer Lee Russell took these photographs at Oklahoma City's streetcar terminal in 1939. A workman climbs to the top of a streetcar to do a repair. A mailman holds a bundle of mail as he waits for a streetcar beside another gentleman. A man reads a newspaper as he waits near the turnstile.

Subways

Since streetcars caused congestion on city streets, people began to think about building streetcar tracks in underground tunnels. London led the way with the London Metropolitan (later called the London Underground), which opened in 1863. Building underground railways was a big investment for private companies, so governments and businesses worked together. The Boston Transit Commission built the

Boston, Massachusetts
Subway Train, Part of Boston's Mass Transit System Called the "T," August 2012

first underground railroad track in the U.S. It opened in 1897. Streetcar companies rented the use of the rails the commission had constructed. The rent repaid the transit commission the money it had invested. See the modern "T" subway on page 798. The famous New York City Subway opened in 1904.

Chicago, Illinois
Chicago Transit Authority
Elevated Train

City Buses

In 1905 the Fifth Avenue Coach Company began offering gasoline-powered bus service in New York City. Like the Atlantic City bus pictured at left, New York's buses were double-deckers. City bus services became popular in many cities.

Atlantic City, New Jersey
City Bus, 1925

Los Angeles, California
Metrolink

A Switch from Private to Public Ownership

By 1905 states had registered 79,000 automobiles. The number of registered automobiles rose to 20,100,000 in 1925. (As of 2006, there were 244,200,000!) As automobiles became more and more popular, mass transit lost business in large numbers. Mass transit changed from a profitable business to one that cost much more to run than it took in. Private companies became less involved in mass transportation and city governments became more involved. When cities became unable to provide enough money for mass transit systems, the Federal government began giving money to cities to help them continue to operate. Though some mass transit systems are still run by private companies, most are owned and operated by local, state, or the Federal government.

Look at the mass transit photographs at right. Many cities find that the best mass transit solution today is a combination of buses that travel on streets and trains that travel on rails. Rail transportation is often a combination of transportation on the ground, under the ground, and on elevated tracks

Charleston, South Carolina
Charleston Area Regional
Transit Authority

Atlanta, Georgia
Metropolitan Atlanta
Rapid Transit Authority

above ground. Ferries continue to provide mass transit along America's coastlines.

Mass Transit in Everyday Life

Fred works as a communication specialist for the state government of West Virginia. His office is near the state capitol in Charleston. He lives with his family in the nearby city of Huntington. For several years, Fred drove every weekday morning and evening along Interstate 64 to travel to and from work. He

Newark, New Jersey
Newark Light Rail,
a System Operated by New Jersey Transit

spent about an hour on the road each way, longer if he had traffic delays. He began to realize that he was tired when he arrived at work each morning after the drive and was even more exhausted when he got home in the evening. He decided to try using the bus service between Huntington and Charleston offered by the Kanawha Valley Regional Transportation Authority. To catch the bus, his wife has to drive him to the bus station each morning by 6:45 a.m. He arrives in Charleston at the stop nearest his office at 8:00 a.m. In the evening, he catches the 5:15 p.m. bus and arrives back at the Huntington bus station at 6:45 p.m. He uses his time on the bus to rest, read the Bible and the newspaper, and stay caught up on his e-mail.

Seventeen-year-old Tony and his sister, fifteen-year-old Monica, live in Newark, New Jersey. They take clarinet and cello lessons on Tuesday afternoons at a studio across town. They use the Newark Light Rail train service to get to their lessons. They leave from the Davenport Avenue station at 1:10 p.m. and arrive at Newark Penn Station at 1:22 p.m. in time to walk to their 1:30 p.m. lessons. They return home from the Newark Penn Station on the 2:52 train. A Newark Light Rail train is pictured above.

Bass Harbor, Maine

Kelly lives on Swan's Island, Maine, with her husband, a lobsterman, and their young twin sons. Swan's Island is a tiny community with about 350 year-round residents and about 1,000 in the summer. The State of Maine operates a ferry service between Swan's Island and Bass Harbor. One Saturday every month, Kelly travels to Bass Harbor on the mainland to buy the family's groceries and do other errands. See picture at left.

Kelly boards the *Captain Henry Lee* ferry at 8:15 a.m. The six-mile crossing takes about 40 minutes. Kelly usually meets a friend for lunch and tries to buy everything her family will need for the next month. She catches the 3:00 p.m. ferry back to Swan's Island, or if she's running late, the 4:30 p.m. ferry. See Maine ferry at right.

Maine
Ferry

When people use mass transit to get where they want to go, they pay a fare to ride. When Jonah ran away because he didn't want to obey God, he paid a fare, too.

But Jonah rose up to flee to Tarshish from the presence of the Lord.
So he went down to Joppa, found a ship which was going to Tarshish,
paid the fare and went down into it to go with them . . .
Jonah 1:3

Lesson Activities

Vocabulary — Copy these words in your notebook, each on a separate line: suburb, streetcar, dismantle, congestion, profitable. Look up each word in a dictionary. Next to each word, write what part of speech it is according to the way the word is used in this lesson.

Literature — Read "New York Subway Opened" in *The Citizen's Handbook* pages 151-152, and chapters 8-9 in *The Wright Brothers: How They Invented the Airplane*.

Creative Writing — In your notebook, make a chart comparing the benefits of mass transit and the benefits of driving personal vehicles. Give each at least 5 benefits for each.

Find Out! — Are there any options for mass transit in your town (trains, airport, bus, subway, or rail)?

Student Workbook or Lesson Review — If you are using one of these optional books, complete the assignment for Lesson 128.

Working in TRANSPORTATION

Each day many skilled workers keep American travelers and their goods safely and efficiently on the move around town and around the country.

Secretary of Transportation

The U.S. Secretary of Transportation is a member of the President's Cabinet. He or she advises the President on everything related to transportation on the Federal level of government. The Secretary is responsible for reviewing the entire U.S. transportation system to make sure that it meets the needs of the country. The Secretary serves as the head of the Department of Transportation, created by Congress in 1966. The purpose of this Department is to "serve the United States by ensuring a fast, safe, efficient, accessible, and convenient transportation system that meets our vital national interests and enhances the quality of life of the American people, today and into the future." Read about the career of one U.S. Secretary of Transportation below.

Using Talents to Serve: Secretary of Transportation Ray LaHood

Ray LaHood became the 16th Secretary of Transportation on January 23, 2009, following a long career in other public sector jobs. LaHood graduated from Bradley University in Peoria, Illinois. During his career, LaHood:

★ Was a junior high school teacher.

★ Worked as chief planner for a regional planning commission (planning commissions help citizens and government use land wisely).

★ Was elected to the Illinois state legislature.

★ Served on the staffs of two U.S. Congressmen.

★ Was elected to the U.S. Congress from the 18th District of Illinois where he served for 14 years.

In Congress LaHood served on the House Transportation and Infrastructure Committee and the House Appropriations Committee.

The Secretary makes transportation agreements with other countries and proposes laws about transportation for Congress to consider. He oversees about 55,000 U.S. Department of Transportation employees.

Manhattan, New York
School Crossing Guard

School Crossing Guard

Early each school day morning, Donna puts on her black uniform and bright reflective vest and drives to her part-time job at George Washington Elementary School. As a school crossing guard, Donna's job is to keep children safe as they arrive at school in the morning and leave in the afternoon. She stands in the middle of the intersection nearest the school to direct pedestrians and traffic. After school begins for the day and the children are safely inside, Donna returns home. She goes to the school again before dismissal time to make sure children are safe when they leave school.

Donna is an employee of her local police department. When she trained for her job, the police department taught her how to use her hands and also a hand-held stop sign to give directions to cars and to children crossing the street. They also gave her instructions about how to report the license plate numbers of reckless drivers as well as suspicious activity in the school zone. Donna enjoys greeting the children who walk to and from school. She is glad her job allows her to know and help children in her community.

Road Construction Heavy Equipment Operator

Bill has always loved big machines. After working for several years in road construction, Bill asked to train to use the heavy equipment. Bill is now an expert at using big, expensive construction machines such as reclaimers, pavers, compactors, and planers. Bill also wears bright, reflective clothing so that he can be spotted by drivers and other construction workers. Bill works in all kinds of weather and at all times of day and night. Road construction often takes place at night and on weekends when traffic is lighter.

Oregon
Removing Pavement on I-405

Bill is an employee of Rock Solid Road Construction, a privately-owned construction company. Bill's employer and other construction companies make contracts with cities, states, and the Federal government to do road-building projects. Bill is appreciated and respected by his employer because he works efficiently while taking great care to be as safe as possible.

Air Traffic Controller

Sam works for the Federal government in the Federal Aviation Administration (FAA) as an air traffic controller. He makes sure airplanes fly safely along designated routes with enough distance between them. Sam, like most air traffic controllers, never sees the airplanes he helps. He works at an air traffic control center where he watches radar screens and talks with pilots. Radar picks up the location of planes and sends the information to air traffic control centers, which might be hundreds or thousands of miles away from the airplane itself. FAA controllers are responsible for directing each airplane in American skies from the moment it leaves the gate of one airport until it reaches the airport gate of its destination. With the heavy air traffic in the United States, Sam's work is essential for the safety of passengers and crews.

Air Traffic Controllers

Tractor-Trailer Driver

Al drives an eighteen-wheeler truck for a private shipping company. He picks up goods at regional distribution centers and delivers them to stores in several different states. Since he drives a commercial vehicle, Al has a Commercial Driver's License (CDL). To get this special license, Al had to pass all the requirements for a regular driver's license, be over 21 years old, pass an oral test, and pass a test demonstrating his skills with a commercial vehicle. Al must be careful to obey all traffic laws. He knows that he must be a safe driver and follow the rules in order to keep his job.

Al usually drives on the Federal Interstate Highway System. These spacious, efficient roads allow him to make good time. To prevent trucks from damaging roads, the Federal government has established weight limits for large vehicles using the Interstates. Each state is responsible for enforcing the weight limits. When Al sees an open weigh station along his route, he pulls off to get in line behind the other commercial vehicles. When his turn comes, he pulls his truck onto a truck-sized scale to be weighed.

Behind the cab in Al's truck is a sleeper berth. With its bed, television, DVD player, dining table and chairs, microwave, stove, sink, water heater, and refrigerator/freezer, it is Al's home away from home. When he's not working, Al lives at an apartment in his hometown. He usually spends two to three days a week at his apartment, but sometimes he is on the road for a few weeks at a time.

Colorado
Motor Carrier Enforcement Officer Inside Weigh Station

The Federal government has laws about how many consecutive hours a commercial driver can be behind the wheel. Al and his shipping company calculate his driving time and the required breaks carefully so that he is in compliance. When traveling on his usual routes, Al looks forward to breaks at his favorite restaurants and truck stops and knows many of their employees by name. He has gotten to know other drivers who travel similar routes. Al enjoys his work handling a large truck and seeing our beautiful country from behind the wheel.

Adopt-a-Highway Program Coordinator

Wanda works for her state department of transportation (DOT) as the program coordinator for the Adopt-a-Highway program. Most states have implemented an Adopt-a-Highway program to recruit citizen volunteers to keep roadways clean of litter. Wanda and her staff developed an application form, guidelines, and safety rules for Adopt-a-Highway groups.

When a church, club, business, or family wants to adopt a section of highway, a representative of the group fills out an online application which Wanda's staff reviews. When the group is approved, a member of Wanda's staff helps it select a two-mile section of highway near their community. The state DOT places a sign at both ends of the highway section recognizing the group's service to the community. These are the guidelines that Wanda and her staff established:

Hawaii
U.S. Navy sailors participate in an Adopt-a-Highway program.

★ The group must commit to performing the Adopt-a-Highway service for at least two years.

★ Each volunteer must wear a safety vest provided by the state.

* The group must pick up trash at least three or four times a year.

* Volunteers must be at least twelve years old and any workers under the age of eighteen must have adult supervision.

* Volunteers must leave filled trash bags near the roadside for pickup by the DOT.

As program coordinator, Wanda hires a district Adopt-a-Highway coordinator for each of the twelve DOT districts in her state. Every year Wanda signs certificates of appreciation for all of the Adopt-a-Highway groups. She organizes an annual Adopt-a-Highway Appreciation Day in the state capital. She and her staff plan a picnic and hire a band to play live music. At the picnic, Wanda gives a speech, expressing her appreciation to all Adopt-a-Highway volunteers for their valuable help in keeping the state's highways clean and beautiful!

Locomotive Engineer

Jack drives freight trains for a privately-owned railroad company. Five years ago the company hired him as a brakeman with responsibilities for inspecting the train and assisting the conductor. Two years later he became a conductor who coordinated the crew.

Jack decided to train to become an engineer. His training took place in a classroom and on the job. Jack became certified in accordance with the rules of the Federal Railroad Administration and met the requirements for a locomotive engineer license. His qualifications included good hearing and vision, obedience to rules about drug and alcohol use, and a good record of safety when handling trains and when driving motor vehicles. Jack passed a test of his knowledge and a skills test in train operation. He must be retested regularly to make sure he continues to be a safe locomotive engineer.

After months of waiting for a job opening, Jack became a locomotive engineer. He transports a variety of goods including grain, lumber, coal, and manufactured products. Jack feels good knowing that many people are counting on him to do his job well.

Near Wright, Wyoming
Coal Train

City Traffic Engineer

The member of the city commission who serves as Commissioner of Transportation appointed Dale to be traffic engineer for his city. Dale is responsible for keeping the city's traffic flowing smoothly. He works to find solutions for areas where many accidents occur and is involved in planning traffic solutions when new subdivisions or businesses are constructed.

Dale and his staff enforce local laws about obstructions such as trees, fences, billboards, or new buildings that block the view of drivers. Dale's office staff takes calls and answers e-mails from citizens who have complaints or suggestions about traffic in the city.

When Dale drives around town, he watches with pride as traffic moves in a safe, efficient, and orderly manner. When he notices a problem, he immediately gets to work to fix it. Dale and his wife have two teenage children who are new drivers. He thinks of them when he makes decisions about making the roads in his city safer.

Columbia, Missouri
Citizens discuss a city road project.

Cargo Handler

Roger works for his state's port authority as a cargo handler. The seaport where he works is a busy place where container ships arrive and depart many times a day. Roger stays busy all day moving things in and out of cargo containers. He must work as part of a team with other cargo handlers and supervisors to move cargo safely and efficiently. Sometimes he moves cargo by hand or uses a dolly. Sometimes he uses a motorized vehicle, such as a forklift. One of Roger's job requirements is the ability to lift up to fifty pounds several times a day. Roger's work keeps him in excellent shape! He also uses his strength to open and close heavy shipping container doors. One of Roger's favorite parts of his job is driving automobiles in and out of containers for transport. He enjoys the challenge of parking cars in exactly the right spot. Roger works both in the bright, open sunshine and in dark, tight spaces inside containers. Every day he wears a hard hat, safety shoes, reflective vest, hearing protection, and a fall protection harness. Roger is proud that his state port authority and the port's customers trust him to handle valuable cargo with skill.

Secretary of the Department of Transportation, school crossing guard, road construction heavy equipment operator, air traffic controller, tractor-trailer driver, Adopt-a-Highway program coordinator, locomotive engineer, city traffic engineer, cargo handler—these are a few of the hundreds of occupations in the public and private sector of the U.S. transportation industry. When you travel or

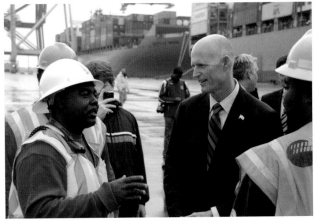
Jacksonville, Florida
Governor Rick Scott talks with port workers.

enjoy goods shipped to you or to a store near you, remember all the dedicated people that make U.S. transportation work and that for many centuries people have depended on others who work in transportation.

Do you see a man skilled in his work?

He will stand before kings;

He will not stand before obscure men.

Proverbs 22:29

Lesson Activities

Thinking Biblically — Copy Proverbs 22:29 into your notebook.

Vocabulary — Look up each of these words in a dictionary and read their definitions: accessible, vital, consecutive, supervision, qualification.

Literature — Read chapter 10 and "About the Photographs" and "Places to Visit" in *The Wright Brothers: How They Invented the Airplane.*

Creative Writing — In your notebook, make a list of at least 10 transportation workers that serve your family.

Picture This! — Take a photograph or draw a picture of a transportation worker.

Student Workbook or Lesson Review — If you are using one of these optional books, complete the assignment for Lesson 129.

★ Remember to choose an American Holiday to study this week! ★

UNIT 27 — HELPING PEOPLE IN NEED

BOOKS USED IN UNIT 27

- The Citizen's Handbook
- Student Workbook (optional)
- Lesson Review (optional)

San Antonio Food Bank, San Antonio, Texas

People HELPING PEOPLE

Being a good citizen includes helping others. When you buy snacks to put in a hospital waiting room, take food to shut-ins like the ladies at right below, or raise funds for a children's camp like the young people at left below, you are making a positive contribution to the life of your community. Citizens should look out for one another's needs. Sometimes we are in a position to help others and sometimes we are the ones needing help. When we need help, one of the best things we can do is to let someone help us.

Michigan
*Raising Funds for a Camp
for Children with Special Needs*

Gainesboro, Tennessee
Volunteers provide meals for people who are confined to their homes.

The Call of Compassion

Jesus had a heart of compassion for each person. Once a man with leprosy begged Jesus to heal him. "Moved with compassion, Jesus stretched out His hand and touched him, and said to him, 'I am willing; be cleansed'" (Mark 1:41). Jesus had compassion for the crowds also. "When Jesus went ashore, He saw a large crowd, and He felt compassion for them because they were like sheep without a shepherd; and He began to teach them many things" (Mark 6:34). After teaching them, Jesus then fed the crowd of five thousand men.

Jesus taught His disciples to have compassion for others. He told them, "And whoever in the name of a disciple gives to one of these little ones even a cup of cold water to drink, truly I say to you, he shall not lose his reward" (Matthew 10:42). This teaching is repeated in many ways in the New Testament. For example:

> So then, while we have opportunity, let us do good to all people, and especially to those who are of the household of the faith.　　　　　　　*Galatians 6:10*

> If a brother or sister is without clothing and in need of daily food, and one of you says to them, "Go in peace, be warmed and be filled," and yet you do not give them what is necessary for their body, what use is that?　　　　　　　*James 2:15-16*

> But whoever has the world's goods, and sees his brother in need and closes his heart against him, how does the love of God abide in him? Little children, let us not love with word or with tongue, but in deed and truth.　　　　　　　*1 John 3:17-18*

When Jesus described the last judgment in Matthew 25, He said that those who will inherit the kingdom will be those who have fed the hungry, given shelter to the stranger, clothed the naked, and visited those in prison (Matthew 25:31-40). Helping others in these ways reflects the love of God.

San Antonio, Texas
Counselor at the San Antonio Food Bank speaks with people in need.

Texas
A minister with Prison Fellowship preaches at a women's prison.

Colorado Springs, Colorado
Volunteers from Woodman Valley Chapel's ACTS Ministry give away a truckload of clothing on Valentine's Day, 2009.

Port Jefferson, New York
Hope House Ministries on Long Island provides shelter, counseling, and practical help for people in their community.

Gastonia, North Carolina
*These boys, ages twelve to fourteen, who work
in a textile mill throughout the week
return home from Sunday school, 1908.*

The early church helped widows (1 Timothy 5:16) and the poor (Romans 15:26). Through the centuries, Christians have cared for abandoned children, provided food and shelter for the needy, and served people in many other ways in the name of Christ. For instance, Christians in Britain began Sunday schools in the 1780s to provide education in the Bible as well as in academic subjects for children who were unable to attend school because they worked in factories.

As seen in the photos below, Americans have started and taught Sunday schools for children for much of our history. During the Great Depression, thousands of Americans migrated to California seeking a better life. Many hoped to find work on California farms. The Federal government set up Farm Security Administration camps to house migrant farm workers and their families. The children pictured below are attending Sunday school at one of these camps. In the photos on page 813, children attend a VBS on a military base.

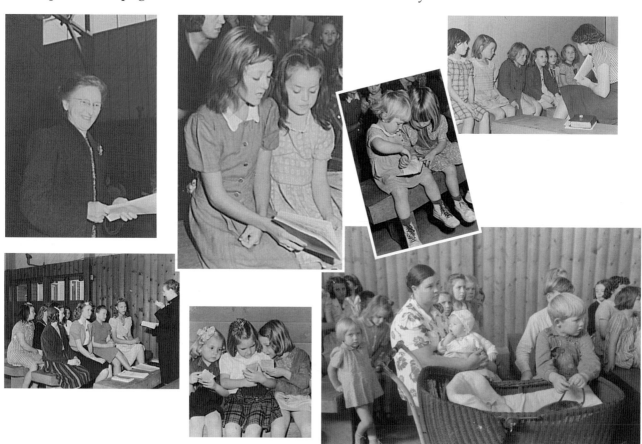

Woodville, California
*Children living in a migrant worker camp set up by the Farm Security Administration attend Sunday school.
The teacher (top left photo) is the wife of a migrant farm worker.*

Vacation Bible School

Soldiers at a military base hold an annual Vacation Bible School for children.

Genuine compassion for people is the motivation for many who help others. Another motivation is the conviction that, because we have been given much, we should give to others. Christians help others in order to bring honor to the Lord.

Helping others is one of the most satisfying things you will ever do. It is a good use of your time, money, and talents. The Lord calls us to think about the needs of others instead of concentrating on ourselves and our own desires.

One Person Helping on His Own

People who are willing to help others do not have to be part of a formal program. They do not have to organize a large group in order to serve. They can simply pay attention to the needs they see around them. In a parable that Jesus told, the Good Samaritan did not have to sign up for a program or organize a group of volunteers to help the man who had been beaten, robbed, and left by the side of the road. He simply responded to the need that he saw (Luke 10:30-37).

Guam
A Navy seaman explains math concepts to a student at a middle school.

Helping with a Large Group

Many large organizations need volunteers. Churches, for example, rely on volunteers to accomplish many tasks, such as cleaning the church building, mowing the church property, working in the church's adult or children's library, or teaching Bible classes.

Palos Verdes, California
Library Volunteers

Churches also offer opportunities for volunteers to meet the spiritual and physical needs of others, from those who live nearby to those who live on the other side of the world.

Hospitals utilize volunteers in many ways. Volunteers sit at information desks to help visitors find their way. They assist customers in hospital gift shops. They take mail and florist deliveries to patients' rooms. Other organizations like Ronald McDonald House help families with children who are in the hospital. See photo at right.

Philadelphia, Pennsylvania
Volunteers prepare a meal at the Ronald McDonald House near St. Christopher's Hospital for Children.

Helping with Government Programs

Volunteers help schools by tutoring students in math, science, computer skills, and English as a Second Language. Volunteers like the ones above provide assistance for public libraries. Volunteers staff county museums so that people can visit them. Volunteers work at local animal shelters. These and many other volunteers help communities in practical ways and save taxpayers money.

The Difference One Person Can Make

You never know whom you will influence by your service and your example. President Theodore Roosevelt's father was Theodore Roosevelt Sr., pictured at right. He was a wealthy businessman in New York City who had a great concern for the poor. One of the many ways he gave to others was by helping to found the Newsboy's Lodging House and Children's Aid Society for poor and homeless children of the city.

Oyster Bay, New York
Portrait of Theodore Roosevelt Sr. at Sagamore Hill

In the mid-to-late 1800s, many children in New York City lived in terrible conditions. They worked at odd jobs. One such job was selling newspapers on the street. Boys who did this were called newsboys. The Newsboys' Lodging House provided clean housing for five cents a night for newsboys and other needy children. Two of those who slept there are pictured at right. Theodore Roosevelt Sr. taught a Bible class there every Sunday evening.

One young man whom Roosevelt helped was John Brady. Brady was born in poverty in 1847. John worked at various odd jobs and was at times a newsboy. He often slept in a cardboard box or beside a building in Chatham Square. Brady spent some time at the Newsboys Lodging House and got to know the elder Roosevelt.

The Children's Aid Society sometimes sent homeless children west to

New York City, New York
These boys slept at the Newsboys Lodging House in February 1908.

live with families in the country. The Society sent Brady to live with a family in Indiana. He eventually attended Yale University and Union Seminary and went into the ministry. Brady worked as a missionary in the Alaska Territory. He helped to start a college for Alaska Natives and later became a businessman so that he would have money to help them.

President William McKinley appointed Brady to two terms as Governor of Alaska Territory. Then in 1904 President Theodore Roosevelt Jr. appointed him to serve a third term. The son of the man who had helped Brady when he was a poor boy in New York City was now President of the United States. Brady had the opportunity to meet the President and express his appreciation for his father.

Brady died in 1918. Alaska Natives who had become his friends conducted his funeral. John Brady was buried in the national cemetery in Sitka, Alaska. The epitaph on his tombstone reads, "A life ruled by faith in God and man." The influence and impact of Theodore Roosevelt Sr. were significant. You may never know how the help you give to one person will make a difference in that person's life and in the lives of the people that person touches. When we do good for the poor, we honor God.

One who is gracious to a poor man lends to the Lord,

And He will repay him for his good deed.

Proverbs 19:17

Lesson Activities

Thinking Biblically — Make a small poster featuring Galatians 6:10, James 2:15-16, or 1 John 3:17-18.

Literature — Read "My Father" in *The Citizen's Handbook*, page 153.

Creative Writing — Write a poem or song of at least ten lines about helping others.

Picture This! — Take a photograph or draw a picture of someone volunteering in the service of others.

Student Workbook or Lesson Review — If you are using one of these optional books, complete the assignment for Lesson 131.

Federal HELPING PROGRAMS

For many years, churches, private charities, and individuals helped people in need. Citizens did not expect the Federal government to give individuals money or to provide programs to help them because the Constitution did not give the Federal government authority to do this.

However, over time the Federal government began various kinds of assistance programs. For example, during and after the Civil War, the United States government provided pensions for veterans who had been injured in the war and later for widows of Union soldiers. Near the end of the 1800s, the former Confederate states began providing pensions to Confederate veterans and the widows of Confederate soldiers.

Government programs that assist individuals and families are often called social programs. One of the earliest social programs begun by the Federal government was the Children's Bureau begun in 1912. Its purpose was to improve infant health and to help children who were working in factories. The Bureau celebrated its 100th anniversary in 2012.

The Impact of the Great Depression

Millions of individuals and families had significant needs during the Great Depression of the 1930s. Churches and helping organizations actively helped people during this time, but some people thought that the government should get involved. Many of the Federal government's New Deal programs during the Depression were social programs.

Chicago, Illinois
The Library of Congress labeled this photo, "Child Welfare Bureau: Infant Welfare, Chicago," c. 1923.

Providence, Rhode Island
The Library of Congress labeled this photo, "For Child Welfare Exhibit 1912." These girls, aged six, nine, and eleven, are working on chain bags, probably for a factory.

A nurse weighs a baby in a basket on a scale, 1912.

817

Since then, the Federal government has taken on more and more responsibility in providing assistance to Americans who have physical, medical, and financial needs. One department in the executive branch of the Federal government, the Department of Health and Human Services, oversees about 300 programs and spends almost one-fourth of the entire Federal budget.

Fortieth Birthday of the Children's Bureau, 1952

The teachings of Jesus have had great influence on Americans. Even people who are not Christians believe many of the principles passed down to them because of America's Christian heritage. Part of the motivation for government assistance programs is an honest belief that people should help others.

This lesson looks at some of the main ways that the Federal government assists individuals and families. People must meet certain qualifications in order to receive these benefits. What each person or family receives depends on income, health problems, whether the person or family has a home, and whether the person or someone in the family has a job.

SNAP EBT Cards

Los Angeles, California
This store accepts only WIC payments and no cash.

Food Assistance for Families

The Women, Infants, and Children (WIC) program provides food and nutritional education for women who are expecting a baby, for new mothers, and for children up to age five. The Supplemental Nutrition Assistance Program (SNAP) is also designed to give families with low incomes help with purchasing food. SNAP replaced a former food assistance program called the food stamp program. Families who receive SNAP benefits receive an Electronic Benefit Transfer (EBT) card. When they want to purchase food, they use the EBT card just like a debit card. EBT cards are intended to provide food and can be used only for specific items. They cannot, for example, be used to purchase dog food. The Food and Nutrition Service of the U.S. Department of Agriculture oversees the WIC, SNAP, and school breakfast and lunch programs. See photos at left and at the top of page 819.

Fairfax, Virginia
The school lunch poster at right was created by the Works Progress Administration (WPA) Oklahoma Art Project, c. 1940. The WPA was a New Deal program. First Lady Michelle Obama (left) and celebrity chef Rachael Ray (center) visit Parklawn Elementary School to discuss new Federal standards for school lunches, January 2012.

Assistance with Housing

The Department of Housing and Urban Development in the executive branch of the U.S. government provides assistance to low income families for renting a home. This is how the program works. A private company agrees to operate an apartment complex for low-income renters. These renters pay less than what the company needs in order to stay in business. The amount of rent that a family pays depends on the family's income. Some families pay nothing. The Federal government then pays the company the difference between what the family pays and what the company needs to stay in business. This type of housing is called subsidized housing. In return for this help, residents must keep their apartments in good condition and not use illegal drugs. The owner of the apartment complex must keep the property in good condition. Former President Jimmy Carter and his family once lived in subsidized housing. It is pictured below.

The Federal government also encourages people to buy their own homes. Most families borrow money to purchase a home. A home loan is called a mortgage. Banks normally require a potential homeowner to pay a certain percentage of the price of a home up front and then loans him or her the remaining amount. The money paid up front is called a down payment. Homeowners then pay the lender a certain amount each month for several years until the mortgage has been paid.

One way the Federal government helps low- and middle-income families to buy their own homes is through the

Plains, Georgia
When future President Jimmy Carter and his wife Rosalynn first took over his father's peanut farm, their income was low. They and their three sons lived for a time in this government-subsidized apartment.

Federal Housing Administration (FHA). A family can obtain an FHA loan with a smaller down payment than a private bank would require for a loan. Private banks issue FHA loans, but the FHA provides insurance for the loan. This means that if the homeowner cannot make his mortgage payments, the FHA makes sure that the bank does not lose money.

Assistance for the Elderly

Two of the best known helping programs of the Federal government are Social Security and Medicare. Social Security began in the 1930s to provide a minimum level of income for retired persons. The program also provides income for disabled persons and for widows and orphaned children. Medicare pays for health care for elderly Americans. President Truman supported the Federal government helping Americans pay for health care. When President Johnson signed the Medicare bill, he held the ceremony at the Truman Library. See photo

Independence, Missouri
President Lyndon Johnson, First Lady Lady Bird Johnson, Senator Hubert Humphrey, Former President Harry Truman, and Former First Lady Bess Truman at the Truman Library when the Medicare Act was signed, 1965.

at right. Employed Americans pay taxes to provide the money for the Social Security and Medicare programs. However, those who receive Medicare services also pay a small monthly premium like they would if they were paying for health insurance.

Jobs, Unemployment, and Tax Credits

The Federal government offers training in many fields to help people become qualified to hold responsible, well-paying jobs. In addition, if a worker loses his job, the government will provide several months of unemployment benefits. Income from these benefits is lower than what a worker was earning when he still had his job, but the money helps the worker and his family pay for their basic needs while the worker looks for another job.

Working Americans pay income tax to the Federal government, but people who do not receive much income receive tax credits so that they pay little or no income tax. Many families with low incomes actually receive more assistance from the Federal government than they pay in taxes.

Benefits for Veterans

The Federal government gives medical assistance to men and women who once served our nation in the military and are now veterans. The government also provides money to pay for college and vocational education for veterans and insures mortgages to help veterans purchase homes.

Health Information and Research

The Centers for Disease Control and Prevention (CDC) collect and publish information about outbreaks of influenza and other diseases, health problems caused by pollution in the environment, diseases that spread as a result of problems in the nation's food supply, and many other health concerns. The National Institutes of Health provides money for medical research.

The programs in this lesson are just a fraction of the many Federal programs that try to help Americans be well-fed and healthy, have comfortable homes, and find work so that they can have a good income. In the next lesson, we will look at some helping programs that state governments carry out. The Federal government provides the money for many of these state programs.

Christians can assist people in need in many ways, especially by praying for them.

Beloved, I pray that in all respects you may prosper and be in good health,

just as your soul prospers.

3 John 2

Lesson Activities

Vocabulary – Write five sentences in your notebook, using one of these words in each: motivation, subsidized, potential, lender, premium. Check in a dictionary if you need help with their definitions.

Creative Writing - In your notebook, write one or two paragraphs answering the question: What is the government's responsibility in helping Americans with their basic needs?

Picture This! - Draw a picture of a family standing in front of their newly-purchased home.

Student Workbook or Lesson Review — If you are using one of these optional books, complete the assignment for Lesson 132.

State and Local
HELPING AGENCIES

Americans pay taxes to the Federal government. The President proposes a Federal budget that gives details about how he believes that money should be spent. Congress examines the President's budget and makes the final decision about how Federal funds will be spent.

Washington, D.C.
Taxpayer Rally

The President and the executive branch he oversees are then responsible for carrying out the spending plans that Congress has passed.

Many Americans worry about the amount of money that the Federal government spends, especially since it spends much more than it takes in. Borrowing money to pay for additional programs has resulted in a large national debt. In the photo at left, citizens have come to Washington, D.C., to express their desire for a smaller Federal government.

Over fifty percent of the Federal budget is used for programs that give assistance to people. Many citizens who believe that the Federal budget should be reduced think that government should spend much less on these programs. The Federal government sends much of the money budgeted for social programs to the fifty states. States oversee programs, using a combination of Federal and state funds.

Temporary Assistance for Needy Families

The Temporary Assistance for Needy Families (TANF) program began in 1997. It replaced an earlier welfare program that had operated for many years. Under the old welfare system, people who received assistance from the government did not have to try to find work and never had to quit receiving the assistance. As a result, some people became dependent on government assistance for many years. Sometimes children who grew up receiving assistance expected to have it when they grew up and had children of their own. As a result, some families came to expect government assistance generation after generation.

TANF provides money to low-income families to help with food and child care expenses. TANF programs vary from state to state, but in most states the adults in a family

Upper Marlborough, Maryland
*Lt. Governor Anthony Brown speaks
at the Prince George's County Health Department.*

must find a job within two years after they start receiving this assistance. Single parents who receive TANF benefits must work at least thirty hours per week, and the adults in two-parent families must work a total of thirty-five to fifty-five hours per week. A family can only receive TANF benefits for a maximum of five years during an adult's lifetime.

Health Care

State and local governments try to help their citizens stay well by encouraging healthy conditions in communities. This is called public health. One way they do this is by inspecting restaurants to make sure they are clean. States also oversee and operate health care clinics that provide health services. See photos at top and below. These clinics provide basic services such as immunizations. Pictured on page 824 is a statue of Dr. Florence Sabin, a physician who made great contributions to the public health of Colorado.

Johnson County, Indiana
Health Department Vehicle and Parking Space

The State of Colorado donated this statue of Dr. Florence Sabin to Statuary Hall in the United States Capitol. Sabin was the first woman to graduate from Johns Hopkins Medical School. In 1917 she became the first woman to become a full professor at a medical college. In 1944 the Governor of Colorado asked Sabin to be chairwoman of a subcommittee on health. Her work resulted in the "Sabin Health Laws."

Many people who live in rural areas do not have access to the level of health care that people in larger cities enjoy. Rural health care providers do not usually have as many patients as those in cities, and many times those rural patients cannot afford to pay the full cost of the medical care they receive. The Federal government and state governments work to make better health care available in rural areas. They provide financial assistance to doctors, small hospitals, and clinics.

Federal and state governments work together to pay for Medicaid programs. Medicaid provides health care for low-income individuals and families. People who receive Medicaid assistance must meet certain requirements to be eligible and must use doctors and nurse practitioners who agree to work with the Medicaid program.

In 2012 about one-fourth of all Americans received health care from either Medicare (see Lesson 132) or Medicaid. For most of American history, the majority of Americans have paid for their own health care or used private insurance companies.

In many countries in Europe, the national government oversees its country's entire health care system. Americans have different opinions about whether this would be good for the United States. As illustrated in the photos on page 825, Americans are divided. Some believe that the Federal government should pay for health care for all Americans, while others strongly oppose national health care. Those who oppose it believe that private health care takes better care of people and that government involvement would make health care more expensive overall. They also believe that people should be able to make all of their own choices about health care. Congress passed the Patient Protection and Affordable Care Act and President Obama signed into it law in 2010. It greatly increases the Federal government's involvement in health care for all Americans.

Help from Cities and Counties

Some cities have programs to help their citizens. For example, some city electric departments help low-income residents pay their utility bills. All electric customers have the opportunity to pay a small extra amount each month over and above their actual charge for electric usage. The utility company uses this money to help families who have difficulty paying their electric bills.

Demonstrators in Favor of National Health Care	Demonstrators Opposed to National Health Care

The city of New York distributes used furniture to people who live in subsidized housing. The city of Chicago helps provide taxis that can be used by people in wheelchairs. The city of Los Angeles has a Restaurant Meals Program that provides prepared meals for homeless, elderly, and disabled people who have difficulty preparing meals for themselves.

Questions about the best ways to help people in need are a dilemma for those who want to help. The reasons people are in need are many. Some people will always need assistance because they do not have the mental and physical capabilities to care for themselves. Some people in need receive help for a short time and learn how to work hard and become people who are able to assist others. Some people are truly victims of circumstances, while others have made bad choices that have caused them to end up where they are. Sometimes the best way to help someone is not to give them anything at all because he or she needs to learn to take responsibility. At other times, we would be wrong not to assist someone. It takes wisdom to know the difference. Though the Bible is clear in 2 Thessalonians 3:10 that "if anyone is not willing to work, then he is not to eat, either," it also says:

Is this not the fast which I choose,
To loosen the bonds of wickedness,
To undo the bands of the yoke,
And to let the oppressed go free
And break every yoke?
Is it not to divide
your bread with the hungry
And bring the homeless poor into the house;
When you see the naked, to cover him;
And not to hide yourself
from your own flesh?
Isaiah 58:6-7

Harrisburg, Pennsylvania
The Capitol Hunger Garden sits just outside the state capitol. It was established in 2010 by the Legislative Caucus on Hunger, which brings together concerned Federal, state, and local government officials and community volunteers.

Lesson Activities

Thinking Biblically — Read James 2.

Vocabulary — Find each of these words in a dictionary, then find the definition that corresponds to the way the word is used in this lesson: excessive, clinic, immunization, dilemma, capability. Copy the words and definitions into your notebook.

Creative Writing — In your notebook, write a short story of at least one page about someone who helped another person.

Find Out! — Talk to your parents about how they feel about a national healthcare system.

Student Workbook or Lesson Review — If you are using one of these optional books, complete the assignment for Lesson 133.

Private Groups That HELP OTHERS

Part of civics is learning how individuals can participate in and improve the civic life of their communities. Private individuals, churches, and other groups in America were helping those in need long before the Federal government became involved. One important way that individuals serve is by joining together with others who also want to help people in need. Notice the volunteers below.

Americans: A Generous People

Researchers have collected information about how people give money and to what causes they give. The results of many studies reveal that Americans are the most generous people in the world. We give around $300 billion in charitable donations each year. About 80% of this is given by individuals and families. Businesses and foundations give the rest.

The very wealthy are not the only Americans who make charitable donations. About half of all charitable donations are made by families with incomes of $100,000 or less. In fact, people with average incomes are often more generous than people with high incomes. People who are members of churches or who consider themselves religious are much more likely to be generous givers than those who are not religious.

The largest single category of donations is money given to religious organizations. These include churches and missionary causes. Donations to educational institutions (such as schools and colleges)

Angel Tree, a program of Prison Fellowship, reaches out to the children of people in prison. They mentor them, give them gifts at Christmas, and provide summer camp experiences like this.

827

are the next largest category. Other popular causes for donations are related to health needs, other benevolent causes, and international causes, such as giving to help victims of natural disasters. Americans respond generously when a natural disaster strikes the United States as well. In addition to giving money, Americans volunteer to go to scenes of disaster in order to help rebuild homes, prepare meals, and provide other emergency services for the people in need.

Faith-Based Organizations

Religious groups or individuals who share a common faith sometimes form helping groups that are called faith-based organizations. These groups depend on churches or other religious organizations and individuals for much of the money they need; but many of them also apply for grants from the Federal government. Generally speaking, faith-based organizations can apply for Federal grants on the same basis as secular groups, but they have to agree not to use the Federal money to promote their religious beliefs or activities.

The Salvation Army

In 1852 William Booth began preaching in London, England. However, he shared the gospel not in church buildings but on the streets of London with the poor and the outcasts of society. Booth made the gospel message central to his work, but he also sought to help people with their practical needs. Many people came to believe in Jesus through his message. Other preachers and helpers began to assist him. By 1874 there were forty-two evangelists and one thousand volunteers working with Booth. Four years later, Booth gave the organization the name by which it is still known today, The Salvation Army. The "Salvationists" sometimes received criticism from people in traditional churches. At times street gangs and others who opposed their work attacked them physically. But they brought tens of thousands to faith in the Lord.

Harrisburg,
Pennsylvania

Eliza Shirley brought The Salvation Army movement to the United States. She held the first meeting in America in 1879 in Philadelphia. The next year a group came from England to New York and established the first permanent Salvation Army effort in this country. The ministry grew rapidly and had a strong influence on people.

The Salvation Army is an example of a faith-based organization. The organization helps homeless people and those who are trying to recover from bad decisions they have made in their lives, such as those who have become addicted to alcohol or drugs. The Salvation Army provides disaster relief in times of crisis. The Salvation Army also offers youth camps for children during the summer. They have a special ministry of teaching children about music and how to play instruments. Perhaps you have seen people volunteering to be bell ringers who collect money for The Salvation Army in the weeks before Christmas.

Individuals can help The Salvation Army by contributing money, volunteering in many different ways (over three million people do volunteer work with The Salvation Army), and working in and contributing items to Salvation Army Thrift Stores. These stores sell second-hand items, and the proceeds go to help ministry activities. Another way that people help the group is by donating cars, which are then sold and the money contributed to the ministry.

Still today, the first priority of proclaiming the gospel of salvation in Christ guides all of the organization's helping activities.

Civic Organizations

Hundreds of thousands of Americans are involved in civic organizations, also called civic clubs. A civic club is an organization whose members join together to accomplish good in their communities. It is not surprising that a country like America with its foundation on Christian ideals and its tradition of giving to others would be the place where so many civic organizations have been founded. Three of America's many civic clubs are Rotary, Kiwanis, and Civitan. Examples of their service are illustrated at right.

Monrovia, California
This area of the public library was donated by the local Rotary and Kiwanis clubs.

Civitan International was founded in 1920. Civitan comes from the Latin word *civitas* which means citizenship. From the beginning, the club's focus was service. Civitans in Knoxville, Tennessee, raised $100,000 to build a hospital in 1923 for poor patients who were suffering from tuberculosis. In 1929 Civitans in Rogersville, Alabama, raised $40,000 to build a new high school. In the early years of

Sand Springs, Oklahoma

the organization, Civitans paid for surgery for disabled children. They served as big brothers to boys who needed attention. They registered people to vote. Civitans eventually decided to focus on helping children with developmental disabilities. In 1992 the club dedicated the Civitan International Research Center at the University of Alabama at Birmingham. The center researches developmental disabilities. Famous Civitans include inventor Thomas Edison, U.S. Supreme Court Justices Hugo Black and Ed Sanford, and Presidents Coolidge, Franklin D. Roosevelt, Truman, and Kennedy. See Civitans at right.

Homeless Shelters

It might be hard for you to imagine someone not having a home—a safe, secure, and warm place to go every night. In the United States, there are thousands of people who are in just this situation. One way that people help others in their communities is by providing homeless shelters for people who do not have a place to live.

In many cities, people have realized this need and have formed organizations that purchase or build buildings to serve as places where people without a home can go for shelter and food. A church sometimes organizes a shelter in its building or secures a separate building for this purpose. The group might receive some government money, but it relies mostly on private donations and volunteers to serve those in need. Many charitable organizations help with homeless shelters that other groups sponsor. The photo at right gives an example of this.

Habitat for Humanity

A homeless shelter is important as a temporary home. However, many people have the goal of owning a home of their own. Habitat for Humanity is a private organization that helps low- to moderate-

Washington, D.C.
President Herbert Hoover (at lower right) met with attendees of the 1932 Civitan International convention.

Pullyup, Washington
Several churches work together to provide food and shelter at the Freezing Nights shelter, 2009.

income families own a decent home. Habitat volunteers build the homes. President and Mrs. Jimmy Carter became two well-known volunteers after he left the presidency. Often at least some of the materials and the required professional labor (such as the services of a roofer or an electrician) are donated free of charge. This lowers the cost of a home considerably. Families that Habitat chooses to receive homes must donate labor themselves. The family receives a no-interest loan, and the

North Dakota
Members of the North Dakota National Guard work at a Habitat home site. Guard members adopted two immigrant families from Iraq who moved to North Dakota.

payments they make go toward the costs of helping to build other homes. Owning a home gives a family a sense of security and of being part of their community. Many cities in the U.S. have Habitat chapters that plan and build homes for local citizens. See photo above.

Food Banks and Food Pantries

The definition of a food bank is a place where people who have the means to donate food do so and people who need food can withdraw it. In 1967 John van Hengel was serving dinner to people in need at a Phoenix charity when a woman told him that she was struggling to feed her children. He talked to his church, which gave him $3,000 and an abandoned building. Van Hengel used these to found St. Mary's Food Bank Alliance, the first food bank in the world. Now food banks exist in many cities around the U.S. and in many other countries.

Many churches operate food pantries, which give canned food and other non-perishable items to people who come to the churches for assistance. Church members have the opportunity to donate food to the food pantry, to organize the food that is collected, and to help carry food

to the cars of people who come for assistance. Churches can also often purchase food at reduced prices from food banks and other organizations. See photo at right.

One American President made a tremendous impact by feeding the hungry. Businessman and future President Herbert Hoover was in London on business when World War I began. Upon the request of the U.S. consul, Hoover organized the evacuation

Boston, Massachusetts
Boston Food Bank

San Antonio, Texas
San Antonio Food Bank

of 120,000 Americans who were trapped in Europe. During the war, Germany invaded Belgium causing widespread hunger. Hoover organized a private charity called the Committee for the Relief of Belgium. He raised several million dollars that provided food and medicine to help the devastated Belgians.

Meals for the Poor and Elderly

Charitable organizations have provided meals for the poor for centuries. During the Great Depression of the 1930s, many people waited in breadlines for free food. The origin of the term breadline can be traced to the late 1800s when Charles Fleischmann gave bread to the poor from his Fleischmann's Model Vienna Bakery on Broadway in New York City. He and his brother Maximillian founded the well-known Fleischmann's Yeast company.

Volunteers work in soup kitchens across America each day to provide food for people who are hungry. The food to feed them comes from many places, from food banks, from private contributors, and from U.S. Department of Agriculture donations of excess food produced by American farmers.

About 5,000 local organizations provide daily meals for over one million older Americans through a program called Meals on Wheels. The first Meals on Wheels program began in England during World War II. A program with the same name delivered meals to people in Philadelphia in the 1950s. Today some older Americans go to local senior citizen centers for their meals, but volunteers deliver many meals to people in their homes. These local organizations might be churches, agencies of local government, or other groups; but they all depend on an army of volunteers to get the food to the people receiving the meals. This "volunteer army" has been estimated to be about one million people.

Paris, Texas
Meals on Wheels Volunteers

Run 4 Don

Thousands of helping organizations exist in the United States. Many are well known—the American Cancer Society, the American Red Cross, Big Brothers Big Sisters, Goodwill Industries, the YMCA. How did they get started and why? Each began with a desire to make things better for other people. Here is the story of one small organization centered in a town of 1,000 people in middle Tennessee.

Donald Wayne "Don" Chaffin had a career in the public sector and retired as a plant supervisor with the U.S. Army Corps of Engineers. Those who loved Don knew him as a husband, father, grandfather, preacher, and Christian gentleman. He was passionate about helping young people and served as the co-director of a Christian youth camp. His friends and family were saddened when this godly man was diagnosed with Amyotrophic Lateral Sclerosis (ALS). Don kept preaching even when confined to a wheelchair. In 2011 Don went to be with the Lord. His memory lingers in the hearts of those who knew him and in the Run 4 Don organization his friends and family began before he died. Each September hundreds gather in tiny Gainesboro, Tennessee, for a 5K race which they Run 4 Don. Don attended the first race in 2010, just four months before he died.

Run 4 Don is a non-profit organization whose purposes are to provide scholarship funds to young Christian men and women, to raise awareness and money for research into ALS, and to honor Donald Chaffin and

Gainesboro, Tennessee
Run 4 Don, 2010 and 2012

Sleepy First Place Winner in the Girls 0-10 Age Group with Her Father

others for their strong and courageous battle with ALS. Three hundred and forty-two people ran (or walked) in the third race in 2012, and the event raised $31,568!

Jesus said that His followers are the light of the world. He said that, as others see the good works that Christians do, they will glorify God. Make a difference in someone's life.

Let your light shine before men in such a way
that they may see your good works,
and glorify your Father who is in heaven.
Matthew 5:16

Lesson Activities

Thinking Biblically — Read Matthew 5:1-16.

Vocabulary — In your notebook, write your own definition for each of these words: benevolent, secular, society, criticism, proceeds. Look in this lesson for clues for the meaning of the words. When you are finished writing your definitions, look in a dictionary for comparison.

Literature — Read "To Love and Care for Our Neighbor" in *The Citizen's Handbook*, pages 154-157.

Find Out! — Find out if there are local chapters of the Civitans Club, Habitat for Humanity, Meals on Wheels, or The Salvation Army in your area.

Student Workbook or Lesson Review — If you are using one of these optional books, complete the assignment for Lesson 134.

★ Remember to choose an American Holiday to study this week! ★

UNIT 28 — EDUCATION AND THE ARTS

BOOKS USED IN UNIT 28

- The Citizen's Handbook
- Student Workbook (optional)
- Lesson Review (optional)

Homeschool Day at the Colorado State Capitol

The Education of
A PRESIDENT

America had never seen a President like Theodore Roosevelt when he assumed the office in 1901. He had bold ideas about the kind of nation that the United States should be, and he had the willingness to work hard to accomplish his dreams. He had been a police commissioner in New York City and a cattle rancher in the Dakota Territory. He was an amateur boxer, and he had written and published fifteen books. In addition to Theodore Roosevelt Island Park mentioned in Lesson 49, Theodore Roosevelt has been honored with statues, memorials, a national park, and many other tributes in the more than one hundred years since he left the presidency. Photos of some of these memorials are on the pages of this lesson.

Clockwise from Top Left: Theodore Roosevelt High School in Des Moines, Iowa; Theodore Roosevelt Memorial Monument in Glacier National Park in Montana; Roosevelt Hotel in Seattle, Washington; President Roosevelt laid the cornerstone of the Roosevelt Arch in Yellowstone National Park in 1903; former President Roosevelt dedicated the Theodore Roosevelt Dam near Phoenix, Arizona, in 1911; Theodore Roosevelt Senior High School in Washington, D.C.; the USS Theodore Roosevelt aircraft carrier was placed into active service in 1986.

Statues of President Theodore Roosevelt (From Top Left)

1) The bust of Vice President Theodore Roosevelt is in the U.S. Capitol.

2) This statue of Roosevelt is part of the "City of Presidents" collection in Rapid City, South Dakota.

3) This statue portrays Roosevelt during the years he worked on his ranch in Dakota Territory. It stands in front of the Stark County Courthouse in Dickinson, North Dakota. The county and city, along with the Theodore Roosevelt Center at Dickinson State University (DSU), and the DSU Foundation unveiled it in 2011. The artist was a DSU graduate.

4) The Presidents carved on Mount Rushmore are George Washington, Thomas Jefferson, Theodore Roosevelt, and Abraham Lincoln.

5) While in Dakota Territory, Roosevelt became friends with Dr. Henry Waldo Coe. Dr. Coe donated this "Theodore Roosevelt Roughrider" statue to Portland, Oregon. It stands in Roosevelt Square. President Calvin Coolidge broke ground for it in 1922. It was unveiled later that year. Dr. Coe also donated a smaller version of the same statue to Mandan, North Dakota. President Roosevelt's widow and all five of his surviving children attended its dedication in 1924 as did members of the Mandan, Gros Ventre, Arikara, and Sioux tribes of Native Americans. The Portland and Mandan sculptures were created by Alexander Proctor, who knew Roosevelt personally.

What experiences helped to create this extraordinary person? What influences shaped his personality and his outlook? How was he able to carry out the great responsibilities he carried?

An Active, Loving Family

The Roosevelt family came to America from the Netherlands during the colonial period of our nation's history. For several generations, they were successful in business and prominent in New York society. As mentioned in Lesson 131, the future President's father, Theodore Roosevelt Sr. (called Thee), was a respected businessman. He was also a civic leader. The future President's mother Martha (called Mittie) was from a prominent family from Georgia. They were married on December 22, 1853. They loved each other but they had differing views about the most important issues facing the country at the time. During the Civil War, Thee actively supported the Union army while Mittie supported the Confederate army.

The Roosevelts had four children: Anna, Theodore Jr., Elliott, and Corinne. According to the Theodore Roosevelt Center in Dickinson, North Dakota, and Harvard University Press, they were called Bye or Bamie (short for bambino), Teedie, Ellie, and Conie within the family circle. However, since Teddy is the nickname used for him today, we'll call Theodore Teddy.

Anna suffered from a spinal handicap. Caring for her and seeking the best medical treatment for her was a big part of what Theodore Sr. did. Though Anna always suffered from her handicap, she grew into a woman of strong character, married, and had a son. When Teddy became President, he visited often at her home in Washington, D.C., and sought her advice.

The Roosevelts put first things first. Mr. Roosevelt began each day with Bible reading and prayers with his family. He took his seat on the couch with room for one child between him and the arm of the couch. Teddy and his younger siblings would scurry to get that privileged position, and after one of them did the other two would take seats on his other side.

In addition to his work with the Children's Aid Society and the Newsboys' Lodging House, Theodore Sr. helped found the New York Orthopedic Dispensary and Hospital to help other children like Anna. Mr. Roosevelt also helped establish the Metropolitan Museum of Art and the American Museum of Natural History.

Teddy's parents were able to provide costly opportunities for their children such as tours of Europe when he was ten and again when he was fourteen, but the greater influence on them was their parents' strong devotion to them and to what was best for them. The children loved being outdoors, spending their summers in the country, roaming and exploring, riding horses, and climbing trees. In his diary, Teddy recorded notes about animals he saw. On the third floor of their New York City townhouse, the parents tore out the back wall so that their children would have an open-air play area.

Education and Experiences

None of the Roosevelt children attended a formal school. Their aunt (their mother's sister) lived with them and was their tutor. The children studied the usual academic subjects; but primarily the parents encouraged their children to read, learn, and investigate on their own. Mr. and Mrs. Roosevelt did not let them read the cheap, unwholesome novels that were popular in the day, but the children were avid readers in their father's extensive library. See a quote from Teddy on page 839. The children asked many questions of their parents, their aunt, and other adults whom they met. Their aunt nourished their imaginations with many stories about life in the South. Young Teddy also enjoyed stories about adventures in the western United States. During the summers, Dr. Hilborne West, an uncle, would visit with them for several weeks. He read to them from Shakespeare and performed Shakespeare's plays for them under the trees. This fascinated them and further encouraged their desire to learn.

★ ★ ★

"The books are everywhere. There are as many in the north room and in the parlor . . . as in the library; the gun room at the top of the house . . . contains more books than any of the other rooms . . . . Let me add that ours is in no sense a collector's library. Each book was procured because someone of the family wished to read it."

★ ★ ★

During the family's tour in Europe and the Middle East when Teddy was fourteen, the children spent the summer with a German family. Teddy loved German poetry and always felt close to the German people because of this experience.

Teddy had a passionate interest in science. He loved reading about birds and reptiles and making drawings of them, but he loved even more collecting specimens of animals for what he called the Roosevelt Museum of Natural History. His father paid for lessons in taxidermy, which is the preparing and mounting of bodies of animals for display. The household servants and Teddy's siblings sometimes complained about the mess and the smells of Teddy's hobby, but Roosevelt later recalled in his autobiography, "My father and mother encouraged me warmly in this, as they always did in anything that could give me wholesome pleasure or help to develop me." While in his twenties, Teddy offered his nearly 250 labeled and mounted specimens to the Smithsonian. Some are pictured at top right.

Roosevelt expanded his knowledge of and love for nature while in Dakota Territory. Portions of his land there are now part of Theodore Roosevelt National Park. See photos of the park and Roosevelt's cabin at right.

Smithsonian National Museum of Natural History

Teddy collected this ruffed grouse on February 3, 1875, and the bat on August 29, 1875, at Oyster Bay on Long Island, New York. He collected the squirrel at Garrison, New York, on March 10, 1877.

North Dakota
Above are wild horses in Theodore Roosevelt National Park. At right is Roosevelt's cabin, which is located within the park.

839

American Museum of Natural History in New York

At left is the entrance to the American Museum of Natural History, co-founded by Theodore Roosevelt Sr., with its equestrian statue of Teddy Roosevelt standing in front. At right is the Theodore Roosevelt Rotunda, which serves as the museum's grand entrance. Decorating the room are three murals which illustrate milestones in Teddy's life. The room also features quotations about Youth, Manhood, Nature, and The State from Teddy's writings. In the center is a snowy owl which Teddy mounted in 1876 when he was seventeen years old. He gave the specimen to the museum in 1911.

Overcoming Physical Limitations

Teddy had a serious difficulty in childhood—severe asthma. Many nights he found it difficult to breathe, and his father would carry him around the house or take him into the streets in a carriage, hoping that the cold night air would open his lungs and help him to breathe. Because of this illness, Teddy had a weak body. His father challenged him to build up his body through exercise and provided exercise equipment for him at home. Teddy used it regularly. He largely overcame his problems with asthma by the time he was in college. The strong adventurer that comes to mind when we think of Theodore Roosevelt came about by the opportunity that his father provided and the hard work and dedication of young Teddy.

Teddy also took up boxing to build up his strength. Though he did not do well at it because he was not big or strong like other boxers, he stayed with the sport. When he was Governor of New York, he would occasionally go a few rounds with a boxer in a boxing ring he had installed in the Governor's mansion.

Another physical limitation that Roosevelt had to overcome was poor eyesight. He did not realize that anything was wrong with his vision until he was twelve years old. His poor eyesight showed up when he could not hit targets well with his gun. When his friends talked about what they read on billboards, Teddy could not even see the letters. He was fitted with glasses, and later he wrote that the spectacles "literally opened an entirely new world to me. I had no idea how beautiful the world was until I got those spectacles."

College Years

Teddy studied under a tutor to prepare for entrance exams to Harvard. He later recalled that when he began with the tutor, "In science and history and geography and in unexpected parts of German and French I was strong, but lamentably weak in Latin and Greek and mathematics." Harvard admitted Teddy. He enrolled when he was not quite eighteen years of age. When he went to college, Theodore Sr. wrote to his son,

Many historic actors have portrayed Teddy Roosevelt at historic sites and festivals, including Joe Wiegand above and Case Hicks at lower right. The real Teddy Roosevelt is at top right.

"Take care of your morals first, your health next, and finally your studies." Roosevelt complied. He later looked back and wrote, "I left college and entered the big world owing more than I can express to the training I had received, especially in my own home; but with much else also to learn if I were to become really fitted to do my part in the work that lay ahead for the generation of Americans to which I belonged."

The Influence of His Father

Theodore endured a crushing blow when his father died unexpectedly of cancer while Teddy was in college. A short time later Teddy wrote in his diary, "How I wish I could ever do something to keep up his name." His father's example and ideals were always in his mind. Later in life he said that whenever he faced a difficult decision, he tried to envision what his father would do and then follow through on that course of action to the best of his ability. Roosevelt looked back and observed, "My father, Theodore Roosevelt, was the best man I ever knew. He combined strength and courage with gentleness, tenderness, and great unselfishness."

Theodore Roosevelt showed that he learned the lessons his father had taught by word and example. He was devoted to his own children, loved being with them, and wrote them letters of encouragement and instruction. He devoted his life to public service.

A Thankful Spirit

Roosevelt Elk

"Here Stood Theodore Roosevelt"
Floor of Pennsylvania State Capitol

The Washington Nationals baseball mascots are from left to right, George Washington, Thomas Jefferson, Abraham Lincoln, and Theodore Roosevelt.

Teddy Roosevelt's parents gave themselves to their children. They provided Teddy an encouraging atmosphere to help him become all he could be. When he turned eighteen during his first semester at Harvard, he wrote the following in a letter to his mother:

> *It seems perfectly wonderful, in looking back over my eighteen years of existence, to see how I have literally never spent an unhappy day, unless by my own fault! When I think of this, and also of my intimacy with you all (for I hardly know a boy who is on as intimate and affectionate terms with his family as I am), I feel that I have an immense amount to be thankful for.*

This is the man who lived life to the fullest, who devoted his life to serving his country, who sought to do as much good as he could, and who became the 26th President of the United States. All his life, Teddy Roosevelt remembered the lessons he learned in his youth.

My son, observe the commandment of your father
And do not forsake the teaching of your mother.
Proverbs 6:20

Lesson Activities

Thinking Biblically - Copy Proverbs 1:8 into your notebook.

Vocabulary — Look up each of these words in a dictionary and read their definitions: amateur, nourish, specimen, asthma, lamentably.

Literature — Read "Work, Study, Exercise, and Play" in *The Citizen's Handbook*, pages 158-159.

Creative Writing — In your notebook, make a list of five things you would like to learn about and five things you would like to accomplish in your life.

Picture This! — Take a photograph or draw a picture of someone in your family doing one of their regular mind-building activities.

Student Workbook or Lesson Review — If you are using one of these optional books, complete the assignment for Lesson 136.

The Education of
A NATION

The adults of every generation have the responsibility to pass on to their children the beliefs, knowledge, skills, and behaviors that they learned from their parents and from their own experiences. Parents also want to teach their children how to learn, so that the next generation can explore new topics, gain additional knowledge, and accomplish even more than their parents have. One of the civic duties that people have is to equip the next generation to be prepared and responsible citizens who can carry on the society and the communities into which they were born. Young citizens have the responsibility to be like young Teddy Roosevelt and to pursue learning with a spirit of gratitude. This is education.

Throughout history, parents have taught their children in many ways. Parents and grandparents have given instruction and admonition, told stories, and sung songs to teach life skills and to pass on their culture to the next generation. Christian parents have taught their children what the Bible says as they go through their days and as they set aside time for family worship and instruction. In the last two centuries, the emphasis in education has become giving children formal instruction while they sit at desks. However, as we saw in the lives of the Roosevelts, schooling is actually only part of education. As illustrated at right, education is visiting historic festivals, going to clogging classes, dressing up in costumes, following a snapping turtle across the yard, watching a family of ducks waddle down the road and learning from books like *Uncle Sam and You*!

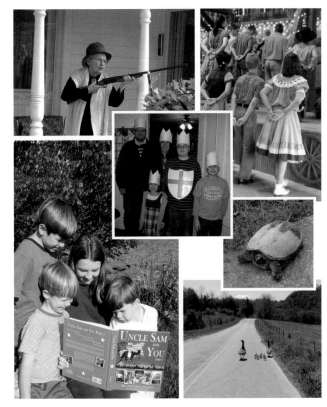

Education in History

Moses commanded the nation of Israel to teach their children the Law that they received at Mount Sinai (Deuteronomy 6:4-9). Israelite parents, like the parents in every nation around them, also taught their children such life skills as farming, hunting, and craft techniques.

In the ancient world, formal education was usually available only for young men who were going to become priests or government workers and for the children of the very wealthy. Greek and Roman philosophers sometimes set up schools to teach a select group of students their perspectives on life and the world around them. Rabbis received special training at the time of Jesus.

Formal education increased at different times in history through the efforts of leaders committed to it. For instance, the emperors of the Eastern Roman Empire in Constantinople encouraged the study of science and history. Charlemagne, king of France (ruled 768-814 A.D.), admired education and made learning available for church leaders and members of his court. The University of Paris in France began around 1200 A.D. and was one of the first universities in Europe. Oxford and Cambridge began in England a short time later. These universities at first emphasized religious studies, medicine, the law, and the arts.

For many centuries, the practice of apprenticeships, in which master craftsmen trained young men in a particular profession, was a common way to teach skills to the younger generation. Historians generally believe that, from ancient times through the Middle Ages, only a small percentage of people could read or write.

The invention of movable type in the 1430s led to an increase in the number of books available, especially copies of the Bible. Reformers such as John Wycliffe and William Tyndale worked to make the Bible available in the everyday language of the people. Church leaders Martin Luther and John Calvin believed that everyone ought to be able to read the Scriptures. Both men encouraged local governments to establish school systems to enable more people to read the Bible. During the 1500s, Catholic religious orders established schools for the poor in Europe and for Native Americans in Spain's colonies in the New World. People in England and Scotland who wanted to improve the lives of the poor established elementary schools in some communities.

Education in the American Colonies

English settlers in America brought with them the desire to provide formal education for children to help them read the Bible and to be good citizens. As the colonists formed communities, they often (but not always) organized schools. Education was important in the Massachusetts colony. In 1647 the colony passed a law that required each township that had fifty households to establish a school or pay a penalty if it did not. The law required towns of one hundred families to establish a grammar school to teach students enough to be able to enter college. The law stated schools needed to be established because Satan is a deluder who wants to keep people ignorant of the Scriptures.

Education in the New United States

At first, American parents made the decision about whether to send their children to the community school. In 1852 Massachusetts became the first state to require children to attend school. In 1918 Mississippi became the 48th state to require children to go to school. When Alaska and Hawaii became states in 1959, they required children to attend school.

Schooling in America began as a local effort. In 1837 Massachusetts established the first state board of education. Other states created departments of education in the decades that followed. These departments developed requirements that local schools had to meet. In the late 1950s, after the Soviet Union shocked the world by sending the Sputnik satellite into space, the Federal government gave money to local school districts to hire teachers in math and science to try to "catch up" with the Soviets. Congress created the U.S. Department of Education in 1979.

Churches established the first colleges in America. Later, states founded colleges. The Federal government gradually got more involved in college education. During the Civil War, the government authorized money from the sale of certain public lands to establish what were called land-grant universities that specialized in the study of agriculture and industry. After World War II, Congress passed the G.I. Bill, which provided money for veterans to attend college or trade schools. During the 1960s, the Federal government helped to establish two-year community colleges in many places around the country. Today universities receive grants from the Federal government to conduct research in many fields.

c. 1874

American Education Today

Educators divide formal schooling into the elementary (kindergarten through the eighth grade) level and the secondary (ninth through twelfth grade) level, which is called high school. Some school systems have middle schools, which can include fifth through eighth grades or possibly fourth through eighth grades.

About 55 million people between the ages of five and seventeen live in the United States today. Of that number, about 85% attend public schools. Charter schools are public schools that receive a special charter from the state government. They do not have to follow the typical rules and regulations for public schools. Instead, they have special goals such as higher student achievement or an emphasis on particular areas of study such as the sciences or the arts. Over six million adults work in the public school systems of our country. Eleven percent of American students attend private schools, and 83% of private schools are religious-based. About four percent of American students, or around two million, are homeschooled. Each state sets its own regulations for homeschoolers, such as what kind of testing is required and how long a school day must be.

The Big Yellow School Bus

The big yellow school bus is widely recognized as a part of public and private schools. The Blue Bird Company is one of the best-known manufacturers of school buses. Schools use Blue Bird buses across the United States and in over sixty other countries. The company, which is based in Fort Valley, Georgia, employs over one thousand workers. Blue Bird began in 1927 on the basis of Christian principles. An original sign from 1927 that says "God is our Refuge & Strength" still hangs in the corporate headquarters. Blue Bird employs a full-time chaplain who holds regular non-denominational services during business hours for any employees who want to take part. The company follows the principles of integrity, trustworthiness, reliability, mutual respect, and appreciation for its employees and customers.

New York
Sign to Jamestown Business College

A College Education

College education involves undergraduate study (which leads to a two-year associate's degree or a four-year bachelor's degree) and graduate study (which leads to master's degrees and to doctoral degrees). Law school and medical school are professional schools. About 21.6 million persons are students in American colleges and universities. Hundreds of thousands of adults take courses in technical or trade schools, for self-improvement, or to prepare for tests to earn the GED (General Educational Development) certificate. The GED is an alternative to a high school diploma. About 700,000 persons take the GED test every year.

Denver Public Library

Libraries

An important source of education in communities across America are local public libraries. Here all citizens have access to printed materials like books and magazines and to computers. The first libraries in America were private. Today most local public libraries are supported by local taxes. The U.S. has many kinds of libraries in addition to local public libraries, including school libraries, university libraries, state libraries, and, of course, the Library of Congress.

Presidents Who Were Teachers

Several Presidents were teachers at some point in their lives before they became President. John Adams taught for a while in a one-room school soon after he graduated from Harvard.

Millard Fillmore taught elementary school as did his wife. She taught Millard himself before they were married—he was seventeen and she was nineteen.

James Garfield taught in Ohio and also taught penmanship at an academy in Vermont. His Vice President Chester Arthur, who became President when Garfield died, had been principal at the same school three years earlier.

Grover Cleveland was an assistant teacher at the New York Institute for the Blind in Manhattan (where he became friends with hymnwriter Fanny J. Crosby).

Lyndon Johnson served as principal of a small Texas elementary school attended by Hispanic children and later taught public speaking at Sam Houston High School in Houston.

Woodrow Wilson was a college professor and President of Princeton University. Presidents Taft, Clinton, and Obama taught in law schools.

You are receiving an education. God gave parents the responsibility to teach their children the ways of God, what their children need to know in order to live well, and how their children can continue growing and learning throughout life. Part of your education is the formal schooling your parents teach you in various subjects from year to year. Schooling takes place in many ways in the United States today, but the heart of education is still one generation of citizens preparing the next generation to be God's servants in their families, their churches, their communities, and their nation—just like Thee and Mittie Roosevelt did for Teddy and his sisters and brother.

> For I give you sound teaching;
> Do not abandon my instruction.
> When I was a son to my father,
> Tender and the only son in the sight of my mother,
> Then he taught me and said to me,
> "Let your heart hold fast my words;
> Keep my commandments and live."
> Proverbs 4:2-4

Lesson Activities

Thinking Biblically — In your notebook, write a paragraph answering the question: What good things can a Christian do with his or her education?

Vocabulary — In your notebook, write a paragraph that uses all of these words: behavior, emphasis, apprenticeship, deluder, regulation. Consult a dictionary if you need help with their definitions.

Literature — Read "The Teacher's Dream" in *The Citizen's Handbook*, pages 160-161.

Find Out! — Ask your parents how they have received formal and informal education in their lives.

Student Workbook or Lesson Review — If you are using one of these optional books, complete the assignment for Lesson 137.

A Home for AMERICAN ART

Birmingham, Alabama
Needlework in Highlands Methodist Episcopal Church in Five Points

Art is all around us. We create art on quilts, barns, gates, and cakes. America has many artists to admire. Using the full breadth of artistic styles, American artists have created paintings, drawings, photographs, textiles, and sculpture that beautifully showcase our country and the people who live in it. Art museums, dotted throughout the country, preserve original pieces of art and display them for the education and enjoyment of Americans and our visitors. These museums and the collections they protect do not just happen—they are the result of intentional efforts of artists, their admirers, and public and private organizations that make the effort to keep American art safe for future Americans to enjoy.

Kentucky
Painted Quilt on Barn

Forkland, Alabama
Tin Man Art in Hayfield

Savannah, Georgia
Wrought Iron Gate

Marietta, Ohio
Birthday Cake for Smokey Bear

848

John James Audubon Center at Mill Grove – Audubon, Pennsylvania

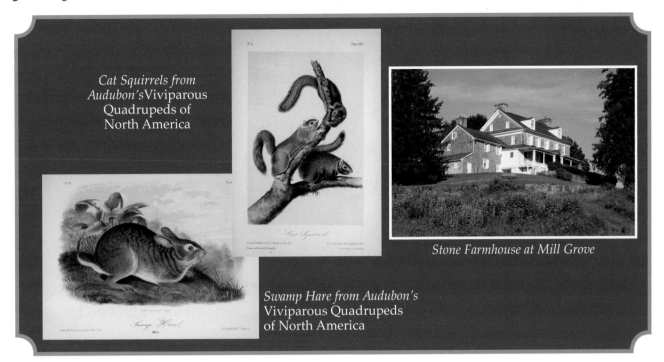

Cat Squirrels from Audubon's Viviparous Quadrupeds of North America

Swamp Hare from Audubon's Viviparous Quadrupeds of North America

Stone Farmhouse at Mill Grove

John James Audubon was born in 1785 in what is now Haiti. He was raised in France. In 1803, when John James was eighteen, his father sent him to manage Mill Grove, his estate in Pennsylvania. While exploring the lush countryside of his first American home, Audubon fell in love with the animals, birds, and plants of America. Here he began a hobby of drawing nature that eventually became his career. The first installment of his *Birds of America* was published in 1827. This collection contains 435 life-sized paintings of birds. John James Audubon's other major work, *Viviparous Quadrupeds of North America*, contains 150 hand-colored drawings of animals. Audubon settled in New York City and died in 1851 at the age of 65.

In 1813 the Audubon family sold Mill Grove to Samuel Wetherill of Philadelphia. The Wetherill family owned the estate until Herbert J. Wetherill sold it to the Montgomery County Commissioners in 1951. Montgomery County opened it to the public as the Mill Grove Museum and Audubon Wildlife Sanctuary. In 2003 the Montgomery County Department of Parks & Heritage Services and the National Audubon Society, which was named for John James Audubon, formed a partnership for the ownership and operation of Mill Grove, now called the John James Audubon Center at Mill Grove. The Pennsylvania office of the National Audubon Society manages Mill Grove as a combination museum and bird sanctuary. The estate has 175 acres with seven miles of walking trails. Over 175 species of birds and over 400 species of plants have been identified on the property. The estate's historic three-story stone farmhouse is a museum honoring John James Audubon. It preserves and displays his original prints, paintings, and family artifacts. The John James Audubon Center at Mill Grove hosts 20,000 visitors a year.

The South Dakota Art Museum – Brookings, South Dakota

Harvey Dunn was born in a claim shanty near Manchester, South Dakota, in 1884 to parents Tom and Bersha Dunn. Young Harvey helped on the homestead, attended a one-room school, and practiced sketching in the evenings with his mother. In 1901 Dunn entered South Dakota Agricultural College, now South Dakota State University (SDSU). His art teacher there, Ada Caldwell, encouraged him to further his education at the Art Institute of Chicago, which he did in 1902. Dunn met American artist Howard Pyle when Pyle lectured at the Art Institute and soon moved to Delaware to study with Pyle. In 1906 Dunn set up his own studio and began a successful career as an illustrator, working for magazines such as *Scribner's*, *Harper's Weekly*, *Collier's Weekly*, and *The Saturday Evening Post*. During World War I, the Army assigned Dunn to be an artist with the American Expeditionary Forces. He traveled in Europe and painted scenes from the war. At right is a poster he created during the war.

After he returned home, he moved his family to Tenafly, New Jersey, and continued painting. He made many visits to his home State of South Dakota. He is best known for his paintings that capture the beauty of the prairie and the courageous spirit of its pioneer settlers. In the 1950s, Harvey Dunn donated forty-two of his works to SDSU. The Harvey Dunn collection forms the cornerstone of the South Dakota Art Museum on the university campus.

Harvey Dunn created this United States Food Administration (USFA) poster. The purpose of the USFA was to save food for American troops fighting in World War I. Future President Herbert Hoover headed the USFA under President Woodrow Wilson. Hoover took no salary. He encouraged American citizens to "Go back to simple food, simple clothes, simple pleasures. Pray hard, work hard, sleep hard and play hard. Do it all courageously and cheerfully."

The museum also houses a large collection by Yanktonai Indian artist Oscar Howe (1915-1983). Howe was born on South Dakota's Crow Creek Indian Reservation and was educated at Pierre Indian Boarding School and Santa Fe Indian School. Howe used bright colors, sharp lines, and dramatic motion in his paintings depicting Native American traditions.

From 1948 to 1971 Oscar Howe designed the annual art on the Corn Palace. Since 1892 residents of Mitchell, South Dakota, have welcomed visitors to its Corn Palace. The current

structure, the town's third, was built in 1921. Each year the Corn Palace, pictured at right, is decorated with elaborate artistic designs made of corn cobs in many varieties. The theme changes from year to year. Many of Howe's designs had Native American themes.

The South Dakota Art Museum is also home to the world's largest collection of Marghab Linens. Emile Marghab of Cyprus and his wife Vera, a native of Watertown, South Dakota, founded the linen company in 1932 and operated it on the Portuguese island of Madeira. In 1970 Vera Marghab and the trustees of her estate donated almost 800 pieces of Marghab Linens to the museum.

Paul Goble was born in England in 1933. As a child, he loved learning about Native American life. His mother read Native American stories to him; and as he grew up, he read everything he could about Native American culture. He and his wife Janet moved to South Dakota in 1977. In 1979 Goble's picture book, *The Girl Who Loved Wild Horses*, won the Caldecott Medal for the year's best illustrated book for children. Paul Goble personally donated original paintings to the South Dakota Art Museum.

Mitchell, South Dakota
At top is the Corn Palace in 1908. The other three photographs are from 2009, when the annual theme was America's Destinations. The third photograph has the Space Shuttle, the Statue of Liberty, and the Space Needle. The fourth destination pictured is of the Corn Palace itself.

Georgia O'Keeffe Museum – Santa Fe, New Mexico

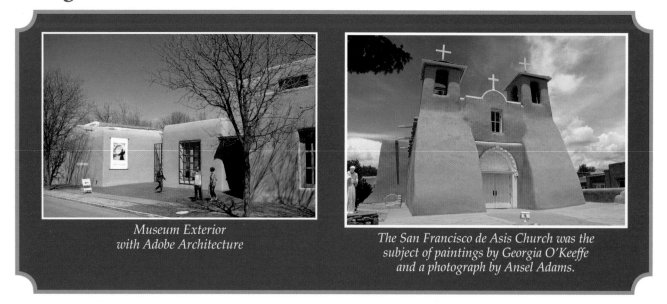

Museum Exterior
with Adobe Architecture

The San Francisco de Asis Church was the
subject of paintings by Georgia O'Keeffe
and a photograph by Ansel Adams.

Georgia O'Keeffe was the second of seven children in a farming family from Sun Prairie, Wisconsin. She had art lessons at home during her childhood, and as she grew up, her teachers at school noticed and encouraged her art. By the time she finished high school, Georgia knew she wanted to be a professional artist. From 1905 to 1908, O'Keeffe studied at the Art Institute of Chicago and New York's Art Students League. She absorbed the instruction in the type of art popular at the time, but soon grew frustrated and quit producing, knowing that her personal artistic style was very different from the kind of art she had learned. In 1912 she took a summer course for art teachers at the University of Virginia under Alon Bement. Bement introduced O'Keeffe to the ideas of artist Arthur Wesley Dow. Dow's theories helped O'Keeffe experiment and discover her own personal style, and the distinctive art of Georgia O'Keeffe was born.

In 1929 O'Keeffe spent her first summer painting in New Mexico, with many such visits to follow. In 1940 she bought a house, sixty miles northwest of Santa Fe and surrounded by the stunning New Mexico desert. In 1945 O'Keeffe bought a 5,000 square-foot Spanish colonial-era compound called Abiquiu that stood in ruins. She supervised its restoration over the next four years. In 1949 she moved permanently to New Mexico and divided her time between her two homes. Her works depicting New Mexico's desert landscapes are some of her best known. She is also known for vibrant close-ups of flowers. Georgia O'Keeffe continued to create art nearly until the time of her death in 1986 at the age of 98.

In 1978 Anne Burnett Tandy of Texas used her large fortune to establish the Anne Burnett Tandy and Charles D. Tandy Foundation in memory of her husband, Charles D. Tandy. The foundation gave grants to help organizations and individuals in the areas of education, health, community affairs, human services, arts, and humanities. Mrs. Tandy was an acquaintance of Georgia O'Keeffe and collected her work. She passed on her enthusiasm for O'Keeffe to her daughter, Anne Windfohr Marion. When Anne Burnett Tandy died in 1980, her daughter inherited the successful family ranching and oil businesses. In 1995 Anne Windfohr Marion and her husband John Marion decided to make a large donation from the Burnett-Tandy Foundation (renamed in 1993) to start a Georgia O'Keeffe museum in Santa Fe, New Mexico. At that time, many owners around the world held the original works of Georgia O'Keeffe. The largest single collection of 24 pieces was in the National Gallery of Art in Washington, D.C.

Since the Georgia O'Keeffe Museum opened in 1997, it has had over 2,225,000 visitors from around the world. This museum has the largest O'Keeffe collection in the world with 1,149 pieces. The art of Georgia O'Keeffe has a fitting home in the area that inspired so much of her work which expresses, as O'Keeffe said, "the wideness and wonder of the world as I live in it."

God is creative. He created every person in His image. When people create beauty, they use the talents He gave them, they use materials that He has made, and they reveal that they are creative like their Father.

New Mexico
This scene is near the New Mexico homes of Georgia O'Keeffe. It shows parts of God's creation that inspired her work.

> God created man in His own image,
> in the image of God He created him;
> male and female He created them.
> Genesis 1:27

Lesson Activities

Vocabulary — In your notebook, make a drawing for each of these words that illustrates what it means: breadth, intentional, sanctuary, studio, acquaintance. Write the word under the drawing. Check in a dictionary if you need help with their definitions.

Creative Writing — Write a short story of at least one page about a visit to an American art museum. The museum can be real or fictional.

Find Out! — What art museums are in your area?

Picture This! — Draw a picture of a place in America. Use a photograph to draw from, or draw a picture of a place you can look at in person.

Student Workbook or Lesson Review — If you are using one of these optional books, complete the assignment for Lesson 138.

A Year of
PERFORMING ARTS

The Donovan family sat around the dinner table one January night and discussed a newspaper article Mr. Donovan had read earlier that day: "Bolivian to Give Free Charango Concert at University."

"What is a charango?" asked Mandy.

"And where is Bolivia?" asked Pete.

"Bolivia is in South America, sort of tucked in between Peru and Brazil. And, judging from this photo, a charango looks like a small guitar," answered Mr. Donovan.

"Let's go!" interjected Mrs. Donovan.

"Where?" her family wondered.

"To the concert. It sounds neat! When else will we get a chance to hear a Bolivian, um, what does he play?" said Mrs. Donovan.

"It's a charango," answered her husband, showing her the photograph.

"In fact, I've been thinking. We live in a neat town with lots going on, and the only places we go besides church and the grocery store is the library and the park to watch Pete play baseball, exciting as that is," Mrs. Donovan smiled at her son.

The rest of the family looked at each other. "Will it count as school?" Mandy asked.

Her parents laughed. "Yes! It will definitely count as school!" Mr. Donovan answered.

"Hmm. It might not be so bad," said Pete.

Mrs. Donovan continued, "I propose a family challenge. Once a month, every month this year, let's go to a different performance at a different place right here in town. And they will all count as school!"

January 15: Folk Tradition of Latin America: An Evening with Ricardo César Botero

The Donovan family arrived at the State University concert hall, found seats near the front, and studied the program while they waited for the concert to begin. All the names of the songs were in Spanish, so they did not recognize any of them. However, they thoroughly enjoyed the concert of beautiful charango music. The musician was enthusiastic and talented, and he talked about his family and his life in Bolivia between songs. As soon as they got home, Pete got an envelope, wrote "CHARANGO FUND" on the outside, and put in $2.00 from his wallet.

Universities and colleges with music programs showcase performances of music students, professors, and visiting musicians. Often, a visiting musician is from a university in another state or country. During a visit, he or she will commonly give special classes for music students during the day and a concert in the evening. Music students give a certain number of recitals as part of their degree program. Faculty and students form special groups or ensembles, such as with jazz instruments or stringed instruments. University music school concerts range from folk to classical to jazz, from solo performances to the university orchestra and choir. These concerts are often free or low-cost. Attending them is a great way to encourage young performers and to hear a wide range of beautiful music.

Charango

February 10: *The Wizard of Oz*

As Mrs. Donovan, Mandy, and Pete were walking out of the grocery store, Mandy noticed a bright green flyer posted beside the door: "Community Theater Presents: *The Wizard of Oz*." "Look, Mom!" she said. They read the flyer and Mom made a note of all the details. The play opened that weekend. Mr. Donovan gave the plan a thumbs-up, so Mrs. Donovan called the local theater box office for tickets. She saved money by buying tickets for the Sunday matinee. They were very surprised to see their dentist, Dr. Watts, playing the Tin Man. It was a fun play and they talked about their favorite scenes on the way home. Everyone hummed the songs all during the following week.

Community theater allows local amateur actors, adult and youth, the chance to perform. These theater groups do plays and musicals, elaborate to simple, classic to modern. They might perform in a theater owned by the city or in a school or in a church gymnasium. In 1856 Louisa May Alcott helped to form the Concord Dramatic Union in Concord, Massachusetts. In 1921 the group added a professional stage to a local armory building. Now called the Concord Players, this community theater group stages three plays per year. Every ten years, the Concord Players stage a performance of *Little Women*.

March 31: Folk Highlights from Bach's *Easter Oratorio*

Bonnie, one of Mr. Donovan's coworkers, is in the choir at First United Methodist Church. She mentioned to him that the choir was presenting Bach's *Easter Oratorio* on Easter Sunday. She thought his family might enjoy it. When Mr. Donovan got home, he looked up "oratorio" in a dictionary so he would be ready if anyone in the family asked.

Birmingham, Alabama
Methodist Church Choir and Orchestra

Sure enough, Pete asked, and Mr. Donovan was ready. "It's like an opera with a Biblical subject. It uses orchestra, soloists, and choir. This is a famous one by Bach." The church orchestra and choir were very small, but they did a wonderful job. It was unlike anything the Donovans had heard before. It made them think about the Resurrection story in a new way. They waited to talk to Bonnie after the concert, and she was delighted to see them.

Church music has been part of religious and community life all over the world for hundreds of years. Some of the best-known composers wrote music for church services. Many churches have a full-time or part-time music minister. Sometimes churches also pay a pianist or organist to play during church services. Church members volunteer to sing in a choir or play an instrument. The main venue for church musicians is the regular Sunday service, but churches sometimes give special concerts.

Music Recital

April 22: Newsong School of Performing Arts Spring Recital

Sara, a friend of Mandy's at church, invited her to come to her clarinet recital. Sara is a student at Newsong School of Performing Arts, which offers lessons to public, private, and homeschooled students in drama, dance, voice, and instruments. The Donovans agreed that this was a great choice for their April event. Sara did a good job with her difficult piece. They saw several other performers that they knew from church and their homeschool group. Children as young as four performed on the piano and violin. They were cute and made a lot of squeaks and mistakes. The Donovans exchanged smiles and tried not to chuckle.

May 27: Memorial Day Music by Moonlight

Mr. Donovan kept an eye on the newspaper all month looking for an event for his family to attend. He saw an advertisement from the Community Band: Memorial Day Music by Moonlight. The program included favorite patriotic songs, marches by John Philip Sousa, and medleys of favorite American folk songs. The concert was to take place on the courthouse lawn downtown on Memorial Day evening. Perfect! The Donovans had a wonderful time, tapping their feet and humming along with the upbeat music.

Many small towns and cities in the United States have a community band, mostly comprised of adults who are amateur musicians (people who play as a hobby while holding another job). Bands have a different sound from orchestras because they contain woodwind, brass, and percussion instruments, but generally not string instruments. Cities and universities sometimes sponsor community bands, but some exist as independent organizations. Community bands do not attempt to make a profit. They simply provide an outlet for amateur musicians and they enrich their communities. Many local businesses and individuals make contributions to support community bands. The musicians usually volunteer their services. Many community bands give all or some of their concerts free of charge. The American Band, with musicians from Rhode Island, Connecticut, and Massachusetts, is one of the oldest community bands in the United States. It dates back to 1837.

Newton, North Carolina
Community Band Concert

June 16: Beethoven's Greatest Hits with the City Symphony Orchestra

"I've got our June event!" Mr. Donovan waved a brochure as he walked in the house. "The symphony orchestra is doing a Beethoven concert!"

"I like Beethoven," Mandy said, then started humming "Für Elise."

The Donovans agreed that it was well worth the price of the tickets to hear a live performance of classical music. Mandy and Pete tried to identify each instrument that was listed in the program. Mandy was amazed at how rich "Für Elise" sounded when played by over twenty different instruments. Everyone else in the family looked over to see Mr. Donovan's big smile when the orchestra starting playing selections from Beethoven's 9th Symphony, his favorite.

The musical ensemble we know as the symphony orchestra developed gradually in Europe between the 15th and 19th centuries. Many of the musicians that play with a symphony orchestra are professionals and receive pay for playing in the orchestra. The famous New York Philharmonic symphony orchestra is by far the oldest in America and one of the oldest in the world. A group of local musicians led and directed by Ureli Corelli Hill founded the orchestra in 1842. The New York Philharmonic currently gives 180 concerts a year. It performed its 15,000th concert on May 5, 2010.

Because Mrs. Donovan signed up for the Community Theater mailing list in February, she received a postcard announcing their town's annual Shakespeare in the Park Summer Festival. It was a joint effort of Community Theater and drama students at the university. This year, the festival featured a performance of *Julius Caesar*. It was a free performance, but there would be collection boxes for donations. The postcard advised coming early and bringing lawn chairs or a blanket. The Donovan family brought a picnic dinner and got good "seats" near the small concrete stage. After dark, the park became ancient Rome as actors in authentic costumes performed the classic drama. Though the Donovans could not follow all the dialogue, the play was thrilling. Mandy checked out a copy of *Julius Caesar* from the library the next week so she could understand it better.

New York City's famous Shakespeare in the Park tradition began in 1954. Since 1962 New York's Shakespeare in the Park has called the Delacorte Theater home. It is an open-air theater in Central Park. In 2012 Shakespeare in the Park at the Delacorte Theater celebrated its 50th anniversary. Over five million New Yorkers and visitors have enjoyed annual summer performances. Many other towns and cities across the United States have joined the innovative Shakespeare in the Park tradition, providing a chance to see classic plays without cost.

August 20: A Monticello Afternoon with Thomas Jefferson

Mrs. Donovan read in an e-mail newsletter from her homeschool support group about a special event at a local private school. Wally Howell from Virginia was coming to town to give his performance of "A Monticello Afternoon with Thomas Jefferson." Mrs. Donovan knew this would be fun for her history-loving family! The tickets were $10 each, but they all decided it was worth the cost. It was a fun evening! "Thomas Jefferson" walked onto the stage and pretended that the audience was a group of afternoon visitors at his home, Monticello. He sat comfortably chatting with the "visitors"

College Station, Texas
Art Yeaman performs in the Meet Ben Franklin Storytelling Event at the George Bush Presidential Library, 2010.

for two hours, telling funny stories and first-hand accounts of early American history and his friends Hamilton, Adams, and Washington. The Donovan family greeted and thanked "TJ" in the lobby after the performance. They felt like they were meeting the real Thomas Jefferson.

Historical reprisors, like Art Yeaman pictured above, offer a unique, memorable way to experience history. First-person accounts make history come alive. Historical reprisors wear accurate costumes and may even try to imitate the accent of the person they are portraying. The reprisor must do extensive historical research to portray accurately the person and tell his or her story. Actor Joe Wiegand, pictured on page 841, portrays Theodore Roosevelt in one-man shows across the country. He has presented his interpretation of Roosevelt in all fifty states. In 2008 he presented it at the White House for George W. and Laura Bush and other guests in celebration of Roosevelt's 150th birthday. Wiegand looks so much like Roosevelt that the American Museum of Natural History in New York City (co-founded by Roosevelt's father) used Wiegand in 2012 as a model for a statue of Theodore Roosevelt for the museum.

September 27-29: *Count the Stars*

In August Mr. and Mrs. Donovan signed up Mandy and Pete to participate in their homeschool group's annual drama production. The rehearsals started the first week in September. Mandy and Pete were very excited at the prospect of being in a play for the first time! A mom in their homeschool support group organizes and directs a play every year for local homeschoolers. This year's play, *Count the Stars*, was about Abraham, Isaac, and Jacob. Each year's play is taken either from the Bible or from history. In addition to singing in the choir, Mandy played the part of Abraham's second wife, Keturah, and Pete played young Isaac. Mr. Donovan helped build sets and Mrs. Donovan helped on the costume committee. Many homeschool groups and co-ops provide opportunities in drama for homeschooled students. They perform a wide variety of plays in civic theaters and church auditoriums.

Cookeville, Tennessee
Homeschool Dramatic Society

Cookeville, Tennessee
Homeschool Dramatic Society

October 18: Laugh 'Til It Hurts with Bobby Sullivan

One of Pete's friends from his baseball team told him about a Christian comedian coming to his church. Pete was excited and told his family about it at dinner: "Can we go? It sounds great! And Will's family is going."

Mr. Donovan said, "I'll check into it, okay? Some comedians make some jokes that are not appropriate, and I want to make sure it's a good thing for our family." Later that evening, Mr. Donovan found the comedian's website and watched all the video clips of his performances. His wife came to see what he was doing because she heard him laughing so hard. Mr. Donovan said, "Okay, I think we're safe to go. I like this guy. He even has a note here for parents: 'I don't say anything I wouldn't say in front of my grandmother.' " At Bobby Sullivan's performance at First Baptist Church, the Donovans definitely laughed until it hurt.

November 30: Greet the Season with the Municipal Children's Choir

The Donovans were listening to the radio on an outing to the mall. They heard an announcement for a concert by the Municipal Children's Choir. "I didn't know we have a municipal children's choir!" said Mrs. Donovan.

The concert was surprisingly high-quality. The Donovans enjoyed watching the director lead the children with enthusiasm. Some boys and girls performed beautiful solos. It was hard to believe such beautiful voices came from such small people! The Donovans left the concert in jolly moods and took a brochure so they could learn about upcoming concerts by the Municipal Children's Choir.

Chicago, Illinois
Boys of an earlier Chicago children's choir put on their robes, 1941.

860

Christopher Moore founded the Chicago Children's Choir in 1956. Moore believed that children from multiracial and multicultural backgrounds could understand each other better by learning to make beautiful music together. Today's Chicago Children's Choir works with 3,000 children between the ages of eight and eighteen in fifty-one Chicago schools and eight after-school programs. Chicago Children's Choir selects students for the 90-member Concert Choir, which tours nationally and internationally. The choir seeks to make a difference in the lives of children and youth through teaching musical excellence.

December 13: *Nutcracker*

"So what are we going to do for our last cultural experience of the year?" Pete asked his parents at breakfast one morning in December.

Mrs. Donovan smiled. "Well, I saw something on the local news." She looked significantly at Mandy, who returned her smile. Mrs. Donovan took a deep breath and continued, "The

San Francisco, California
The Nutcracker *Performed by the San Francisco Ballet Company*

Moscow Ballet is coming to the city to perform the *Nutcracker*. I have always wanted to see the *Nutcracker*!" Mr. Donovan and Pete looked at each other with raised eyebrows.

"We have not seen any dance the whole year! We're missing out!" Mandy said.

Mr. Donovan grinned. "What can we say to that, Pete?"

"Well, it counts as school." Pete looked down and blushed. "But don't tell the guys."

Mrs. Donovan and Mandy did not ask Mr. Donovan and Pete afterward if they enjoyed the ballet. They had glanced at them during the performance and suspected that they had.

Ballet originated in the courts of Italian nobles during the 1400s. The San Francisco Ballet Company is America's oldest professional ballet company, established in 1933. It was the first American company to perform the famous ballets *Swan Lake* in 1940 and *Nutcracker* in 1944. San Francisco Ballet Company was the first American company to tour in the Far East, visiting eleven countries in 1956. The San Francisco Ballet Company gives approximately one hundred performances every year. See photo above.

A Year of Performing Arts

"We did it, everyone! Twelve shows in twelve months," Mr. Donovan said as he drove his family home from the ballet.

"It was fantastic! I enjoyed every one, and I think we should do it next year. What do you think, kids?" asked Mrs. Donovan.

"I learned a lot, and it was fun doing it together," Mandy answered.

Granville, Tennessee
Granville United Methodist Church Christmas Concert

"I'd say Performing Arts is my favorite subject in school!" said Pete.

Now these are the singers, heads of fathers' households of the Levites,

who lived in the chambers of the temple free from other service;

for they were engaged in their work day and night.

1 Chronicles 9:33

Lesson Activities

Literature — Read "The Open-Hearted and Courageous Way" in *The Citizen's Handbook*, pages 162-166.

Creative Writing — In your notebook, write one or two paragraphs about an experience you have had with performing arts, either performing yourself or watching others perform.

Find Out! — Find out if there is a community band or symphony orchestra in your community or another community nearby. Find out the date of their next scheduled concert.

Picture This! — Take a photograph or draw a picture of an individual or a group performing.

Student Workbook or Lesson Review — If you are using one of these optional books, complete the assignment for Lesson 139.

★ Remember to choose an American Holiday to study this week! ★

UNIT 29 — DESTINATIONS, USA

BOOKS USED IN UNIT 29

- The Citizen's Handbook
- Lost on a Mountain in Maine
- Student Workbook (optional)
- Lesson Review (optional)

Bald Eagle at the Alaska Zoo in Anchorage, Alaska

How Americans PRESERVE HISTORY

LESSON 141

Abraham Lincoln stayed at the Willard Hotel when he came to Washington, D.C., to be inaugurated as the sixteenth President of the United States. While there he wore the bedroom shoes pictured below. Lincoln was not the only President to stay at the Willard — so did Zachary Taylor, Millard Fillmore, Franklin Pierce, James Buchanan, Ulysses S. Grant, William Howard Taft, Woodrow Wilson, Warren G. Harding, and Calvin Coolidge. Other famous guests include author Charles Dickens and entertainer Buffalo Bill.

Slippers Worn by Lincoln

Oliver Carr (third from right), president of the company that restored the Willard Hotel, and Senator Daniel Patrick Moynihan (to his left) who helped prevent the Willard and nearby buildings from being demolished to build a Federal improvement project.

The Willard Hotel is located at the corner of Fourteenth Street and Pennsylvania Avenue. By 1818 buildings on the spot were being used as a hotel. The Willard family began operating a hotel there in 1847 and continued to expand it. The 1904 expansion was called Washington's first skyscraper. The Willard family owned the hotel until 1946. By the 1960s, the formerly grand "Hotel of Presidents" was in terrible shape. It closed in 1968. In the 1980s, a private company invested more than $100 million to restore the hotel. On page 865 are photos taken during the restoration. At left is a photograph of the ceremony when it re-opened in 1986.

You can know the story of what happened in the past because people have worked to preserve history. Some people preserve historical sites, using them for businesses or homes or opening them to the public. Others research old documents, interview those who were involved in historical events, and write books and articles that tell the story of the past. Still others dig for artifacts or work in museums that display objects from history.

Why Is History Important?

But what difference does history make? Why should you want to know it? We live in this country, with the freedoms and opportunities we have, because people who came before us established and defended our community, state, and nation. History helps us appreciate those who have made a difference. It is good to remember the lover of learning who helped to establish the local library or the person who invented something we now use all the time. Such stories can inspire us to use our lives for a good purpose, too.

History teaches us to avoid the mistakes that people have made in times gone by, but it also teaches about godly people whom we can strive to be like. History helps us appreciate what the people of earlier generations accomplished. Their stories encourage us to do more with what we have.

Think about your community, state, and nation. Many years before you were born, people settled there. They established governments. People in earlier generations paved streets, built church buildings and public buildings, and passed laws that benefit you today. They demonstrated bravery and performed amazing acts of generosity and kindness. It would be a great loss if we did not have the story of the past. As a history professor friend of ours said, "If you don't know history, you don't know who you are."

Preserving History Is Not Automatic

Preserving history does not happen automatically. We have no guarantee that people will preserve historical documents and maintain historic places for future generations to visit. Preserving history takes commitment and action by many people.

Soon after George Washington died, a number of Americans wanted some appropriate memorial to honor the father of our country. However, it was not until 1833 that Chief Justice John Marshall and former President James Madison helped to organize the Washington National Monument Society. The Society laid the cornerstone for the memorial fifteen years later, on the Fourth of July in 1848. Then the Civil War, a lack of funds, and conflict within the Society delayed its completion. The Washington Monument finally opened to the public on October 9, 1888, eighty-nine years after Washington's death.

The first publicly-owned historic site in the United States is Washington's Headquarters State Historic Site in Newburgh, New York, near West Point. The State of New York set it aside in 1850. Here in April of 1782, in a family farmhouse called Hasbrouck House, Washington established his last military headquarters of the American Revolution. During Washington's time here, some Americans encouraged him to become America's first king. He refused. At Hasbrouck House, Washington calmed disgruntled soldiers who wanted to take over the government from the Continental Congress, created the Badge of Military Merit, which is now called the Purple Heart, and wrote letters to each of the thirteen state Governors, sharing ideas that were later included in the U.S. Constitution.

Building memorials and reserving important sites even relating to the beloved George Washington required people who cared about history, leaders able to put ideas into action, people willing to donate money, and decisions by state and national officials. Since so many people, places, and events have contributed to the story of America, preserving its history is a big job. It is one way that many people can contribute to the civic life of our communities, states, and nation.

The Power of One Person

Successful preservation projects often begin with one person who has the vision to see what should be saved. He or she shares that vision with others and inspires more volunteers. Through effort and tireless fund-raising over many years, they accomplish something important for generations. One person can preserve history by writing a history book. Some books of history are read across the land. Other people write about local history that may be interesting to a much smaller audience. All preserve stories that were once important to many people but are now in danger of being forgotten. Ken Burns is an example of one person who had an idea about using technology to preserve history. He founded a production company in 1976 and has continually produced quality documentaries about historical subjects. His work has helped millions of Americans know more about their past.

State and Local History

People have organized state historical societies or historical commissions that preserve state history. State history is important for at least two reasons. First, the history of your state has contributed to what your state is today. People worth knowing about lived in your state, and events that made an impact took place there. Second, state history allows you to experience history. By traveling relatively short distances, you can visit the very places where important events occurred. State historical commissions often oversee state museums and decide on the placement of historical markers along highways that provide information about people and places in history. A study of the names of cities, counties, roads, rivers, and even of the states themselves help you learn history because many were named for people and events of the past.

Harrisburg, Pennsylvania

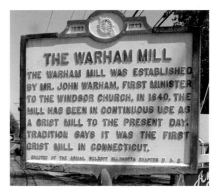
Windsor, Connecticut
Historic Marker

City and county historical societies work to preserve local history. Counties and cities often establish museums. The Baker Heritage Museum in Baker City, Oregon, for example, tells about gold mining and other aspects of life in the part of eastern Oregon that lay along the Oregon Trail. Volunteers are vital to the operation of this and many other small museums. Across America, thousands of people donate their time each week to sell tickets, help in gift shops, serve as tour guides, and perform other tasks necessary to keeping museums open to the public. States and many cities and counties hire archivists who protect and organize public records. Some communities have created veterans halls that honor local men

Franklin, Tennessee
Veterans Hall in the Williamson County Museum

and women who have served in the military. The American Association for State and Local History, begun in 1940, offers programs to state and local museums and historical societies to help them preserve history on the state and local levels. See photos above.

National Organizations

National private groups help keep history alive, too. Foundations preserve specific sites and donate money to historic sites. The National Trust for Historic Places protects numerous historic sites around the country. It once received government funds but now relies completely on private contributions. The American Association of Museums was founded in 1906.

Living History

Living history museums are a fun way to learn about history. In a living history museum, workers assume the roles of people from a particular period. They dress in clothing from the period. At Plimoth Plantation near Plymouth, Massachusetts, for instance, the people you meet pretend to be the actual people who lived there in 1627. See photo above.

Plymouth, Massachusetts
Plimoth Plantation

Another kind of living history is performed by re-enactors. War re-enactors, for example, gather a few weekends each year to dress as soldiers, recreate military encampments, and stage re-enactments of battles. Re-enactors are volunteers who participate in these activities out of a love for history and to help keep the memory of historical events alive.

Haw Branch, North Carolina
Revolutionary War Encampment, 2012

Collecting History

Historians sometimes collect history from the people who lived it. From 1936 to 1938, government employees working in the Federal Writers' Project wrote down the personal stories of people who had been born into slavery. Museums sometimes create oral or video history archives. They interview people such as World War II, Korean War, and Vietnam War veterans and record their responses in audio or video formats. These interviews record the experiences of the everyday people who were eyewitnesses to important historical events. This is an important way to honor those who have served sacrificially to defend our country and to preserve their stories for future generations while it is still possible to do so.

Waco, Texas
Former Slave Patsy Moses, 1937

Federal Government Involvement in Preserving History

Federal and state governments authorize monuments that call special attention to places and heroes from history. In addition to protecting natural areas, the National Park Service (NPS) preserves a number of historic sites.

The United States Postal Service (USPS) helps keep history alive with commemorative stamps. Each year it creates stamps that honor individuals and events from history. Anyone can suggest a person or event to be honored in this way. The USPS receives thousands of suggestions each year. The Citizens' Stamp Advisory Committee meets four times per year to go through the suggestions that other citizens have made and to make recommendations to the Postal Service. The USPS tries to issue stamps that collectors will want to purchase and that people across America will want to use to send mail. The USPS makes the final decisions on what stamps will be issued. The artists who create the stamps use their talents to help the citizens of our nation remember its history.

Haugan, Montana
Savenac Historic Tree Nursery

The National Register of Historic Places (NRHP) is a listing of historic places (homes, buildings, areas in cities, and geographic sites) that the NPS recognizes as being worthy of preservation. The purpose of the Register is to identify properties that have historical significance because of architecture; the people who lived, worked, or visited there; and events that happened there. The National Historic Preservation Act of 1966 created the NRHP. The NPS, which is part of the Department of the Interior, oversees the Register. Over 85,000 places are on the Register, and the NPS adds more each year. The NRHP lists sites in all fifty states, including those pictured at right.

Gainesboro, Tennessee
Town Square

Of the places listed on the NRHP, just over 2,400 or about three percent have been named National Historic Landmarks. These landmarks are in all fifty states, but one fourth are in Pennsylvania, Massachusetts, and New York. The Register also contains about ninety National Historic Sites, which are individual buildings, and about forty National Historical Parks, which include larger areas. Federal agencies, mainly the NPS, oversee all of these.

Coplay, Pennsylvania
Schoefer Kilns

Preserving Your Family History

Many people study the genealogies of their own families. It is exciting to find out that one of your ancestors was a pilgrim on the Mayflower or a soldier in the Civil War. Government agencies can be helpful in the search for your ancestors. Federal census records, military records, and state birth records are a few government records that are useful. When you become a grandparent, the life you are living now will be thought of as history by your grandchildren. It is important to live in such a way that your descendants are proud of what they find out about you.

Nashville, Tennessee
Andrew Jackson VI speaks at the Hermitage, home of President Jackson, on the President's birthday, 2007.

For He established a testimony in Jacob

And appointed a law in Israel,

Which He commanded our fathers

That they should teach them to their children,

That the generation to come might know,

even the children yet to be born,

That they may arise and tell them to their children.

Psalm 78:5-6

Lesson Activities

Kansas City, Missouri
Missouri Valley Room with Books to Help with Genealogical Research

Thinking Biblically — Read Joshua 4:1-7 to learn about a way God gave Israel to remember their history.

Vocabulary — Copy these words in your notebook, each on a separate line: inspire, generation, generosity, conflict, disgruntled. Look up each word in a dictionary. Next to each word, write what part of speech it is according to the way the word is used in this lesson.

Literature — Read "Vermont's Old Constitution House" in *The Citizen's Handbook*, pages 167-168, and chapter 1 in *Lost on a Mountain in Maine*.

Find Out! — Are there any sites on the National Register of Historic Places in your area?

Picture This! — Take a photograph or draw a picture of an historically significant place in your town.

Student Workbook or Lesson Review — If you are using one of these optional books, complete the assignment for Lesson 141.

Saving George WASHINGTON'S HOME

George Washington loved his Mount Vernon estate overlooking the beautiful Potomac River in Virginia, as seen here from his colonnade. His father died in 1743 when young George was eleven years old. At that time, Lawrence Washington, George's elder half-brother, inherited the estate. George and his brother Lawrence were very close, and as a teenager George spent a great deal of time with Lawrence at Mount Vernon. Lawrence died in 1752. George Washington leased Mount Vernon from Lawrence's widow from 1754 until she died in 1761, when he became the full owner. Washington worked devotedly to make improvements to his home and the surrounding land. He regretted the years he had to spend away from his home while he served his country in the Revolutionary War and as its first President. Washington finished his second term as President in 1797 and returned gratefully to Mount Vernon. He died there in 1799 and was buried on the estate.

Honoring the Father of Our Country

Soon after Washington's death, the United States Navy started a tradition to honor George Washington that continues to this day. Official Navy regulations dictate that when a naval ship sailing on the Potomac passes the tomb of George Washington at Mount Vernon between sunrise and sunset, the full guard and band must stand on deck, the ship's bell be tolled, the guard present arms, all on deck salute, and "Taps"

Washington's Tomb

and "The Star-Spangled Banner" be played. The autobiography of Commodore Charles Morris mentions the earliest instance of this solemn ceremony. Morris passed Mount Vernon as a young midshipman on the USS *Congress* in 1801. Look at the Potomac River through the columns on the photo on page 871 and imagine the scene he describes:

> *About 10 o'clock in the morning of a beautifully serene day, we passed Mount Vernon. Every one was on deck to look upon the dwelling where Washington had made his home. Mrs. Washington and others of the family could be distinguished in the portico which fronts the river. When opposite the house, by order of Captain Sever, the sails were lowered, the colors displayed half-masted, and a mourning salute of thirteen guns was fired as a mark of respect to the memory of Washington, whose life had so recently closed, and whose tomb was in our view. The general silence on board the ship and around us, except when broken by the cannon's sound, the echo and re-echo of that sound from the near and distant hills, as it died away in the distance, the whole ship's company uncovered and motionless, and the associations connected with the ceremony, seemed to make a deep impression upon all, as they did certainly upon me.*

Private vessels mark their respect for Washington by tolling their bells when passing the channel that leads to Mount Vernon's wharf.

Louisa Bird and Ann Pamela Cunningham

In 1853 Louisa Bird Cunningham of South Carolina traveled on the Potomac past Mount Vernon. The bell tolled in Washington's honor summoned her to the deck. She wrote to her daughter, Ann Pamela Cunningham, "I was painfully distressed at the ruin and desolation of the home of Washington, and the thought passed through my mind: Why was it that the women of his country did not try to keep it in repair, if the men could not do it? It does seem such a blot on our country."

George Washington's great-grandnephew, John Augustine Washington, owned Mount Vernon then. He struggled to maintain the mansion, manage the farm, and contend with a flood of sightseers. Mrs. Cunningham saw peeling paint and weeds. The portico was dilapidated. The masts of old ships propped it up. John tried to persuade the United States and Virginia to purchase and preserve the home of his illustrious ancestor, but neither were interested.

Louisa Cunningham's letter inspired her daughter, who was then thirty-seven years old. Ann Pamela Cunningham dedicated her life to saving and preserving Mount Vernon. Writing under the pen name of "A Southern Matron," she first appealed to the ladies of the South and then to the entire country to save Mount Vernon.

Mount Vernon Ladies' Association

Miss Cunningham founded the Mount Vernon Ladies' Association in 1853. She said, "Every citizen, irrespective of age or sex, by the subscription of $1.00 can become a member, and one of the purchasers of Mount Vernon." The Association's first job was to purchase Mount Vernon. John Augustine Washington's asking price was high: $200,000. Cunningham appointed a lady to head up fund raising efforts in each state and they appointed ladies in counties and communities.

The Mount Vernon Ladies' Association used many fund-raising methods. They sold Washington memorabilia. A gold-framed Gilbert Stuart portrait of Washington sold for $1.00. They published a monthly magazine, *The Mount Vernon Record*, which listed all donations and told stories about Washington's life. The cost was $1.00 per month.

At that time in history, public speaking was a favorite form of entertainment. Former U.S. Senator, Governor of Massachusetts, and President of Harvard University Edward Everett was the most popular orator of the time. Everett read about the Mount Vernon Ladies' Association's cause in the newspaper and offered his help to Cunningham. Everett had written a speech about Washington's character for a celebration of Washington's birthday at the Mercantile Library in Boston. For five years, Everett traveled the country giving this speech, which he called, "My Washington." He delivered his memorized, two-hour speech 129 times, drawing large enthusiastic crowds. People paid at first $1.00 and later $2.00 each to hear him speak. Everett paid his own travel expenses and gave everything he raised to the Association. This letter to him appeared in *The Mount Vernon Record*:

> *Legation of the United States*
> *Honolulu, Hawaii, January 13, 1859*
>
> *Sir - A number of American ladies of the Hawaiian Islands have contributed one hundred and forty-one dollars, which they have requested me to forward to you, to be appropriated towards the purchase and embellishment of Mount Vernon. I have nowhere met with persons who more properly appreciate the character of Washington, than among the American residents and their descendants on these islands; and I am requested by the ladies who have made this contribution, to return to you their thanks for your exertions to arouse our people to a sense of their duty towards the memory of our great countryman.*
>
> *I have the honor to be, sir,*
> *Your obedient servant,*
> *James H. Borden*

Many groups such as fire companies, infantry companies, and private and public schools got involved and made donations. Augusta, Georgia, hosted a festival lasting several days to raise money. The legislature of Missouri authorized a donation of $2,000 to the Association. Private donations came in from far and wide—from President James Buchanan to newsboys of New York City, who pooled pennies and donated $4.18.

The Mount Vernon Ladies' Association successfully raised the money, purchased the estate, and took over operations at Mount Vernon in 1860. Right away, they opened it to the public for an admission fee. These fees helped the Association continue to raise funds. At first Ann Cunningham herself supervised the restoration work. By 1862, a visitor reported in a Vermont newspaper, "a new and very good wharf has been made, the tomb repaired, the mansion and out-buildings thoroughly put in order. . . . The object has been, not to modernize and embellish Mount Vernon, but to make it look as probably it did in the hands of the thrifty and order-loving old General."

Soon after meeting the enormous challenge of purchasing the estate, the Mount Vernon Ladies' Association faced the challenge of the Civil War. The Association officially declared the grounds to be neutral territory, and both sides respected this declaration. Many soldiers from both sides visited the estate during the war, but they had to come unarmed and not in uniform.

Ann Pamela Cunningham led the Mount Vernon Ladies' Association until 1874, when she resigned due to failing health. She admonished her successors, "Ladies, the Home of Washington is in your charge; see to it that you keep it the Home of Washington. Let no irreverent hand change it; no vandal hands desecrate it with the fingers of progress!" Cunningham died in 1875 at her family's estate in South Carolina.

The Mount Vernon Ladies' Association, the oldest historic preservation organization in the country, still owns and maintains the property which it has restored to its appearance in 1799. Many of the outbuildings have been restored. A few, including a slave cabin, the sixteen-sided barn, the wash house, gristmill, and kitchen, plus Washington's carriage, are pictured on page 875. The Association's mission is, "to preserve, restore, and manage the estate of George Washington to the highest standards and to educate visitors and people throughout the world about the life and legacies of George Washington, so that his example of character and leadership will continue to inform and inspire future generations." They do not accept Federal, state, or local government grants and have never relied on taxpayer money.

Americans honor George Washington because of his life of integrity and sacrifice. Mount Vernon is America's most popular historic estate. It is open 365 days a year and annually welcomes an average of one million visitors.

Slave Cabin Exterior and Interior

Sixteen-Sided Barn

Gristmill

Washington's Carriage

Kitchen

Two Views Inside the Wash House

Mount Vernon on the Fourth of July, 2012

Mount Vernon Gardens

He stores up sound wisdom for the upright;

He is a shield to those who walk in integrity.

Proverbs 2:7

Lesson Activities

Thinking Biblically — Copy Proverbs 2:7 into your notebook.

Literature — Read "The Purest Guardians of a National Shrine" in *The Citizen's Handbook*, page 169, and chapters 2-3 in *Lost on a Mountain in Maine*.

Creative Writing — In your notebook, write a letter as if you were a Civil War soldier writing to your family after visiting Mount Vernon.

Student Workbook or Lesson Review — If you are using one of these optional books, complete the assignment for Lesson 142.

America's STATE PARKS

They welcome over 700 million visitors each year (over two-and-a-half times as many as at national parks!). They provide twenty billion dollars worth of impact on local economies every year. They preserve historic sites and beautiful scenery. They offer places for a fun day trip or a relaxing vacation. What does all of this? America's state parks!

American citizens and visitors from around the world enjoy amazing national parks and well-maintained historic sites all over our country. But did you know that state parks offer similar opportunities, and they are almost in your backyard? The fifty states have about 6,600 state parks. Federal government programs such as the Works Progress Administration and the Civilian Conservation Corps (CCC) helped construct many state parks during the 1930s. The CCC alone, also called Roosevelt's Tree Army, built around eight hundred parks. States continue to create new parks all the time. When you think of state parks, you might think mostly of woods, trails, and perhaps lakes and picnic tables. However, the 6,600 state parks have much more to offer.

State Parks: East, West, and In Between

State parks and state recreational facilities are as varied as the fifty states. Did you know that the American side of Niagara Falls is a state park? Niagara Falls State Park, pictured at right, is the oldest state park in the country. The State of New York established it in 1885. America's largest state park is also in New York. The state created Adirondack Park, pictured at right, in 1885 also. About one-third of the State of New York is in this park, which covers over six million acres in the northeastern part of New York. Adirondack Park is larger than Yellowstone, Yosemite, Grand Canyon, Glacier, and Great Smoky Mountains National Parks combined.

State Parks in New York

Niagara Falls State Park

Adirondack Park

Jersey City, New Jersey
View of New York City from Liberty State Park

Liberty State Park covers over 1,200 acres in Jersey City, New Jersey. Many visitors to the Statue of Liberty leave from Liberty State Park, which offers spectacular views of the New York City skyline.

South Dakota
Custer State Park

Mackinac Island, Michigan
American Fur Company Store and Dr. Beaumont Museum at Mackinac Island State Park

Indian Springs State Park in central Georgia has been a public park since 1825 and became a Georgia state park in 1931. Creek Indians once collected waters from its springs, believing they had healing properties. CCC workers built the stone Spring House there during the 1930s.

Mackinac Island State Park was a national park before the Federal government transferred it to the State of Michigan. The state designated it as a state park in 1895.

The Watkins Woolen Mill State Historic Site near Kansas City, Missouri, takes you back to the nineteenth century with its three-story mill, elegant home, and other buildings constructed

Cannon Beach, Oregon
Ecola State Park

by Waltus Watkins. Watkins Mill State Park is adjacent to the historic site.

Custer State Park near Mount Rushmore in South Dakota offers an amazing variety of scenery and wildlife. Visitors encounter buffalo herds, elk, and prairie dog towns, plus beautiful views.

Ecola State Park on the Oregon coast gives you the opportunity to drive or hike through a coastal rain forest.

What Can You Do at a State Park?

Let's tour Delaware state parks to see the kinds of activities visitors can find in state parks across America.

Play on the Water! Fishing, swimming, boating, and canoeing are favorite state park activities. In Delaware visitors can canoe or kayak a pond or a river or venture out into the open waters of Delaware Bay. Not every state borders an ocean, but twenty-three American states do have ocean or gulf shorelines. Delaware Seashore State Park gives visitors opportunities to surf-fish, deep-sea fish, surf, sail, paddle, and more.

Take a Hike! With over 41,000 miles of trails in our country's state parks, it's easy to do. Hiking trails take visitors to forests, valleys, rock outcroppings, and breathtaking vistas. The Twin Valley Trail in White Clay Creek State Park passes the Arc Corner Monument, the point where Delaware and Pennsylvania meet. The Post Mark Trail cut-off from Bryan's Field Trail takes you to the "Post Mark'd West" monument. This marker designates the spot where the famous Mason-Dixon survey began and ran for two hundred miles due west.

You can hike through a wetland forest in Trap Pond State Park near Laurel, Delaware. This park preserves a part of the freshwater wetlands that once covered much of the area. The bald cypress trees here are the northernmost stand of this species in the United States. Developers in the late 1700s created the pond that gives the park its name. The pond powered a sawmill that milled cypress trees. The Federal government bought the pond and surrounding land during the 1930s, and the CCC began to develop the land for recreation.

If you'd rather ride trails on horseback, Bellevue State Park in Wilmington, Delaware, maintains Wellspring Stables, which offers pony rides, riding lessons, and much more.

Go on a Picnic! Delaware's state recreational areas have many facilities for picnicking. If you want to work up an appetite before your picnic, you can visit a disc golf course, horseshoe pits, or playgrounds, plus courts for basketball, tennis, badminton, and volleyball.

Go Camping! American state parks offer over 207,000 campsites and over 7,100 cabins and lodges. In Delaware, Killens Pond State Park cabin rentals include the use of a canoe and rowboat. And what about yurts? A traditional yurt is a large, round, movable structure with a bent wood frame covered with fabric or sheepskin. Nomads in the steppes of central Asia live in yurts. In 1993 Oregon began offering canvas-covered yurts for campers at its state parks, and at least seventeen other states now offer these alternative camping structures. Lums Pond and Trap Pond State Parks in Delaware feature yurts as a camping alternative.

Learn About Nature! Brandywine Creek State Park at Wilmington has over 900 acres and was once a dairy farm owned by the du Pont family. Stone walls built in the late 1800s divide the fields, which are a treasure trove of wildflowers. Delaware's first two nature preserves are here: Tulip Tree Woods, with 190-year old tulip poplars, and Freshwater Marsh.

State parks are wonderful places to see rare and beautiful bird species. Often park rangers or naturalists can help you know where to look and what you may find. Delaware Seashore State Park lets you see birds that inhabit coastal areas. Brandywine Creek State Park offers monthly bird walks and occasional other events, such as November's Owl Prowl at dusk.

Sharp-eyed visitors to Trap Pond State Park might spot a great blue heron, a bald eagle, or a pileated woodpecker.

Learning is fun at state parks! The Nature Center at Killens Pond State Park in Felton, Delaware, has an environmental education lab where scientists and rangers conduct programs. The building has a covered deck that overlooks a forest and a mill pond. The center

State Parks in Delaware

Brandywine Creek State Park

has a collection of native reptiles and amphibians. Several Delaware state parks regularly schedule stargazing activities that help both amateur and expert astronomers appreciate the wondrous nighttime sky. Many state park systems conduct Junior Ranger programs in which school-age children can study the natural environment and also forest and water safety. Completing certain activities enables students to earn patches and qualify as Junior Rangers.

Experience History! State parks preserve historic structures and sites important in state and American history. State parks host vivid re-enactments of army life at various times in American history, often on or near the anniversaries of important battles.

Trap Pond State Park

The Mount Pleasant Meeting House at Bellevue State Park in Wilmington beautifully preserves a church meeting house and parsonage from around 1838. The original amber windows and curved walnut pews make the meeting house a popular setting for weddings. The meeting house is on the National Register of Historic Places.

The United States Lifesaving Service, a forerunner of the U.S. Coast Guard, built the Indian River Lifesaving Station in 1876 in response to the many shipwrecks that were occurring along the Atlantic coast. The station is now in Delaware Seashore State Park at Rehoboth Beach, Delaware. Workers have restored it to its appearance in 1905. The station is on the NRHP.

Delaware Seashore State Park

The government constructed the granite and brick Fort Delaware at Delaware City in 1859 to protect the ports at Wilmington and Philadelphia. During the Civil War it housed Confederate prisoners. Today at the fort, which is in Fort Delaware State Park, costumed interpreters provide a living history experience as visitors watch a blacksmith, a laundress, and other workers realistically demonstrate what life was like during the Civil War. Visitors can even watch a gunner fire an eight-inch cannon with a live charge.

The Fort Miles Historic Area in Cape Henlopen State Park at Lewes preserves a coastal defense installation from World War II. Harbor defense was an important part of U.S. military strategy before the day of long-range missiles. The site is on the NRHP.

Hold a Special Event! State parks sometimes feature purpose-built or well-preserved facilities that are the perfect location for memorable events. The Judge Morris Estate at White Clay Creek State Park in Newark is a gray fieldstone house constructed in the 1790s. Federal judge Hugh Morris purchased the home in 1930, and the mansion is decorated in the style

he brought to the structure. The 600-acre estate features a pond, beautiful gardens, and a fenced-in courtyard. Groups wanting a fashionable setting for their events reserve the estate. Bellevue Hall at Bellevue State Park in Wilmington is another elegant mansion with a grand foyer, a Crystal Dining Room, and other beautifully decorated rooms; gardens with a gazebo; and rooms especially intended to be used for wedding preparations.

Cape Henlopen State Park

The Blue Ball Barn at Alapocas Run State Park in northern Delaware is named for an inn and meeting house that was once located near the property. During the 18th and early 19th centuries in this part of the country, innkeepers raised a pole with a blue ball on it to let a stagecoach driver know when someone at the inn wanted to ride the stagecoach. Alfred I. du Pont built a concrete and steel barn for his dairy farm in 1914 and named it Blue Ball Barn. After du Pont's death, a series of people owned the farm until it was finally abandoned. The State of Delaware purchased the barn in 1999 and began renovating it five years later. It opened to the public in 2007. Blue Ball Barn is a two-story structure that beautifully combines historic and contemporary architecture. It houses the Delaware Folk Art Collection and features large reception, meeting, and banquet rooms.

Volunteer! State park staffs welcome volunteers. Parks often have work days to clear trails, repair park buildings, pick up litter, and plant native vegetation. Volunteers can help at nature centers or at living history or other special events. State parks need good citizens, too!

He waters the mountains from His upper chambers;
The earth is satisfied with the fruit of His works.
Psalm 104:13

Lesson Activities

Vocabulary — In your notebook, write a paragraph that uses all of these words: spectacular, adjacent, venture, survey, nomad. Consult a dictionary if you need help with their definitions.

Literature — Read "North Head Lighthouse Officially Transferred to Washington State Parks" in *The Citizen's Handbook*, pages 170-171, and chapters 4-5 in *Lost on a Mountain in Maine*.

Find Out! — What is the nearest state park to you?

Picture This! — Draw a picture of a family enjoying a state park in your state.

Student Workbook or Lesson Review — If you are using one of these optional books, complete the assignment for Lesson 143.

Working in
TOURISM

Travel is an important industry in the United States. Americans enjoy taking trips within the United States, and millions of international visitors come every year to see America. Travel is a big boost to the U.S. economy as travelers seek a way to get from here to there, a place to stay overnight, meals to eat, fun things to do, and souvenirs to remember their trip. The tourism industry provides jobs for many Americans. One out of nine jobs in the United States depend on travel and tourism. Travel is in the top ten industries in forty-eight of our states and in the District of Columbia. Millions of Americans work in the United States tourism industry. Tourism jobs are diverse; they range from serving customers in a restaurant to maintaining a rocky wilderness trail in a national park.

La Pointe, Wisconsin
Madeline Island Museum

State Museum Security Guard

Donald works as a security guard at a museum. Donald is a retired police officer. His police work gave him skills he needs for his current job. Donald's post is near a display of historic firearms, but he regularly walks a certain route around the museum to check for any problems. The difficult part of his job is when he must insist that a visitor leave the museum because he or she is being disorderly or breaking other rules. Donald's favorite part of his job is watching children enjoy and learn from the displays of historic artifacts.

Why Americans Travel Within the USA

1. Visiting Relatives
2. Shopping
3. Visiting Friends
4. Dining
5. Beaches

National Park Service Maintenance Worker

Sam works for the Federal government as a maintenance worker at a National Park. His responsibility is maintaining

883

trails. Sam worked in construction and landscaping before taking this job, so he had experience with many of the tools he uses, such as shovels, picks, sledgehammers, chain saws, rock drills, and weed trimmers. Sam's job keeps him in great physical shape. He has to move large rocks and logs and often walks or hikes up to 20 miles a day checking on trails and reaching spots that need maintenance. He enjoys spending his days in the outdoors, though in the extreme cold of winter and heat

Sedro-Woolley, Washington
*A maintenance worker helps maintain
the Little Beaver Trail in North Cascades National Park.*

of summer, he looks forward to getting back to his cabin. Generally he works with only a handful of other people. Since he and his fellow maintenance workers spend a lot of time together, they have had to learn to get along and cooperate well. They have become good friends and enjoy working together to keep national park trails safe and beautiful.

Server at Cafe

Ellen is a server at the Seaside Walk Cafe. She is a high school student who works evenings, weekends, and during the summer. The cafe is in a resort town, where business triples during the summer months. Ellen knows all the regular local customers who frequent the cafe. She enjoys meeting travelers, especially from other countries, and hearing about their homes and their travel experiences. The Seaside Walk Cafe offers local specialties, produce and dairy products from area farms, and seafood caught by local fishermen. Some of the items on the menu are unfamiliar to out-of-town guests, so Ellen is accustomed to describing unusual dishes. Ellen enjoys working for the Cafe's chef, Luke, and his wife Virginia, who are the owners of the Seaside Walk Cafe.

New Harmony, Indiana
*A Rainy Day at the Red Geranium
Restaurant in this Restored Historic
Town in Southwestern Indiana*

Planetarium Director

Kristen is the director of her city's planetarium. The planetarium is state-of-the-art. It attracts a large number of visitors from her city and state, many from other states, and frequently people from foreign countries. Kristen is responsible for a large staff, including an astronomer; people who design and build displays for the museum section; people who run the machines for planetarium shows; clerks in the gift shop; and people who sell tickets and arrange tours for school groups. The city government owns and maintains the planetarium and pays for the building and equipment and staff salaries. However, Kristen works hard to encourage individuals, businesses, and foundations to support the planetarium financially to enable expansion and to pay for new equipment and programs. Kristen enjoys spending time out of her office to see the planetarium in action. She likes to watch visitors, young and old, to find out what parts of the planetarium experience they enjoy the most.

Chicago, Illinois
Adler Planetarium as Seen from the Sears Tower

Bed and Breakfast Owners

Philip and Tina own Autumn Winds Bed and Breakfast. They have been open for business five years. They both wanted a change from their old jobs, so they sold their home in a large city and bought an older home in a beautiful small town popular with tourists. They spent a year remodeling and updating the home before opening for business. They advertise through brochures, a website, listings in online directories, and by word of mouth. Many of their guests say they came to Autumn Winds because a friend recommended

Ashland, Wisconsin
Timber Cove Bed and Breakfast, Carriage House

it. They have enjoyed a steady stream of guests. Philip and Tina enjoy the opportunity to work together. They both clean rooms, maintain the house and yard, and make gourmet breakfasts in the mornings. The couple loves meeting people from all over the country and around the world. They try to give their guests a memorable and restful experience. Some come back every year and have become friends.

State Commissioner of Tourism

Deborah is the Commissioner of Tourism in her state. The Governor appointed her to this position in his cabinet. Deborah is responsible for promoting and expanding tourism. She has a large staff of state employees to assist her. Deborah's goals are to help people around the country know what her state has to offer as a vacation destination and to advertise famous and out-of-the-way attractions. Tourism in the state has grown under Deborah's leadership, with more in-state travel, more visitors from out-of-state, and visitors spending more money.

Florida
Stormy Day at a Welcome Center on I-75

Deborah meets with chambers of commerce around her state to learn about attractions in various communities and to advise them on how to build tourism. Deborah began a state program to remodel and improve welcome centers at her state's borders and to build new welcome centers. The department's website staff has redesigned and expanded the state's tourism website. Deborah directs the development of many travel brochures and an annual vacation guide that lists attractions, festivals, and activities by region. She is currently working with a team to design a user-friendly state map that indicates key tourist destinations. Another team is working on developing and advertising tourism "trails" that will guide tourists to attractions in certain categories, such as the Farm and Food Trail, Civil War History Trail, Wildlife Trail, and Adventure Trail. Deborah's enthusiasm for her state and its exciting destinations inspires her staff and helps her be successful at her job.

Souvenir Designer

Jonathan is a product designer at Treasured Mementos, LLC. His company makes a wide range of souvenir products that museums, zoos, parks, aquariums, historic buildings, and state capitols sell in their gift shops. His company offers many standard souvenirs such as pencils, T-shirts, baseball caps, key chains, and travel mugs, and imprints the names or logos of tourist attractions on these items. Jonathan's job is to design custom products. For example, his most recent client was Heritage Pioneer Village. Jonathan worked with the gift shop manager to design three custom products for the gift shop. They settled on three of Jonathan's designs: a stuffed cow with a bell around her neck that looks like Rosie, a real cow that lives at the village; a real wood refrigerator magnet that looks like a log cabin; and a Christmas ornament that is a miniature version of a real china pitcher from the 1800s which is in the collection of Heritage Pioneer Village. After the store manager approved Jonathan's designs, he submitted them to the engineering team at Treasured Mementos. It is always exciting for Jonathan to see his product designs become real objects. He proudly sent the first completed products to the store manager.

Vintage Pennant Souvenir from Ann Arbor, Michigan

Amusement Park Food Service Associate

Lori works in food service at a large amusement park during the busy summer season. She is a kindergarten teacher who uses her time off in the summer to earn extra money because she and her husband are saving to buy a house. Lori's main position is running a frozen lemonade stand near the carousel, though she sometimes fills in at park restaurants and other food stands. She is usually busy with customers, and sometimes

Ocean City, New Jersey

very busy with a long line of people to serve. She enjoys interacting with people of all ages. The frozen lemonade she serves is delicious, so she knows it will please her customers. When Lori meets someone new at church or in her neighborhood, she enjoys telling them what her job is: "I teach kindergarten, and all summer I run a lemonade stand."

Director, City Convention and Visitors Bureau

Chris is the director of his city's Convention and Visitors Bureau, a department of the local government. The mayor nominated Chris for the position, and the city council approved the nomination. Chris's city has been struggling economically in recent years, so the city council established the Convention and Visitors Bureau to bring in visitors and generate income. His first job was to direct the remodeling and expansion of the city's old convention center to make it more attractive to businesses and organizations holding conferences. Chris's marketing staff

promotes the convention center to groups in other parts of the state and in nearby states. The convention center has had a significant increase in bookings since the improvements, and private companies recently built two hotels nearby to accommodate convention attendees. Chris's media staff has improved the city's tourism website; created brochures listing area hotels, restaurants, and stores; and designed signs to point visitors to local attractions. Chris's events planning staff is currently working on a proposal for a new local festival. Chris meets frequently with the directors and staff of local attractions so that they can share ideas and work together to build the tourism industry in their city.

Mobile, Alabama
Convention Center in Front of RSA Tower

From cities of millions to charming small towns; from amusement parks to local museums; from Grand Canyon National Park to the Statue of Liberty, America is an exciting destination! Skilled tourism workers make our trips possible.

So then, while we have opportunity,

let us do good to all people . . . .

Galatians 6:10

Lesson Activities

Vocabulary — In your notebook, write the vocabulary words and the letter of the definition that goes with each word: maintenance, landscaping, planetarium, remodel, enthusiasm.

    a. a projector that displays celestial images and the room or building that houses the projector

    b. to change the structure and appearance of

    c. the upkeep of an object or place

    d. zeal, passion

    e. the design and maintenance of yards and gardens

Literature — Read chapters 6-7 in *Lost on a Mountain in Maine*.

Creative Writing - In your notebook, write a short story of at least one page about an experience by a tourism worker.

Find Out — Ask your parents if your family knows anyone who works in the tourism industry.

Picture This! — Take a photograph or draw a picture of a tourism worker.

Student Workbook or Lesson Review — If you are using one of these optional books, complete the assignment for Lesson 144.

★ Remember to choose an American Holiday to study this week! ★

International Tourists to the USA

Top Five Countries

1. Canada
2. Mexico
3. United Kingdom
4. Japan
5. Germany

Top Five State Destinations

1. New York
2. Florida
3. California
4. Nevada
5. Hawaii

Top Five City Destinations

1. New York City, New York
2. Los Angeles, California
3. Miami, Florida
4. Orlando, Florida
5. San Francisco, California

Top Five Activities

1. Shopping
2. Dining
3. City Sightseeing
4. Visiting Historical Places
5. Theme/Amusement Parks

Savannah, Georgia
Tour Bus Driver

UNIT 30 – CITIZENS SERVING ONE ANOTHER

BOOKS USED IN UNIT 30

- The Citizen's Handbook
- Lost on a Mountain in Maine
- Student Workbook (optional)
- Lesson Review (optional)

Fire Department of New York (FDNY)

Serving in Three Branches of the
FEDERAL GOVERNMENT

It is a great honor to be able to serve the people of the United States in one of the branches of our Federal government, whether as a U.S. Senator or a Congressman in the legislative branch, a presidential appointee in the executive branch, or as a Federal judge or member of the Supreme Court in the judicial branch. An extremely rare person is he who has had the privilege of serving in all three branches of the Federal government at different times in his life. Only about twenty people in our history have been called upon to serve in these ways. They have had the opportunity and the responsibility to help make laws in Congress, to carry out laws in the executive branch, and to apply and interpret laws as a judge. In this lesson we will look at the careers of some of these exceptional citizens of our country.

John Marshall

Washington, D.C.
*John Marshall Statue in John
Marshall Memorial Park*

Chief Justice John Marshall of Virginia

Probably the best known person who has served in all three branches of the Federal government is John Marshall of Virginia. Marshall was related to Thomas Jefferson, but they had very different ideas about government. Marshall was a Federalist who favored a strong central government while Jefferson was a Democratic-Republican and wanted to limit the powers of the Federal government. Marshall served in the Continental Army during the American Revolutionary War and knew George Washington. After the war, Marshall became an attorney in Virginia and was elected to the Virginia state assembly.

Legislative Branch. In 1799, Marshall was elected to the U.S. House of Representatives.

Executive Branch. He only served in Congress a little more than a year before President John Adams appointed him to be Secretary of State in 1800.

Judicial Branch. Marshall had been Secretary of State less than a year when in 1801 Adams nominated him to be Chief Justice of the U.S. Supreme Court. Marshall served for thirty-four years in this position. By his work as Chief Justice, he helped to make the Supreme Court just as important in the Federal government as Congress and the President.

Chief Justice Salmon P. Chase of New Hampshire

Salmon P. Chase was born in New Hampshire. He began working as a lawyer in Cincinnati, Ohio, in 1830. Chase had a deep Christian faith, which led him to be a strong opponent of slavery.

Legislative Branch. Chase was elected to the United States Senate in 1849 and served one six-year term. He was a leader in the founding of the Republican Party in 1854. Chase was elected Governor of Ohio in 1855 and again in 1857. He wanted to be the Republican nominee for President in 1860, but the party chose Abraham Lincoln.

Executive Branch. Chase was elected to the United States Senate in 1860, but after only two days in office Lincoln asked him to serve as his Secretary of the Treasury.

Judicial Branch. Chase resigned his position as Secretary of the Treasury in 1864, but later that year Lincoln nominated him to serve as Chief Justice of the Supreme Court. The Senate

Salmon P. Chase

confirmed him as Chief Justice the same day that Lincoln submitted the nomination. Chase was the first Chief Justice to admit an African American attorney to argue cases before the Supreme Court. In his role as Chief Justice, Chase presided over the impeachment trial of Andrew Johnson in 1868. Chase died in 1873. In 1928 Chase's portrait appeared on the $10,000 bill of U.S. currency. The bill is no longer printed.

Secretary of the Treasury Salmon P. Chase stands at the left in this portrait of President Abraham Lincoln and his Cabinet.

Chief Justice Fred Vinson of Kentucky

Congressman Vinson (left) visits with House Speaker William Bankhead and Majority Leader Sam Rayburn at a "Congressional Get-Together" before the opening of Congress in 1937.

Fred Vinson was born in Louisa in far eastern Kentucky. His father was the county jailer. Vinson was born in his family's home which was attached to the jail. He became an attorney and won election as the city attorney of Louisa. He then served in the United States Army during World War I.

Legislative Branch. Vinson was elected to the U.S. House of Representatives in 1924.

Judicial Branch. In 1938 President Franklin Roosevelt appointed him to the United States Court of Appeals for the District of Columbia.

Executive Branch. Vinson then served in several positions during the Roosevelt and Truman presidencies, including Secretary of the Treasury.

Judicial Branch. In 1946 Truman nominated Vinson to be Chief Justice of the U.S. Supreme Court, a position which he held until his death in 1953.

Photos of Fred Vinson when he was sworn in as a judge on the United States Court of Appeals for the District of Columbia.

Justice Lucius Quintus Cincinnatus Lamar II of Mississippi

Lucius Quintus Cincinnatus Lamar II was born in Georgia in 1825 and grew up to be a lawyer. He moved to Oxford, Mississippi, in 1849 when his father-in-law, the chancellor of the University of Mississippi, invited him to teach mathematics at the university. He also practiced law and owned a cotton plantation. Lamar returned to Georgia in 1852, and the next year he was elected to the Georgia House of Representatives.

Legislative Branch. Lamar moved back to Mississippi in 1855 and was elected to the U.S. House of Representatives the next year. Lamar served in the House of Representatives until

Lucius Quintus Cincinnatus Lamar II

January of 1861, when he resigned to support the secession of Mississippi from the Union. He wrote the law which declared that Mississippi was no longer part of the United States. Lamar organized a military unit, but then Confederate President Jefferson Davis appointed him to be the South's representative to Russia, Britain, and France (though he never made it to Russia). He lost two brothers and two law partners in the war.

After the war, Lamar was a member of the Mississippi constitutional convention. In 1872 he was once again elected to the U.S. House. Congress passed a special law allowing him to serve, since former Confederate officials had not been allowed to be members of Congress. He was the first Democrat from Mississippi in the House since before the Civil War. Charles Sumner, a strongly anti-slavery Senator from Massachusetts, asked Lamar to deliver a eulogy at his funeral. This took place in 1874, and Lamar's speech was an appeal for the North and the South to be reconciled and unified. In 1877 Lamar became a United States Senator from Mississippi, the first former Confederate leader to serve in the Senate after the Civil War.

Executive Branch. President Grover Cleveland named Lamar as Secretary of the Interior in 1885.

Judicial Branch. Two years later, Cleveland named Lamar to be an associate justice of the U.S. Supreme Court. He was the first southerner to serve on the Court after the war. Lamar was an associate justice on the Supreme Court until his death in 1893.

Ambassador Warren Austin of Vermont

Warren Austin was born in Vermont in 1877. He became an attorney. Republican Austin served as mayor of St. Albans in 1909.

Judicial Branch. In 1917 Austin was appointed as judge for the United States Court for China. This court served as a U.S. Federal district court to enforce American law for American citizens living in China.

Legislative Branch. Austin was elected to the Senate in 1931 and remained in office until 1946.

Executive Branch. In 1946 President Harry Truman (a Democrat) nominated Austin to be the country's first Ambassador to the United Nations.

Senators Royal S. Copeland (left) and Warren R. Austin (right) visited Jerusalem in August 1936.

Justice James F. Byrnes of South Carolina

James F. Byrnes was born in South Carolina in 1882. He became a law clerk for a judge and later an apprentice to a lawyer. He was admitted to the bar to practice as an attorney in 1903, having never attended high school, college, or law school.

Legislative Branch. Byrnes was elected to the U.S. House of Representatives in 1910. He lost a bid for the U.S. Senate in 1924 but won election to that body in 1930 and served for ten years.

Judicial Branch. During the Great Depression, Byrnes was a strong supporter of Franklin Roosevelt's New Deal programs. Roosevelt thanked Byrnes by nominating him to the Supreme Court in 1941, but Byrnes did not enjoy this work and resigned fifteen months later.

James F. Byrnes

Executive Branch. During World War II, Byrnes headed two important offices in the Roosevelt Administration. They dealt with prices and taxes as well as industrial production. He was a close advisor to Roosevelt during the war. President Harry Truman named Byrnes to be Secretary of State, and Byrnes served in this role from 1945 to 1947. He was a close advisor to Truman on the country's relations with other countries. Then in 1950, at the age of sixty-eight, Byrnes was elected Governor of South Carolina and served for four years. A lifelong Democrat, Byrnes became a Republican in his later years. He endorsed the Republican candidate for President in every election from 1952 to 1968. Byrnes died in 1972.

Judge James L. Buckley of New York

James Buckley was born in New York City in 1923.

Legislative Branch. Buckley was elected to the United States Senate from New York in 1970 on that state's Conservative Party ticket. He served one six-year term. While in the Senate, he proposed a human rights amendment to the U.S. Constitution that would have included the unborn child in the definition of "person" as used in the Constitution.

Executive Branch. In 1981 Buckley was confirmed by the Senate as an assistant Secretary of State. The next year, he was selected to head Radio Free Europe/Radio Liberty, a broadcasting service that is similar to the Voice of America program, which was discussed in Lesson 124.

Judicial Branch. In 1985 President Ronald Reagan nominated Buckley to serve as an associate judge on the U.S. Court of Appeals for the District of Columbia. He retired from that court in 2000. Buckley is the brother of the late conservative writer William F. Buckley Jr.

Lives of Service

Leaders in American civic life show courage, a love of their state and country, and a willingness to serve in whatever roles they are needed. The rare individuals who have served in all three branches of our Federal government are examples to all who want to devote themselves to serving their fellow citizens.

Let us consider how to stimulate one another to love and good deeds.

Hebrews 10:24

Lesson Activities

Thinking Biblically — In your notebook, write a paragraph about ways that a Christian can serve others by serving in government positions.

Vocabulary — Find each of these words in a dictionary, then find the definition that corresponds to the way the word is used in this lesson: appointee, privilege, interpret, chancellor, eulogy. Copy the words and definitions into your notebook.

Literature — Read "Thoughts on Education" in *The Citizen's Handbook*, pages 172-173, and chapter 8 in *Lost on a Mountain in Maine*.

Find Out! — What are the names of the Senators and Congressmen currently representing your state in the U.S. Congress?

Student Workbook or Lesson Review — If you are using one of these optional books, complete the assignment for Lesson 146.

A Civics Day
IN THE USA

South Dakota
Badlands National Park

Civics happens around the country, around the clock. It involves many people and takes many forms. Some civic activities get a lot of attention; some happen completely behind the scenes. What happens in the world of civics on a typical day?

8:32 a.m. A National Park Service ranger in Badlands National Park of South Dakota begins the "Geology Walk" with a small group of visitors.

9:03 a.m. A curator at the National Gallery of Art makes a phone call to an art museum in France to discuss borrowing a painting for a special Medieval Art exhibit.

10:45 a.m. A group of homeschooled students watches court proceedings during their tour of the United States District Court for the Eastern District of Michigan in Detroit.

11:21 a.m. A 6th grade class at the Wyoming Indian Middle School on the Wind River Indian Reservation begin their social studies class to continue learning about the Constitution of the United States.

12:46 p.m. A U.S. Senator's intern leaves the pile of mail she is sorting at her desk to grab a quick bowl of

Washington, D.C.
National Gallery of Art
Interior and Exterior

896

soup and a sandwich at the Dirksen North Servery in the basement of the Dirksen Senate Office Building.

1:58 p.m. A Governor who is considering entering the next presidential race arrives at the office of a fellow Governor of the same political party for a meeting to share ideas on the state of the party and to strategize about their political futures.

2:29 p.m. At a White House ceremony, the President of the United States presents the Medal of Honor to an heroic member of the U.S. military.

3:51 p.m. A Federal Emergency Management Agency multilingual phone operator answers the questions of a Spanish-speaking citizen affected by a natural disaster.

Washington, D.C.
President George W. Bush presented the Medal of Honor to retired Lieutenant Colonel Bruce P. Crandall for heroism in Vietnam.

Ford Island, Hawaii
Roy Carter, a survivor of Pearl Harbor (above), and a sailor (right) view the USS Oklahoma Memorial. Each of the 429 marble posts honors one person who lost his life when it sank.

4:03 p.m. A Pearl Harbor survivor views the USS Oklahoma Memorial on Ford Island, Hawaii.

5:35 p.m. The U.S. Consulate General in Rio de Janeiro, Brazil, speaks at the annual Visit USA fair designed to promote Brazilian tourism to the United States.

6:09 p.m. A United States Congresswoman greets gathered constituents at an informal barbecue dinner in her home state.

7:30 p.m. The U.S. Ambassador to China enjoys the first selection of a joint concert of the U.S. Army Band and the People's Liberation Army of China Military Band at the National Center for the Performing Arts in Beijing, China (7:30 p.m. in Beijing).

8:12 p.m. The South African Ambassador to the United States speaks in New York City at a Heritage Celebration for immigrants from his home country.

Fort Meade, Maryland
Twenty-three members of the U.S. Army Field Band re-enlist together.
They are called "The Musical Ambassadors of the Army."

9:39 p.m. A family from Germany arrives at the baggage control area of the Phoenix Sky Harbor International Airport. A U.S. Customs and Border Protection officer checks their baggage for any prohibited items, such as fruit or meats, before clearing the visitors to continue on their way.

Phoenix, Arizona
Daytime Scene at Phoenix Sky Harbor International Airport

10:12 p.m. Before going to bed, a Justice of the Supreme Court finishes reading a brief for an upcoming case.

11:21 p.m. An electrical engineer who has lost his job due to the closure of a manufacturing plant works on submitting an online application for a job at Hoover Dam in Arizona.

Nevada and Arizona
Hoover Dam

12:12 a.m. A Secret Service agent patrols the grounds of the White House.

1:37 a.m. A nurse in the emergency room of the Veterans Administration Medical Center in Bath, New York, takes the blood pressure of a patient.

2:19 a.m. A soldier performs overnight guard duty at the gate of the Fort Hood, Texas, Army base.

3:03 a.m. Crew members on the International Space Station capture a nighttime video of North America from space.

4:45 a.m. The Vice President's alarm clock goes off so he can meet Secret Service agents outside his residence for a morning jog.

Astronauts Sunita L. Williams and Michael A. Lopez-Alegria Onboard the International Space Station, 2007

Moose in Idaho

5:09 a.m. A hunter quietly walks through the dense woods in the Idaho Panhandle National Forest, looking for elk, deer, and moose.

6:35 a.m. A group of Christian legislators bow their heads for the opening prayer at a weekly prayer breakfast in a small room in the U.S. Capitol.

7:19 a.m. Amtrak passengers pull out of the St. Louis, Missouri, Amtrak station. Next stop: Alton, Illinois, 8:43 a.m.

Lead me in Your truth and teach me,

For You are the God of my salvation;

For You I wait all the day.

Psalm 25:5

Lesson Activities

Vocabulary - In your notebook, make a drawing for each of these words that illustrates what it means: geology, curator, intern, strategize, multilingual. Write the word under the drawing. Check in a dictionary if you need help with their definitions.

Literature - Read chapters 9-11 in *Lost on a Mountain in Maine*.

Creative Writing - Write an article of 2-3 paragraphs as if you were a newspaper reporter covering a civics event.

Picture This! - Take a photograph or draw a picture of a civics event.

Student Workbook or Lesson Review — If you are using one of these optional books, complete the assignment for Lesson 147.

A Civics Day
IN YOUR TOWN

Just as civics is always happening around the country, your city also never sleeps! Someone is always awake and serving in your town. We can be thankful that whether we are awake or asleep, public and private servants are working for us and others in our community.

8:01 a.m. A ranger unlocks the front gate of the state park parking lot. A family is already waiting to enter the park, their car loaded with a canoe and camping equipment.

9:14 a.m. The Judge explains to the jury the duties and responsibilities they have as jurors as a trial commences at the county court.

10:18 a.m. Transportation workers replace a vandalized stop sign at a neighborhood intersection.

11:01 a.m. The Mayor begins his remarks at the ribbon-cutting ceremony opening a new manufacturing plant on the outskirts of town.

12:36 p.m. At a lunch meeting, the City Special Events Planning Commission starts discussing plans for the annual Sunflower Festival.

1:12 p.m. In a classroom at the fire station, firefighters study first aid procedures in preparation for a continuing education exam.

2:40 p.m. The county clerk telephones an interpreter to come to her office to help her explain to a Chinese couple the process of getting a marriage license.

3:09 p.m. A clerk at the main post office helps a woman mail a care package to her grandson stationed overseas.

4:19 p.m. A science teacher at Washington Middle School starts working on a new wall decoration of the Solar System in her classroom.

5:41 p.m. A doctor at the Community Free Health Clinic finishes seeing his last patient before starting on his paperwork.

6:46 p.m. The director of the Community Band walks down the corridor of the local high school to the band room, unlocks the door, turns on the lights, and prepares for the 7:00 rehearsal of the Community Band.

7:02 p.m. The curtain is ready to rise for the 8:00 p.m. performance of "Peter Pan" by the Community Theatrical Society at the Municipal Performing Arts Center.

8:19 p.m. The first baseman for the Cougars hits a home run to beat the Bumblebees at Woodlands City Park.

9:41 p.m. While they watch a movie, a mother and daughter crochet a baby cap and baby blanket to donate to a local organization that serves mothers and babies in need.

10:12 p.m. After her children are in bed, a homeschooling mother updates her children's school records and grades a few quizzes they took that day.

11:46 p.m. A city councilman finishes answering e-mails from concerned citizens and fellow councilmen. The councilman has a professional job, so his city council work has to wait for the evenings and weekends.

12:23 a.m. A nurse in the hospital's intensive care unit answers the summons of a recovering surgery patient.

1:14 a.m. A tractor-trailer truck driver pulls a B-1 bomber through town on the Interstate, purposely traveling at night when the traffic is lighter.

2:58 a.m. A police officer in a patrol car stops to take care of some paperwork while patrolling city streets.

3:36 a.m. EMTs race in an ambulance to the home of an elderly couple. The husband has called for help because his wife has fallen.

4:00 a.m. A city bus starts its rounds for the day, stopping at a downtown bus stop, where one passenger is waiting.

5:57 a.m. A state representative arrives at his hometown office with coffee and a box of donuts to have a breakfast meeting with his staff members before catching a train for the state capital for a 9:00 a.m. committee meeting.

6:49 a.m. After a car hit a fire hydrant, city utility workers hurry to the scene to shut off the water supply.

7:12 a.m. A waitress at Sunrise Cafe fills coffee cups of members of the Rotary Club as they listen to a presentation by the city's Director of Housing and Community Development.

This is the day which the Lord has made;

Let us rejoice and be glad in it.

Psalm 118:24

Lesson Activities

Vocabulary — In your notebook, write which of the following words belongs in each sentence: public, commence, outskirts, procedure, summons.

1. What is the established _____ when a fire engine needs maintenance?

2. We live on the _____ of the city and it takes us forty minutes to drive to church.

3. Greg received a _____ to serve on a jury.

4. After three decades of _____ service, the former Governor will begin working as a manager in a large corporation.

5. The ceremonies will _____ with a prayer by an Army chaplain.

Literature — Read chapter 12 and the Afterword in *Lost on a Mountain in Maine*.

Creative Writing — In your notebook, write a fictional story of at least one page in which you encounter several different civics events in your town in a single day.

Find Out! — What is your mayor's name, office address, and office phone number?

Picture This! — Take a photograph or draw a picture of a civics event in your town.

Student Workbook or Lesson Review — If you are using one of these optional books, complete the assignment for Lesson 148.

Uncle Sam
AND YOU

One Nation Under God

Three Levels of Government—Federal, State, and Local

Three branches of government—Legislative, Executive, and Judicial

Symbols and Ideals

Electing Officials to Lead Us

The Military

Our Relations with Other Nations

Justice and Security

Economics and Natural Resources

Technology, Communication, and Transportation

Native American Tribes

Education, the Arts, and Tourism

What Does This Mean for You?

Uncle Sam and You has discussed some big ideas. You have learned how our great country works: what government does, what private citizens and businesses do, and how government and individuals work together.

What does all of this mean for you, the young citizen? What is your responsibility? What is your opportunity? What can you do now, and what can you prepare yourself to do in the future?

Our country needs good people on every level of government. It needs good citizens involved at the local, state, and national levels. We need people who will work to protect and defend what should stay the same and who will work to change what will make our country better. As we have seen again and again, one person can make a difference. America is stronger when many people work together, but any group working together begins with individuals.

America needs citizens who are devoted to what is good for themselves, their families, our communities, and our nation as a whole. We need citizens who stay informed and who do good for their fellow citizens. When you offer yourself in service to help your community and your nation, you are helping yourself at the same time. Think about the possibilities of what God might do through you.

Love Your Neighbor as Yourself

If we could put all of these ideas into a single thought, it would be to love your neighbor as yourself. Jesus said that the greatest commandments are to love God with your whole being and to love your neighbor as yourself—in other words, as though your neighbor were you (Matthew 22:35-40). The Golden Rule, "Treat people the same way you want them to treat you" (Matthew 7:12), is simply another way of expressing the commandment to love your neighbor as yourself.

Jesus told the parable of the Good Samaritan in Luke 10 to explain how a person is to love his neighbor as himself. The Good Samaritan was a good citizen. He saw someone in need, and he did something about it. This is acting in love, and this is what we would want someone to do for us if we were in need.

Being good managers of our natural resources is a way to love our neighbors as ourselves. We share our natural resources, so we should be considerate of others in how we use them, including people who are not yet born. The United States should be a good neighbor to the other countries in the world and conduct our relations with them the way we want other nations to treat us.

Citizens in a community often come together to work on a common task. They might work to clean up litter or to create a park. When a community is struck by a tornado, volunteers work together to prepare food, remove fallen trees, rebuild homes, provide temporary housing, and meet other needs. After Hurricane Katrina hit New Orleans and the nearby Gulf Coast in 2005, people from many parts of the country went there to provide help of many kinds. In the photo at right, volunteers are installing wireless service to help people be able to use computers again. Citizens from all over the country treated others the way they would want to be treated if their lives had been turned upside down by a hurricane.

Hurricane Katrina Volunteers

Citizens helping others is an important, meaningful, and practical way to build and maintain a strong civic life. Sometimes the citizens of one community help the people of another community. The following story shows how the people of one city "loved their neighbors" in another city who were in need, and how many years later the help flowed in the opposite direction.

Northerners Helping Southerners

In the closing months of the Civil War, a Union army took control of Atlanta and Savannah, Georgia. The army then turned north and took over other areas of the South. By February of 1865, Union troops had arrived in Columbia, South Carolina, the state capital. A devastating fire broke out in Columbia. Southerners believed that Union troops started the fire, while Northerners said that people in Columbia set bales of cotton on fire to keep them from being captured by Union soldiers. Whatever the cause, the fire destroyed a large part of the city. Among the materials lost was Columbia's fire fighting equipment. As the city rebuilt following the war, volunteer firemen had to line up in bucket brigades to put out fires.

Harper's Weekly included this illustration entitled "The Burning of Columbia, South Carolina, February 17, 1865" *on page 217 of its April 8, 1865, edition. Artist William Waud drew the illustration. The print shows a large group of Union soldiers under the command of General Sherman, watching Columbia burn. Inhabitants of the city, who are mostly women, are seen fleeing both the fire and the soldiers.*

The New York (City) Firemen's Association learned of the situation in Columbia and began raising money to buy a new fire hose wagon for the city. Many of the New York City firemen had been Union soldiers. They raised $2,500, with many donations being pennies, and purchased the wagon. They sent it to Columbia on a ship, but the vessel sank off the North Carolina coast and the wagon was lost. The New York firemen then raised the money for another wagon, and it arrived safely in Columbia.

The president of the New York Firemen's Association presented the wagon to the city of Columbia at a ceremony in 1867 in a park near where Confederate ammunition had been made. He said, "We call upon our fellow citizens of the two great sections to emulate our example and thus hasten a restoration to its normal condition and grand proportions of our once beautiful and still united national fabric." The leader of the Columbia fire department responded by saying, "These noble efforts of yours to assist us must forever remain green in our memory." A former Confederate colonel spoke on behalf of the city of Columbia and promised to return the favor "should misfortune ever befall the Empire City." The colonel said that he hoped the people of Columbia would be able to "obey that golden rule by which you have been prompted in the performance of this most munificent kindness to a people in distress."

Southerners Helping Northerners

One hundred and thirty-four years later, on September 11, 2001, terrorists destroyed the World Trade Center in New York City. Over three hundred firefighters lost their lives trying to save people in the burning buildings. The Fire Department of New York (FDNY) also lost about one hundred pieces of equipment when the buildings collapsed.

New York City
World Trade Center in Manhattan, August 2001

Windsor Locks, Connecticut
The Connecticut Fire Academy has a scrap from the World Trade Center in a memorial to the firefighters who died in the 9/11 attack.

Fire Department of New York (FDNY)

Lower Left: On September 8, 2011, New York Fire Department Chief Jack Prichard stood aboard the USS New York as this amphibious transport dock ship was about to pass the National September 11 Memorial. Northrop Grumman Ship Systems shipyard in Avondale, Louisiana, built the ship. Shipbuilders included 7.5 tons of steel from the World Trade Center in the bow of the USS New York.
Posters: Created by the Federal Art Project During the Great Depression

Individuals, companies, and cities around the country raised money to help the FDNY get new equipment. Companies that build fire equipment donated several pieces. People in Akron, Ohio, and surrounding communities raised $1.4 million in just over a month to buy new materials to send to New York City.

Nancy Turner, the principal of White Knoll Middle School in West Columbia, South Carolina, and teachers at the school, encouraged the children at their school to raise money to buy a new fire truck for the FDNY. When Turner was doing research about what kind of truck they might buy and how much it would cost, she discovered the records of the long-ago gift that New York City had given to Columbia. This gave an additional motivation to those involved in raising the money.

The students held car washes and bake sales, sold T-shirts, and collected money at football games. William Murray, an attorney in New York City who had ties to South Carolina, donated $100,000. An anonymous donor gave $50,000. The brother of a firefighter who died at the World Trade Center on September 11 sent a donation. In about two months, the drive raised over a half million dollars. Students from the school traveled to New York in November of 2001 and presented a check to New York City Mayor Rudy Giuliani. While in New York, they rode in Macy's Thanksgiving Day parade. Members of the FDNY unit that received the truck visited White Knoll Middle School in December to say thank you.

Numerous connections between Columbia, South Carolina, and New York City, New York, existed at the time or developed later. The fire chief in Columbia in 2001 was a native of New York and had worked with the FDNY. Owens Steel, a company in Columbia, made a four-ton steel beam that became part of the 9/11 Memorial built on the site of the World Trade Center. In 2008 the White Knoll High School marching band was invited to give a performance at Carnegie Hall in New York City. Some of the band members had been students at the middle school at the time of the fund drive. They got to visit the fire station that had received the truck that their efforts had helped to purchase. The truck bears a plaque with the names of the men from that unit who died on September 11, 2001, and it flies the South Carolina state flag.

Who Is Your Neighbor, Citizen?

Who is someone who needs your help? What is a project or cause about which you care deeply? How can you show your commitment to the principles that have made our nation great? In what way can you be a neighbor to others in your community, state, and nation? This is the task that is before Uncle Sam—and you!

Matchbook from the World War II Era

Jesus answered, "The foremost is, 'Hear, O Israel! The Lord our God is one Lord; and you shall love the Lord your God with all your heart, and with all your soul, and with all your mind, and with all your strength.' The second is this, 'You shall love your neighbor as yourself.' There is no other commandment greater than these."

Mark 12:29-31

Lesson Activities

Thinking Biblically — Copy Mark 12:29-31 into your notebook.

Literature — Read "Makers of the Flag" in *The Citizen's Handbook*, pages 174-175.

Creative Writing — In your notebook, write a paragraph about what you want to do for your country.

Picture This! — Draw a picture or ask someone to take a photograph of you holding the flag of the United States of America.

Student Workbook or Lesson Review — If you are using one of these optional books, complete the assignment for Lesson 149.

★ Remember to choose an American Holiday to study this week! ★

AMERICAN HOLIDAYS

Martin Luther King Day - Third Monday in January

National Freedom Day - February 1

Groundhog Day and Valentine's Day - February 2 and 14

Washington's Birthday - Third Monday in February

St. Patrick's Day - March 17

Tax Day - April 15

Good Friday and Easter - Between March 22 and April 25

National Arbor Day - Last Friday in April

Loyalty Day and Law Day - May 1

National Day of Prayer - First Thursday in May

Mother's Day - Second Sunday in May

Armed Forces Day - Third Saturday in May

Memorial Day - Last Monday in May

Flag Day - June 14

Father's Day - Third Sunday in June

2008 Memorial Day Parade in Chicago, Illinois

MARTIN LUTHER KING DAY
Third Monday in January

Martin Luther King Jr. was a leader in the civil rights movement in the 1950s and '60s. After his death in 1968, his wife Coretta led the effort to establish Martin Luther King Day as a Federal holiday to honor her husband's legacy. A bill to create the holiday was proposed to Congress in every legislative session from 1968 until 1983, when it finally passed and was signed by President Ronald Reagan. The holiday was observed for the first time nationwide in 1986.

King's Early Life

Martin Luther King Jr. was born on January 15, 1929, in the house pictured below that still stands in Atlanta, Georgia. At birth he was named Michael after his father, but his father later changed his own name and his son's name to Martin Luther. Martin Jr.'s father, grandfather,

Atlanta, Georgia
Birthplace of Martin Luther King Jr.

and great-grandfather were all Baptist ministers. His mother's father was a sharecropper. Martin had one sister and one brother.

Martin graduated from high school when he was fifteen years old. He attended Morehouse College, the same school attended by his father and grandfather, and received his degree when he was 19. He then studied at a theological seminary in Pennsylvania, from which he graduated two years later. He attended Boston University and received his doctorate in 1955 at the age of twenty-six. During his time in Boston, King met and married Coretta Scott. The couple had two sons and two daughters: Yolanda, Martin, Dexter, and Bernice.

Working for Civil Rights

King became the pastor of Dexter Avenue Baptist Church in Montgomery, Alabama, in 1954. The church's building is pictured at right. King also became a leader in the National Association for the Advancement of Colored People (NAACP), a group that works for civil rights for African Americans. At this time in Montgomery, Alabama, black people and white people were not treated equally. White people received better treatment just about everywhere. In 1955 a woman named Rosa Parks refused to give up her seat to a white man on a Montgomery city bus. What she did was against the law, so

Montgomery, Alabama
Dexter Avenue Baptist Church

Rosa Parks was arrested. This led to a citywide bus boycott, led by Martin Luther King Jr., in which African Americans protested this unfair treatment by not using the city bus system. The boycott lasted over a year and received worldwide attention. During the boycott, King was arrested. He was abused and people threw bombs at his home. King handled this unfair treatment with dignity, and through the ordeal he came to be widely respected as a leader among the African American people and the civil rights movement.

Dr. King was elected president of a civil rights organization called the Southern Christian Leadership Conference in 1957. During the next eleven years, King traveled over six million miles promoting nonviolent action to gain civil rights for African Americans. He spoke over 2,500 times during these years. He also wrote books and articles. King was arrested nearly twenty times, but he never game up. *Time* magazine chose King to be its Man of the Year in 1963. Also in 1963, King directed a March on Washington, a peaceful demonstration at which he delivered his famous "I Have a Dream" speech. Dr. King received the distinguished honor of being chosen as the recipient of the Nobel Peace Prize in 1964 when he was thirty-five years old. At the time he was the youngest person ever to receive the award. As part of the prize King received over $50,000. He donated this money to the civil rights movement. The picture at left shows King the year he received the Nobel Peace Prize.

Dr. Martin Luther King Jr., 1964

Dr. King's Legacy

In April of 1968, King was staying at a hotel in Memphis, Tennessee. He was there to lead a peaceful march supporting city garbage workers. On the evening of April 4, King was standing on the hotel balcony when he was assassinated by a white man named James Earl Ray.

Despite King's death, the civil rights movement continued to make advances. Today African Americans are able to enjoy a much greater degree of justice and equality than they experienced in the past thanks to the work of Dr. King and many others. King's legacy is honored around the world by people seeking justice and peace.

Washington, D.C.
Coretta Scott King, 1988

After Dr. King's assassination, his wife Coretta established the King Center in Atlanta, Georgia, to carry on her husband's nonviolent philosophy. King's ideas have accomplished much good and have kept much evil from happening. Coretta Scott King is pictured above making a speech in Washington, D.C., in 1988.

Washington, D.C.
Martin Luther King Jr. Memorial

Martin Luther King Jr. Memorial

Today the large granite memorial pictured at left stands in Washington, D.C., as a tribute to the life and work of Martin Luther King Jr. A wreath-laying ceremony took place at the memorial on Martin Luther King Day in 2012.

The process of erecting a memorial such as this is a long one that requires many people working for many years. It also takes a large amount of money. Read the timeline below that describes just some of the many steps that had to take place before the Martin Luther King Jr. Memorial was completed and dedicated.

★ January 1984 – A group of men who were members of the Alpha Phi Alpha Fraternity, of which Martin Luther King Jr. was a member, sit around a dinner table and talk about the idea of a national memorial to honor Dr. King. The idea is presented to the fraternity's board of directors later in the month.

★ September - October 1996 – The U.S. Senate and House of Representatives pass resolutions to authorize Alpha Phi Alpha to establish a King memorial in Washington, D.C.

★ November 12, 1996 – President Clinton signs the legislation to create the King memorial.

★ February 15, 1999 – Architects, designers, and artists are invited to enter a competition for the design of the memorial.

* December 2, 1999 – A panel of judges is named to select the winning design. The panel includes architects and artists from Washington, D.C.; California, Michigan, New York, and Florida; and China, India, Mexico, and Switzerland.

* September 12, 2000 – A design from a group in San Francisco, California, is selected as the winner from over 900 submitted designs.

* March 2001 – General Motors becomes the first major sponsor to help raise the $120 million that is needed to complete the memorial.

* July 2002 – Public Service Announcements are created to raise awareness about the project.

* November 2002 – An assessment is made of the chosen site to make sure building the memorial will not harm the environment.

* August 28, 2002 – Yahoo! puts information about the memorial on their homepage to help raise awareness and to help raise money.

* June 28, 2005 – The U.S. Senate agrees to provide $10 million for the project.

* February 28, 2006 – The Walt Disney Company Foundation donates $2.75 million.

* April - September 2006 – State Farm Insurance, PepsiCo, ExxonMobile, and FedEx each donate $1 million. The government of South Africa also commits $100,000. Others also make significant donations over the next few years.

* October 2006 – The memorial's design team travels to China to tour possible granite quarries and fabrication sites for the monument.

* November 13, 2006 – A groundbreaking ceremony takes place on the site of the future King memorial. That night, a dinner is held at the Kennedy Center in Washington, D.C., that raises $5.2 million for the project.

* January 15, 2007 – An announcement is made telling which quotes by Dr. King have been selected to be included on the memorial. Also, Chinese Master Lei Yixin is announced to be the sculptor who will carve the image of Dr. King.

* September 18, 2007 – Several popular music artists perform The Dream Concert at Radio City Music Hall in New York City to raise money for the memorial. Attendees pay between $150 and $1,000 each for their tickets.

* August 12, 2008 – Site preparation begins for the memorial.

* November 20, 2008 – Wal-Mart gives a $12.5 million letter of credit (a loan) to the Martin Luther King Jr. National Memorial Project Foundation so that there will be enough funds to begin construction of the memorial. The Foundation will pay Wal-Mart back after they raise more funds.

* March 17, 2009 – Facebook is used as a tool to raise funds.

* August 2010 – A cargo ship arrives in Baltimore, Maryland, after making a 47-day trip from China. The ship is carrying 159 granite sculpture blocks that were quarried and carved in China.

* October 8, 2010 – Dr. and Coretta King's children, Bernice and Martin III, visit the construction site.

* June 2011 – Nick Benson, a stone carver from Rhode Island, finishes carving the quotes from Dr. King on the memorial's inscription walls.

* August 22, 2011 – The memorial opens to the public!

* August 28, 2011 – The memorial is scheduled to be formally dedicated on this day, but the ceremony is postponed due to a hurricane headed for the area.

* October 16, 2011 – Over twenty-eight years after the project was first discussed, President Barack Obama speaks to over 10,000 people at the dedication of the Martin Luther King Jr. Memorial.

Martin Luther King Jr. Day of Service

Dr. King once said, "Life's most persistent and urgent question is, 'What are you doing for others?'" In 1994 Congress designated the Martin Luther King Day as a national day of service. Americans are encouraged to find a place where they can serve others on this day, which is observed each year on the third Monday in January. Serving our communities is one way we can carry on the work of Dr. King. He sought to make the world a better place, something each of us can also do. Below are just a few of the service projects in which Americans across the country have participated on Martin Luther King Day.

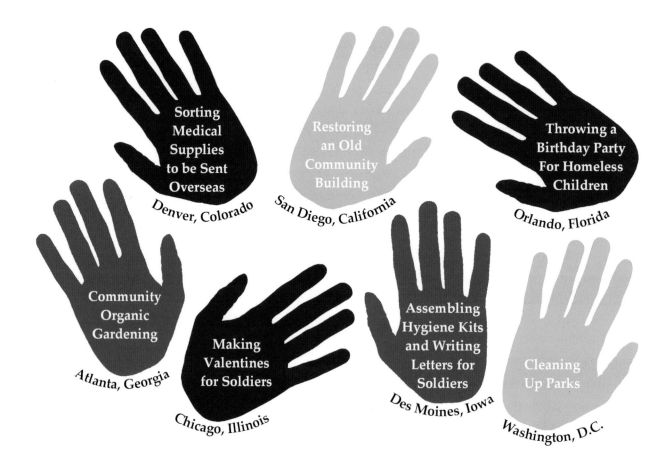

In the photo at left, two girls show the certificates they received after volunteering at their local library on Martin Luther King Day. Some communities remember Dr. King's legacy with parades, concerts, and other events. Look at the images on the next page that show some of the events that have been held in different parts of the country.

Roackaway, New Jersey
Martin Luther King Day of Service Volunteers, 2010

Seattle, Washington
Community March, 2003

Magnolia, Arkansas
March at Southern Arkansas University, 2008

San Antonio, Texas
Performance by a Children's Choir, 2010

Greenbelt, Maryland
Performance at NASA's Goddard Space Flight Center, 2011

Martin Luther King Day is a wonderful opportunity to find a way to serve others. Whether on that day or on any of the other 364 days of the year, look for ways that you can be the hands and feet of Jesus by reaching out and serving your fellow American citizens.

For even the Son of Man did not come
to be served, but to serve,
and to give His life a ransom for many.
Mark 10:45

Washington, D.C.
Preparing a Meal for People in Need, 2012

Family Activity

Create a "What Are You Doing for Others?" poster. Instructions are on page 1006.

NATIONAL FREEDOM DAY

February 1

Richard Robert Wright Sr., 1903

Richard Robert Wright Sr. knew what it meant to be free, and he knew what it meant to be denied freedom. Wright was born into a Georgia slave family in 1855. After slavery was abolished in the United States, Wright took hold of opportunities in front of him and rose high above the challenges he had faced as a young boy. Wright served as a major during the Spanish-American War. He was the first African American to become Army paymaster. He founded a high school and Georgia State Industrial College for Colored Youth (now called Savannah State University) in Georgia and served as the school's first president from 1891 until 1921. The building below was built on the school's campus in 1901. The portrait of Wright above was taken in 1903.

Wright moved to Philadelphia, Pennsylvania, in 1921 where he opened the Citizens and Southern Bank and Trust Company. It was the only bank in the North that was owned by an African American at that time. Wright also owned several newspapers.

Wright encouraged African Americans to pursue higher education. He knew that people should keep learning no matter how old they are. He enrolled in Wharton Business School in Philadelphia when he was sixty-seven years old.

One of Wright's lasting contributions to American society is National Freedom Day, observed each year on February 1. Wright chose February 1 since that was the day in 1865 when Abraham Lincoln signed the Thirteenth

Savannah, Georgia
Savannah State University

Amendment to the Constitution that abolished slavery in the United States. Wright wanted a day to promote goodwill, harmony, and equal opportunity among all citizens. He also wanted the United States to rededicate itself each year to the ideal of freedom.

On February 1, 1941, Wright gathered national and local leaders together in Philadelphia to make plans for establishing National Freedom Day. The next year the first community-wide observance was held in Philadelphia. Around 3,500 people came together for the celebration. They recited the Pledge of Allegiance in front of the Liberty Bell and held a parade with forty automobiles decorated with flags.

Wright continued to work to make the observance nation-wide. He went on a national speaking tour and worked with various legislators. Finally a bill establishing National Freedom Day was passed in the U.S. House of Representatives and the U.S. Senate. It was signed into law by President Harry Truman on June 30, 1948, as pictured at right. Sadly, Wright had died the year before and so did not get to see his dream become reality.

Washington, D.C.
President Harry Truman Signs the Bill Proclaiming February 1 as National Freedom Day, June 30, 1948

President Truman issued this proclamation in 1949 for the first nation-wide observance of National Freedom Day:

By the President of the United States of America
A Proclamation

WHEREAS, near the end of the tragic conflict between the Northern and Southern States, the Congress adopted a joint resolution proposing an amendment to the Constitution which would outlaw slavery in the United States and in every place subject to its jurisdiction; and

WHEREAS the resolution was signed by President Lincoln on February 1, 1865, and thereafter led to the adoption of the Thirteenth Amendment to the constitution; and

WHEREAS that Amendment is a corner stone in the foundation of our American traditions, and the signing of the resolution is a landmark in the Nation's effort to fulfill the principles of freedom and justice proclaimed in the first ten amendments to the Constitution; and

WHEREAS, by a joint resolution approved June 30, 1948 (62 Stat. 1150), the Congress authorized the President to proclaim the first day of February of each year as National Freedom Day in commemoration of the signing of the resolution of February 1, 1865; and

WHEREAS the Government and people of the United States wholeheartedly support the Universal Declaration of Human Rights approved by the General Assembly of the United Nations on December 10, 1948, which declares that "recognition of the inherent dignity and of the equal and inalienable rights of all members of the human family is the foundation of freedom, justice and peace in the world":

NOW, THEREFORE, I, HARRY S. TRUMAN, President of the United States of America, do hereby designate February 1, 1949, and each succeeding February 1, as national Freedom Day; and I call upon the people of the United States to pause on that day in solemn contemplation of the glorious blessings of freedom which we humbly and thankfully enjoy.

IN WITNESS WHEREOF, I have hereunto set my hand and caused the Seal of the United States of America to be affixed.

DONE at the City of Washington this 25th day of January in the year of our Lord nineteen hundred and forty-nine, and of the Independence of the United States of America the one hundred and seventy-third.

HARRY S. TRUMAN

"Tell 'Em We're Rising!"

Even when Richard Robert Wright Sr. was a young boy, he knew that he wanted to rise to do great things. When he was nine years old, he traveled two hundred miles with his mother to

General Oliver O. Howard

meet retired Union General Oliver O. Howard, pictured at left. Young Richard gave the General a message to tell Northerners who were curious about the former slaves in the South. He said, "Tell 'em we're rising."

A poet named John Greenleaf Whittier seized on the boy's statement and incorporated it into a poem he wrote about the event called "Howard at Atlanta."

"Tell 'em we're rising!" became a motto for many former slaves who wanted to rise above their lives of slavery, embrace their new freedom, and do good and noble things.

Howard at Atlanta (excerpt)

by John Greenleaf Whittier

Right in the track where Sherman
Ploughed his red furrow,
Out of the narrow cabin,
Up from the cellar's burrow,
Gathered the black people,
With freedom newly dowered,
Where, beside their Northern teacher,
Stood the soldier, Howard.

Transformed he saw them passing
Their new life's portal!
Almost it seemed the mortal
Put on the immortal.
No more with the beasts of burden,
No more with stone and clod,
But crowned with glory and honor
In the image of God!

He said, "Who hears can never
Fear for or doubt you;
What shall I tell the children
Up North about you?"
Then ran round a whisper, a murmur,
Some answer devising;
And a little boy stood up: "General,
Tell 'em we're rising!"

O black boy of Atlanta!
But half was spoken:
The slave's chain and the master's
Alike are broken.
The one curse of the races
Held both in tether:
They are rising,—all are rising,
The black and white together!

Slave Cabin

National Freedom Day Association

As a part of his efforts to promote National Freedom Day, Richard Robert Wright Sr. founded the National Freedom Day Association. The purpose of the association is "Promoting the observance of National Freedom Day on February First in Commemoration of the Adoption of the Thirteenth Amendment to the Constitution of the United States of America and for the Annual Re-Dedication of all citizens to the idea of freedom, the basis of our Democracy." The association's motto is the same phrase that is inscribed on the Liberty Bell: *Proclaim liberty throughout all the land to all the inhabitants thereof. Leviticus 25:10* In the photo at left the mayor of Philadelphia is presenting a city tribute to the association.

Philadelphia, Pennsylvania
Mayor Michael Nutter (left) Presents a City Tribute to
Lorenzo Cruger Sr., President of the
National Freedom Day Association

Observing National Freedom Day

Even though every President since Harry Truman has issued National Freedom Day proclamations encouraging all Americans to commemorate the day, the observance has largely remained localized in Philadelphia. Each year a wreath is placed at the Liberty Bell to commemorate the day, as pictured below. Other events such as a banquet and school programs are also held.

Placing a Wreath at the Liberty Bell on National Freedom Day

National Slavery and Human Trafficking Prevention Month

In 2010 President Barack Obama helped to renew interest in National Freedom Day. Obama designated January as National Slavery and Human Trafficking Prevention Month, building up to the observance of National Freedom Day on February 1. Even though slavery was officially outlawed long ago in the United States and other countries, slavery still exists today in many forms. Men, women, and children around the world are bought and sold and forced to work against their will in factories, in fields, and through military service. Obama's administration wanted to raise awareness of these realities so that Americans will be educated about the facts and will be more able to fight against these injustices.

The apostle Paul wrote a letter to the Christians in Ephesus. Some of the Christians there were slaves and some were slave masters. Paul told the slaves that they should be obedient to their masters and serve them well, as if they were serving the Lord. He told the slave masters that they should not threaten their slaves. Paul said that to God there is no difference between a slave and a free man. He loves us all the same.

Whatever good thing each one does,
this he will receive back from the Lord,
whether slave or free.
Ephesians 6:8

Family Activity

Have a Freedom Day Banquet. Instructions are on pages 1007-1008.

GROUNDHOG DAY
AND VALENTINE'S DAY
February 2 and February 14

Groundhog Day

The American tradition of Groundhog Day is tied to an ancient European celebration called Candlemas Day. Candlemas Day, celebrated on February 2, marked the mid-point between the beginning of winter and the beginning of spring. According to legend it was the day Jesus

was taken to the temple to be circumcised forty days after His birth. On this day Catholic priests would bless the candles for the year and give them out to the people. Many people placed lighted candles in their windows on Candlemas night.

Some people believed that the weather on Candlemas Day predicted the weather for the rest of the winter. An ancient English rhyme said:

> *If Candlemas be fair and bright,*
> *Come, Winter, have another flight;*
> *If Candlemas brings clouds and rain,*
> *Go Winter, and come not again.*

In Germany people looked at the hedgehog on Candlemas Day to see if he cast a shadow. If the day was clear and the hedgehog cast a shadow, the people expected six more weeks of wintery weather. If the day was overcast and no shadow appeared, the people anticipated an early spring.

When German settlers came to America and settled in what is now Pennsylvania, they brought many traditions with them, including Candlemas Day. There were not any hedgehogs in the German settlers' new homeland, but groundhogs were plentiful and became the animal associated with February 2 in America.

Punxsutawney Phil

Punxsutawney, Pennsylvania
Punxsutawney Phil

In the mid-1880s, a man named Clymer H. Freas worked as city editor of the *Punxsutawney Spirit* newspaper in Punxsutawney, Pennsylvania. Freas wrote a story about a group of men known as the Punxsutawney Groundhog Club. The men had a tradition of holding a groundhog hunt followed by a picnic with barbecued groundhog as the main dish. Freas claimed that the Punxsutawney groundhog was the official weather forecaster for the coming of spring. Freas named the groundhog Punxsutawney Phil. Freas kept writing stories about the Punxsutawney Groundhog Club, embellishing the stories as the years went by. Other newspapers began publishing his tales, and before long the whole country started looking to Punxsutawney Phil to find out when they could expect spring to come. The club members of today claim that the current Punxsutawney Phil, pictured above, is the same groundhog who has been predicting the weather since the club was founded. They say they give him a special drink once a year that gives him seven more years of life. This claim, however, has never been proven as fact! Phil has made quite a name for himself, though. In 1986 he even traveled to Washington, D.C., to meet President Ronald Reagan!

The National Oceanic and Atmospheric Administration's National Climatic Data Center created a comparison chart to judge Punxsutawney Phil's accuracy in his weather predictions. Their conclusion was that Phil showed "no predictive skill." His predictions are accurate about 39% of the time.

Despite Phil's track record, he still draws tens of thousands of people to Gobbler's Knob, a hill in Punxsutawney that is the scene of the annual ceremony. The gates open at 3:00 a.m. Visitors who arrive early enough can enjoy a bonfire, live entertainment, and a pre-dawn fireworks display. Around 7:25 a.m., Phil comes out of the simulated tree stump pictured at left and the crowd watches to see whether or not his shadow is visible.

Punxsutawney Phil's Tree Stump

Groundhog Day is a large source of income for the State of Pennsylvania. Hotels up to one hundred miles away from Punxsutawney are packed in early February. It is estimated that tourists spend an average of $200 per day on gas, food, lodging, and souvenirs.

As Pennsylvania Governor Tom Corbett said in 2012, "The economic impact of this multi-day event is tremendous."

The town of Punxsutawney has created additional tourist attractions, including the Punxsutawney Weather Discovery Center housed in an old Federal Building and Post Office that was built in 1914.

The Punxsutawney Groundhog Club and Northwest Pennsylvania's Great Outdoors Visitors Bureau worked together to bring the "Phantastic Phils! Public Art Project" to the town in 2004. One by one throughout that year, 32 six-foot fiberglass groundhog statues were placed in various locations in Punxsutawney. Each statue had a sponsor and was decorated by a local or regional artist. The one pictured at right was sponsored by the owner of the local McDonald's restaurant. Other groundhog statues are creatively clothed as a mailman, a fireman, a pizza man, a newspaper reporter, a Scottish bagpipe player, and the Statue of Liberty, just to name a few.

Punxsutawney, Pennsylvania
Punxsutawney Phil

While Punxsutawney is unmistakably the "Weather Capital of the World," other towns across the country still have their own weather-predicting mascots, including:

Staten Island Chuck
Staten Island, New York

Buckeye Chuck
Marion, Ohio

Jimmy
Sun Prairie, Wisconsin

French Creek Freddie
French Creek, West Virginia

Birmingham Bill
Birmingham, Alabama

Sir Walter Wally
Raleigh, North Carolina

General Beauregard Lee
Atlanta, Georgia

Pierre C. Shadeaux
New Iberia, Louisiana

Valentine's Day

No one knows exactly how Valentine's Day came about, but the most common story dates back to the 200s A.D. in Ancient Rome. According to the story, the Roman Emperor Claudius II issued an order forbidding young men to marry. A Roman priest by the name of Valentine defied the order and performed marriage ceremonies anyway. Claudius had Valentine arrested. While he was in prison, Valentine befriended the jailer's blind daughter. The girl was cured of her blindness and Valentine wrote her a note and signed it "from your Valentine." Valentine was executed in 269 A.D. Around the year 500 A.D., Pope Gelasius designated a day to honor Valentine and called it St. Valentine's Day.

Geoffrey Chaucer, an English poet, wrote a poem in the 1380s that mentioned Valentine's Day. Chaucer wrote the poem in honor of the first anniversary of King Richard II's engagement to his queen, Anne of Bohemia. The poem is the first known connection made between Valentine's Day and romantic love.

The modern celebration of Valentine's Day began in Great Britain in the 1600s. By the mid-1700s, people were giving their sweethearts small tokens and notes of affection. Printers began making Valentine's Day cards in the early 1800s.

Mother of the American Valentine

A woman from Massachusetts named Esther Howland received a fancy English valentine card in 1847. This card gave her an idea. Her father owned a book and stationery store in Worcester, Massachusetts. Esther asked him to order paper lace and other supplies from England and New York. After Esther received the supplies, she started making cards. She hoped that she could sell $200 worth of cards.

Esther's brother took twelve samples of the valentines when he went on a sales trip. When he came home, he brought Esther orders for $5,000 worth of cards! Esther had to get help from her friends and family to fill all the orders. She established her own company, which eventually made $100,000 a year. Esther's valentines were similar in style to the one pictured at right that was made in 1890. Her valentines often contained a verse such as this one:

1890 Valentine

> *Thou are beautiful, young lady*
> *But I need not tell you this,*
> *For few have borne unconsciously*
> *The spell of loveliness.*

Esther and a man named Edward Taft worked together to establish the New England Valentine Company in 1879. They sold their business in 1881 to George C. Whitney so that Esther could care for her aging father. Whitney's son ran the business until it was forced to close during World War II because of a shortage of paper.

Even though she created countless valentine cards during her lifetime for one lover to give to another, Esther herself never married.

Today an estimated 190 million Valentine's Day cards are sold each year, not counting the millions of valentines exchanged by school children. The valentines on this page are from World War I. Notice the nurse and soldier on the card at right. "Over There" was a popular song during that time about U.S. soldiers going off to fight in the war.

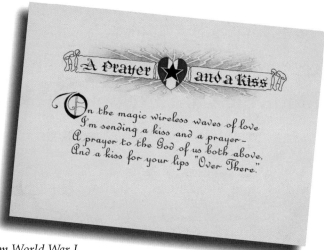

Valentines from World War I

Valentine, Nebraska

Nestled in the Sandhills of Nebraska lies the small town of Valentine. The town was named for U.S. Congressman E. K. Valentine who represented the state from 1879 to 1885. Valentine was incorporated as a village in 1884.

Today the town has less than 3,000 residents. A heart theme is obvious throughout the city in places such as the street signs pictured on the next page. The county in which Valentine is located is larger than the size of Connecticut, but it only has around 6,000 people. That means each person in the county could have his own square mile!

Valentine is a special destination for weddings. Some couples travel hundreds of miles to get married there. The town also offers a service called Cupid's Mailbox. People from anywhere in the world can prepare a valentine for someone they love, address it, put a stamp on, then put it in a larger envelope and mail it to Valentine. There the large envelope will be opened and someone will stamp a special Valentine, Nebraska, postmark on the valentine card, and put it back in the mail. The post office in Valentine, Texas, offers the same service.

Valentine, Nebraska
Heart-Themed Street Signs

Valentine, Nebraska, holds an annual Valentine's Day Coronation sponsored by the Valentine Chamber of Commerce. The celebration dates back to the 1930s. School students from each grade are elected to participate in a special ceremony. A King and Queen of Hearts are crowned from among the members of the high school senior class.

The Chamber of Commerce also hosts an annual Chili Cook-Off around Valentine's Day, as well as a Chocolate Lover's Experience. Area restaurants share the love by serving foods such as heart-shaped steaks.

Love

February 14 has become a day to remind people we love just how much we love them. While we can show them our love by giving cards and gifts and flowers on Valentine's Day, the most important way to show someone we love them is to be kind and sweet and loving in our thoughts and words and actions every day of the year.

Jesus said the most important commandment each of us must follow is to love the Lord our God with all our heart, soul, mind, and strength. The second most important is to love our neighbors as ourselves (Mark 12:29-31).

If I have all faith, so as to remove mountains,

but do not have love, I am nothing.

1 Corinthians 13:2

Family Activity

Make Valentine's Day Decorations for some elderly people where you live.

Instructions are on page 1009.

WASHINGTON'S BIRTHDAY

Third Monday in February

George Washington Mosaic,
Created in 1930

President George Washington was born in Virginia on February 11, 1731. In 1752, when Washington was twenty-one years old, England and its colonies in America and around the world began using a slightly different calendar system. This changed Washington's birthday to February 22. The mosaic of Washington at left was created in 1930.

Americans began celebrating Washington's birthday even before he became the country's first President. The first official Federal observance of February 22 as a holiday was on the one hundredth anniversary of Washington's birth in 1831. Congress did not meet that day as a way of showing respect to the memory of the "father of our country."

Congress declared Washington's birthday an official holiday in 1879. The holiday remained on February 22 until 1968 when Congress changed it to the third Monday in February. This change went into effect in 1971. Since February 22 fell on a different day of the week from year to year, Congress made this decision to give workers a consistent three-day weekend. Interestingly, changing the holiday to the third Monday in February meant that it would

never be celebrated on Washington's actual birthday. The third Monday in February can never be later than February 21! The sign at right was printed around the year 1900 to notify customers of a printing company that the business would be closed on February 22 in honor of Washington's birthday. Government offices, schools, and some businesses still close each year in honor of this day.

Sign for Customers of a Printing Company, c. 1900

During the second half of the twentieth century, some Americans began to think of this February holiday as a day to honor both George Washington and Abraham Lincoln, who was also born in February. Since states have the right to declare their own official holidays, some states chose to call the holiday "Presidents' Day." Many calendars, newspapers, and other sources began to use this name, but Congress has never officially changed the name of the Federal holiday. According to the United States government, the holiday remains "George Washington's Birthday."

Celebrating at Mount Vernon

Washington's birthday is celebrated each year at his Mount Vernon estate near Washington, D.C. Admission is free of charge that day. The observance begins with a wreath-laying ceremony at Washington's tomb. Visitors can enjoy patriotic music and performances by members of the military dressed in Revolutionary uniforms. A man dressed as General Washington greets the public and attends a "surprise" birthday party held in his honor.

Mount Vernon, Virginia
Celebrating George Washington's Birthday, 2008

Celebrating in Alexandria, Virginia

Alexandria, Virginia, is proud to bear the title of birthplace of George Washington. The citizens of this city have been celebrating his birthday since the days of the Revolutionary

War. The official program of the 1908 celebration is pictured below. Here are some of the ways Alexandrians celebrate Washington's birthday today:

★ Men and women dressed in historic costumes take part in a Revolutionary War re-enactment as they show visitors what it was like to live in a camp and be a part of military skirmishes.

★ At the Swordsmen's Rendezvous, children and adults can try their hand at learning swordplay, a skill learned by gentlemen of the 1700s.

★ In 1798 the Washingtons attended the second Birthnight Banquet and Ball held at Gadsby's Tavern in Alexandria. The first ball was held in 1797, but Washington was not able to attend that year. The tradition of this birthday celebration continues to this day. Visitors can enjoy delicious food and participate in traditional English country dances, just like George and Martha did.

Official Program for the Celebration of George Washington's Birthday, 1908

★ Runners take part in the George Washington Classic 10-K Race that helps fund the city's annual parade.

★ In honor of the legend about George Washington and the cherry tree, local restaurants participate in a Cherry Challenge, a competition to see who can create the best appetizer, main dish, dessert, or drink using cherries. If you order a cherry dish at one of the participating restaurants, you get to cast your vote in the challenge.

★ The biggest event in Alexandria's celebration is the annual parade. It is the largest parade in the country held in honor of George Washington. Alexandria's parade tradition started around 1923. The man and woman in the photo at right are dressed up as George and Martha Washington for the 2012 parade.

Alexandria, Virginia
Washington's Birthday Parade, 2012

Celebrating in a Farm Worker's Camp

During the late 1930s and early 1940s, the Farm Security Administration operated dozens of farm worker camps in California and other western states. The camps were home to migrant farm workers who had moved west during the Great Depression. They were also home to migrant workers from Mexico.

The camp in Tulare County, California, was called the Visalia Migratory Labor Camp. Its name was changed in the 1940s to the Tulare Farm Workers Community. In a 1942 edition of the community's newspaper, the camp manager said the community existed "to conserve our national resources by preventing human erosion caused by poverty, sickness, insecurity and the loss of real home life and community responsibility." The camp manager also said that, "From the very beginning, our Farm Workers' Communities have been organized and governed in the true American way— through self government." Members of the camp elected their own council and the council was authorized to enact legislation. Members also elected a community court and several committees that oversaw specific activities. The camp manager, however, could veto any legislation that violated laws of the county, the state, or the nation.

The photos on this page were taken at the Tulare camp during the President's Birthday Ball held in February of 1942 in honor of George Washington's birthday.

Tulare County, California
President's Birthday Ball, 1942

935

A Senate Tradition

Each year around Washington's birthday, one United States Senator receives a special honor. He or she is asked to read George Washington's Farewell Address aloud to the Senate. This tradition dates back to the Civil War. In 1862 Tennessee Senator Andrew Johnson suggested the reading of Washington's Farewell Address to boost morale. He wanted his fellow Senators to be encouraged to "recur back to the days, the times, and the doings of Washington and the patriots of the Revolution, who founded the government under which we live."

The second time the Address was read in the Senate was in 1888, one hundred years after the U.S. Constitution was ratified. Beginning in 1896, the Address has been read every year on or around Washington's birthday. At the end of each reading since 1900, the Senator who was chosen to read the document writes a few comments and signs his name in a special black leather book called the Farewell Address Notebook. The book is kept by the Secretary of the Senate. Read the three entries from the notebook printed below and on the following page.

Read according to custom by appointment of the Vice President Charles Warren Fairbanks this 22nd. day of February, 1907.
Burkett
U.S.S. Nebraska

Feb. 21, 1983
I pray that the spirit of ardent patriotism, joyous adventure, and religious zeal that marked the life and words of George Washington will live again in our land
Paul Trible
U.S. Senator Virginia

In these days, when the troubles of the mind and the conscience are multiplying, as we tend to turn more to the material and less to the spiritual for the solutions to them, it is correct that Americans pause to remember their basic sources of strength. These sources are carefully outlined in the documents left us by those wise men who, thru God, created our republic. It will forever be a source of pride that it fell my lot to read to my colleagues & thru them, the American people, the inspiring and thought provoking Farewell message of George Washington on this 22nd day of Feb. 1957——

> Barry Goldwater
> USS Arizona

The Past is Prologue—Study the Past

Our hearts should always been open and willing to learn from the past. The book of Nehemiah describes a time in the history of Israel hundreds of years after God gave the Israelites the laws He wanted them to follow. Many Israelites had forgotten the Lord and were worshipping other gods. In Nehemiah chapter 8, we read about a large group of Israelites gathering in a city square and asking Ezra to read to them the book of the law of Moses so they could know their past and what God expected of them.

> Then Ezra the priest brought the law before the assembly of men, women
> and all who could listen with understanding . . .
> and all the people were attentive to the book of the law.
> Nehemiah 8:2-3

Family Activity

Enjoy your own Cherry Challenge meal. Instructions are on pages 1010-1011.

ST. PATRICK'S DAY

March 17

Ireland
Statue of St. Patrick

Patrick was born into a wealthy British family around 390 A.D. When he was sixteen he was captured and taken as a slave to Ireland where he was forced to tend sheep for seven years. Even though he had been born to Christian parents, Patrick did not show interest in Christianity until after he was captured. While in Ireland he became a deeply religious man.

According to legend, Patrick escaped from Ireland on a pirate ship and returned to Britain. After being reunited with his family, Patrick is said to have heard a voice telling him to return to Ireland. Patrick became a priest and went back to Ireland to spend the rest of his days working to convert the Irish to Christianity.

According to tradition, Patrick died on March 17 about the year 493. He was largely forgotten after his death, but over time myths and legends began to circulate about his life and Patrick was later named the patron saint of Ireland. The statue at left stands in Ireland as a memorial to St. Patrick.

St. Patrick's Day Parades

The American tradition of celebrating St. Patrick's Day with a big parade does not have a long Irish tradition as you might think. The custom was established in America before the Revolutionary War when British military units (which included some Irish men) marched to various houses throughout New York City that were inhabited by Irish immigrants. This was on March 17, 1766. With very few exceptions, New York City has held a St. Patrick's Day parade every year since. It is said to be the longest running civilian parade in the world. Millions of people gather on the streets to watch and participate in the event. Only after the tradition of holding a St. Patrick's Day parade was firmly established in America did the Irish begin holding their own parades in Ireland.

Other towns and cities across America also hold St. Patrick's Day parades and have their own special traditions. If you have the best float in the parade in Kansas City, Missouri, you could win two tickets to Ireland! The parade in Dublin, Ohio, is over a mile long.

Savannah, Georgia, holds one of the country's largest celebrations. Here fountains are dyed green for the occasion. You can also find special menu items at local restaurants, including green grits! Chicago has an even more elaborate city decoration than Savannah. The photos below show the Chicago River dyed green, as it has been every March since 1962. The idea originated with some plumbers who used a green dye to check for leaks. The formula for dyeing the river has changed over the years. The current recipe is a closely guarded secret, but it has been tested and deemed acceptable for the environment.

Chicago, Illinois
The Chicago River Dyed Green for St. Patrick's Day, 2012

Shamrocks

According to tradition, St. Patrick used the three leaves of a shamrock plant to teach Irish people about the trinity of the Father, the Son, and the Holy Spirit. The shamrock has become a symbol of Ireland and of St. Patrick's Day. The shamrock shape can be found on a wide variety

St. Patrick's Day Cupcake

of seasonal items, such as clothing, dishes, decorations, and food, like the cupcake pictured at left.

White House St. Patrick's Day Reception

On St. Patrick's Day in 1952, the Irish ambassador to the U.S. gave President Harry Truman a gift of a box filled with Irish shamrock. Truman was out of town, so the ambassador just left his gift at the White House.

That first unimpressive presentation was the start of an annual White House tradition. Ireland had only recently become an independent republic, so sending an ambassador to the U.S. was something new for them. The ambassador wanted to use St. Patrick's Day as a way to strengthen ties between the United States and Ireland.

President Eisenhower received Ireland's shamrock gift the next St. Patrick's Day at a formal ceremony. The ceremonies have varied in extravagance and importance over the years, depending on who is President and on various political issues that might be happening at the same time. The presentation has become an annual reminder of the close ties between Ireland and the United States.

At modern ceremonies the shamrock are presented by the Prime Minister of Ireland in a crystal bowl specially made for the occasion. According to White House security regulations, any food, drink, or plant that is presented to the President is to be handled according to Secret Service policy. That means that

Washington, D.C.
President Reagan Receiving a Shamrock Gift from Ireland's Prime Minister Garret FitzGerald, 1986

after the fancy ceremony the Secret Service has to destroy the lovely shamrock that traveled all the way across the Atlantic for the occasion. The President gets to keep the crystal bowl,

White House Fountain Dyed for St. Patrick's Day, 2009

however. President Reagan used one of his to hold jelly beans! Reagan is pictured above receiving his bowl of shamrock in 1986.

In 2009, First Lady Michelle Obama added to the St. Patrick's Day decor by having the water in the fountains outside the White House dyed green, as seen in the photo at left. Mrs. Obama is a native of Chicago, so having green water on St. Patrick's Day is customary for her!

St. Patrick's Day Luncheon

In 1983 the House of Representatives established a new Washington tradition of holding a St. Patrick's Day luncheon. The event was hosted by Speaker of the House Thomas P. "Tip" O'Neill and was attended by members of the House and the Senate, as well as President Ronald Reagan. The event was planned to ease the political tension that existed between Speaker O'Neill and President Reagan. St. Patrick's Day was chosen for the luncheon because both men were Irish-Americans. Since then the luncheon has become an annual event at the United States Capitol. The photo at right was taken at the luncheon held in 2009.

President Barack Obama, House Speaker Nancy Pelosi (center), and Ireland's Prime Minister Brian Cowen (right) at the St. Patrick's Day Luncheon at the U.S. Capitol, 2009

A Message from the President

Presidents often issue statements on special days throughout the year, including St. Patrick's Day. Below is the message that President George W. Bush sent out for St. Patrick's Day in 2008.

> I send greetings to those celebrating St. Patrick's Day.
>
> On this day, we commemorate the great faith of St. Patrick and celebrate the rich heritage of the Irish people. The Apostle of Ireland was committed to preaching a gospel of peace even in the face of great hardship, and people of all faiths can be inspired by his remarkable example. During St. Patrick's Day, we join together with the many children of Erin who have come to our shores full of hope and purpose, and found success.
>
> Americans are grateful for our country's Irish traditions and the deep friendship that exists between Ireland and the United States. Irish Americans have valiantly defended our Nation, enriched our culture, and contributed to our prosperity. We are reminded, in celebrating, of our history as a Nation of immigrants and of our responsibility to remain a welcoming society.
>
> Laura and I send our best wishes for a blessed and joyous St. Patrick's Day.
>
> George W. Bush

St. Patrick's Day in the Military

The U.S. military has been celebrating St. Patrick's Day for a long time. The illustrations below show the Irish Brigade of the Army of the Potomac celebrating the holiday in 1863. These soldiers enjoyed a little time off from duty during the Civil War to compete against each other with races and games. According to an article from *The New York Times* that told about the event, the brigade's General Meagher believed that "the morale of his troops would not be injured by a little wholesome amusement." The article went on to describe the day's festivities.

> *Every preparation was therefore made, such as the building of speaker stands, digging of ditches, erecting of hurdles, &c., &c., and at 1 o'clock this morning the ball opened with the beating of drums and other accompanying noises, which startled the soldiers in the various encampments for miles around; and well they might, for the music of the drums at that unnatural hour of the night is suggestive of nothing else save the long roll and coming of the enemy. The rebs, however, did not make their appearance.*
>
> *. . .*
>
> *About 1 o'clock Gen. MEAGHER mounted the platform near his tent, and announced that the day's sports were not over "by a long shot," but that among other things to follow would be a foot-race, all privates and non-commissioned officers being permitted to enter the lists, the winner to receive $5; a wheelbarrow-race, the competitors to be bound hand and foot, the one first reaching the goal to receive $7; a wrestling match, the contestants to be inclosed in sacks; and as a finale, a chase for a greased pig, the one succeeding in holding him to be declared the lawful owner and possessor.*

At the time the article was written, however, it was unknown whether or not the last event would actually take place because the competitors still needed a pig! One had been located at a farm nearby, but the woman who owned the animal wanted $30 for it. If the soldiers were able to talk her down to $15, they would have their chase.

St. Patrick's Day at the Army of the Potomac Sports of the Irish Brigade, 1863

Military personnel still participate in St. Patrick's Day competitions. The photos on this page were taken on St. Patrick's Day in 2010 at Camp Hansen in Okinawa, Japan. The competition was between Combat Engineers from the U.S. Air Force's Detachment 1554, Red Horse Squadron and Marines from the 9th Engineer Support Battalion. They competed to see who were the ultimate "gung ho warriors." The top left photo shows a competitor in the pull-up competition. The next photo shows a man participating in the caber toss. The lower left photo shows men preparing for a tug of war. The last photo shows the Humvee pull competition.

Okinawa, Japan
St. Patrick's Day Field Meet at Camp Hansen, 2010

America is a nation made up of people from around the world. It is good to recognize and honor the various heritages that make America the strong and diverse country it is.

I will give thanks to You, O Lord, among the peoples;

I will sing praises to You among the nations.

Psalm 57:9

Family Activity

Hold a St. Patrick's Day Field Meet. Instructions are on page 1012.

TAX DAY

April 15

It takes a great deal of money to run the United States of America, and that money has to come from somewhere. The largest single source of revenue for the government is the income tax paid by individual American citizens.

Establishing the Federal Income Tax

Before the Revolutionary War, most revenue to fund the war came from taxes on whiskey and tobacco. The colonies also borrowed money from other countries. After the war was over, the government of the new country knew they needed more money.

It was a struggle for the new Federal government to raise the funds it needed from the new thirteen states, but it managed to raise $15 million from each state in 1779. That figure grew over the years. During the Civil War the United States government began collecting an income tax, but it was only a temporary source of revenue to help pay for the expense of the war.

Income Tax Cartoon, 1894

President Grover Cleveland worked toward establishing a regular income tax in 1894. Look at the political cartoon from that year pictured at left. It shows a jester holding an "Income Tax Law." The woman represents "Democracy" and the chair in which she is sitting is labeled "Congress." "Democracy" is holding a quill pen and appears to be uncertain as to whether or not she should sign the bill. Behind her is a man with a ballot box warning her not to sign it. The U.S. Supreme Court soon declared the income tax to be unconstitutional.

Politicians who supported the idea of an income tax worked to pass an amendment to the Constitution that would allow it. As with most political decisions, some people were in favor of the idea, and others were opposed to it. The political cartoon below was published in 1909. It suggests other ways the United States government might collect revenue, instead of "putting it all over on the poor old Consumer." The cartoon says, "Why not impose a stamp tax on divorces—And on American heiresses—And on sidewhiskers—And on amateur elocutionists—And on the chap who says: 'Have you heard this one?'—And on poodles and other precious pups—And on rubber plants."

Tax Cartoon, 1909

Congress finally passed the 16th Amendment to the U.S. Constitution in 1909. It was ratified in 1913 and became law. The Amendment reads:

> *The Congress shall have power to lay and collect taxes on incomes, from whatever source derived, without apportionment among the several States, and without regard to any census or enumeration.*

In other words, after this amendment was passed, it was legal for Congress to collect taxes on the incomes of American citizens.

Income Tax Deadline

April 15 is the deadline for filing tax returns for the previous year, but this has not always been the case. When Congress passed the 16th Amendment, the date agreed upon was March 1. In 1918 the date was changed to March 15. The poster at left from 1945 was created to remind citizens of their need to fill out an income tax return by March 15 if their 1944 income was over $500. In 2012 Americans were required to pay income taxes if their annual income was over $9,500.

In 1954 the date for the filing deadline was changed again, this time to April 15. This deadline has remained in place unless April 15 falls on a weekend. In that case, the deadline is moved to the Monday following.

Income Tax Poster, 1945

The filing deadline for 2012 was an exception. April 15 fell on a Sunday. Monday, April 16, would have become the deadline, but the District of Columbia observes a holiday known as Emancipation Day on that date. Because of that observance, the deadline was moved to Tuesday, April 17.

Taxpayers do not have to wait until the last minute to pay their taxes. They can pay anytime between January 2 and April 15. If a taxpayer wants to, he may file for an extension. This means that his deadline for filing his personal or business return is extended for a set amount of time. A person might file for an extension if he doesn't have enough cash on hand to pay his taxes. The extension gives him more time to earn the money he needs for his taxes.

The majority of Americans don't particularly enjoy paying their income taxes and going through the hassle of filling out forms. Some businesses try to make people feel a little better by offering tax day freebies on April 15, such as coffee, frozen yogurt, chicken sandwich, curly fries, or mini cinnamon bun!

Tax Day Freebies

What Is the IRS?

The Internal Revenue Service (IRS) is the largest office within the U.S. Department of the Treasury. The IRS is responsible for collecting taxes and checking the accuracy of the returns filed by Americans. The IRS also enforces tax laws and regulations. In 2011 the IRS collected $2.4 trillion from American taxpayers.

The 10-story IRS building at right was completed in the Washington, D.C., suburb of New Carrollton in 1997. About 4,000 IRS employees work at this location. As of the end of 2011, the IRS employed 88,308 full-time employees and 3,072 part-time and seasonal workers.

New Carrollton, Maryland
Internal Revenue Service Building

How Are Tax Returns Filed?

Some taxpayers hire an accountant to figure out how much they owe in Federal income tax. Other people figure out their taxes on their own. Americans have been wrestling over their tax returns for a long time! The photo at right shows a man working on his taxes around 1943. In the photo at right below a woman is getting free tax advice at an Army tax center in 2012.

Many people file online using services that make figuring out all the complicated details a little easier. In 2011 the IRS processed over 143 million individual income tax returns, and 77% of those returns were filed electronically.

Camp Lee, Virginia
Preparing an Income Tax Return, c. 1943

Deductions

The amount of taxes each American pays to the Federal government depends on how much the person earned, on personal exemptions granted by the tax laws, and on certain deductions the person can take.

Fort Meade, Maryland
Fort Meade Joint Installation Tax Center, 2012

Exemptions and deductions can be subtracted from a person's taxable income. This means she will not have to pay as much to the Federal government. Here are some of the deductions that people are permitted to take if they qualify for the specifications of each one:

Refunds

Let's say that Freddie Frank works for the Peter Piper Pickle Company. Freddie makes $12 an hour, but the Peter Piper Pickle Company doesn't pay him that full amount. They keep a portion of Freddie's earnings to send directly to the Department of the Treasury to cover what Freddie will owe in income tax for that year. After the end of the year, when Freddie figures up his taxes, he might find that the Peter Piper Pickle Company sent the Treasury more of his money than he really owes. If that is the case, the Treasury will send Freddie a check for the extra money the Peter Piper Pickle Company sent in. That is called an income tax refund.

Let's say that Maggie McGillicutty owns her own business called the Clip and Curl Beauty Salon. Since Maggie doesn't have an employer to send her tax money to the Treasury for her, she has to take care of it herself. Four times a year, Maggie makes what is called an estimated payment to go toward what she will owe on her income taxes and payroll taxes for that year. These estimated payments are just a guess because Maggie does not know how many customers she will have at the Clip and Curl and how much money she is going to make. After the end of the year, she might discover that she didn't send in enough money in estimated payments and will have to pay more by April 15. If Maggie sent in too much money, however, she will get a refund check just like Freddie.

In 2011 the IRS sent out almost $416 billion in refund checks to American taxpayers.

Tax Freedom Day

Tax Freedom Day is not a national holiday, but it is the day when the average American worker has worked enough to pay his tax bill for the year. For example, the average American worker will have to use 29.2% of his income to pay Federal, state, and local taxes in a given year. That means he must work an average of 107 days to cover his tax bill. Tax Freedom Day is a name given to the 107th work day in a calendar year. Tax Freedom Day in 2012 fell on April 17. April 17 was merely an average calculation, though. Tax Freedom Day actually varies depending on the state in which a person lives since state and local taxes vary widely.

When we look at the dates on which Tax Freedom Day has fallen in recent history, we can see how much taxes have increased. In 1917 the average American had earned all the money he would need to pay his taxes for that year by January 24. In 1933 the date was March 6. In 1943, largely due to the cost of World War II, Tax Freedom Day was not until April 5. It fell back into March by the late 1940s, but it has not been that early in the year since then.

Paying What We Owe

When a person sends in his tax money, that money is used to fund things that the Federal government pays for. Most Americans do not agree with everything the government pays for, but they still have to pay their taxes. It would not be right for a person to say, "Well, I don't believe that what the government is going to do with my money is how God would want me to spend my money, so I'm not going to send it in." As American citizens, God expects us to follow the laws of this country and submit to the authority of our government.

In Luke chapter 20, we read an account of a time when scribes and chief priests came to Jesus, as shown in the illustration at right. They tried to trick Jesus into saying something that would give them legitimate reason to arrest Him. They asked Jesus if it was lawful for the Jews to pay taxes to Caesar. The Jews did not agree with everything the Roman government did, so should they give Rome their money? Jesus' answer was clear then, and it is clear for us today:

Jesus with the Chief Priests

> Render to Caesar the things that are Caesar's,
> and to God the things that are God's.
> Luke 20:25

Family Activity

Make a "Why We Are Thankful for Income Tax" poster. Instructions are on page 1013.

GOOD FRIDAY AND EASTER

Between March 22 and April 25

Easter is the name given to the annual celebration of the resurrection of Jesus after His crucifixion. Good Friday is the Friday before Easter and is traditionally observed as the day Jesus died. The date on which Easter falls varies from year to year. The calculation for deciding when it will occur dates back to 325 A.D. in the Roman Empire.

Deciding on a Date

Emperor Constantine began ruling parts of the Roman Empire in 306 A.D. A statue of Constantine is pictured below. Before Constantine came to power, Christians in the Roman Empire were often severely persecuted. Constantine expressed belief in the God of the Christians and declared that their persecution would end. Constantine gained ultimate control of the entire Roman Empire in 324.

York, England
Statue of Constantine

Around this time, a man in Egypt began teaching false doctrine. Many church leaders felt that the church needed to have an established doctrine that all Christians should believe. Constantine called together a group of bishops at the town of Nicea to discuss the controversy. Their gathering was called the Council of Nicea. The leaders at the council made many decisions that they expected true Christians to accept. Some were vital decisions; others were not as important. One of the decisions they made involved when the resurrection of Jesus should be celebrated each year. They decided on the first Sunday after the first full moon in spring. This is still how Western countries calculate the observance of Easter. When calculated in this way, Easter can fall on any Sunday between March 22 and April 25.

950

Sunrise Services

Many churches and communities hold an annual sunrise service on Easter morning. The services are a special time to celebrate the fact that Jesus rose from the grave early in the morning. It is a time to be especially thankful that He offers the gift of eternal life to all of His followers throughout the centuries and around the world. Look at the images on this page that show sunrise celebrations of the resurrection of Jesus.

Puyallup, Washington
Church Pastor Beside a Wooden Cross with Flowers, 2010

San Bruno, California
Bagpipe Player on Sweeney Ridge, 2008

Arizona
At the Grand Canyon, 2011

Arabian Sea
Aboard an Amphibious Assault Ship, 2012

Baghdad, Iraq
Camp Prosperity, 2010

Kabul, Afghanistan
Camp Eggers, 2008

Sunrise Service at Arlington

For many years, an Easter sunrise service has been held at the amphitheater in Arlington National Cemetery near Washington, D.C., as pictured at right. Thousands of people attend the event each year, which is sponsored by the U.S. Army Military District of Washington.

La Procesion De Viernes Santo

Outside Tucson, Arizona, rises a mountain called Sentinel Peak. It is known locally as "A" Mountain. The mountain earned this name after a large letter "A" was whitewashed on the side of it in 1915 by fans of the University of Arizona who were celebrating a football victory. The mountain offers a spectacular view of the city of Tucson.

Fort Myer, Virginia
Easter Sunrise Services at Arlington National Cemetery, 1938 and 2006

In the late 1960s, a man named David G. Herrera, pictured at right below, wanted to do something that would encourage young people in Tucson to get involved in religion. In 1969 he initiated La Procesion De Viernes Santo (The Good Friday Procession). This first procession had twenty-five participants and became an annual tradition. Herrera never dreamed it would grow to attract hundreds of participants year after year. Each year on Good Friday, a sixteen-foot cross that weighs 242 pounds is carried by participants up "A" Mountain, as pictured below. This is intended to remind people of what it was like for Jesus to carry His cross to Calvary. A sunrise service is held on the mountain every Easter morning.

Tucson, Arizona
Left: Participants Carry a Large Cross Up "A" Mountain; Right: David G. Herrera, Age 93, 2012

Easter Parades

Over the years, since people dressed up to attend a church service on Easter Sunday, traditions developed for getting a new dress or a new suit to wear on that day. The tradition of an Easter parade was developing in New York City by the mid-1800s. After wealthy citizens of the city attended Easter services at various churches on Fifth Avenue, they enjoyed taking a walk outside and showing off their finery. Easter parade traditions sprang up in other cities as well. A parade on the boardwalk in Atlantic City is pictured above.

Atlantic City, New Jersey
Easter Parade, c. 1905

Easter parades still take place on Fifth Avenue in New York City. Participants often wear elaborate (and sometimes ridiculous!) hats like the one pictured at right.

New York City, New York
Easter Parade, 2006

Bunnies and Eggs

The connection of bunnies and Easter apparently dates back to thirteenth century Germany before Christianity was widely practiced there. The Germans worshipped several gods and goddesses. At the beginning of spring they held feasts in honor of the goddess of springtime and fertility. The rabbit was the symbol associated with this goddess. After Christianity was accepted by many German people, some of their old traditions mixed with their new beliefs, like bunnies and Easter.

Easter Illustration, 1903

The earliest writing about the legend of an Easter Bunny is from the 1500s. In 1680 a story was published about a rabbit laying eggs and hiding them in a garden. German immigrants brought these traditions with them when they immigrated to America. Over time a basket with grasses came to be thought of as a good place for the imaginary Easter Bunny to leave gifts for children. The illustration at left was published in 1903. Hiding eggs for children to find on Easter has become a tradition at family and community gatherings across the country.

White House Easter Egg Roll

During the 1800s, children of Washington, D.C., enjoyed playing on the grounds of the United States Capitol. By the 1870s it had become a tradition to gather there on the day after Easter for egg rolling activities. An egg roll is done by placing a hard-boiled egg on the ground and rolling it with a spoon, seeing whose egg can reach the finish line first.

Washington, D.C.
White House Easter Egg Roll, 1939

Members of Congress were frustrated by the event. The landscaping around the Capitol was not complete and they did not have enough money to finish the work and maintain it, let alone recover from a big event like an egg roll! Congress passed a law that forbade the Capitol grounds being used as a playground.

On the day before Easter in 1878, a newspaper announcement told the public that the new law about the Capitol grounds would be enforced on Monday. But the children of Washington would not be stopped! Some of them talked to President Rutherford B. Hayes while he was out for an Easter walk and asked him if they could have their egg roll on the South Lawn of the White House. After he returned to the White House, Hayes issued an official order that any children who wanted to roll an egg on the White House grounds should be permitted to do so. The children came and a tradition was established! The photo above was taken during the Egg Roll in 1939.

The White House Easter Egg Roll has been held every year since, except when the weather was bad and when it was canceled during World War I and World War II. It has included various other activities through the years, such as sporting events, live entertainment, storytime, crafts, cooking demonstrations, and dancing, as pictured below.

Maypole Dance at the Easter Egg Roll, 1929

The White House Easter Egg Roll is the largest event held at the White House. About 30,000 people attended in 2012. To control attendance, people who want to attend are invited to enter an online drawing. Entering is free and tickets are free for the people who are randomly selected, but everyone who attends must have a ticket. Photos from the 2010 and 2012 Easter Egg Rolls are pictured on the next page.

At the Easter Egg Roll in 2010, signs such as this one helped attendees navigate through the huge crowd.

At the 2012 Easter Egg Roll, the Obama family shared a book with children who attended the event.

Where do all those hard-boiled eggs that are rolled across the White House lawn come from? In 2011 about 6,000 of them were prepared at the DC Central Kitchen, pictured at right. This kitchen provides culinary job training for men and women who have been through homelessness, addictions, and prison. When they are not boiling eggs for the Easter Egg Roll, the workers at DC Central Kitchen are preparing about 5,000 meals a day for homeless shelters, transitional homes, nonprofit organizations, and children from low-income families.

Remembering Jesus

The story of Jesus' death, burial, and resurrection is one that Christians should celebrate not just on Easter, but on every day of the year. It is the story that gives us hope.

Preparing Hard-Boiled Eggs for the 2011 Easter Egg Roll at the DC Central Kitchen

Blessed be the God and Father of our Lord Jesus Christ,
who according to His great mercy has caused us to be born again to a living hope
through the resurrection of Jesus Christ from the dead
1 Peter 1:3

Family Activity

Hold an Easter Egg Roll on your lawn. Instructions are on pages 1014-1015.

NATIONAL ARBOR DAY

Last Friday in April

In 1854 journalist J. Sterling Morton decided to leave Detroit, Michigan, and head west. He and his wife Caroline settled in what would become Nebraska Territory. They both loved nature and began planting flowers, shrubs, and trees around their new homeplace.

Near Nebraska City, Nebraska
Date Unknown

Morton worked as a farmer and as editor of the *Nebraska City News*. The newspaper gave Morton a chance to share his love of nature by publishing information on agriculture. Through his newspaper articles and editorials, Morton encouraged individuals, civic organizations, and other groups to plant trees. Trees were scarce on the Nebraska prairie. The settlers needed them for windbreaks and to keep the soil of their farms in place. They also needed them to use for firewood and building materials.

Morton became a prominent citizen in his area. He helped survey Nebraska City and was active in politics. He eventually became secretary of Nebraska Territory. This gave him another outlet to promote his belief in the importance of planting trees. He later became president of the State Board of Agriculture. At a meeting of the board in January of 1872, Morton suggested having a tree-planting holiday later in the year. The idea caught on. Morton proposed that the holiday be called Arbor Day. The holiday was set for April 10. When the first Arbor Day

Downtown Nebraska City, c. 1908

arrived, Nebraskans planted an estimated one million trees. Counties and individuals that planted the most received prizes. "Arbor Day is not like other holidays," Morton once stated. "Each of those reposes on the past, while Arbor Day proposes for the future."

Nebraska Governor Robert W. Furnas issued an official proclamation for a state-wide Arbor Day observance in 1874. Arbor Day became a legal holiday in Nebraska in 1875. The date chosen was April 22, the birthday of J. Sterling Morton.

Nebraska City's celebration in 1885 began with schoolchildren planting trees. It was established that each grade would continue to care for the tree or trees they planted. After the children had planted their trees, they formed a parade and headed to the city's opera house. About one thousand children were in the march. They carried brightly colored banners made of silk and satin and trimmed with gold fringe. Other townspeople joined in the parade as it went along. They crammed into the opera house until it was nearly bursting.

Mr. Morton delivered a speech and the children concluded the celebration by singing "America." The *Nebraska City News* reported that, "To say that it was a complete success but faintly expresses it. A celebration of this kind results in good to all, and is worthy of imitation by every school in the state."

Nebraska City, Nebraska
Statue of J. Sterling Morton

Other states followed Nebraska's example of establishing Arbor Day. Today the last Friday in April is the most common day for a state to observe Arbor Day, but since climates differ dramatically across the United States, some states choose a different day. Some southern states hold Arbor Day as early as January, while some northern states wait until May. Several U.S. Presidents have issued Arbor Day proclamations, but the day has never become an official Federal holiday.

Sterling Morton served as Secretary of Agriculture under President Grover Cleveland from 1893 to 1897. He supported Cleveland's efforts to set up national forest reservations. Morton was chosen as one of the Nebraskans to be featured in National Statuary Hall at the U.S. Capitol. Another statue of Morton, pictured at right, stands in Nebraska City. Morton's farmland is now a state park.

Many of the trees growing in America today were planted as a result of the work of J. Sterling Morton. Morton knew that trees were important, and he wanted to encourage Americans

Washington, D.C.
Planting a Tree in Memory of J. Sterling Morton, 1920

to plant them to be enjoyed by themselves and by future Americans. Morton is quoted as saying:

> *. . . all the people strive on Arbor Day to plant many, many trees, both forest and fruit. May the day and the observance thereof be cherished in every household, and its name and fruits become a shower of blessing to the long lines of generations who shall succeed us.*

The photo at left shows members of the District of Columbia Federation of Women's Clubs in Washington, D.C., planing a tree in 1920 in memory of J. Sterling Morton.

Arbor Day Foundation

The Arbor Day Foundation was established in 1972, the one hundredth anniversary of the first Arbor Day celebration. It is based in Morton's hometown of Nebraska City, Nebraska. The foundation is a nonprofit conservation and education organization dedicated to planting trees. Their motto is: *We inspire people to plant, nurture, and celebrate trees.*

The foundation has a 260-acre farm, pictured below, where visitors can enjoy a variety of attractions such as a fifty-foot treehouse, a hiking trail, a preservation orchard where rare apple trees grow, and a greenhouse where hundreds of thousands of tree seedlings are grown every year. Visitors can take home a free tree from the greenhouse. Arbor Day Farm was named Nebraska's Outstanding Nature Tourism Entity in 2011.

Nebraska City, Nebraska
Arbor Day Farm

The Arbor Day Foundation gives out several awards each year to individuals, clubs, and organizations who "have demonstrated the very best in tree planting and care, Arbor Day celebrations, partnerships, community projects, and environmental education." In 2011 the local Boy Scout and Cub Scout troops from Palmer, Alaska, received one of the Arbor Day Celebration Awards. Around one hundred people turned out for the small town's observance of the holiday. Participants ranged in age from a seven-year-old Cub Scout to a ninety-seven-year-old World War II veteran.

Tree City USA

The Arbor Day Foundation, the U.S. Department of Agriculture, and the National Association of State Foresters sponsor a program called Tree City USA. The program gives recognition to urban and community forestry programs in cities across the country. To qualify as a Tree City USA community, a town or city has to meet four requirements. It must have:

Bismarck, North Dakota

* ★ a local Tree Board or Department,

* ★ a tree care ordinance,

* ★ a community forestry program with an annual budget of at least $2 per resident,

* ★ and an Arbor Day proclamation and observance.

More than 3,400 towns and cities across the country have been recognized by the Tree City USA program. Three of them are pictured on this page.

Portland, Maine

Sandy, Utah

The Morton Arboretum

Sterling and Caroline Morton's son Joy carried on his parents' love of nature by establishing in 1922 The Morton Arboretum in Lisle, Illinois, near Chicago. The arboretum collects and studies trees and other plants from around the world. Visitors can learn about caring for trees and plants as they enjoy 1,700 acres of woodlands, wetlands, and prairies. One of the arboretum's attractions is the one-acre Garden Maze pictured at right. A lookout platform built around a large sycamore tree offers a bird's- eye view.

In addition to establishing the arboretum, Joy Morton incorporated the Morton Salt Company in Chicago in 1910.

Lisle, Illinois
Garden Maze at The Morton Arboretum

Observing Arbor Day Today

The Arbor Day Foundation has many suggestions for ways that Americans can observe Arbor Day. These are some of them:

Hold an Arbor Day ceremony and honor the good stewards of your community.

Organize a community-wide search for the biggest or oldest tree in your area.

Plant a tree.

Ask your mayor to issue an Arbor Day proclamation.

Write a story, play, or skit about trees.

Clean up a local park or public area in your town.

Read a book about trees.

Sponsor a craft show with exhibits of crafts made from natural materials.

Learn to identify the trees in your yard by their leaves, bark, and seeds.

Make a bark rubbing using paper and a crayon.

Have an Arbor Day Birthday Party and serve tree-shaped cookies.

Offutt Air Force Base, Nebraska
An Arbor Day tree has been planted on this Air Force base every year since 1987. The photo at left shows an Eastern Red Bud that was planted in 2009. Notice the ceremonial gold shovels. At right is a Northern Red Oak being planted in 2010.

960

All the trees, flowers, lakes, rivers, and everything else in Creation show us how glorious and amazing our God is. Psalm 148 gives a beautiful picture of the whole earth praising God: sun and moon, wind and snow, animals, princes, and children. We should always join in with the created world in praising God by letting His glory be seen in us.

Praise the Lord from the earth . . .

Mountains and all hills; fruit trees and all cedars . . .

Let them praise the name of the Lord,

for His name alone is exalted;

His glory is above earth and heaven.

Psalm 148: 7, 9, 13

Family Activity

Celebrate Trees! Instructions are on page 1016.

Violet, Louisiana

LOYALTY DAY AND LAW DAY

May 1

During the early part of the twentieth century, as the threat of Communism was increasing overseas, some Americans began to worry that Communism was going to take over America. They became suspicious of their immigrant neighbors, wondering if they had come to America to try and take it over for the Communists.

The National Americanization Committee was formed in New York in 1915 to promote education in citizenship and civic affairs throughout the United States. Americanization Day began to be celebrated in conjunction with the Fourth of July. The observance was primarily for the benefit of new American citizens. An article in *The New York Times* from 1915 stated:

> *On these occasions, it is proposed to present the advantages of citizenship and the study of English and civics, all designed to awaken interest in a more popular participation in American life and affairs by the naturalized population.*

The same year, the *Milwaukee Sentinel* in Milwaukee, Wisconsin, reported:

> *Uncle Sam has asked the American people to combine Americanization day with the Independence day celebration this year and in every large city of the country special arrangements in accordance with the American government's request have been made.*
>
> *The flags, the candy and the other things to gladden the hearts of the children next Monday have all been distributed . . . and a celebration of citywide extent is assured.*

The patriotic parade pictured at right took place in Boise, Idaho, around 1918. Beginning in 1921, Americanization Day was celebrated on May 1. This day was chosen because it was the same day when many Communists celebrated the Russian Revolution. America wanted to combat this Communist celebration with one of their own. Interest in Americanization Day grew. On May 1 in 1930, around ten thousand veterans gathered for an Americanization Day rally in Union Square in New York City to promote patriotism.

Boise, Idaho
Patriotic Parade, c. 1918

Congress adopted a resolution in 1949 to designate May 1 as Loyalty Day (instead of Americanization Day). An estimated five million Americans participated in Loyalty Day rallies held across the country in 1950. Congress passed a law in 1958 that permanently designated May 1 as Loyalty Day. Its purpose was stated as being "for the reaffirmation of loyalty to the United States and for the recognition of the heritage of American freedom." The law requests that Presidents issue an annual Loyalty Day proclamation.

President Dwight D. Eisenhower issued the first proclamation in 1959. A copy of the proclamation, including the presidential seal, is pictured at right. The proclamation stated that "Loyalty to the United States of America, its democratic traditions and institutions, and the liberties embodied in our Constitution is essential to the preservation of our freedoms." Eisenhower went on to say that "it is fitting and proper that we reaffirm our loyalty to our country and our gratitude for the precious heritage of freedom and liberty under law."

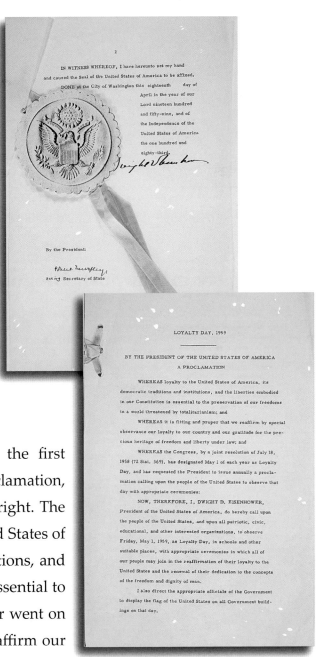

President Dwight D. Eisenhower's
First Loyalty Day Proclamation, 1959

The photos at left and below were taken during a Loyalty Day parade on Osan Air Base in South Korea in 2005. The parade honored U.S. servicemen and women of the past and the present. The men in the photo below are dressed in historic military uniforms.

Pyeongtaek City, South Korea
Veterans and Active Members of the U.S. Military Participate in a Loyalty Day Parade on Osan Air Base, 2005

Loyalty Day in Newport, Oregon

On May 1 in 1938, about two thousand people attended the first annual Crab Festival in Newport, Oregon. The attendees gobbled up six thousand free crabs that were given away at the event. Organizers were hoping that the festival would provide an economic boost for the area as it suffered through the Great Depression. The illustration below shows Newport in the early 1900s.

Newport, Oregon
Illustration from the Early 1900s

World War II got in the way of the Crab Festival during the early 1940s. After the war was over, however, the fishermen returned home from the fighting and the fishing boats were no longer needed by the military to patrol the coast. The Crab Festival was revived, complete with a Crab Festival Queen and a raffle for a new car.

Anxiety over the threat of Communism was high in the United States, and in 1953 the Crab Festival was replaced with Loyalty Days. The local veterans' organization held a small parade. Over time, the more sombre feel of Newport Loyalty Days became more like the frolicsome Crab Festivals of decades past.

The event continued to grow and expand. There were almost fifty entries in the parade in 1970. Over the years visitors to the annual event have been able to enjoy air shows, boat races, horse shows, scuba diving contests, crab running contests, carnival rides, boat tours, and yacht races. A special ceremony takes place each year to honor the men and women from Oregon who have died while defending our freedom. The name-reading ceremony takes place in a park overlooking the Pacific Ocean.

Newport, Oregon
Newport Harbor, 2012

As the threat of Communism has diminished in recent years, most places have let the observance of Loyalty Day fall by the wayside. Loyalty Day is alive and well in Newport, however, and the annual event is a source of community pride. The photo at right shows how Newport looks today.

Law Day

Between the time that Loyalty Day began to be celebrated in America and when it became a permanent observance, another holiday was initiated in our country. Law Day was established as a day to celebrate the rule of law and the freedom Americans enjoy under it.

Charles S. Rhyne served as president of the American Bar Association and as a legal counselor to President Dwight D. Eisenhower. In 1957 Rhyne began promoting his idea for Law Day. He believed that respect for the rule of law was a key factor in individual freedom and justice.

Rhyne had observed the coverage American media gave to the Soviet Union's annual May Day parade like the one pictured at right. The Communists used these celebrations as a way to display their new war weapons. Rhyne wanted Americans to appreciate the contrast between the United States' reliance on the rule of law with the Soviet Union's rule by force.

St. Petersburg, Russia
Communist May Day Celebration, 1917

Rhyne's close relationship with President Eisenhower's administration made it easier for his idea to become reality. Eisenhower issued the first Law Day proclamation in 1958. Before the first Law Day observance, Eisenhower issued a statement broadcast on radio and television in which he said, "On this Law Day, then, we honor not only the principle of the rule of law, but also those judges, legislators, lawyers and law-abiding citizens who actively work to preserve our liberties under law." Read the words of Eisenhower's proclamation below. A statue of Eisenhower is pictured at right.

Abilene, Kansas
Statue of President Eisenhower

By the President of the United States of America
A Proclamation

WHEREAS it is fitting that the people of this Nation should remember with pride and vigilantly guard the great heritage of liberty, justice, and equality under law which our forefathers bequeathed to us; and

WHEREAS it is our moral and civic obligation, as free men and as Americans, to preserve and strengthen that great heritage; and

WHEREAS the principle of guaranteed fundamental rights of individuals under the law is the heart and sinew of our Nation, and distinguishes our governmental system from the type of government that rules by might alone; and

WHEREAS our Government has served as an inspiration and a beacon light for oppressed peoples of the world seeking freedom, justice, and equality for the individual under laws; and

WHEREAS universal application of the principle of the rule of law in the settlement of international disputes would greatly enhance the cause of a just and enduring peace; and

WHEREAS a day of national dedication to the principle of government under laws would afford us an opportunity better to understand and appreciate the manifold virtues of such a government and to focus the attention of the world upon them:

NOW, THEREFORE, I, DWIGHT D. EISENHOWER, President of the United States of America, do hereby designate Thursday, May 1, 1958, as Law Day.

I urge the people of the United States to observe the designated day with appropriate ceremonies and activities, and I especially urge the legal profession, the press, and the radio, television, and motion-picture industries to promote and to participate in the observance of that day.

IN WITNESS WHEREOF, I have hereunto set my hand and caused the Seal of the United States of America to be affixed.

DONE at the City of Washington this third day of February in the year of our Lord nineteen hundred and fifty-eight, and of the Independence of the United States of America the one hundred and eighty-second.

DWIGHT D. EISENHOWER

Every President since Eisenhower has also issued Law Day proclamations. Congress passed a joint resolution in 1961 that permanently designated May 1 as Law Day, U.S.A. The resolution stated that Law Day "is a special day of celebration by the people of the United States . . . in appreciation of their liberties and the reaffirmation of their loyalty to the United States and of their rededication to the ideals of equality and justice under law in their relations with each other and with other countries."

The American Bar Association chooses a theme each year for Law Day programs. They publish an annual planning guide with lesson plans and ideas for classroom and community programs.

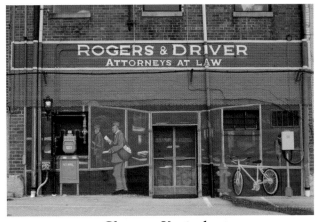

Glasgow, Kentucky
Law Office of Rogers & Driver, Attorneys at Law
Notice how the building has a flat front,
but is painted to look like it has an inset entryway.

God wants His people to be good, law-abiding citizens of the countries in which they live. As long as obeying the laws of the land does not require Christians to disobey God's law, they must respect their authorities and follow the laws that have been made.

Remind them to be subject to rulers, to authorities, to be obedient,
to be ready for every good deed, to malign no one, to be peaceable, gentle,
showing every consideration for all men.
Titus 3:1-2

Family Activity

Make a "Laws Kids Have to Follow" book. Instructions are on pages 1017-1018.

NATIONAL DAY OF PRAYER

First Thursday in May

Conrad Hilton was born on Christmas Day in 1887 in territorial New Mexico. His parents instilled in him a sincere faith in God. They trained him to believe in the importance of hard work and dreaming big.

When Conrad grew up he served as a representative in New Mexico's first state legislature. He then enlisted in the military to serve in World War I. After he came home, Hilton settled in Texas. There he purchased his first hotel. Over the next several decades, Hilton made a name for himself in the hotel industry as he developed his Hilton Hotels chain. He lived by his philosophy that "man with God's help and personal dedication is capable of anything he can dream."

Conrad Hilton was known for being optimistic, honest, and unfailing. He became exceedingly wealthy through his business dealings. When he died, he left almost all of his fortune to the Conrad N. Hilton Foundation, an organization dedicated to providing relief to the suffering, distressed, and destitute, without regard to race, religion, or country. The inscription on Hilton's tombstone reads: *Charity is a supreme virtue and the great channel through which the mercy of God is passed on to mankind. Christmas is forever.* Several members of the Hilton family now serve on the Conrad N. Hilton Foundation's board of directors and staff.

During his lifetime, Hilton worked as a patriot and international statesman. He worked with Senator Frank Carlson of Kansas to initiate a bill in Congress that would establish an annual National Day of Prayer. The bill was passed in 1952 and President Harry S. Truman issued the first National Day of Prayer proclamation.

By the President of the United States of America

A Proclamation

WHEREAS from the earliest days of our history our people have been accustomed to turn to Almighty God for help and guidance; and

WHEREAS in times of national crisis when we are striving to strengthen the foundations of peace and security we stand in special need of divine support; and

WHEREAS the Congress, by a joint resolution approved on April 17, 1952 (66 Stat. 64), has provided that the President "shall set aside and proclaim a suitable day each year, other than a Sunday, as a National Day of Prayer, on which the people of the United States may turn to God in prayer and meditation"; and

WHEREAS I deem it fitting that this Day of Prayer coincide with the anniversary of the adoption of the Declaration of Independence, which published to the world this Nation's "firm reliance on the protection of Divine Providence":

NOW, THEREFORE, I, HARRY S. TRUMAN, President of the United States of America, do hereby proclaim Friday, July 4, 1952, as a National Day of Prayer, on which all of us, in our churches, in our homes, and in our hearts, may beseech God to grant us wisdom to know the course which we should follow, and strength and patience to pursue that course steadfastly. May we also give thanks to Him for His constant watchfulness over us in every hour of national prosperity and national peril.

IN WITNESS WHEREOF, I have hereunto set my hand and caused the Seal of the United States of America to be affixed.

DONE at the City of Washington this 17th day of June in the year of our Lord nineteen hundred and fifty-two, and of the Independence of the United States of America the one hundred and seventy-sixth.

HARRY S. TRUMAN

The original law signed in 1952 did not establish a specific date for the annual National Day of Prayer. That choice was left to each President. In 1961 President John F. Kennedy chose October 4. President Gerald Ford designated December 18 in 1974. The dates varied through the years until the law was amended in 1988 to establish that the first Thursday in May would be America's annual National Day of Prayer. The new law was signed by President Ronald Reagan. Every President since then has issued a proclamation each year encouraging Americans to observe a National Day of Prayer on the first Thursday in May.

Washington, D.C.
A Young Girl Prays in Front of the U.S. Capitol, 2008

Earlier Days of Prayer

While President Truman was the first President to issue a National Day of Prayer in accordance with a law, several earlier Presidents called on the American people to pray at various times throughout our nation's history. The first to do so was President George Washington.

Elias Boudinot was a member of the House of Representatives from New Jersey. In 1789 he proposed the idea of Congress requesting that the President recommend that the citizens of the newly formed United States of America observe a day of public thanksgiving and prayer.

The House appointed a committee to present the idea to the President. Two Senators were also appointed to the committee. Washington liked the idea and issued the proclamation on October 3.

President Washington sent a copy of the proclamation to the Governor of each state, saying, "I do myself the honor to enclose to your Excellency a Proclamation for a general Thanksgiving which I must request the favor of you to have published and made known in your State in the way and manner that shall be most agreeable to yourself." Many newspapers printed the proclamation as well and public observances were scheduled across the new nation. A painting of George Washington praying is pictured at right.

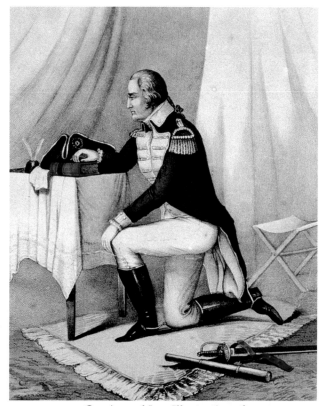

Currier and Ives Illustration of George Washington at Prayer, created c. 1850

James Madison issued proclamations recommending days of prayer during the War of 1812. President Franklin D. Roosevelt did the same during World War II. Other Presidents also called on the citizens of the United States to lift up our country in prayer in a special way on specific days.

National Day of Prayer Task Force

The National Day of Prayer Task Force was founded in 1983 with a mission to "mobilize prayer in America and to encourage personal repentance and righteousness in the culture." It is a privately-funded group that is not connected to any government agency. The organization promotes personal and corporate prayer on the National Day of Prayer, as well as throughout the year. It seeks to preserve America's heritage of faith and to defend the religious freedoms granted in the U.S. Constitution. It emphasizes the importance of prayer in government, military, media, business, education, church, and family. The National Day of Prayer Task Force also works to promote unity among believers.

On the National Day of Prayer, tens of thousands of events are held across the country at which Americans gather to pray for our leaders and our country as a whole. Men, women, and children gather at a variety of events and locations, including churches, school flagpoles, sports stadiums, courthouses, and state capitol buildings. Many of these events are listed on the National Day of Prayer Task Force website so that people can find out about events being held in their area. The photos on this page show National Prayer Day events in St. Paul, Minnesota, and Bakersfield, California.

St. Paul, Minnesota
National Day of Prayer Gathering at the State Capitol, 2010

Bakersfield, California
*National Day of Prayer Gathering
at the Kern County
Superior Court Building, 2011*

Praying for Our Leaders

The Bible teaches about the importance of praying for our leaders. Romans 13:1 tells us we must be in subjection to the governing authorities. This is tough when a person doesn't agree with what their government is doing, but Romans 13:1 goes on to tell us that God establishes all authority.

In Paul's first letter to Timothy, he wrote of the importance of praying for all who are in authority over us.

Therefore I want the men in every place to pray, lifting up holy hands,
without wrath and dissension.
1 Timothy 2:8

Family Activity

Go pray. Instructions are on page 1019.

MOTHER'S DAY

Second Sunday in May

The restaurant door is continually opening and closing all day, but especially around lunchtime. The servers and cooks are exhausted. They have been handing out menus and taking orders and refilling drinks until the whole day is a blur in their minds. This day, the second Sunday in May, has been their busiest day of the year! It's Mother's Day, and according to the National Restaurant Association, this is the most popular holiday on which Americans go out to eat. Many families choose going to a restaurant as a way to honor their moms and give them a break from cooking and washing dishes. Many people mail or give their mom a greeting card on Mother's Day. Sales for Mother's Day greeting cards in the U.S. rank third after cards for Christmas and Valentine's Day. Florists sell more flowers in May than in any other month.

The tradition of honoring mothers goes all the way back to the time of the Bible.

Honor your father and your mother,
That your days may be prolonged in the land
Which the Lord your God gives you.
Exodus 20:12

Hear, my son, your father's instruction
And do not forsake your mother's teaching;
Indeed, they are a graceful wreath
to your head
And ornaments about your neck.
Proverbs 1:8-9

My son, observe the commandment
of your father
And do not forsake the teaching
of your mother;
When you walk about, they will guide you;
When you sleep, they will watch over you.
Proverbs 6:20, 22

A wise son makes a father glad,
But a foolish son is a grief to his mother.
Proverbs 10:1

Let your father and your mother be glad,
And let her rejoice who gave birth to you.
Proverbs 23:25

The United States has celebrated Mother's Day as an official holiday since 1914, but the history of the holiday in this country goes back a little farther.

The History of Mother's Day

Anna Jarvis from West Virginia is considered to be the mother of Mother's Day. In May of 1907, two years after her mother's death, Miss Jarvis hosted a gathering of friends in her home to celebrate her mother's life—a life of service to her community and her nation. At this gathering, Miss Jarvis told her friends of an idea she had of a national celebration to honor mothers. The next year, Miss Jarvis suggested that the church where her mother had taught Sunday School for twenty years have a special time of celebration in honor of mothers. She chose to use the white carnation as a symbol for the observance.

Miss Jarvis continued to promote her idea of Mother's Day and the idea eventually caught on. The Governor of West Virginia issued the first Mother's Day proclamation in 1910. The United States Congress passed a resolution to establish Mother's Day as an official holiday in 1914. The resolution was approved by President Woodrow Wilson, and Mother's Day has been celebrated on the second Sunday in May ever since.

Anna Jarvis, c. 1900

Miss Jarvis was displeased with the commercialism that exploded after Mother's Day became an official holiday. She preferred that mothers be honored in a quieter and simpler way. She wanted Mother's Day to be a time when people went to visit their mothers and didn't just send a card or buy them a box of candy. She thought of buying a printed card as "a poor excuse for the letter you are too lazy to write." She wanted people to go out of their way to honor, as she phrased it, "the woman who has done more for you than anyone in the world." When Miss Jarvis was eighty-four years old, she was arrested for disturbing the peace as she protested against the commercialization of Mother's Day.

Even though Mother's Day did not turn out to be exactly what Miss Jarvis was hoping for, her efforts were not in vain. Mother's Day has become a special day for our country.

Anna Jarvis never had children of her own, but she still received thousands of Mother's Day cards and letters from people all over the world. One of her favorites was a letter from a little boy that read, "I am six years old and I love my mother very much. I am sending you this because you started Mother's Day." Sewn onto the letter was a one dollar bill.

Read President Wilson's 1914 Mother's Day proclamation below.

BY THE PRESIDENT OF THE UNITED STATES OF AMERICA

A PROCLAMATION.

WHEREAS, By a Joint Resolution approved May 8, 1914, "designating the second Sunday in May as Mother's Day, and for other purposes", the President is authorized and requested to issue a proclamation calling upon the government officials to display the United States flag on all government buildings, and the people of the United States to display the flag at their homes or other suitable places on the second Sunday in May as a public expression of our love and reverence for the mothers of our country;

AND WHEREAS, By the said Joint Resolution it is made the duty of the President to request the observance of the second Sunday in May as provided for in the said Joint Resolution;

Now, Therefore, I, Woodrow Wilson, President of the United States of America, by virtue of the authority vested in me by the said Joint Resolution, do hereby direct the government officials to display the United States flag on all government buildings and do invite the people of the United States to display the flag at their homes or other suitable places on the second Sunday in May as a public expression of our love and reverence for the mothers of our country.

In witness whereof I have set my hand and caused the seal of the United States to be hereunto affixed.

Done at the City of Washington this ninth day of May, in the year of our Lord one thousand nine hundred and fourteen, and of the Independence of the United States one hundred and thirty-eight.

Woodrow Wilson

By the President:

William Jennings Bryan
Secretary of State.

President Woodrow Wilson's First Mother's Day Proclamation, 1914

International Mother's Day Shrine

The church building in Grafton, West Virginia, where Miss Jarvis' mother taught Sunday school now houses a museum and is known as the International Mother's Day Shrine. The structure was built in 1873. The International Mother's Day Shrine Foundation was established in 1972. The group exists to "preserve, promote and develop through education, the Spirit of Motherhood, as exemplified by the lives of Ann Maria Reeves Jarvis and Anna Jarvis, and the institution of Mother's Day that they established." Visitors may tour the building on weekends and visit the gift shop where plates, bells, mugs, and other souvenirs are available. Visitors might come upon a wedding ceremony taking place in the building. The foundation rents out the space to brides and grooms, but they better say their vows and snap their pictures in a hurry! Each couple has a one-hour time slot in which to have their wedding and they only have one hour to decorate before the ceremony begins.

Grafton, West Virginia
International Mother's Day Shrine

Mother's Day Around the World

Many countries around the world have their own Mother's Day traditions. Some countries, including Denmark, Belgium, Japan, and Italy, have followed the pattern of the United States and celebrate the holiday on the second Sunday in May. Other countries have chosen different days. Many Arab countries celebrate the holiday on March 21, a day that is close to the beginning of spring. People in Panama honor their mothers on December 8, the same day that Catholics honor Mary the mother of Jesus. Mothers in Thailand receive special honor on August 12, the birthday of their beloved Queen Sirikit.

Japan

Thailand

Whether your family takes your mom out to eat or prepares a special meal at home, or whether you make her a card or buy one, make sure that on the second Sunday in May your mom knows how much you love and appreciate her. In fact, make sure she know that every day of your life.

The most important way to honor a Christian mother is to follow her example of faith. In a letter the apostle Paul wrote to Timothy, Paul spoke of Timothy's faith and how he had learned it from his mother and grandmother. Timothy not only learned about God from them; He embraced their faith and made it his own.

Mother's Day Postcard, 1915

For I am mindful of the sincere faith within you,
which first dwelt in your grandmother Lois
and your mother Eunice,
and I am sure that it is in you as well.
2 Timothy 1:5

Family Activity

Write biographical sketches of your mom and grandmothers.
Instructions are on page 1020.

ARMED FORCES DAY

Third Saturday in May

The first observance of Armed Forces Day occurred in 1950. Before that, each branch of the military had its own special day.

Navy Day

The Navy League of the United States established the first Navy Day observance in 1922. It was not a national holiday, but it did receive attention from President Warren Harding. In a note about the observance to the Secretary of the Navy, Harding wrote:

> *From our earliest national beginnings the Navy has always been, and deserved to be, an object of special pride to the American people. Its record is indeed one to inspire such sentiments, and I am very sure that such a commemoration as is planned will be a timely reminder.*

Washington, D.C.
Navy Day at the Washington Navy Yard, 1938

October 27 was chosen as the date for the observance to honor the legacy of Theodore Roosevelt, who was born on that date in 1858. Roosevelt served as Assistant Secretary of the Navy from 1897 to 1898, three years before he became President of the United States. October 27 was also the day when a special committee of the Continental Congress issued a report stating they wanted to purchase merchant ships to establish the new American Navy in 1775. The photo at left shows the crowd that visited the Washington Navy Yard on Navy Day on October 27, 1938.

Army Day

Army Day was first celebrated on May 1, 1928. Communists held an annual celebration on this day, so the Army wanted to establish a counter-celebration. (The Communists' May 1 celebration was discussed in the lesson on Loyalty Day and Law Day.) Before the 1928 celebration, the Amy had participated in Defense Test Day in 1924 and 1925. Congress, however, soon forbade the Army from holding this observance again.

The purpose of Army Day was to make the American public aware of what the Army did. It was also a day to let America know of the need for the country's military to be prepared for whatever might happen in the world.

President Franklin D. Roosevelt issued a proclamation in 1936 designating April 6 as Army Day across the country. The photo at right shows congressional leaders signing the resolution that officially established Army Day in 1937.

The photo below shows an Army Day parade in 1937. Members of both Houses of Congress watched the parade pass the U.S. Capitol. The photos at right were taken during the Army Day parade in 1939. World War II was looming on the horizon. Thousands of people showed up to see soldiers and veterans march by. The Army also displayed its latest types of tanks.

Washington, D.C.
*Congressional Leaders Sign
National Army Day Resolution, 1937*

Army Day Parades near the U.S. Capitol, 1937 and 1939

Air Force Day

President Harry Truman declared the first Air Force Day on August 1, 1947. This was the fortieth anniversary of the beginning of the Air Force. When the Air Force was established in 1907, it was called the Aeronautical Division in the Office of the Chief Signal Officer of the Army. In establishing the observance of Air Force Day, Truman was trying to raise awareness "of the priority of importance of air forces in any system of national security." Truman wanted Americans to realize that with the development of aviation technology, the oceans that bordered our country on the east and west were no longer a sure defense against attack from our enemies. Truman wanted all American citizens to remember that air power was necessary to preserve our liberty and that "the continued development of the science of air transportation is vital to the trade and commerce of a peaceful world."

Kabul, Afghanistan
Cutting a Marine Birthday Cake, 2011

Marine Corps Day

The United States Marine Corps began celebrating its birthday on July 11, 1799, one year after it was established under that name. It was celebrated on that date until 1921 when it was changed to November 10. November 10 was the date the Continental Marines was established during the Revolutionary War. The Continental Marines was a precursor to the Marine Corps.

Marine Corps Day is celebrated around the world with exhibits, parades, performances, and speeches. On this day Marines in many places enjoy a Marine birthday cake, like the one pictured at left. Marines have been celebrating their day with a birthday cake since at least 1937.

Coast Guard Day

Coast Guard Day is celebrated each year on August 4. This was the date the Revenue Cutter Service was established in 1790. The Revenue Cutter Service was renamed the Coast Guard when it joined with the Lifesaving Service in 1915.

Grand Haven, Michigan, was given the official title of Coast Guard City USA. Coast Guard personnel started a picnic in 1924 that grew into an annual festival starting in 1937. It draws about 300,000 attendees each year. It takes place over several days around August 4 and offers many attractions, including parades, ship tours, a street dance, carnival rides, a car show, and a craft fair. The Coast Guard National Memorial Service also occurs during the festival.

Creating Armed Forces Day

The Army, the Navy, and the Air Force were united into one Department of the Federal government in 1947. At first it was called the National Military Establishment, but the name was soon changed to the Department of Defense.

Navy Day, Army Day, and Air Force Day were each observed for the last time in 1949. Each branch was asked to drop its own observance and join together for a united observance called Armed Forces Day. The United States Marine Corps and the U.S. Coast Guard participate in Armed Forces Day, but they also each maintain celebrations for their own specific days.

According to President Truman, the first Armed Forces Day was to be a "parade of preparedness." The theme of the first observance was "Teamed for Defense." The government wanted Americans to have an increased awareness and understanding of the armed forces. It was a day for the military to display their new equipment. It was also a time to honor and show appreciation for the people who had served and were serving in the military.

Americans across the country participated in parades, open houses, receptions, and air shows on the first Armed Forces Day in 1950. President Truman and everyone else gathered in Washington, D.C., watched 10,000 veterans and active members of the military parade past. Around 33,000 people celebrated in New York City and beheld a display of 250 military planes flying overhead. German citizens in Berlin watched a parade of 1,000 U.S. troops who were stationed in Germany at the time.

An article in *The New York Times* in 1950 commented that for many who were active members of the military, Armed Forces Day would not be a time for parades and receptions; it would be a day to be on duty doing their job and perhaps even giving their lives for our country.

Armed Forces Day Posters, 1951-2011

Observing Armed Forces Day at Aberdeen Proving Ground

After the United States became involved in World War I, it became urgent for the military to find a place where they could test field artillery weapons, ammunition, trench mortars, air defense guns, and railway artillery. They needed a place that was near factories, but far away from heavily populated areas. A site of about 80,000 acres was chosen near the town of Aberdeen, Maryland. The area contained rich farmland and was home to about 3,000 people. The residents, their animals, and even old family cemeteries had to be moved. After the government took control of the area in 1917, the Army began to build testing facilities.

After the war, Aberdeen Proving Ground (APG) continued to be used for research and development of munitions. During World War II over 25,000 military personnel and civilians worked in research, development, and training at APG. Aberdeen Proving Ground has continued to be used by the military during times of peace and times of war.

One tradition at APG is their observance of Armed Forces Day. The week-long festivities include musical performances and displays from a variety of military groups, such as a chemical response team and canine units. It is a time for civilians to learn about what the military does and how it operates. The highlight for many attendees is the live fire demonstration. Photos from this part of the event are pictured below.

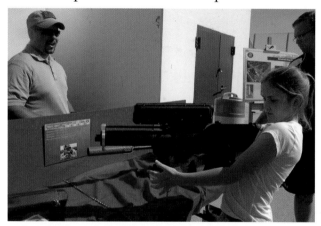

Aberdeen Proving Ground, Maryland
Live Fire Demonstration on Armed Forces Day, 2012

Words from Our Presidents

Through the years, our Presidents have issued proclamations, given radio addresses, and spoken at various gatherings on or around Armed Forces Day. As Commander in Chief, each President bears a great responsibility to our country and to each man and woman in uniform. It is on the President's shoulders to keep American citizens at home and around the world safe and secure. Read the words from some of our Commanders in Chief below.

And that whole world today is watching to see whether the Star-Spangled Banner still waves over the land of the free and the home of the brave. Well, together let us prove that it does. Let us so conduct ourselves at home that we truly remain the land of the free. And let us so meet our responsibilities in the world as to show that we are still, more than ever, the home of the brave.

And then we can look to the future with confidence that Armed Forces Day in the years to come will be not only a day of pride but also a day of peace for America and for all the people of the world.

Richard Nixon, 1973

One last thought for Armed Forces Day and every day: If you see someone in uniform, would you go up, shake their hand, and thank them.

Ronald Reagan, 1988

The first Armed Forces Day celebrated service unity, honored those in uniform, and reassured Americans that our military was ready for whatever challenges lay ahead. Fifty years later we can look back proudly on a half-century in which America's best have more than met those challenges. We are as secure at home and safe from external threat today as we have been at any time in our long history. For that, we owe every American in uniform and everyone who has served before an eternal debt.

Bill Clinton, 2000

Nations have been going to war against each other for thousands of years. Many wars took place during Bible times. War is a terrible thing, but it has been a part of this world almost since the beginning. One day, though, God promises that wars will all be over. At the end of time, God's people will live in peace forever.

Nation will not lift up sword against nation, and never again will they train for war.

Each of them will sit under his vine and under his fig tree,

With no one to make them afraid, for the mouth of the Lord of hosts has spoken.

Micah 4:3-4

Family Activity

Design the next Armed Forces Day poster. Instructions are on page 1021.

MEMORIAL DAY

Last Monday in May

The heart-wrenching scenes of the Civil War were still fresh in the mind of Major General John A. Logan in 1868. General Logan is pictured below. The war had ended three years before. General Logan had been involved in much of the bloody conflict. At the Battle of Fort Donelson, Logan was wounded three times. He survived his wounds and was promoted to brigadier general. After his brave service during the Battle of Vicksburg, he was promoted to major general. After the war, Logan helped to establish the Grand Army of the Republic, an organization of Union veterans.

General John A. Logan

During the war, General Logan had watched men become heroes. He had watched men give the supreme sacrifice—their lives—for their country. He knew that there were countless mothers and fathers, aunts and uncles, wives and children who were still mourning the men they loved who had died in the war. In 1868 General Logan worked to establish Decoration Day, a day set apart to place flowers on the graves of Civil War veterans.

Decoration Day was observed at Arlington National Cemetery near Washington, D.C., on May 30, 1868. A stereo card of the event is pictured below. Around five thousand people were in attendance. They listened to speeches and then watched as children from the Soldiers' and Sailors' Orphan Home, along with members of the Grand Army of the Republic, walked through the cemetery saying prayers, singing hymns, and placing flowers on Union and Confederate graves. Small American flags were also placed on the graves.

Washington, D.C.
President Grant and General Logan in the Reviewing Stand at the First Official Decoration Day, 1868

People in various parts of the country had already begun traditions of placing flowers on the graves of veterans even before General Logan proposed the idea. Two years earlier in Columbus, Mississippi, for example, a group of women decorated the graves of Confederate soldiers who died in the Battle of Shiloh. As they placed flowers on the graves, they saw the bare graves of Union soldiers nearby. Even though the men buried there were from the enemy army, the women decorated their graves as well.

The idea of Decoration Day spread, and by the early 1900s many communities across the country were holding annual ceremonies on May 30 to honor Civil War veterans. The photo at right shows schoolchildren with flowers that were gathered for Decoration Day. The date written on the chalkboard is May 30, 1899. Decoration Day was eventually renamed Memorial Day. The photos below were taken during a Memorial Day gathering in Ashland, Maine, during World War II.

Decoration Day, 1899

Ashland, Maine
Memorial Day Ceremony, 1943

Congress and President Lyndon Johnson declared the city of Waterloo, New York, the official birthplace of Memorial Day in 1966, one hundred years after that town held its first annual ceremony. Other cities also claim to be the birthplace of Memorial Day, but according to the United States government, the title belongs to Waterloo. This town was chosen because its annual celebrations were community-wide events when businesses closed and citizens decorated the graves of veterans.

Modern Memorial Day Observances

After World War I, May 30 became a time to honor veterans of all American wars, not just those from the Civil War. Congress made the holiday official in 1971 and placed it perpetually on the last Monday in May (instead of on May 30). Many states in the South have added an additional holiday to honor their Confederate Civil War veterans.

Memorial Day parades and other observances from coast to coast are pictured below. For many Americans, Memorial Day means a day off from work and school, with maybe a cookout or a trip to a park. It has also come to signify the beginning of summer. No matter how we spend the last Monday in May, we should always be thankful to God for the freedoms we enjoy in this country. We should also be thankful for the men and women who have served in our country's military, both those who are living and those who have died.

Cambridge, Massachusetts

Eugene, Oregon

Millburn, New Jersey

Ukiah, California

Congress passed a resolution in the year 2000 to establish an annual National Moment of Remembrance. Each Memorial Day at 3:00 p.m. local time, American citizens are encouraged to pause as they think about the men and women who have died serving our country.

Arlington National Cemetery

Arlington National Cemetery is an important landmark connected with Memorial Day. It was here that General Logan's first official Decoration Day ceremony took place in 1868. The cemetery lies on the banks of the Potomac River across from Washington, D.C. The land that is now the cemetery was once the grand estate called Arlington that belonged to George Washington Parke Custis, a grandson of Martha Washington.

George Washington Parke Custis' daughter Mary Anna inherited the estate after her father's death. Mary Anna was married to Confederate General Robert E. Lee. The Lees lived on the Arlington estate until 1861 when Virginia seceded from the Union. Robert E. Lee became a major general in the Confederate army. He knew that his wife was not safe at Arlington, so he told Mary Anna that she must leave. It was hard for the Lees to be separated from their beloved home. Federal troops soon took it over. When Mary Anna did not pay her taxes in person during the war, the Federal government confiscated the property. It was put up for auction and sold. A tax commissioner purchased it for "government use, for war, military, charitable and educational purposes." The grounds were designated a military cemetery in 1864.

After Robert E. Lee died, his oldest son, Custis, claimed that the land was rightfully his. He said that the property had been confiscated illegally. The case was taken to the U.S. Supreme Court, who ruled in favor of Custis and returned Arlington to him. Custis sold the property to Congress the next year and it became a military reservation.

Each year on Memorial Day, it has become a tradition for the President, Vice President, or another government official to place a wreath of flowers on the Tomb of the Unknowns and deliver a Memorial Day address in the cemetery's amphitheater. About 5,000 people attend this ceremony each year. The photos at right show Presidents Warren Harding and Barack Obama at two Arlington ceremonies that took place ninety years apart.

Fort Myer, Virginia
Memorial Day Observances at
Arlington National Cemetery, c. 1921 and 2011

Decorating Graves at Arlington National Cemetery, 1943 and 2010

Memorial Day Poppies

John McCrae was a doctor in the Canadian army during World War I. McCrae wrote a poem in 1915 called "In Flanders Fields." McCrae wrote the poem after witnessing horrific scenes of battle in a place called Flanders, located in western Belgium and northern France.

In Flanders Fields

by Lieutenant Colonel John McCrae, M.D.

In Flanders Fields the poppies blow
Between the crosses row on row,
That mark our place; and in the sky
The larks, still bravely singing, fly
Scarce heard amid the guns below.
We are the Dead. Short days ago
We lived, felt dawn, saw sunset glow,
Loved and were loved, and now we lie
In Flanders fields.
Take up our quarrel with the foe:
To you from failing hands we throw
The torch; be yours to hold it high.
If ye break faith with us who die
We shall not sleep, though poppies grow
In Flanders fields.

Poppy

McCrae's poem was published in London and touched many hearts. As a result of the poem, the poppy flower has come to symbolize remembering and honoring veterans. The poem had a profound impact on many people, including Anna E. Guerin of France and Moina Michael of the State of Georgia. They came to be known as the "Poppy Lady of France" and the "Poppy Princess."

Anna E. Guerin and Moina Michael worked hard to promote the idea of selling poppies to raise money for orphans and others who were severely impacted by World War I. The Poppy Lady of France and the Poppy Princess called on the Veterans of Foreign Wars (VFW) organization to help them in their cause. The VFW named the poppy their official memorial flower in 1922. The organization distributed many poppies, and people were encouraged to wear them in remembrance of soldiers who had died. There was a poppy shortage the next year, but the VFW had the idea that unemployed and disabled veterans could make money by creating artificial poppies to sell. These artificial poppies came to be called "Buddy Poppies." The poppy makers chose this term to honor their buddies who had served with them in war but who either didn't come home or who came home scarred or wounded. The VFW has continued their poppy tradition, and they distribute around fourteen million artificial poppies each year.

Many Americans have a loved one who has died while serving in the military. There are many things in this life that break our hearts and make us cry, but God has given His people hope. He has promised that He will comfort us here, and He has promised us that one day we will be with Him in Heaven forever where:

He will wipe away every tear from their eyes;
and there will no longer be any death;
there will no longer be any mourning, or crying, or pain;
the first things have passed away.
Revelation 21:4

Family Activity

Make a Memorial Day bouquet and place it somewhere special.
Instructions are on page 1022.

FLAG DAY

June 14

lag Day is the birthday of our nation's flag. On June 14, 1777, the Second Continental Congress approved a design for a flag to represent the United States of America:

Resolved, that the Flag of the thirteen United States shall be thirteen stripes, alternate red and white; that the Union be thirteen stars, white on a blue field, representing a new constellation.

San Francisco, California
Historic American Flag Reproduction at City Hall

But that was all! The resolution did not specify how many points each star would have or how the thirteen stars would be arranged on the blue field. As a result, the early flags that were created for our country were not all the same. The flag design was not officially standardized until 1912 when William Howard Taft was President. The flag pictured at left is a reproduction of a design that was popular during the Revolutionary War. This flag flies at City Hall in San Francisco, California. It is commonly called the Betsy Ross flag, referring to the story about George Washington commissioning Philadelphia seamstress Betsy Ross to create an American flag in 1776.

Congress changed the specifications for the flag in 1794 after Kentucky and Vermont became states. The new design had fifteen stars and fifteen stripes. This flag remained in use until 1818. A Navy captain named Samuel C. Reid suggested that Congress adopt a new tradition of adding only a new star to represent each new state and keeping the original thirteen stripes.

By 1912 the flag had gained a total of 48 stars. Two more were added after Alaska and Hawaii became states in 1959.

Bernard J. Cigrand

Several communities claim to be the first to have observed Flag Day, including New York City, New York; Philadelphia, Pennsylvania; and Waubeka, Wisconsin. In 2004 Congress recognized Waubeka as the true birthplace of Flag Day.

Bernard J. Cigrand was born in Waubeka in 1866. His parents were immigrants from Luxembourg. As a child, Cigrand earned money to buy books by selling scrap iron and rags. He began working for the U.S. Book and Bible Club when he was twelve years old. At this job he earned a commission of twenty-five cents for every book he sold.

Bernard J. Cigrand

When he grew up he taught school at Waubeka's Stony Hill schoolhouse. His teaching salary plus the money he made selling books was enough for him to pay his way through dental school. In 1886, while nineteen-year-old Cigrand was teaching school, he placed a small American flag in an inkwell and assigned his students to write essays on what the flag meant to them personally. That same year he wrote an article that was published in a Chicago newspaper promoting his idea for an annual observance of the birth of the American flag on June 14.

Cigrand was a strong patriot. He had a keen interest in American history. He encouraged others to respect and honor the United States and her flag. In 1888 he was appointed editor of a magazine called *American Standard*. The publication sought to encourage its readers to respect the symbols of America.

Cigrand wrote hundreds of articles for magazines and newspapers over the years to encourage the establishment of an official Flag Day observance. In addition to his editorial work, Cigrand also authored several books, including *The Story of the American Flag*, *Story of the Great Seal of the United States*, and *History of American Emblems*. Cigrand also wrote a pamphlet titled "Laws and Customs Regulating the Use of the Flag of the United States."

Flag Day Movement

The first national observance of Flag Day took place on June 14, 1877, the one hundredth anniversary of the adoption of the original flag resolution by the Second Continental Congress. Over 300,000 Chicago schoolchildren participated in a city-wide Flag Day observance in 1894 on the third Saturday in June. A similar event was held the following year. One by one, mayors in other cities and Governors in various states began calling for Flag Day observances.

A Flag Day movement began to sweep the country as patriotic organizations and veterans groups began to push for the establishment of a permanent national observance of the day. President Woodrow Wilson issued a Flag Day proclamation in 1916, but Congress did not make the observance a permanent one until 1949. The legislation was signed by President Harry Truman.

Washington, D.C.
Flag Day Celebration, 1919

The photo at right was taken on Flag Day at the U.S. Capitol in 1919. At the time, the flag on the front of the building was the largest flag in the world. It was 90 feet tall and 165 feet wide! The photo at right shows the Old Post Office Building in Washington, D.C., decked out for Flag Day in 1914.

Annin Flagmakers

Brothers Benjamin and Edward Annin began a flag company in New York City in 1847. Annin Flagmakers has been producing flags ever since and is still a family-owned business.

The company's flag sales spiked during the 1860s as a result of the Civil War. This was

Old Post Office Building Decorated for Flag Day, 1919

the first time in U.S. history that large numbers of private citizens displayed flags at their homes. The company experienced more spikes in sales during World War I and World War II. The company opened a new plant in Verona, New Jersey, in 1917. After Alaska and Hawaii became states, Annin received a flood of orders from people who wanted to replace their outdated flags that had only forty-eight stars with new ones that had fifty. Sales rose again in 1976 for America's Bicentennial, and also after the September 11, 2001, terrorist attacks.

Annin Flagmakers prides itself on the top-quality American flags they sell that are made in America out of American-made fabric. The company now has additional facilities in Virginia and Ohio and employs about 500 people.

The Federal Flag Code

The Federal government has established rules and regulations regarding the proper way to handle, display, and use the American flag. These regulations are called the Federal Flag Code. On the next page are just a few of the regulations outlined in the code.

- The flag should never touch anything beneath it, such as the ground, the floor, water, or merchandise.

- The flag should never be carried flat or horizontally, but always aloft and free.

- The flag should never be used for advertising purposes in any manner whatsoever. It should not be embroidered on such articles as cushions or handkerchiefs and the like, printed or otherwise impressed on paper napkins or boxes or anything that is designed for temporary use and discard.

- When displayed either horizontally or vertically against a wall, the union should be uppermost and to the flag's own right, that is, to the observer's left.

- The flag should be displayed during school days in or near every schoolhouse.

- The flag should be hoisted briskly and lowered ceremoniously.

- The flag should never be used as a receptacle for receiving, holding, carrying, or delivering anything.

The Story of the Pledge of Allegiance

Francis Bellamy

Francis Bellamy was born in 1855 in Mount Morris, New York. Francis' father was a Baptist minister who died when Francis was about nine years old. Francis enrolled in the University of Rochester in 1872 where he studied to become a Baptist minister like his father.

Bellamy's first position as a minister was with a church in Little Falls, New York, beginning in 1880. The next year he married Hattie Benton. The couple had two sons. From his pulpit, Bellamy preached in support of prohibition (the outlawing of liquor) and campaigned for the candidate of the National Prohibition Party.

The Bellamy family moved to Boston in 1885. Francis was passionate about encouraging and uplifting factory workers and their families through his ministry. He wanted to help solve the economic, social, political, and religious problems the workers were facing. Francis also continued to speak in favor of prohibition.

Youth's Companion

Bellamy's sermons and his work among the poor caught the attention of Daniel Ford, who was the publisher of *Youth's Companion*, a popular children's magazine published in Boston. Bellamy resigned as a minister in 1891 and began working with Ford on *Youth's Companion*.

Ford gave Bellamy the task of working with James Upham on the 1892 National Public School Celebration in honor of the four hundredth anniversary of the arrival of Christopher Columbus. *Youth's Companion* had been put in charge of promoting this event and publishing a program to help schools know what to do for the occasion.

National Public School Celebration

Youth's Companion asked its young readers to support the celebration by talking to their teachers and members of their local school board. Bellamy sent information about the celebration to thousands of newspapers across the country. The American flag was to be an important part of the celebration. President Benjamin Harrison wanted the flag to "float over every school house in the country" for the celebration. The drawing at left shows a flag flying over a school in the 1890s.

Washington, D.C.
Flag Flying Over High School, 1890s

Francis Bellamy was assigned to write the program for the celebration. The program he created included reading a proclamation from President Harrison, raising and saluting the flag, praying or reading Scripture, singing, and speeches. James Upham tried several times to write a salute to the flag for the ceremony, but he couldn't come up with one that satisfied him. He asked Francis Bellamy to write one instead.

A principal in New York City had written a flag salute in 1889 that said, "We give our heads and our hearts to God and our country; one country, one language, one Flag." Upham and Bellamy wanted the new salute to include a promise of allegiance to the American flag. The pledge that Bellamy wrote for *Youth's Companion* was slightly different from the pledge recited today. The original version was: *I pledge allegiance to my Flag and the Republic for which it stands, one nation, indivisible, with liberty and justice for all.*

Millions of Americans across the country took part in the National Public School Celebration in October of 1892. At Boston's celebration, Bellamy listened to thousands of schoolchildren recite in unison the pledge that he had written.

Saluting the Flag

In the late 1800s and early 1900s, the salute was made by raising the right hand up and out toward the flag. After the Italian Fascists and German Nazis began using a similar salute in their countries, some Americans were concerned that our salute was too much like these other groups. In 1942 Congress established that the proper way for an American citizen to salute the flag would be to place his right hand over his heart. The photo at right shows schoolchildren saluting the flag before the change was made. Also in 1942, Bellamy's Pledge of Allegiance was established as part of the Federal Flag Code.

Southington, Connecticut
Saluting the Flag, 1942

Changes to the Pledge

Slight changes to the wording of the pledge have been made over the years. The word "to" was added before "the Republic" to give the pledge a better rhythm. At a National Flag Conference in the 1920s, "my Flag" was replaced with "the Flag of the United States of America."

In the 1950s, the Catholic organization called the Knights of Columbus, as well as other groups, campaigned for the words "under God" to be added to the pledge. When President Eisenhower attended a church service in 1954, the minister spoke of his view that this phrase should become a part of the pledge. The minister spoke to Eisenhower personally after the service. The next day Eisenhower began to work with Congress to get the phrase added. The bill passed and Eisenhower signed it into law on Flag Day of that same year. The pledge now states:

I pledge allegiance to the Flag of the United States of America and to the Republic for which it stands, one nation, under God, indivisible, with liberty and justice for all.

Some Christians do not feel comfortable pledging allegiance to the flag because they know their true allegiance is only to God. Whatever a person's convictions are on this issue, it is still important to respect the leaders of our country and to live as obedient citizens.

In the Bible, God made it clear that one day, after the world has come to an end, every person—even the people who are not Christians—will realize that God is God and everyone will bow down and worship Him.

I have sworn by Myself,
The word has gone forth from My mouth in righteousness and will not turn back,
That to Me every knee will bow, every tongue will swear allegiance.
Isaiah 45:23

Family Activity

Play Flag Trivia. Instructions are on pages 1023-1025.

FATHER'S DAY

Third Sunday in June

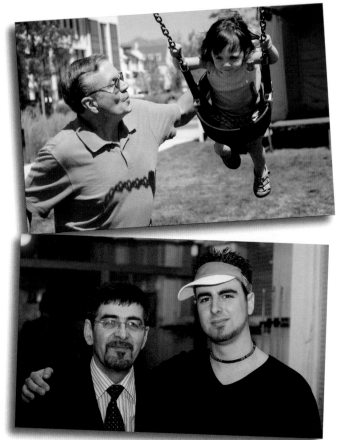

Father's Day is celebrated in America each year on the third Sunday in June. It is a day for Americans to honor their fathers and grandfathers. Some people also take the opportunity on Father's Day to honor another special man who has been important to them, such as a step-father, an uncle, or a friend who has been like a father. Some people give gifts. Special outings, neckties, and electronics are popular choices. Many people buy or make a Father's Day card for their dad. The Hallmark Greeting Card Company began printing Father's Day cards in the 1920s.

Honoring our Fathers is not just a nice thing to do. According to the Bible, it is something we are commanded to do.

Hear, O sons, the instruction of a father,
And give attention that you may gain
understanding.
Proverbs 4:1

Grandchildren are the crown of old men,
And the glory of sons is their fathers.
Proverbs 17:6

The father of the righteous
will greatly rejoice,
And he who sires a wise son
will be glad in him.
Proverbs 23:24

He who keeps the law is a discerning son,
But he who is a companion of gluttons
humiliates his father.
Proverbs 28:7

Listen to your father who begot you,
And do not despise your mother
when she is old.
Proverbs 23:22

The Idea for Father's Day

As Sonora Smart Dodd sat in the Central Methodist Church in Spokane, Washington, on Mother's Day in 1909, she listened to a sermon about mothers. A painting of the building is pictured at right. At the time Sonora was expecting her first and only child and knew she would soon be experiencing the joys and responsibilities of being a parent. Sonora's own mother had died eleven years earlier when Sonora was sixteen. Sonora and her five younger brothers were left to be cared for by their father, William Jackson Smart, a veteran of the Civil War. Sonora described her father as "a very strict man, a real disciplinarian," but said he was also "kind and loving" and kept the family "together and happy." Sonora loved her father, and she wanted him to be honored. The Mother's Day sermon she listened to that Sunday in 1909 started her thinking. She decided to embark on a mission of establishing another holiday—a special day to honor fathers. Look at the photograph of Spokane around this time below.

Spokane, Washington
Painting of the Central Methodist Church

Spokane, Washington
c. 1908

Sonora Smart Dodd

Working to Establish Father's Day

Sonora, pictured at left, worked hard to convince others that her idea was a good one. She succeeded! The following year, Father's Day was celebrated in the city of Spokane. The month of June was chosen for the special day since that was the birth month of Sonora's father, who was still living at the time. Ministers across Spokane delivered Father's Day sermons. The mayor of Spokane and the Governor of Washington state issued Father's Day proclamations. It was on this first Father's Day that the tradition began of fathers wearing red roses on Father's Day. Family members were also encouraged to wear roses in honor of their fathers—a red one if their father was living and a white rose if their father had died.

News of the Father's Day celebration in Spokane began to travel across the country. Seven national newspapers published articles about it. Sonora started receiving letters from all over the country. She replied to the letters as she could, but sometimes she received as many as one hundred in a single day! She eventually asked some other women to help her handle the correspondence. Many people wrote about how they wanted their own communities to observe Father's Day.

Some politicians, including William Jennings Bryan and Woodrow Wilson, were in favor of the holiday, but it took a long time for it to become official. Calvin Coolidge encouraged the observance of Father's Day in 1924, saying it was a time to "establish more intimate relations between fathers and their children and to impress upon fathers the full measure of their obligations." Coolidge is pictured at right with his two sons. This advanced Sonora's cause, but the job wasn't finished. The holiday still was not official.

President Calvin Coolidge with His Sons, John and Calvin Jr., 1924

Finally, fifty-six years after the first Father's Day celebration in Spokane, President Lyndon Johnson signed a proclamation in 1966 that declared the third Sunday in June the first nation-wide official observance of Father's Day. Sonora Dodd said that she was "happy that this could have come to pass in my lifetime." She was eighty-four years old. In 1972 President Richard Nixon made the observance of Father's Day a permanent one. Nixon is pictured at right with his daughter Tricia, who got married at the White House while her father was President.

President Richard Nixon with His Daughter, Tricia, 1971

More About the Mother of Father's Day

Sonora was born in Arkansas in 1882. When she was seven years old, she and her family moved to Washington State. She married John Bruce Dodd in 1899. Sonora was once described as being "gentle, retiring, and gracious." In honor of Sonora's efforts to make Father's Day an official national holiday, she received many special recognitions and awards. Among these was the "Friend in Deed" medal awarded to her by the Columbia Broadcasting System in

1939. She was honored as the founder of Father's Day at the New York World's Fair in 1940 and at the 1974 World's Fair Expo in Spokane. In 1971 the National Father's Day committee presented her with a silver bowl and named her the "Mother of Father's Day."

William Jackson Smart

In a 1939 newspaper article, Sonora said of her father, "His kindness and the sacrifices he made inspired me. Besides that, at that time the pendulum of disrespect for fathers had swung too far, I thought. . . . I thought that fathers should be revered as mothers always had been." Speaking again of her father in a 1955 article, Sonora said, "He felt fatherhood was a lifelong task and he never relinquished its duties and responsibilities until his death in 1919. Even after my brothers and I were married, he was mindful of his obligations for he was a golden rule type of father." Sonora's father is pictured above.

While promoting her idea for Father's Day was a significant part of Sonora Dodd's life, she was also involved in a variety of other pursuits. Sonora was the author of a series of children's books about Native Americans called *Children of the Sun*. She was also a poet. Her poem about her home town of Spokane became the city's official welcome poem. Sonora created many Native American dolls, some of which she gave away as gifts. She presented one of her dolls to the Royal Museum of Romania in 1926. She was a member of many different clubs and organizations. Sonora died in 1978 at the age of ninety-six.

Honoring Fathers

Honoring our fathers is clearly something that God wants His followers to do. Honoring our fathers is something God wants us to do not only when we are children, but also when we are grown up. When we live in a way that shows we are wise, we make our fathers glad (Proverbs 15:20). When we honor our fathers, we make God glad, too.

The song lyrics below were published in 1865. They tell of the importance of being thankful when we have had a kind and loving father.

Oh! Write Me a Song of My Father

by C. Henry

Oh! write me a song of my Father,
And tell me the reason, I pray,
You ever write songs about Mother,
Not a word of dear Father you say.
Is his love and affection less ardent?
Does his heart less emotion bestow?
Though the sun to the moon is less argent,
Still but one light from both o'er us glow.

Oh! think of him, when in your childhood,
With dear Mother, he'd fervently pray,
And call you his child and his darling,
And that God might protect you alway:
Then blessings and kisses he'd give you,
And call you his own pretty boy,
When scarce you could lisp the word: Father!
And your heart free from earthly alloy.

And now that you've grown into manhood,
Be grateful to him whose fond care
Ever guarded both you and your Mother,
And as oft dried the sorrowful tear.
Oh! love him, think not of him lightly;
Cheer his heart, let it not be opprest.
Love your Mother, but don't forget Father.
Let the one with the other be blessed.

A Compassionate Father

The Bible gives us a clear picture of God as a loving Father to all of His children. Exodus 34:6 describes God as "compassionate and gracious, slow to anger, and abounding in lovingkindness and truth." God wants us to trust Him just like a little child trusts a good and loving daddy to take care of him and give him what he needs. God wants to take care of us and give us what we need as well.

> Just as a father has compassion on his children,
> So the Lord has compassion on those who fear Him.
> Psalm 103:13

Family Activity

Write biographical sketches of your dad and grandfathers. Instructions are on page 1026.

FAMILY ACTIVITIES

Each of these activities goes with one of the lessons on American holidays. Have fun creating, eating, laughing, talking, and making memories together as a family. Please keep in mind that children should be supervised when using sharp tools, using the stove or oven, climbing ladders, looking up information online, and visiting public places.

MARTIN LUTHER KING DAY

"WHAT ARE YOU DOING FOR OTHERS?" POSTER

Dream together with your family about making a difference in your world.

Supplies:

poster board

old magazines and/or newspapers

colored paper

scissors

glue

marker

pens or pencils

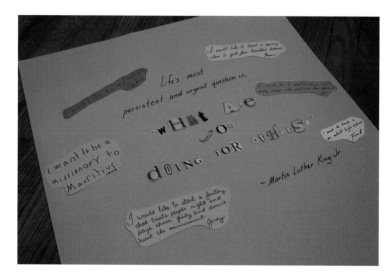

Instructions:

★ In the center of the poster board, write: *Life's most persistent and urgent question is,*

★ Look through old magazines and/or newspapers to find each of the letters you need for these words: *"What are you doing for others?"* Glue these letters in the center of the poster board under the words you wrote. Under the letters you glue on, write: —*Martin Luther King Jr.*

★ As a family, talk about the meaning of Dr. King's quote. Talk about things your family has done, is doing, and would like to do to help others. Give each person in your family a piece of paper. Have everyone write something they would like to do in their lifetime to make a difference in the world. Bubble cut around each person's words and glue them to the poster board.

★ Hang the poster in your house as a reminder to be a family who serves.

NATIONAL FREEDOM DAY

FREEDOM DAY BANQUET

Write a proclamation, make a wreath, and celebrate the freedoms your family enjoys!

Supplies (see detailed instructions below):

Freedom Day proclamation

Freedom Day wreath

food for a special dinner

Instructions:

★ Look again at the words of President Truman's National Freedom Day Proclamation on pages 921-922. Using Truman's words as a pattern, write a proclamation for your family's observance of the day. Write or print it on nice paper. Sign your name at the bottom. Here is a sample proclamation to give you some ideas:

WHEREAS the Harper family has lived in the United States of America and enjoyed the blessings of life, liberty, and the pursuit of happiness for six generations; and

WHEREAS the Harper family feels grateful for the freedom of speech, the freedom of religion, and the many other freedoms we enjoy in this country; and

WHEREAS we would like to thank God for these freedoms:

NOW, THEREFORE I, FREDDIE HARPER, middle child of the Harper family, do hereby designate February 1, 20__, as Harper Family Freedom Day; and I call upon the Harper family to pause on that day in solemn contemplation of the glorious blessings of freedom which we humbly and thankfully enjoy.

IN WITNESS WHEREOF, I have hereunto set my hand.

DONE at the town of Walhalla, North Dakota, this 27th day of January in the year of our Lord 20__, and of the Independence of the United States of America the ____.

FREDDIE HARPER

Continued on the following page.

★ Make a wreath similar to the one at right that was created for the National Freedom Day Association's observance of National Freedom Day. You may choose to use a real or artificial wreath. You can make your own wreath by cutting a circle out of cardboard and coloring or painting it green. Decorate your wreath with red, white, and blue ribbon or yarn. You might want to cut miniature Liberty Bells and American flags out of paper or cardboard.

★ Prepare a special meal for your family's Freedom Day banquet. The food can be anything your family likes to eat. Set the table with a nice tablecloth, napkins, and dishes.

★ When all of your family is gathered for the banquet, read the proclamation you have written. Designate someone in the family to place the wreath in a special location in the room.

★ As you enjoy your special meal, go around the table and have everyone talk about a particular freedom they are thankful we can enjoy in our country. When everyone has had a turn, have someone read Galatians 5:13-14 and discuss the meaning of the passage.

GROUNDHOG DAY AND VALENTINE'S DAY

VALENTINE'S DAY DECORATIONS

Show some elderly people in your town how much you love them!

Supplies:

white, pink, or purple index cards

hole punch

small artificial flowers

white, pink, or purple ribbon

scissors

pens or markers

Instructions:

★ Call a local nursing home or assisted living facility in your area and ask if you can make Valentine's Day decorations for the residents there. Find out how many decorations you need to make.

★ Fold each index card in half. On each one, write the words: *Happy Valentine's Day!* Choose one of the verses from the list below to write on each card as well.

- Love never fails. 1 Corinthians 13:8
- The God of love and peace will be with you. 2 Corinthians 13:11
- Love one another, for love is from God. 1 John 4:7
- God is love. 1 John 4:8

★ Punch two holes in the index card, as seen in the illustration at right. Cut a piece of ribbon about 14 inches long. Thread the ribbon through the holes. Lay the stem of an artificial flower between the holes and tie it to the card.

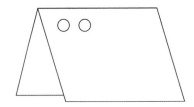

★ Deliver your valentines to the facility on or before Valentine's Day. Ask the facility staff if you can distribute the valentines yourself. You might be able to go around to the different tables during a meal time to give them to the residents.

Washington's Birthday

Cherry Challenge

Celebrate Washington's birthday with a meal made of cherries!

Supplies:

white, red, green, and brown paper

scissors

glue

pencils

bowl (approximately 8 inches in diameter)

black marker

cherry-themed or red and white linens

a meal that includes at least three items made with cherries

Instructions:

★ Use the bowl and pencil to trace two circles on two pieces of red paper. Cut out the circles. Write *Cherry* on one and *Challenge* on the other.

★ Cut out two green leaves and two brown stems. Glue the cherries, leaves, and stems together to make the Cherry Challenge centerpiece pictured above.

★ If you have any tablecloths, napkins, or placemats that have cherries, use them to decorate your table. If not, use red and white linens.

★ Prepare a meal that includes at least three items made with cherries. Here are some ideas of recipes to look up that can include cherries: ham, chicken, fruit salad, bread, muffins, turnovers, pie, cookies, smoothies.

★ Trace the axe on the next page onto white paper. Cut it out and use it as a pattern to cut more axes out of brown paper. Cut out one axe for each cherry dish you are serving at your Cherry Challenge meal. Write the name of one of your cherry dishes on each of the axes to label them for the meal.

★ During the meal, have someone read the following story.

George Washington and the Cherry Tree

Shortly after George Washington's death, a man named Mason Locke Weems wrote a biography of Washington's life called *A History of the Life and Death, Virtues and Exploits, of General George Washington*. Weems' book was full of made-up stories about the American hero, and his writing was immensely popular. One of the stories he apparently created was the legend of George Washington and the cherry tree. Weems' tale went like this:

When George . . . was about six years old, he was made the wealthy master of a hatchet! of which, like most little boys, he was immoderately fond, and was constantly going about chopping everything that came in his way. One day, in the garden, where he often amused himself hacking his mother's pea-sticks, he unluckily tried the edge of his hatchet on the body of a beautiful young English cherry-tree, which he barked so terribly, that I don't believe the tree ever got the better of it. The next morning the old gentleman, finding out what had befallen his tree, which, by the by, was a great favourite, came into the house; and with much warmth asked for the mischievous author, declaring at the same time, that he would not have taken five guineas for his tree. Nobody could tell him anything about it. Presently George and his hatchet made their appearance. "George," said his father, "do you know who killed that beautiful little cherry tree yonder in the garden?" This was a tough question; and George staggered under it for a moment; but quickly recovered himself: and looking at his father, with the sweet face of youth brightened with the inexpressible charm of all-conquering truth, he bravely cried out, "I can't tell a lie, Pa; you know I can't tell a lie. I did cut it with my hatchet."—"Run to my arms, you dearest boy," cried his father in transports, "run to my arms; glad am I, George, that you killed my tree; for you have paid me for it a thousand fold. Such an act of heroism in my son is more worth than a thousand trees, though blossomed with silver, and their fruits of purest gold."

St. Patrick's Day

Field Meet

Find out who can run the fastest, jump the farthest, and catch the pig!

St. Patrick's Day Field Meet Participant

Supplies:

white and green paper

scissors

pen

hole punch

yarn or string

Instructions:

★ Make one shamrock medal for each participant. Trace the shamrock shape above onto white paper. Cut it out and use it as a pattern to cut more shamrocks out of green paper. Write "St. Patrick's Day Field Meet Participant" on each shamrock. Punch a hole in each one and attach a piece of yarn or string long enough to go over someone's head.

★ Decide on a schedule of various races and competitions for your field meet. Here are some ideas of events to include:

- tug of war
- relay race
- wheelbarrow race

- three-legged race
- shoe kick
- throwing objects at a target

- long jump
- football toss
- catch the pig

For the catch the pig event, assign the smallest person in your family to be the pig and have her run around the yard while everyone else tries to catch her. To make it harder, all of the chasers could be assigned a partner and have to run as in a three-legged race. If you have a pet such as a dog, a cat, or a pig, you could chase him instead of your youngest sibling.

★ Ask everyone to dress in green for the field meet. When all the events are completed, present everyone with a shamrock-shaped participation medal.

Tax Day

"Why We Are Thankful for Income Tax" Poster

It's easy to complain about having to pay income tax. Let's be thankful instead!

Supplies:

- poster board
- green paper
- scissors
- glue
- markers

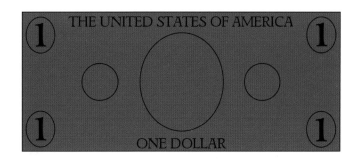

Instructions:

★ Turn the poster board sideways. Across the top write *Why We Are Thankful for Income*

★ Cut out fifteen green rectacles that each measure 3 1/2 inches by 1 1/2 inches. Decorate each one to look like a dollar bill, as seen in the image above.

★ It's easy to complain about having to send part of our money to the government in taxes, especially when we don't like everything the government does with our money. However, there are things that we can be thankful the government does, such as paying for the military, printing our money, investigating crimes through the Federal Bureau of Investigation (FBI), looking into possible problems through the Central Intelligence Agency (CIA), building Interstates, sending ambassadors to other countries, maintaining foreign embassies, issuing passports, mainting historic buildings in Washington, D.C., and maintaining our National Parks. As a family, come up with fifteen things you are thankful the United States government pays for. Write one thing in the center oval of each dollar bill.

★ Glue the dollar bills onto the poster to form the word *Tax*, as seen at right.

Good Friday and Easter

Easter Egg Roll

Pretend your house is the White House and have an Easter Egg Roll on your lawn.

Supplies:

hard boiled eggs

spoons to roll the eggs

four stakes

ribbon

story to read

pole, ribbons, and music for Maypole Dance (see instructions on the following page)

Instructions:

★ Before your event, decide where in your yard the race course will be. The length you mark off should depend on the ages of those who will be participating. To mark the staring line, drive two stakes into the ground about ten feet apart. Tie a ribbon to the top of each one. Mark the finish line the same way.

★ Prepare one hard boiled egg for each participant. Dye the eggs in water tinted with food coloring after they are cooked.

★ Gather one spoon for each participant.

★ Your Easter Egg Roll can be enjoyed by just your family, or you can invite other families to participate with you. Ask everyone to dress up. Pretend your house is the White House. Have Mom and Dad be the President and First Lady.

★ To begin your event, have the President or First Lady read a story to everyone. Choose a book related to Easter or read the story of Jesus' resurrection in Matthew 28, Mark 16, Luke 24, or John 20.

* Have an Easter Egg Roll. If you have more than six participants, divide into younger and older groups. Have everyone stand behind the start line and lay their hard boiled egg on the ground in front of them. At the word "Go!" everyone uses a spoon to push his egg across the race course to the finish line. The first one to get his egg across the finish line wins. Note that eggs must be rolled, not picked up with the spoon and tossed!

Maypole Dance Instructions

* A Maypole Dance is an optional event you may choose to add to your festivities. Look again at the picture of the Maypole Dance that took place at the White House in 1929 pictured on page 954.

* You will need a basketball pole that is firmly cemented in the ground. If you do not have one at your house, you could choose to hold your event at a park or playground.

* Cut lengths of wide ribbon or plastic party streamers about twice as long as the pole. You will need one ribbon for each dancer. You will need to have an even number of dancers (between 6 and 20). Firmly attach the ribbons to the top of the pole below the backboard. Use strong tape if necessary. If you use a ladder, be sure to have someone stand at the bottom of the ladder to hold it firmly in place. Children should not use a ladder unattended.

* To begin a dance, have the dancers stand evenly spaced around the pole, each holding a ribbon. Below are the steps for two Maypole dances. Choose an Irish or English folk tune with a lively beat to play while dancing.

Maypole Dance #1

Dancers skip eight steps toward the pole, then eight steps back out. Skip around the pole clockwise until ribbons are almost completely wound. Turn and skip until ribbons are unwound. Continue to repeat as long as the music lasts.

Maypole Dance #2

Before the dance begins, dancers number off as ones and twos. All skip eight steps toward the pole, then eight steps back out. Skip eight steps clockwise, then turn and skip eight steps counter-clockwise. At this point, all ones face clockwise and all twos face counter-clockwise. Each dancer should hold her ribbon with her hand that is farthest from the pole so she can use her inside hand to guide her ribbon over and under the other dancers. Begin to weave the ribbons around the pole by going over, under, over, under. When you have gone completely around the pole twice, turn and go the opposite way.

NATIONAL ARBOR DAY

CELEBRATE TREES!

Follow the motto of the National Arbor Day Foundation and plant, nurture, and celebrate trees!

Supplies:

a tree ready for planting

shovel

water

pruning tools

paper

drawing or painting supplies

Instructions:

★ Plant a Tree! Purchase a tree ready for planting from a local nursery or greenhouse or from the Arbor Day Foundation. Follow the instructions that come with the tree so that you are sure you are planting it properly.

★ Nurture a Tree! Tend to a tree in your yard that needs some attention by watering, pruning, and/or mulching it. Children should not use pruning tools unsupervised.

★ Celebrate a Tree! Find a unique tree near your home and draw or paint it. Look for features such as height, interesting twists, old age, damage from a storm, or unusual bark.

★ Read Psalm 1 together as a family and discuss its meaning.

Loyalty Day and Law Day

"Laws Kids Have to Follow" Book

Make a book to help little kids understand the concept of obeying the laws of our country.

Supplies:

8.5″ x 11.5″ paper
computer (optional)
drawing supplies
8.5″ x 11.5″ heavy paper
hole punch
ribbon or string

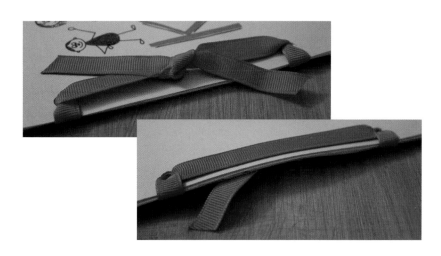

Instructions:

★ Refer to the next page to see the text for each page of the book you are making. You may either write the words on the pages of your book or type them on a computer and print them off. Make each page of your book the size of half of a sheet of paper.

★ Illustrate each page by drawing a picture. Illustrate a cover on heavy paper. Use a second piece of heavy paper for the back.

★ Punch two holes in the side of the two covers and each page of your book. Use a piece of ribbon or string about 20 inches long to thread the pages of your book together. First pull the two ends of the ribbon up through the holes from the back. Then thread the ribbon over the side edge and back up through the holes from the back. Tie the ribbon together on the front of the book and cut the ends to make them even. Refer to the photos above. You may keep the book for your family or give it to a family you know who has small children.

Laws Kids Have to Follow

Page 1: The United States of America is a country that is run by the rule of law. This means that there are laws that have been made, and it is the responsibility of every citizen to obey them.

Page 2: Some laws are mostly for adults, but there are a lot of laws that adults and kids have to follow.

Page 3: Kids have to wear a seatbelt or sit in a carseat when riding in a car.

Page 4: It's the law that kids have to be in school, either at home or in a public or private school.

Page 5: If there's a law that says dogs have to be on a leash when outside, a kid has to keep his dog on a leash.

Page 6: Kids have to obey laws about where they can and cannot ride their bikes.

Page 7: It's against the law for kids to write any graffiti on a public structure.

Page 8: Kids have to keep out if there is a "No Tresspassing" sign posted.

Page 9: Kids have to obey laws about when and where to cross the street.

Page 10: Kids are not allowed to drive a vehicle on the road until they have a permit or license.

Page 11: If there is a law against littering, that means kids can't leave their trash on the ground.

Page 12: Kids can't call 9-1-1 unless there is a real emergency.

Page 13: Kids can't steal.

Page 14: If we are going to continue to enjoy liberty, justice, and equality in the United States, everyone in the country needs to obey the laws that have been established —

Page 15: Even kids!

NATIONAL DAY OF PRAYER

GO PRAY

Take a trip to your local courthouse with your family and pray for your country.

Supplies:

paper

pencils, colored pencils, or pens

Instructions:

* Find out the names of specific leaders in your community such as the city mayor, county mayor, and county clerk.

* Write a note for each of the people on your list. Decorate your notes with red, white, and blue stars or other patriotic illustrations. Here is suggested wording you might use:

Thank you for serving our community. We are praying for you.

The _____ Family

* Take the notes with you and go to your local courthouse or town hall. As a family, hold hands around the flagpole and pray for the leaders of your community. Pray for your Governor and other elected officials. Pray for the President of the United States.

* When you are finished praying, deliver the notes to the offices of the officials on your list.

* Remember to continue praying for the government officials of your community, state, and country.

MOTHER'S DAY

BIOGRAPHICAL SKETCHES

Preserve the stories of your mom and grandmothers to pass on to future generations.

Supplies:

paper

pen or pencil

computer (optional)

Instructions:

★ Write a biography of your mom and both of your grandmothers. You might also want to write biographies of your great-grandmothers. Use the questions below and any other questions you would like to ask to interview your mother and grandmothers. If your family member is no longer living, interview other relatives who knew them.

★ Include a photograph with each biography. If possible include a picture of your mom or grandmother as a young girl and a picture of them with you.

Suggested Questions

1. Where and when were you born?
2. What are the names and birth years of all your siblings?
3. How did your parents earn a living?
4. Did you have any pets as a child?
5. Where did you go to school?
6. How did you meet your husband?
7. When and where did you get married?
8. What jobs have you had?
9. Where have you lived?
10. What did you enjoy about being a mother when your children were small?
11. What do you enjoy about being a mother/grandmother now?
12. What is something you learned from your mother?
13. What is something important you want me to remember?

ARMED FORCES DAY
POSTER

Imagine that you have been hired to design next year's Armed Forces Day poster!

Supplies:

poster board

colored pencils, paint, markers, or pens

Instructions:

★ Design a poster to promote next year's Armed Forces Day observance. Look at the examples on page 983 and below to help get your creative juices flowing!

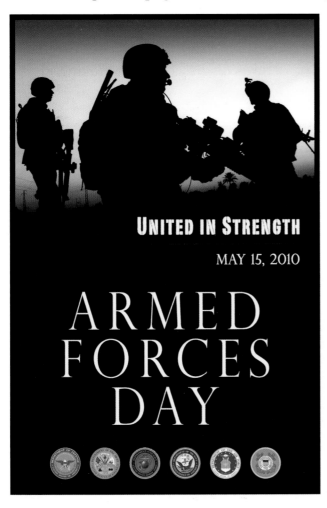

MEMORIAL DAY
MEMORIAL FLOWERS

Honor the fallen heroes from your community.

Supplies:

flowers

patriotic ribbon

Instructions:

★ Make a bouquet with flowers and greenery you gather yourself or purchase from a florist. Use red, white, or blue ribbon to tie your bouquet together.

★ Many communities have a war memorial outside the courthouse. If your community has one, make a trip there together as a family and place your flowers beside it. If there are names included on the memorial, take turns reading each name aloud.

★ If there is not a war memorial in your community, place your bouquet in a local cemetery. Look for the graves of soldiers who are buried there.

★ Pray together and ask God to continue to bless and comfort the families who are grieving the loss of a loved one who died in the military.

FLAG DAY

THE FLAG GAME

Learn about the American flag (and have fun while you're at it!). For 2-6 players.

Supplies:

white poster board (28 inches by 22 inches)

red crayon, colored pencil, or marker

blue construction paper

glue

white paper

yardstick

pencil

scissors

black marker

25 index cards

coins for game pieces

one die

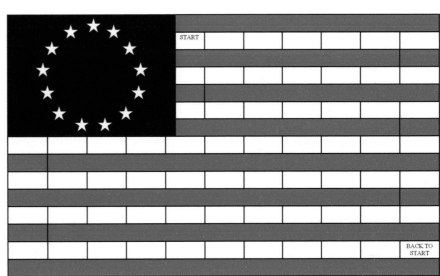

Instructions:

* ★ To make the flag game board, cut the short side of your poster board down to 16 1/4 inches. Use a yardstick to divide the board into thirteen stripes that are each 1 1/4 inches wide. (Hint: Make marks on both ends of the poster board, then turn your yardstick sideways and use it to draw straight lines between the marks.)

* ★ Beginning at the top, color every other stripe red.

* ★ Cut a rectangle of blue construction paper that measures 11 inches by 8 3/4 inches. Glue this in the upper left corner of the game board.

* ★ Use the pattern at right to trace 13 stars on white paper. Cut out the stars, but do not glue them to the flag.

Continued on the following two pages.

* Divide the white stripes into spaces, according to the diagram above. Also draw a space on one end of each red stripe, alternating right and left as in the diagram above. Use a pencil first and then darken your lines with a black marker.

* Draw a star on 3 random spaces on your game board.

* Draw a question mark on 20 random spaces.

* Draw an exclamation mark on 15 random spaces.

* Cut the 25 index cards in half to make 50 cards. On the blank side of 30 of them, draw a question mark. On the lined side, write one of each of the questions and answers below.

1. How many stripes are on the American flag?
   thirteen
2. Who is the author of the Pledge of Allegiance?
   Francis Bellamy
3. How many stars were on the original American flag?
   thirteen
4. When was the American flag design standardized?
   1912
5. What two states added the last two stars to the flag?
   Alaska and Hawaii
6. What Wisconsin man worked to establish Flag Day?
   Bernard J. Cigrand
7. Who signed legislation to make Flag Day an official annual observance by the Federal government?
   Harry Truman
8. What year did Flag Day become an official annual observance?
   1949
9. What is the name of the collection of rules about the proper use of the American flag?
   The Federal Flag Code
10. In what was the Pledge of Allegiancce first published?
    Youth's Companion
11. What was the original salute to the American flag?
    raising the right hand toward the flag
12. When did it become proper to salute the American flag by placing the right hand over the heart?
    1942
13. Why did the original salute to the American flag become unpopular?
    It looked like the salute of Nazis and Fascists.
14. When was the phrase "under God" added to the pledge?
    June 14, 1954
15. Which President added "under God" to the pledge?
    Dwight D. Eisenhower
16. How many stars are on the current American flag?
    50

17. What nickname has been given to the flag pictured on this game board?
    Betsy Ross Flag
18. What group approved the original design for the American flag?
    Second Continental Congress
19. According to the original description of the design of the American flag, what do the stars represent?
    a new constellation
20. On what date was the original design for the American flag approved?
    June 14, 1777
21. What city was home to seamstress Betsy Ross?
    Philadelphia
22. How many stars and stripes were on the flag of 1794?
    fifteen
23. How many stars were on the flag of 1912?
    forty-eight
24. What city is considered the birthplace of Flag Day?
    Waubeka, Wisconsin
25. What was the date of the first national observance of Flag Day?
    June 14, 1877
26. What was the significance of the date chosen for the first national observance of Flag Day?
    It was one hundred years after the flag design was approved by the Second Continental Congress.
27. What is the proper way to hoist the American flag?
    briskly
28. What is the proper way to lower the American flag?
    ceremoniously
29. The American flag is never supposed to be carried flat or horizontally, but always how?
    aloft and free
30. The Pledge of Allegiance was originally written for what celebration?
    four hundredth anniversary of Columbus' arrival

★ On the blank side of 20 of the index cards, draw an exclamation mark. On the lined side, write one of the instructions below.

1. Close your eyes and draw an American flag.
2. Close your eyes and draw 13 stars.
3. Spell "American flag" backwards.
4. Do 13 jumping jacks.
5. Pat the top of your head with one hand while you rub your stomach with the other as you count to 13.
6. Do 13 toe touches.
7. Count to 50 in less than fifteen seconds.
8. Close your eyes and write "June 14, 1777."
9. Blink 50 times.
10. Think of four words to describe America that begin with the four letters in the word "flag."
11. Use the hand you do not normally use to write "red, white, and blue."
12. Use the hand you do not normally use to draw an American flag.
13. Use the hand you do not normally use to draw a star.
14. Close your eyes and draw a girl with her right hand over her heart.
15. Close your eyes and draw a boy saluting the flag the originial way with his left hand outstretched.

16. Name thirteen things you like about America.
17. Name thirteen American cities or towns you have visited.
18. Name thirteen things that are red.
19. Close your eyes and draw something that is blue.
20. Say "I am proud to be an American" five times using five different accents.

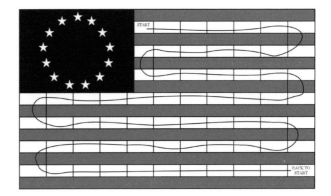

Game Instructions:

★ Before the game starts, arrange the 13 white stars on the blue paper as seen in the diagram above. Have some paper and a pencil handy.

★ Give each player a coin to use as a game piece. Roll the die to see who goes first. On a player's turn, the player rolls the die and moves that many spaces forward according to the diagram above.

★ If a player lands on a star, he takes one of the stars off the blue paper as his own.

★ If a player lands on a question mark, the player to his right draws a question card and reads it. If the player answers the question correctly, he keeps the card.

★ If a player lands on an exclamation mark, he draws an exclamation mark card, reads it, and performs the action described. If he performs the action satisfactorily (the other players judge), he keeps the card.

★ When a player has earned 3 cards (question or exclamation mark), he may take a star from the blue paper.

★ When a player reaches the last space, he goes back to START to begin his course again.

★ If playing with 2-3 people, game continues until one player has received 4 stars. If playing with 4-6 people, game continues until one player has received 3 stars.

Father's Day

Biographical Sketches

Preserve the stories of your dad and grandfathers to pass on to future generations.

Supplies:

paper

pen or pencil

computer (optional)

Instructions:

★ Write a biography of your dad and both of your grandfathers. You might also want to write biographies of your great-grandfathers. Use the questions below and any other questions you would like to ask to interview your father and grandfathers. If your family member is no longer living, interview other relatives who knew them.

★ Include a photograph with each biography. If possible include a picture of your dad or grandfather as a young boy and a picture of them with you.

Suggested Questions

1. Where and when were you born?
2. What are the names and birth years of all your siblings?
3. How did your parents earn a living?
4. Did you have any pets as a child?
5. Where did you go to school?
6. How did you propose to your wife?
7. What jobs have you had?
8. What is a special trip you have taken?
9. What is a special gift you have received from someone?
10. What did you enjoy about being a father when your children were small?
11. What do you enjoy about being a father/grandfather now?
12. What is something you learned from your father?
13. What is something important you want me to remember?

States and
CAPITALS

State	Capital	Date Admitted	Order of Admission
Alabama	Montgomery	December 14, 1819	22
Alaska	Juneau	January 3, 1959	49
Arizona	Phoenix	February 14, 1912	48
Arkansas	Little Rock	June 15, 1836	25
California	Sacramento	September 9, 1850	31
Colorado	Denver	August 1, 1876	38
Connecticut	Hartford	January 9, 1788	5
Delaware	Dover	December 7, 1787	1
Florida	Tallahassee	March 3, 1845	27
Georgia	Atlanta	January 2, 1788	4
Hawaii	Honolulu	August 21, 1959	50
Idaho	Boise	July 3, 1890	43
Illinois	Springfield	December 3, 1818	21
Indiana	Indianapolis	December 11, 1816	19
Iowa	Des Moines	December 28, 1846	29
Kansas	Topeka	January 29, 1861	34
Kentucky	Frankfort	June 1, 1792	15
Louisiana	Baton Rouge	April 30, 1812	18
Maine	Augusta	March 15, 1820	23
Maryland	Annapolis	April 28, 1788	7
Massachusetts	Boston	February 6, 1788	6
Michigan	Lansing	January 26, 1837	26
Minnesota	St. Paul	May 11, 1858	32
Mississippi	Jackson	December 10, 1817	20
Missouri	Jefferson City	August 10, 1821	24
Montana	Helena	November 8, 1889	41
Nebraska	Lincoln	March 1, 1867	37
Nevada	Carson City	October 31, 1864	36

State	Capital	Date Admitted	Order of Admission
New Hampshire	Concord	June 21, 1788	9
New Jersey	Trenton	December 18, 1787	3
New Mexico	Santa Fe	January 6, 1912	47
New York	Albany	July 26, 1788	11
North Carolina	Raleigh	November 21, 1789	12
North Dakota	Bismarck	November 2, 1889	39
Ohio	Columbus	March 1, 1803	17
Oklahoma	Oklahoma City	November 16, 1907	46
Oregon	Salem	February 14, 1859	33
Pennsylvania	Harrisburg	December 12, 1787	2
Rhode Island	Providence	May 29, 1790	13
South Carolina	Columbia	May 23, 1788	8
South Dakota	Pierre	November 2, 1889	40
Tennessee	Nashville	June 1, 1796	16
Texas	Austin	December 29, 1845	28
Utah	Salt Lake City	January 4, 1896	45
Vermont	Montpelier	March 4, 1791	14
Virginia	Richmond	June 25, 1788	10
Washington	Olympia	November 11, 1889	42
West Virginia	Charleston	June 20, 1863	35
Wisconsin	Madison	May 29, 1848	30
Wyoming	Cheyenne	July 10, 1890	44

Cheyenne, Wyoming
Wyoming State Capitol

SOURCES

Articles and Reports

Antsaklis, Panos. "The Dates of Easter Sunday," University of Notre Dame

Bellune, Mark. "South Carolina, NYC continue special friendship," *Lexington Chronicle*, September 8, 2011; retrieved October 20, 2012

Bogo, Jennifer. "Why Texans See Green Gold in Renewable Resources." *Popular Mechanics*, December 18, 2009; retrieved February 15, 2012

Burnett, John. "Winds of Change Blow into Roscoe, Texas, " NPR, November 27, 2007; retrieved February 15, 2012

Cain, Amanda. "A Mountain service marks Easter dawn," *Tuscon Sentinel*, April 9, 2012

"Celebrating America's Freedoms: The Origins of Flag Day," U.S. Department of Veterans Affairs

"Children repay 134-year-old debt of kindness," *Victoria Advocate*, November 10, 2001; retrieved October 20, 2012 from www.news.google.com/newspapers

"From Plans to Pavement: How a Road Is Built," Michigan Department of Transportation, www.michigan.gov/mdot, retrieved December 30, 2011

Gay, Wayne Lee. "Making a Home for Georgia O'Keeffe," *Fort Worth Star-Telegram*, December 27, 1995; retrieved October 10, 2012

Greenbaum, Hilary and Dana Rubinstein. "The Stop Sign Wasn't Always Red," *The New York Times Magazine*, December 9, 2011, retrieved October 1, 2012

Ellen Terrell. "History of the US Income Tax," Library of Congress, Business Reference Services, February 2004

"How a Road Gets Built," Virginia Department of Transportation, www.virginiadot.org, retrieved December 30, 2011

Kaufman, Wendy. "Why Tax Day Falls On April 17 This Year," NPR

Kershner, Jim. "A Prime Mover," The Spokesman-Review, June 19, 2010

Kratz, Steven. "Governor Corbett Opens Groundhog Day Festivities, Punxsutawney Phil Predicts Six More Weeks of Winter Weather," Pennsylvania Department of Community and Economic Development

Krause, Jason. "Charlie Rhyne's Big Idea," *ABA Journal*, May 1, 2008

Luckey, John R. "The United States Flag: Federal Law Relating to Display and Associated Questions," Congressional Research Service Report for Congress

Mires, Charlene. "National Freedom Day," Encyclopedia of Greater Philadelphia

"NY Firefighters Thank SC Students Who Raised Money For New Fire Truck," www.eng202lad101.tripod.com, December 10, 2001; retrieved October 20, 2012

"National 9/11 memorial tour begins in SC," *USA Today*, September 10, 2007; retrieved October 20, 2012

O'Grady, Eileen. "E. ON completes world's largest wind farm in Texas," *Reuters*, October 1, 2009; retrieved February 15, 2012

Perry, Leonard. "Shamrocks for St. Patrick's Day," University of Vermont Extension Department of Plant and Soil Science

Pinsker, Matthew. "Why is Feb. 1 Designated as National Freedom Day?" National Constitution Center

Poole, Brad. "Procession up 'A' Mountain will be tomorrow," *Tuscon Citizen*, April 13, 2006

Roach, John. "St. Patrick's Day 2011: Facts, Myths, and Traditions," National Geographic News

"S.C. teens visit truck they gave to NYFD," *New York Daily News*, March 30, 2008; retrieved October 20, 2012

Sack, Kevin. "Southern City Hopes to Return Favor to New York," *The New York Times*, October 22, 2001; retrieved October 20, 2012

"School raises money to buy N.Y. fire truck," *Lodi News-Sentinel*, December 3, 2001; retrieved October 20, 2012

Shami, Hamooda. "America's Best St. Patrick's Day Parades," U.S. News and World Report: Travel

"Tax Day Freebies," Fox News Network, LLC, April 12, 2012

Vaccaro, Bob. "From the Ashes," *Journal of Emergency Medical Services*, retrieved October 20, 2012

"What Does the Easter Bunny Have To Do With Easter?" Analysis by Dnews Editors, Discovery Communications, LLC, April 6, 2012

Wunner, Bill (CNN International Senior Producer). "Presidential shamrock ceremony had inauspicious beginning," CNN, March 17, 2010

Zezima, Katie. "Sure, the Bridge Is a Marvel, But How About the View?" *The New York Times*, July 10, 2007; retrieved February 15, 2012

Books

Colson, Charles. *Born Again*. Lincoln, Virginia: Chosen Books, 1976

McCullough, David. *Mornings on Horseback*. New York: Simon and Schuster, 1982

Morris, Edmund. *The Rise of Theodore Roosevelt*. New York: Ballantine Books, 1979

Roosevelt, Theodore. *An Autobiography*. New York: Macmillan, 1913

Business and Tourism Organizations

AA Truck Sleeper, LLC
Annin Flagmakers
AT&T
Averitt Express, Inc
American College of Surgeons
Caterpillar
Delta Airlines
E. ON Climate and Renewables North America
Festivals and Events
Greeting Card Association
Kansas Wheat Commission/Kansas Association of Wheat
  Growers
King Arthur Flour
National Asphalt Pavement Association
National Registry of Emergency Medical Technicians
National Restaurant Association
New Mexico Solar Energy Association
Pierce Manufacturing
Platts Energy Information
Power-Technology
Roscoe Wind Council
Stop Sign Xpress
TurboTax
United States Postal Service
Wyoming Mining Association

Civic, Historical, and Other Organizations

AlmonStrowger.com
American Alliance of Museums
American Association for State and Local History
American Bar Association
American Library Association
The American Presidency Project, Online by Gerhard Peters
  and John T. Woolley
  John F. Kennedy: "Proclamation 3406 - Loyalty Day,
    1961," April 12, 1961. http://www.presidency.ucsb.edu/
    ws/?pid=24134
  Harry S. Truman: "Proclamation 2978 - National Day of
    Prayer, 1952," June 17, 1952.
    http://www.presidency.ucsb.edu/ws/?pid=87332
  William J. Clinton: "Remarks at the 50th Anniversary
    Celebration of Armed Forces Day in Suitland,
    Maryland," May 19, 2000. http://www.presidency.ucsb.
    edu/ws/?pid=58513
  Richard Nixon: "Remarks at Armed Forces Day
    Ceremonies, Norfolk Naval Base, Virginia.," May 19,
    1973. http://www.presidency.ucsb.edu/ws/?pid=3853
  Ronald Reagan: "Radio Address to the Nation on Armed
    Forces Day ," May 21, 1988. http://www.presidency.
    ucsb.edu/ws/?pid=35862
Arbor Day Foundation
The Augustine Club at Columbia University
Baker (Oregon) Heritage Museum
Brotherhood of Locomotive Engineers and Trainmen
Carlton H. Hilton Foundation
C-SPAN
Clare Booth Luce Policy Institute
Corporation for National and Community Service
DC Central Kitchen
Georgia O'Keeffe Museum
George Washington Birthday Celebration Committee
Grand Haven Coast Guard Festival
International Mother's Day Shrine Foundation
Joe Foss Institute

The Jimmy Stewart Museum
The King Center
Legacy Project
Metropolitan Tuscon Convention & Visitor's Bureau
Mike Thornton
The Morton Arboretum
Mother's Day Central
Mount Vernon Ladies' Association
National Audubon Society, Inc.
National Conference of State Legislatures
National Day of Prayer Task Force
National Flag Day Foundation
Newport Loyalty Day & Sea Fair Festival Association
Nobel Media
Plimoth Plantation
Points of Light Institute
Prison Fellowship
Prison Fellowship International
Punxsutawney Area Chamber of Commerce
The Punxsutawney Groundhog Club
Scholastic, Inc.
Schuylkill River (Pennsylvania) National and State Heritage
  Area
Spokane Regional Convention & Visitor Bureau
Stormfax, Inc.
Supreme Court Historical Society
Tax Foundation
Texas State Historical Association
U.S. Travel Association
Valentine Chamber of Commerce
Valentine Cherry County Economic Development Board
Veterans of Foreign Wars
Wisconsin Historical Society

Government Agencies

Alabama State Government
Alaska Department of Commerce, Community, and
  Economic Development
The American Folk Life Center (Library of Congress)
Amtrak
Architect of the Capitol
Arizona Department of Transportation
Bureau of Indian Affairs
Campbell County (Wyoming) School District
Cedar City, Utah
Chester County, Pennsylvania Courts
City of Burlington, Iowa
City of Carrolton, Maryland
City of Davis, California Fire Department
City of New York
City of Portland, Oregon
City of Trenton, New Jersey
Civil Air Patrol
Consulate General of the United States, Rio De Janeiro,
  Brazil
Delaware Art Museum
Economic History Association
Embassy of the United States, Beijing, China
Federal Aviation Administration
Federal Bureau of Investigation
Federal Judicial Center
Federal Reserve System
Florida Department of Agriculture and Consumer Services
Honolulu International Airport
Idaho State Government

Internal Revenue Service
  2011 Internal Revenue Service Data Book
Iowa State Government
Joint Chiefs of Staff
Judiciary of England and Wales
Kanawha Valley (West Virginia) Regional Transportation
  Authority
Kelly Bean, Mayor's Administrative Assistant, Mackinac
  Island, Michigan
Kent, Washington School District
Library of Congress
Los Angeles County Metropolitan Transportation Authority
Maine State Government
  Department of Inland Fisheries and Wildlife
  Maine State Ferry Service
Maryland State Government
Mercer County, New Jersey
Minnesota Department of Transportation
Minnesota House of Representatives House Research
Morgan County West Virginia Prosecutor's Office
Nashville (Tennessee) Police Department, School Crossing
  Guard Section
National Archives and Records Administration
National Oceanic and Atmospheric Administration
National Park Service
  Grand Canyon National Park
National Weather Service
Navajo Nation
New Jersey Transit Authority
New Mexico State Police
New Mexico Motor Vehicle Division
New York State Parks
North Dakota State Legislature
North Dakota Wheat Commission
Phoenix (Arizona) Sky Harbor International Airport
Recreation.gov
Roanoke, Virginia City Government
Senate Historical Office
Smithsonian Institution
South Carolina Ports Authority
South Dakota Art Museum, South Dakota State University
South Dakota State Government
Swan's Island, Maine
Tennessee State Government
  Department of Tourism Development
  Department of Transportation
U.S. Air Force
U.S. Army
  Aberdeen Proving Ground
  Arlington National Cemetery
U.S. Census Bureau
U.S. Coast Guard
U.S. Congress
U.S. Courts
U.S. Department of Agriculture
  Idaho Panhandle National Forests
U.S. Department of Defense
U.S. Department of Education
U.S. Department of Energy
U.S. Department of Homeland Security
  Citizenship and Immigration Services
  Customs and Border Protection
U.S. Department of the Interior
U.S. Department of Justice
U.S. Department of Labor, Bureau of Labor Statistics

U.S. Department of the Treasury, Bureau of Engraving and
  Printing
U.S. Department of Veterans Affairs
U.S. Environmental Protection Agency
U.S. Department of Transportation
U.S. Geological Survey
U.S. House of Representatives
  Office of the Clerk
U.S. Marine Corps
U.S. Marshals Service
U.S. Military Academy
U.S. Navy
  Naval History and Heritage Command
U.S. Office of Personnel Management
U.S. Secret Service
U.S. Senate
  Washington's Farewell Address Notebook
U.S. Senate Dining Services
U.S. Supreme Court
Utah State Government
West Virginia State Parks
Wyoming Indian Schools
Wyoming State Government

Magazines, Newspapers, and News Organizations
A&E Television Networks, LLC
The Badger Herald, Wednesday, March 9, 2005
BBC
Fox 11, Tuesday, April 12, 2011
Dispatch Magazine On-Line
Milwaukee Sentinel, July 4, 1915
National Geographic
News Press Journal
The New York Times
Washington Life Magazine
Wharton Alumni Magazine, Spring 2007

Reference Websites
Encyclopedia of Arkansas
Google Maps
Handbook of Texas Online
Rand McNally

Universities
California Community Colleges Chancellor's Office
California State University
  College of Business Administration and Public Policy
Cornell University Law School
  Legal Information Institute
George Washington University, Planet Forward
Kansas State University
Maine Maritime Academy
Massachusetts Institute of Technology
Rutgers University School of Communication and
  Information
Savannah State University
University of California
University of Maine
University of Virginia
  American Studies
  Miller Center for Public Affairs

Video
American Experience: The Telephone, PBS

IMAGE CREDITS

Numbers indicate the page numbers of images. The meanings of the letters t, m, b, l, and r are as follows: t - top of page; m - middle; b - bottom; l - left; r - right.
Images marked CC BY-SA 1.0 are licensed through the Creative Commons Attribution-ShareAlike 1.0 Generic License. For more information, visit http://creativecommons.org/licenses/by-sa/1.0/
Images marked CC BY 2.0 are licensed through the Creative Commons Attribution 2.0 Generic License. For more information, visit http://creativecommons.org/licenses/by/2.0
Images marked CC BY-SA 3.0 are licensed through the Creative Commons Attribution-Share Alike 3.0 Unported License. For more information, visit http://creativecommons.org/licenses/by-sa/3.0/
Images marked CC BY 3.0 are licensed through the Creative Commons Attribution 3.0 Unported License. For more information, visit http://creativecommons.org/licenses/by/3.0/

Homeschooling Families
Abby Bedsaul, 574b, 731 (North Carolina)
Amanda Gosline, 571t, 690tr/br, 730bm/br, 783bl
Ann Kite, 730 (utility payments), 787 (Florida)
Annette Wilson, 570 (West Virginia), 731 (West Virginia)
Ashton Thompson, 570b, 730tr
Caleb Beasley, 722bm
Ethan Russell, 579t
Faith Free, 654tl, 787 (Georgia)
Lynn Riedel, 843bl
Nancy Goff, 572b
Rachel Gaffney, 574tl, 576b, 653, 657 (Arkansas)
Ruth Pell, 541br
Sam Schlagel, 727
Torie Pendleton, 785 (Alaska)
Wendy Janzen, 541 (Phoenix), 728br

Notgrass Family
Bethany Poore, 604
Charlene Notgrass, 539, 540m, 541t, 546, 547, 548bl/br, 549, 550, 551, 555t, 563b, 566, 569m/b, 570 (except t), 572tl/tr/mr, 573b, 574tm, 575, 576 (except b), 578, 580, 581, 582bl/m/tr, 585t, 607, 616, 634 (museum, Galveston), 643, 646, 648, 650 (inset), 652t/m, 653tr/bl, 655, 656, 657 (except Arkansas), 658br, 659tl/bl/br, 660 (Waco), 670b, 672t, 674 (except bm), 675, 677br, 679b, 680 (second), 681, 683, 684, 686b, 691, 692, 704 (North Dakota, Texas, Minnesota, Georgia, Tennessee), 705, 706, 709, 713t, 714t, 716b, 718 (Gold Medal, Pillsbury), 721, 724, 728mr/bl, 729t/b, 730bl, 731b, 733b, 734 (bottom three), 737b, 741, 742, 743b, 744l, 747b, 748 (Tennessee), 750 (sign), 751b, 754b, 760, 767, 770t, 772b, 774b, 783 (top six), 784tr, 785 (Virginia, Wisconsin, Kentucky, Texas), 786 (Georgia, Wisconsin, Tennessee, South Dakota, Louisiana, Kansas), 787 (New York, South Dakota, Tennessee, North Carolina, Kentucky), 788tm/tr/ml/br, 796m, 810r, 819br, 823bl/br, 826, 828, 833, 834, 841tl, 842m, 843 (except bl), 846t/m, 848m/bm, 856b, 859, 860tl/tr, 862, 867t/b, 869m, 878tm, 883, 884b, 885b, 888

Mary Evelyn McCurdy, 526, 541 (Little Rock), 569t, 570m, 572m, 582br, 657bl, 674bm, 680t, 730tm, 731 (Wyoming), 768 (Wyoming), 776, 777b, 784bl, 785 (California), 786 (California), 787bl, 806, 870t, 928b, 946b, 948, 962, 968l/r, 969m, 1004, 1005, 1006, 1009, 1010, 1016, 1017, 1018, 1020tl, 1026tl
Notgrass Family Collection, 1020tr/b, 1026tr/b
Ray Notgrass, 744r

Library of Congress
Prints & Photographs Division, 516t, 542t, 545tl, 592, 593, 594, 595, 611, 624b, 625, 626, 627, 644, 645t, 659bm, 668bl, 694b, 757t, 762t, 763t, 765t, 769 (except t), 797, 798ml/m/mr, 799l, 812, 815, 817, 819tr, 841tr, 845, 850b, 851t, 861, 868b, 890t, 891, 892, 893, 894, 908, 910 (posters), 914, 915b, 916t, 922, 923, 929, 930, 932, 935, 942, 944, 945, 947m, 949 (William Hole), 952t (Harris & Ewing), 953t/b, 954 (Harris & Ewing), 956, 958t, 963t, 965, 968m (Ralph Amdursky), 971 (Charles Currier), 976, 980 (Harris & Ewing), 981 (Harris & Ewing), 986, 987t/b (John Collier), 989t, 990tl, 994b, 996 (Frances Benjamin Johnson), 997, 1000m, 1001
Carol M. Highsmith's America, 523tl, 542 (Clarkson S. Fisher Building), 543br, 631, 637b, 673, 676m, 677tr/m, 678, 680 (bottom two), 695, 697, 699t, 702, 728tr/ml, 738, 754t, 755t, 758t, 765b, 784m, 785 (Alabama), 788bl, 836tl, 836 (hotel, high school), 837mr, 848tl/bl, 851 (except t), 860b, 864, 865, 868t, 887b, 890b, 899t, 909, 915t, 947t

U.S. Military
401st Army Field Support Brigade/401st_AFSB (Flickr, CC BY 2.0), 517tm
807th Medical Command (Deployment Support)/807MDSC (Flickr, CC BY 2.0), 517tr
Aberdeen Proving Ground (Flickr, CC BY 2.0), 984

1032

DVIDSHUB (Flickr, CC BY 2.0), 773ml, 951bl (Sgt. Melissa Shaw)

Fort George G. Meade Public Affairs Office/Fort Meade (Flickr, CC BY 2.0), 813t (Nate Pesce)/813 (except t, Brendan Cavanaugh), 898t, 947b (Nate Pesce)

Fort Rucker (Flickr, CC BY 2.0), 722tl

Fort Wainwright Public Affairs Office (Flickr, CC BY 2.0), 518b, 614 (top six), 654tr

ISAF Public Affiars/isafmedia (Flickr, CC BY 2.0), 555b, 804 (U.S. Air Force Staff Sgt. Joseph Swafford), 982 (U.S. Army Photo by Sgt. April Campbell)

Kentucky National Guard Public Affairs Office/KYNGPAO (Flickr, CC BY 2.0), 540t

National Guard (Flickr, CC BY 2.0), 517br, 640 (Bagram Airfield, Iraq)

Offutt Air Force Base (Flickr, CC BY 2.0), 960b

U.S. Air Force, 667tl (Senior Airman Joshua Strang), 773tl (Staff Sgt. Brian Ferguson), 964t/m (Airman Melinda Fields) Official U.S. Air Force (Flickr, CC BY 2.0), 520t

U.S. Army, 519 (Jerome Howard CIV)
U.S. Army (Flickr, CC BY 2.0), 514t (Sgt. Resolve Savage), 515t (Sgt. Bryanna Poulin), 516b, 517m (1st Sgt. Carl Adams)/bl, 518t, 637t, 640tr, 831t (U.S. Air Force photo by Senior Master Sgt. David H. Lipp), 897t
U.S. Army Africa (Flickr, CC BY 2.0), 514m, 517tl, 724ml
U.S. Army Public Affairs - Midwest (Flickr, CC BY 2.0), 913, 990tr (Public Affairs Specialist Jacqueline Leeker)
U.S. Army's Family and MWR Programs/familymwr (Flickr, CC BY 2.0), 919ml (Rob Dozier)

U.S. Army Corps of Engineers
Kansas City District (Flickr, CC BY 2.0), 622
norfolkdistrict (Flickr, CC BY 2.0), 614 (bottom five/Patrick Bloodgood)
USACEpublicaffairs (Flickr, CC BY 2.0), 574tr, 630, 634 (boat safety)

U.S. Department of Defense
Secretary of Defense (Flickr, CC BY 2.0), 624t , 983, 989br (Mass Communications Specialist 1st Class Chad J. McNeeley), 1021
U.S. Department of Defense Current Photos (Flickr, CC BY 2.0), 514b, 515b, 520b, 521, 523tr, 524, 525t, 534bl

U.S. Marine Corps, 943 (Lance Cpl. Audrey Graham)
Marine Corps Archives & Special Collections (Flickr, CC BY 2.0), 533tr
U.S. Marine Corps New York (Flickr, CC BY 2.0), 641 (Sgt. Randall. A. Clinton)
United States Marine Corps Official Page (Flickr, CC BY 2.0), 525b, 533tl/tm/bl/br, 534tl/tr, 535, 536, 537, 538

U.S. Navy, 836bl (Mass Communications Specialist Seaman Eben Boothby), 897br (Chief Mass Communication Specialist Bart Bauer), 951br (Petty Officer 1st Class David M. Votroubek)
Naval History & Heritage Command (Flickr, CC BY 2.0), 911
Official U.S. Navy Imagery (Flickr, CC BY 2.0), ii (James Woods), 522b, 523b, 634 (space shuttle), 640 (USS Essex), 722tr, 773tr, 805b (Mass Communication Specialist 1st Class Jay C. Pugh), 814t (Information Systems Technician 2nd Class Alexavier Allen), 897bl, 910bl (Mass Communication Specialist 1st Class Corey Lewis), 951mr (Mass Communication Specialist 1st Class David McKee)

West Point Public Affairs (Flickr, CC BY 2.0), 513, 527, 529, 530, 531, 532

Government Agencies

Architect of the Capitol, 608, 609, 610, 693t/b, 694m, 755b, 824t, 837tl

JAXPORT (Flickr, CC BY 2.0), 807b (Meredith Fordham Hughes)

Maryland GovPics/MDGovpics (Flickr, CC BY 2.0), 554b, 604, 823t, 902t

Montgomery County Planning Commission (Flickr, CC BY-SA 2.0), 849 (Mill Grove)

NASA, 899b
NASA Goddard Photo and Video (Flickr, CC BY 2.0), 669t, 775
NASA Goddard Space Flight Center (Flickr, CC BY 2.0), 919mr

National Archives, 602bl, 676b, 694t, 699b, 730tl (Ansel Adams), 737, 739, 757b, 818t, 820, 963b, 977, 994t

National Park Service, 839 (cabin), 884t (Michael Silverman)
GlacierNPS (Flickr, CC BY 2.0), 722bl, 785 (Montana/David Restivo)
Grand Canyon NPS (Flickr, CC BY 2.0), 591, 602 (dancer/Michael Quinn), 615, 666, 723m/b

NOAA/National Ocean Service (Flickr, CC BY 2.0), 784tl
NOAA Photo Library (Flickr, CC BY 2.0), 668br, 670t, 671, 672br, 878b, 880b

North Cascades National Park (Flickr, CC BY 2.0), 884t

Oregon Department of Transportation/OregonDOT (Flickr, CC BY 2.0), 559, 560, 669 (three br), 707, 728tl, 733t/m, 783 (bikers), 786 (Oregon), 787 (Oregon), 791, 792, 793, 794, 803b, 805t, 904t

Seattle Municipal Archives (Flickr, CC BY 2.0), 919tl

U.S. Citizenship and Immigration Services, 642

U.S. Department of Agriculture, 728tm, 748t (Scott Bauer)
USDAgov (Flickr, CC BY 2.0), 555m, 596 (Alice Welch), 602 (veterans/Bob Nichols), 603 (rice/Las Vegas), 613 (#1/#2/#5 - Bob Nichols; #3 - Steven Thompson), 617, 619br, 620b, 704 (Pennsylvania), 750 (eggs/Bob Nichols), 809, 811t, 818m, 819tl/tm, 832t, 919br, 955tr (Bob Nichols)

U.S. Department of Labor (Flickr, CC BY 2.0), 639

U.S. Department of Transportation, 802

U.S. Fish and Wildlife Service
Northeast Region (Flickr, CC BY 2.0), 772t, 788tl (Catherine J. Hibbard/USFWS)
USFWS Mountain Prairie (Flickr, CC BY 2.0), 556m, 667bl, 723t, 841br (Betty Mulcahy, National Elk Refuge volunteer)
U.S. Fish and Wildlife Service - Midwest Region, 999bm (Rick L. Hansen)

U.S. Forest Service, 654br
Northern Region (Flickr, CC BY 2.0), 869t, 900

U.S. General Services Administration, 678t

U.S. Immigration and Customs Enforcement (Flickr, CC BY 2.0), 621

U.S. Treasury Department, 701, 708, 710, 711

U.S. Senate, 934, 937

US Mission Canada (Flickr, CC BY 2.0), 633 (bottom three)

Voice of America, 779b

Wayne National Forest (Flickr, CC BY 2.0), 848br (Alex Snyder)

vastateparksstaff (Flickr, CC BY 2.0), 901t

The White House Photostream (Flickr, CC BY 2.0), 941 (Pete Souza)

Libraries & Universities

Biodiversity Heritage Library (Flickr, CC BY 2.0), 849 (birds)

George Bush Presidential Library and Museum/Bush 41 Library (Flickr, CC BY 2.0), 662b, 858

Monrovia Public Library - Monrovia, California (Flickr, CC BY 2.0), 829t

Palos Verdes Library District (Flickr, CC BY 2.0), 814m

Ronald Reagan Library, 940m

Southern Arkansas University (Flickr, CC BY 2.0), 919tr

Theodore Roosevelt Center at Dickinson State University, 837br

Theodore Roosevelt Collection, Harvard College Library, 840m

University of Arkansas Division of Agriculture, 750 (peanuts/ Kerry Rodtnick)

University of North Texas Digital Library, 946t

Other Sources

(vincent desjardins) (Flickr, CC BY 2.0), 753

Adam Bartlett/adam*b (Flickr, CC BY 2.0), 734tr

Alan Levine/cogdogblog (Flickr, CC BY 2.0), 768t

Alex E. Proimos (Flickr, CC BY 2.0), 629m, 910ml

Alex Polezhaev/sashapo (Flickr, CC BY 2.0), 565

Alisha Vargas/AlishaV (Flickr, CC BY 2.0), 585 (Nevada), 749 (Rhode Island Red)

Alternative Heat (Flickr, CC BY 2.0), 715m

Amanda Hirsch/creativedc (Flickr, CC BY 2.0), 881br

Amy Gizienski/amy.gizienski (Flickr, CC BY 2.0), 589tl

Anders Carlsson/andersc77 (Flickr, CC BY 2.0), 889

Anders Sandberg/Arenamontanus (Flickr, CC BY 2.0), 896b

Angel Tree, 827

Angie Garrett/smoorenburg (Flickr, CC BY 2.0), 1003

Anna Guthermurth (Flickr, CC BY 2.0), 969l

Anna/bcmom (Flickr, CC BY 2.0), 975b

Antti T. Nissinen/V31S70 (Flickr, CC BY 2.0), 863

apium (Flickr, CC BY 2.0), 752

Appalachian Encounters (Flickr, CC BY 2.0), 572ml

babsteve (Flickr, CC BY 2.0), 999tm

Barbara Eckstein/beckstei (Flickr, CC BY 2.0), 785 (Rhode Island yacht)

Bart Everson/Editor B (Flickr, CC BY 2.0), 577t

Beatrice Murch/blmurch (Flickr, CC BY 2.0), 667br

Ben Pecka/Ben Josephs (Flickr, CC BY 2.0), 661t

Beverly & Pack (Flickr, CC BY 2.0), 667tl

Bill Bradford/mrbill (Flickr, CC BY 2.0), 748b

Bill Morrow/bill85704 (Flickr, CC BY 2.0), 952b

Bill Rand/randwill (Flickr, CC BY 2.0), 836br

Billy Hathorn (CC BY-SA 3.0), 737t

Bob Dass (Flickr, CC BY 2.0), 988bl

Bob Vonderau/vonderauvisuals (Flickr, CC BY 2.0), 650t, 669bm

Bob With/D.C.Atty (Flickr, CC BY 2.0), 904m

bombust (Flickr, CC BY 2.0), 998m

Brad Holt/brad_holt (Flickr, CC BY 2.0), 872, 875 (wash house)

Bradley Gordon/bradleygee (Flickr, CC BY 2.0), 782

Brett Neilson/brettneilson (Flickr, CC BY 2.0), 647, 998t

Brian Fitzgerald/Brianfit (Flickr, CC BY 2.0), 606

Brian Pennington/Penningtron (Flickr, CC BY 2.0), 704 (West Virginia)

Bruce Fingerhood/Slideshow Bruce (Flickr, CC BY 2.0), 789

Bunches and Bits {Karina} (Flickr, CC BY 2.0), 1014

Carissa Rogers/GoodNCrazy (Flickr, CC BY 2.0), 974m

Carl Lender (Flickr, CC BY 2.0), 787 (Maine)

Carl Wycoff/cwwycoff1 (Flickr, CC BY 2.0), 586 (Tulip Time tower, boy with broom, girl in black dress and white headcovering, and windmill), 587tr/b, 716m

Carlos "Chacho" Pacheco (Flickr, CC BY 2.0), 974b

Casey Fleser/somegeekintn (Flickr, CC BY 2.0), 967

Casey Helbling/caseyhelbling (Flickr, CC BY 2.0), 837bl

Central United Methodist Church, Spokane Washington, 1000t

Chanel Beck/TheChanel (Flickr, CC BY 2.0), 782

Charles Knowles/The Knowles Gallery (Flickr, CC BY 2.0), 715b, 716t

Chris Waits/waitscm (Flickr, CC BY 2.0), 719, 1022

Chuck Abbe/ChuckthePhotographer (Flickr, CC BY 2.0), 972r

Civitan International Archives, 830t

Claire Gribbin/gribbly (Flickr, CC BY 2.0), 842t

Clark Gregor/clgregor (Flickr, CC BY 2.0), 952m

Clarkston SCAMP (Flickr, CC BY 2.0), 810l

cliff1066™ (Flickr, CC BY 2.0), 557bl, 629t/b, 660tr, 712b, 779t

ClintJCL, 771

Clinton Little (Flickr, CC BY 2.0), 561tr

Colin Grey/www.cgpgrey.com (Flickr, CC BY 2.0), 782

ColoradoSenateGOP (Flickr, CC BY 2.0), 541bl, 835

curimedia (Flickr, CC BY 2.0), 634 (seaplane)

Cyndy Sims Parr/cyanocorax (Flickr, CC BY 2.0), 750 (sorghum)

Cyril Bèle/kanjiroushi (Flickr, CC BY 2.0), 978bl

Dan Dawson (Flickr, CC BY 2.0), 654bl

Daniel Hartwig/dwhartwig (Flickr, CC BY 2.0), 548 (2nd and 3rd), 552

Daniel Lobo/Daquella manera (Flickr, CC BY 2.0), 661b, 770b

Dave Conner/conner395 (Flickr, CC BY 2.0), 602t, 659 (patch), 660 (patches), 662t, 663, 664, 665, 722 (patch), 735

Dave Williss (Flickr, CC BY 2.0), 540b, 558r, 957

David Becker/loyaldefender2004 (Flickr, CC BY 2.0), 561br, 589tr, 958

David Brodbeck/gull@cyberspace.org (Flickr, CC BY 2.0), 777t

David DeHetre/davedehetre (Flickr, CC BY 2.0), 596t

David Friedel (Flickr, CC BY 2.0), 846b

David Herrera/dherrera_96 (Flickr, CC BY 2.0), 633 (top two), 751t

David Schott/dave_mcmt (Flickr, CC BY 2.0), 903tr

Davidwhitewolf of Random Nuclear Strikes blog/ davidwhitewolf (Flickr, CC BY 2.0), 747t

DaVonte Johnson/Davonteee (Flickr, CC BY 2.0), 773b

dbking (Flickr, CC BY 2.0), 601t, 758b, 940b

DC Central Kitchen (Flickr, CC BY 2.0), 955m/b

Derek Kaczmarczyk/dkaz (Flickr, CC BY 2.0), 649, 960t

diaper (Flickr, CC BY 2.0), 887t

diosthenese (Flickr, CC BY 2.0), 896t

Doc Searls/dsearls (Flickr, CC BY 2.0), 563t

D'oh Boy (Mark Holloway) (Flickr, CC BY 2.0), 650b, 651, 653tl/m

Don Hankins (Flickr, CC BY 2.0), 988tr

Donald Hobern/dhobern (Flickr, CC BY 2.0), 562bl

Donald Lee Pardue (Flickr, CC BY 2.0), 868m

Donovan Shortey/dshortey (Flickr, CC BY 2.0), 598

Doug Wertman/doug_wertman (Flickr, CC BY 2.0), 585 (Arkansas)

DualD FlipFlop/dualdflipflop (Flickr, CC BY 2.0), 645b

Dwight Sipler/photofarmer (Flickr, CC BY 2.0), 736t

Dylan/Dylerpillar (Flickr, CC BY 2.0), 938

Edd Prince/princedd (Flickr, CC BY 2.0), 961

Eddie~S (Flickr, CC BY 2.0), 927, 928t

edenpictures (Flickr, CC BY 2.0), 975bm, 999br

Edi Hargett/EdiSellsTulsa (Flickr, CC BY 2.0), 829b

Edward Stojakovic/akasped (Flickr, CC BY 2.0), 724tl

INDEX

Page numbers 1-512 are in Part 1. Page numbers 513-1026 are in Part 2. CH refers to The Citizen's Handbook. *Bold numbers indicate a photo or illustration related to that topic.*

Also Available from Notgrass Company

America the Beautiful by Charlene Notgrass

America the Beautiful is a one-year American history, geography, and literature course. It combines the flexibility and richness of a unit study with the simplicity of a textbook-based approach to history. Ages 10-14.

_____

The *Walking In* Series by Mary Evelyn McCurdy

Each workbook is a 30-lesson study of what the Bible says about a particular topic such as faith, peace, and truth. Ages 7-12.

_____

A Record of the Learning Lifestyle by Charlene Notgrass

This simple and effective record-keeping system helps you focus on the most important things and feel good about what you are accomplishing. All ages.

_____

Exploring World History and *Exploring America* by Ray Notgrass

Each of these courses allows your child to earn one year of credit in history, English (literature and composition), and Bible. Engaging history lessons combined with primary sources provide a rich understanding of the past. High school.

_____

Exploring Government and *Exploring Economics* by Ray Notgrass

These one-semester studies give your child a historical perspective on and a contemporary understanding of the subjects covered. High school.

_____

For more information about our homeschool curriculum and resources, call 1-800-211-8793 or visit www.notgrass.com.